FISH MICHIGAN

100 UPPER PENINSULA LAKES

by

Tom Huggler

Friede Publications

FISH MICHIGAN
100 UPPER PENINSULA LAKES

Text: Tom Huggler
Maps: Gary W. Barfknecht
Cover Design: Gail Dennis

Photo Credits
Front Cover: Outdoor Images/Tom Huggler
Lures: Outdoor Images/Randy Carrels
Back Cover, top two photos: Richard P. Smith
Back Cover, bottom two photos: Outdoor Images/Tom Huggler

Friede Publications
2339 Venezia Drive
Davison, Michigan 48423

Printed in the United States of America

First Printing, February 1994
Second Printing, March 1995

ISBN 0-923756-06-X

MAP SYMBOLS

 PUBLIC ACCESS SITE, which includes a boat launch as described in the text.

Fish symbols on the lake maps indicate primary locations to catch the following species:

 BLACK CRAPPIE

BLUEGILL

CISCO

LARGEMOUTH BASS

LAKE TROUT

GREAT LAKES MUSKIE

 NORTHERN MUSKIE

 NORTHERN PIKE

 PUMPKINSEED SUNFISH

 RAINBOW TROUT

SMELT

 SMALLMOUTH BASS

 SPLAKE

 TIGER MUSKIE

 WALLEYE

WHITEFISH

YELLOW PERCH

INTRODUCTION

With this book our series of Michigan inland fishing lakes is complete. Like the southern Michigan and northern Lower Peninsula guides, this book includes only lakes with public access. Each affords good to excellent angling opportunities and is capable of taking additional pressure.

That last call is the toughest to make because it is largely subjective. The DNR does not survey most of these lakes on an annual basis, and some have not been researched in years or at all. How much pressure is too much pressure? Lake Gogebic, for example, is so huge and has so many walleyes the DNR has relaxed minimum length restrictions. Nobody worries about Lake Gogebic being overfished. On the other hand, several bluegill and brook trout lakes I had initially planned to include were scrapped along the way because they were too small, too fragile and could be wiped out by someone without a conservation conscience.

If some of these lakes were turned into no-kill lakes with shortened seasons and tight regulations — including a ban on live bait — I would not hesitate to include them here. Wakely Lake in Crawford County near Grayling, for example, is such a catch-and-release trophy lake. I almost included Fumee Lake in Dickinson County for the same reason except that as we went to press, no fishing was allowed and a battle for control between the county and state appeared to be heading to court.

As I did while researching the other books, I relied heavily on the recommendations of DNR fisheries biologists, arguing with some, negotiating with others. Most of these professionals are fishermen, too, and some of them are overly protective for either selfish or noble reasons. I cannot read people's minds, but I know my responsiblity is first to the resource and then to my readers.

What I can do, and did do, is research as thoroughly as possible. Each lake has a personality; in order to discover it, I paged through more than 60 years of musty file materials, then contacted literally hundreds of knowledgable people to flesh out details about the best times and tactics, lures and locations. Fisheries biologists, conservation officers, bait and tackle shop owners, local and visiting fishermen and others with information were interviewed. And I fished as many of the lakes in this book as was possible.

Lakes are a lot like people: they were born, they grow, and eventually they die. Lakes change dramatically over their lives. Sometimes the changes are so gradual as to hardly be noticed. consider, for instance, the accumulation or organic material on a lake bottom from trees shedding their leaves each fall. At other times, though, the changes are dramatic, such as when unchecked pollution quickly adds nutrient loading or one species of fish gets the upper hand and eats everything else with fins.

Surveys by DNR and USFS managers are aimed at monitoring a lake's health for water quality and/or for fish stocks. After collecting fish in fyke, trap or gill nets or electroshocking the lake's shallows at night. researchers identify the fish, then measure and record their lengths and let them go. A few are saved for laboratory analysis where other experts age the fish by examining scales or dorsal fin spines and then compare growth rates with the state average. Sometimes the fish are tested for toxins and parasites.

Such information, together with the lake's physical characteristics, its history, and the wishes of property owners, helps the biologists to determine the best management prescription for each lake. Those that are two-story, that is contain basins conducive to both warm-water and cold-water species' survival, can be especially challenging to manage (and to fish successfully).

When white suckers, bullheads or stunted yellow perch take over a lake, some form of reclamation may be necessary. In years past the DNR mostly used rotenone, a powerful chemical that killed all fish. Today, managers are more discriminant. Especially in the U.P., for example, the diets of nesting eagles and loons must be taken into consideration. Managers today increasingly rely on a more selective chemical called antimycin, or they trap and manually remove the undesirable species. These they either give away to interested citizens or transplant in other lakes.

Once the fisheries biologists have control of a lake, they try to keep in balance the ratio of predator species to prey. An unending chore, the task is also all but impossible to achieve, except for a handful of lakes, because of competition at various stages of the food chain. Yellow perch, for example, compete with small splake for the same zooplankton, and so it is difficult to maintain both species as young fish in the same lake. On the other hand, most lakes with a thriving black crappie population also contain just the right number of big northern pike to keep the youngsters thinned and allow some crappies to grow big because of less competition for available food.

Like a kitchen recipe that turns out perfect only once, the cook is both fascinated and frustrated in his attempt to get it right again. Each change, no matter how seemingly insignificant, is a potential catalyst for reaction. Each push has its pull. Consider the walleye, arguably the hottest gamefish at the moment. Caught up in the current angling craze, biologists are stocking walleyes as fast as they can rear them in ponds. But walleyes are among the most efficient piscatorial predators. Virtual grazing machines, they are capable of mowing down other desirable species. Already in some U.P. lakes biologists are discovering they have to stock food for walleyes that have depleted existing sources.

When your family doctor agrees that something is wrong with your health, he enlists other specialists, performs tests, and consults the research in a process of elimination to identify the problem and then try to correct it. In the same way, biologists attempt to manage public waters, and although they can't test everything and can't afford to right every wrong they find, they do have some tools at their disposal. Lakes that are high in acid levels, for example, can be treated cheaply with lime to make them more neutral in pH. In lakes barren of fish cover, adding various shelters and structures can help furnish places to spawn and to hide. Sportsmen's clubs and lakeowner associations often provide the manpower and, in some cases, the money to improve fishing quality.

So, lakes constantly change. The more that people use them and impact them, the faster they change. My goal in the Fish Michigan series is not to burn out any lake. Rather, it is to steer fishermen of all ages and levels of experience to some of our state's best fishing waters in the hope that these anglers, too, will enjoy a quality experience. I have already begun work on a fishing guide to Michigan rivers — not just trout streams but the best rivers for bass, walleye and other species, too. I plan to follow up that guide or guides with a major revision of *Fish Michigan — Great Lakes*, a popular reference that has been out of print now for several years. Then I will revise the inland lake titles, including the newest edition you are holding.

Responsible use of Michigan's excellent water resources prompts the government to manage them for the greater good. This management involves improving access sites — including facilities for handicapped anglers — and increasing field personnel to conduct surveys and to enforce regulations.

The rest is up to us fishermen. If we remember that limits are aimed at regulating the maximum, to eat what we catch, and to let the rest go for Mom, Dad and their kids, there is no reason that all of us cannot enjoy our favorite pasttime for years to come.

Tom Huggler
Lansing, Michigan

CONTENTS

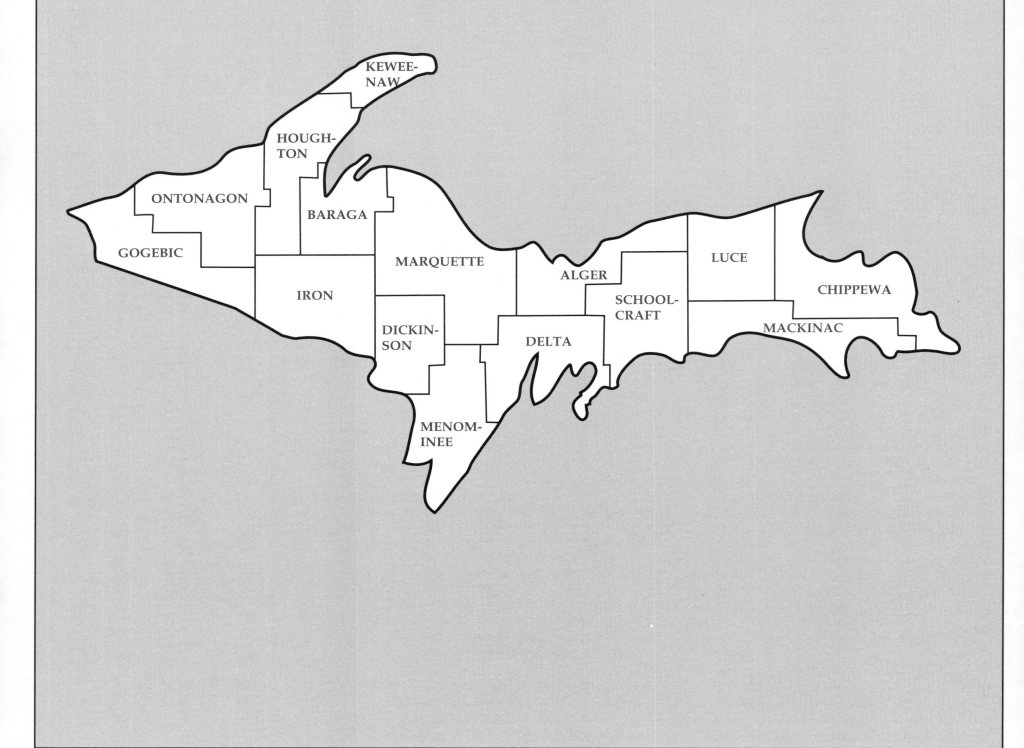

MAP SYMBOLS	ii
INTRODUCTION	iii
HOW TO USE THIS BOOK	vi

ALGER COUNTY

Au Train Lake	1
Bar Lake	2
Beaver Lake	3
Fish Lake	4
Grand Sable Lake	5
Nawakwa Lake	6

BARAGA COUNTY

Craig Lake	7
Crooked Lake	8
Fence Lake	9
King Lake	10
Parent Lake	11
Prickett Dam Backwater	12
Roland Lake	13
Vermilac Lake	14

CHIPPEWA COUNTY

Caribou Lake	15
Carp Lake	16
Frenchman's Lake	17

DELTA COUNTY

Camp 7 Lake	18
Norway Lake	19
Round Lake	20

DICKINSON COUNTY

Lake Antoine	21
Twin Falls Flowage	22

GOGEBIC COUNTY

Cisco Lake	23
Clark Lake	24
Clearwater Lake	25
Crooked Lake	26
Deer Island Lake	27
Duck Lake	28
East Bear Lake	29
Imp Lake	30
Lac Vieux Desert	31
Lake Gogebic	32
Loon Lake	33
Marion Lake	34
Pomeroy Lake	35
Tamarack Lake	36
Thousand Island Lake	37
Whitefish Lake	38

HOUGHTON COUNTY

Bass Lake	40
Bob Lake	39
Clear Lake	40
Lake Gerald	41
Lake Roland	42
Otter Lake	43
Perrault Lake	44
Portage Lake	45
Rice Lake	46
Torch Lake	47

IRON COUNTY

Brule Lake	48
Chicagon Lake	49
Golden Lake	50
Hagerman Lake	51
Lake Emily	52
Lake Ste. Kathryn	53
Ottawa Lake	54
Peavy Reservoir	55
Perch Lake	56
Stanley Lake	57
Sunset Lake	58

KEWEENAW COUNTY

Gratiot Lake	59
Lac LaBelle	60
Lake Medora	61
Manganese Lake	62

LUCE COUNTY

Belle Lake	63
Moon Lake	64
Muskallonge Lake	65
Perch Lake	66
Pike Lake	67
Pretty Lake Quiet Area	68
Round Lake	69
Twin Lakes	70

MACKINAC COUNTY

Big Manistique Lake	71
Brevoort Lake	72
Little Brevoort Lake	73
Milakokia Lake	74
Millecoquin Lake	75
South Manistique Lake	76

MARQUETTE COUNTY

Deer Lake Basin	77
Goose Lake	78
Greenwood Reservoir	79
Lake Independence	80
Lake Michigamme	81
Squaw Lake	82
Teal Lake	83
Witch Lake	84

MENOMINEE COUNTY

Chalk Hills Flowage	85
White Rapids Flowage	86

ONTONAGON COUNTY

Courtney Lake	87
Mirror Lake	88
Sudden Lake	89
Victoria Dam Backwater	90

SCHOOLCRAFT COUNTY

Big Island Lake Complex	91
Dodge Lake	92
Dutch Fred Lake	93
Gulliver Lake	94
Indian Lake	95
Island Lake	96
Petes Lake	97
Swan Lake	98
Thunder Lake	99

ALPHABETICAL LIST OF LAKES	101
THE AUTHOR	103

You bought this book because, like most fishermen, you realize that more than simple luck is involved with catching fish. Between these covers is a wealth of information that can translate to success. All the homework you need is here if you'll take the time to review it carefully. Here is how to get the most value for your investment.

Picking a Lake to Fish

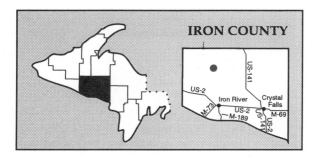

When you are looking for a particular lake in any Upper Peninsula county, check the regional map and table of contents on pages *iv* and *v*. Counties are listed alphabetically, and the featured lakes, all with public access, are listed alphabetically within each county. On page 101 is a single alphabetical list of all lakes included in this book.

At the top of each page containing a lake map, you'll find a small county map featuring main highways and a red dot that will help you generally locate the lake (Figure 1).

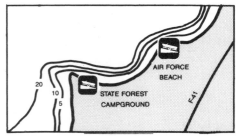

Figure 2

Access: Directions to the public access site(s) are explained in the final paragraph of text for each lake. On the map, public access sites are indicated by the symbols in Figure 2.

Fishing Opportunities: Walleyes, Smallmouth Bass, Ciscoes and Splake—Good to Excellent; Yellow Perch, Northern Pike, Brown Trout—Fair to Good; Rainbow Trout, Lake Trout, Great Lakes Muskies, White Bass, Black Crappies, Smelt, Largemouth Bass and Sturgeon—Available with varying degrees of opportunity.

Figure 3

To focus on the best fishing for northern pike, walleyes, bluegills, trout or any of more than 20 other gamefish species, scan the *Fishing Opportunities* highlights (Figure 3) that are printed in red ink under the boldface lake name on each page. The prioritized ratings we use include Excellent, Good, Fair, Poor and Available.

Picking the Best Time to Fish

The red symbols (Figure 4) that appear on each lake map are good places to begin looking for certain species. As a general rule, these are known summer locations. However, fish may move to different areas in the lake for many reasons, including changes in water temperature and level, food availability, the onset of the spawning period, and the need to escape from predators. If you cannot find fish in the recommended locations, be prepared to try different depths and different spots.

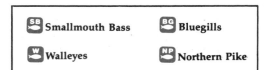

Figure 4 (See page ii for all symbols)

Reading the Lake Maps

A map is effective only if the person reading it knows what to look for. The 100 new lake maps in this book are drawn for accuracy and detail, with an eye to making them easy to read and understand.

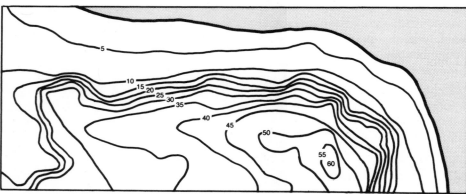

Figure 5

These are contour maps, also called bathymetric or hydrographic maps, because they show changes in depth. Most maps depict these changes as 5- or 10-foot intervals (Figure 5). To find the correct depth of any contour line, simply follow it to the closest number.

Lines that are spaced far apart (Figure 6) indicate a gradually sloping bottom. They are often found in shallow areas of the lake and can be good places to fish in spring and fall. Spawning activity in spring often begins in these areas of level bottom. When they are located away from shore they are often referred to as "flats." Flats are good spots to find resting fish, such as post-spawn walleyes, as well as foraging predators after dark.

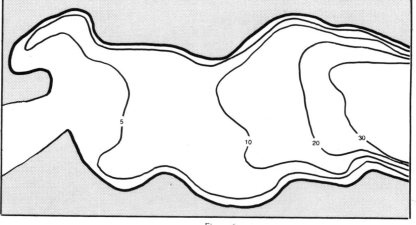

Figure 6

BECOME A BETTER FISHERMAN

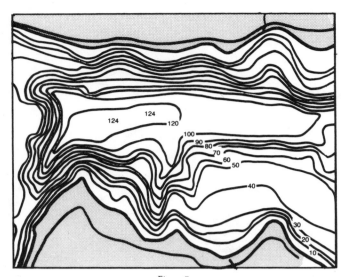

Figure 7

Lines that are spaced close together (Figure 7) denote rapid changes in depth. Such areas provide structure by way of edges, drop-offs, shelves and breaklines, all of which attract and hold a wide variety of gamefish.

Holes and drop-offs are indicated by areas of great depth (Figure 8). In lakes that do not develop a thermocline in summer, fish often concentrate in holes because the water is cooler there. Some of the best fishing spots in winter occur in these same deep areas. On the other hand, if the lake stratifies, fish usually suspend in the life zone or thermocline away from the bottom.

Figure 8

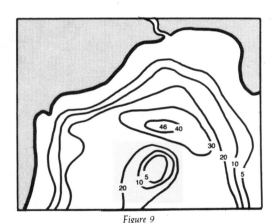

Figure 9

Sunken islands (Figure 9) are depicted by one or more circles with the shallowest depth in the middle. Often called "humps", the special areas of structure can be as small as a bathtub or as large as a football field. Bottom compositions vary and can include rock, gravel, sand, marl or peat. Depending on their depth, sunken islands may or may not contain weeds, but they are usually excellent places to locate fish.

Points, inlets, outlets and narrows (Figure 10) are among many shoreline features that you can easily find on these maps. Fish relate to such areas at various times of the year. A rocky point, for example, may provide spawning habitat for smallmouth bass. Tributaries that flow into the lake are always good places to look for hungry predators. On certain reservoirs, wind-swept points develop a mud line that attracts baitfish and gamefish.

Where manmade reefs and fish shelters are known, we have indicated them on the maps.

In addition to studying the maps, we recommend the use of sonar for finding ministructure and for locating fish.

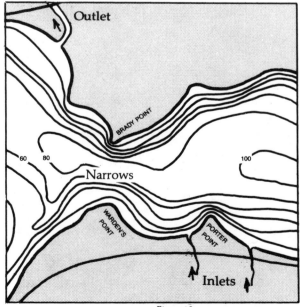

Figure 10

Catching Fish From These Lakes

| Tactics to Try: |

The text that accompanies each map should get you started as to what lures, bait and techniques to try. Experiment, be flexible, and most of all be patient. Although every one of the lakes in this book is among the best inland fishing waters in Michigan, each day is not a good fishing day.

Perhaps that's why we call it fishing and not catching.

AU TRAIN LAKE

Fishing Opportunities: Northern Pike, Ciscoes and Walleyes—Good to Excellent; Smallmouth Bass and Yellow Perch—Good.

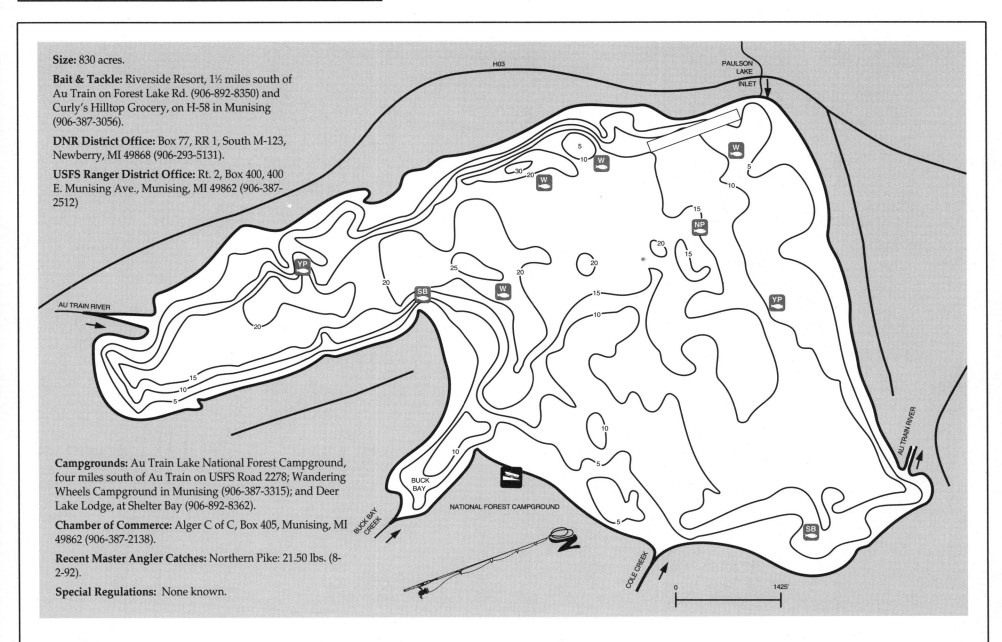

Size: 830 acres.

Bait & Tackle: Riverside Resort, 1½ miles south of Au Train on Forest Lake Rd. (906-892-8350) and Curly's Hilltop Grocery, on H-58 in Munising (906-387-3056).

DNR District Office: Box 77, RR 1, South M-123, Newberry, MI 49868 (906-293-5131).

USFS Ranger District Office: Rt. 2, Box 400, 400 E. Munising Ave., Munising, MI 49862 (906-387-2512)

Campgrounds: Au Train Lake National Forest Campground, four miles south of Au Train on USFS Road 2278; Wandering Wheels Campground in Munising (906-387-3315); and Deer Lake Lodge, at Shelter Bay (906-892-8362).

Chamber of Commerce: Alger C of C, Box 405, Munising, MI 49862 (906-387-2138).

Recent Master Angler Catches: Northern Pike: 21.50 lbs. (8-2-92).

Special Regulations: None known.

Au Train Lake is located in northwest Alger County in the Hiawatha National Forest about nine miles west of Munising. The north and west shorelines are heavily developed with resorts, homes and camps, while most of the south and east shorelines are owned by the U.S. Forest Service. A cedar swamp lies along the northeast side where the Au Train River outlets to Lake Superior. The Au Train River flows in on the south end, an unnamed stream and Paulson Lake flow in from the west side, and Cole and Buck Bay creeks enter from the east side.

The lake's deepest spot is 30 feet, and more than half of it is less than 15 feet deep. Sand and gravel cover the shoal areas, and pulpy peat makes up most of the deep-water bottom. Water color is a light brown, and the water is hard, by U.P. standards, with a pH of 8.5. Bulrushes are common on the south end, along the northeast side and in scattered locations up the west shoreline. Most submergent vegetation is found near the Paulson Lake inlet, in Buck Bay and near the inflow and outflow.

A total of 42 fish shelters were placed throughout the lake along the 10-foot contour in 1975. A 1,500-foot-long artificial reef of rock cobble lies along the northwest shoreline just south of the Paulson Lake inlet. It extends out from the shoreline about 30 feet.

Surveys/Stocking: A September 1991 DNR gill net survey to evaluate the tiger muskie population found no tigers. However, 20-inch walleyes, 20- to 28-inch pike, 16- to 21-inch ciscoes and a 14-inch smallmouth bass were collected. In September 1989 a general fyke and gill net survey found fair numbers of pike, perch and 15- to 23-inch walleyes throughout the lake.

In the spring of 1989, the sucker collection nets also captured 1,500 walleyes, including many fish from 15 to 22 inches long. Each spring for several years the DNR manually removed from 8,000 to 25,000 pounds of suckers. The project has virtually been abandoned because of the inexhaustible supply from Lake Superior.

In May 1993 DNR researchers found good numbers of northern pike in the upper 20-inch range and walleyes from 20 to 25 inches.

In 1991 managers stocked 1,425 smallmouth bass and 67,000 walleyes; in 1992 they released 40,000 smallmouths; and in 1993 they planted out an estimated 13,630 walleyes. All fish stocked were fingerlings. Three miles south of the lake, the DNR annually stocks brown trout yearlings in the Au Train River.

Tactics to Try: Northern pike have been the mainstay for the past 40 years, and they grow fast thanks to a healthy population of suckers and ciscoes. The bigger pike enter from Lake Superior via the Au Train River. Anglers take them in spring and summer by bobber fishing with big sucker minnows — especially along the first-to-warm north shore — and in the winter with tip-up and spear. Good summer spots to try are the weedbeds in the river.

The best place for walleyes is all along the west shore, off the inlets and outlet, and over the artificial reef. Live bait with jigs or spoons and Rapalas work well along structure and over the mixed bottom composition of sand, rock and rubble. Leeches are also good.

Anglers take smallmouth bass each year over boulder piles and around large rocks. The lake also contains a few rock bass, pumpkinseed sunfish and the occasional steelhead and salmon.

Access: The USFS maintains a hard-surfaced boat launch ramp at its Buck Bay campground. Toilets are provided and there is a limited amount of parking. To rent a boat, contact Riverside Resort (see listing under Bait & Tackle) or one of several other resorts on the lake.

BAR LAKE

Fishing Opportunities: Northern Pike—Good to Excellent; Largemouth Bass and Pumpkinseed Sunfish—Fair to Good; Walleyes—Poor; Black Crappies—Available.

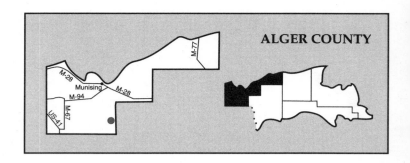

ALGER COUNTY

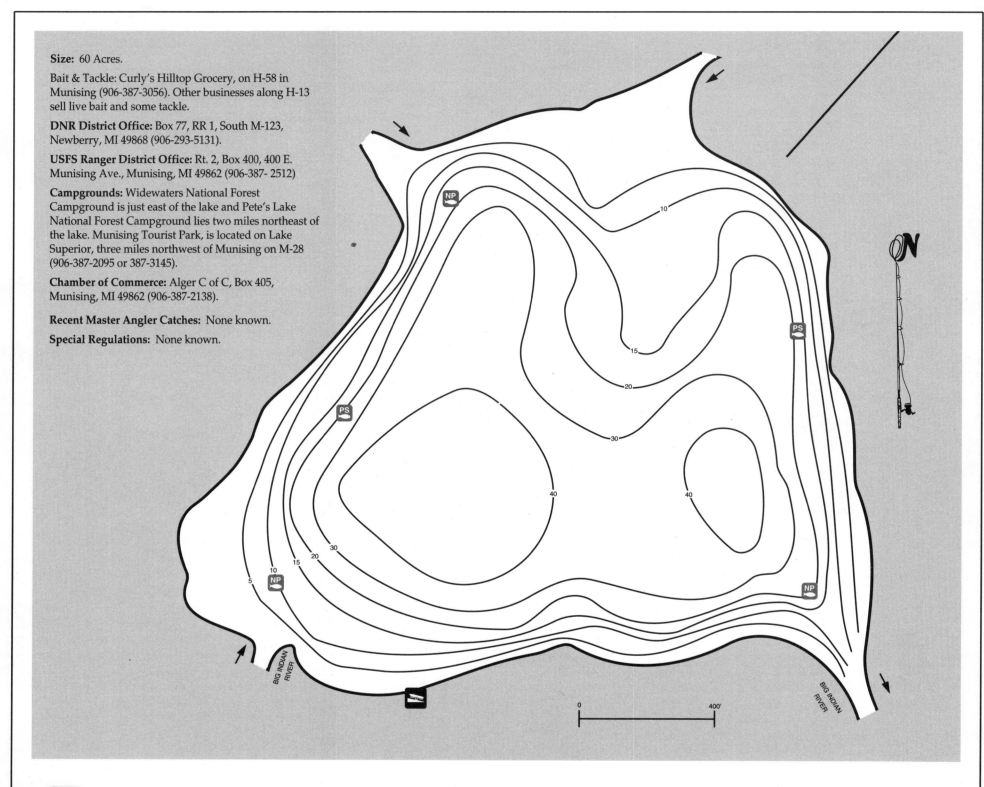

Size: 60 Acres.

Bait & Tackle: Curly's Hilltop Grocery, on H-58 in Munising (906-387-3056). Other businesses along H-13 sell live bait and some tackle.

DNR District Office: Box 77, RR 1, South M-123, Newberry, MI 49868 (906-293-5131).

USFS Ranger District Office: Rt. 2, Box 400, 400 E. Munising Ave., Munising, MI 49862 (906-387- 2512)

Campgrounds: Widewaters National Forest Campground is just east of the lake and Pete's Lake National Forest Campground lies two miles northeast of the lake. Munising Tourist Park, is located on Lake Superior, three miles northwest of Munising on M-28 (906-387-2095 or 387-3145).

Chamber of Commerce: Alger C of C, Box 405, Munising, MI 49862 (906-387-2138).

Recent Master Angler Catches: None known.

Special Regulations: None known.

ar Lake is located in southcentral Alger County on the Upper Big Indian River Chain of Lakes about 15 miles south of Munising. The lake is completely undeveloped and is surrounded by northern hardwoods growing on sandy soil of the Hiawatha National Forest. High hills are found on the south and southwest sides, and fallen trees and deadheads enter the water along this portion of the shore. The Big Indian River enters Bar Lake on the southwest corner and exits on the southeast corner and connects Bar Lake to Fish Lake.

The north and east shores contain bulrushes, lily pads and other pond weeds. The rest of the shoreline shoal area is firm sand, gravel and rock. The bowl-shaped lake is 40 feet deep, and the moderately productive water is clear to slightly stained. In spring and early summer the color is a light green; by September it takes on a reddish tint from vegetation entering via the river.

Surveys/Stocking: Stocking records date to 1930 when 75 largemouth bass were released. Walleyes were introduced in 1979 after a partial chemical reclamation to remove panfish and brown bullheads. DNR biologists last surveyed the lake in August 1983. Their experimental gill net found poor survival of walleyes stocked to date. Many northerns turned up, but they were of small size. A good population of pumpkinseed sunfish was evident.Managers have not stocked the lake in recent years.

Tactics to Try: First-rate pike fishing is available, with fish averaging 21 to 27 inches and trophies to 40 inches caught each year. Good fishing occurs off creek inflows along the lake's north end and near the mouths of the Indian River. A half-inch rainfall is enough to bring food into the lake and turn on the pike. Bobber fishing with 3- or 4-inch shiners, suckers or chubs is a rated tactic, along with casting Mepps Musky Killer spinners and trolling with Rapalas or Jack-of-Diamonds Dardevle spoons.Most other species are caught incidentally to pike.

Access: An undeveloped launch site is accessible for small boats via USFS-2329 on the south side of the lake near the river inlet. Anglers must pull their boats down a big hill to reach the lake. Another option is to paddle upriver from Fish Lake where the USFS maintains a better boat launch. There is no place to rent a boat.

BEAVER LAKE

Fishing Opportunities: Northern Pike and Walleyes—
Good to Excellent; Smallmouth Bass and Yellow Perch—
Fair to Good.

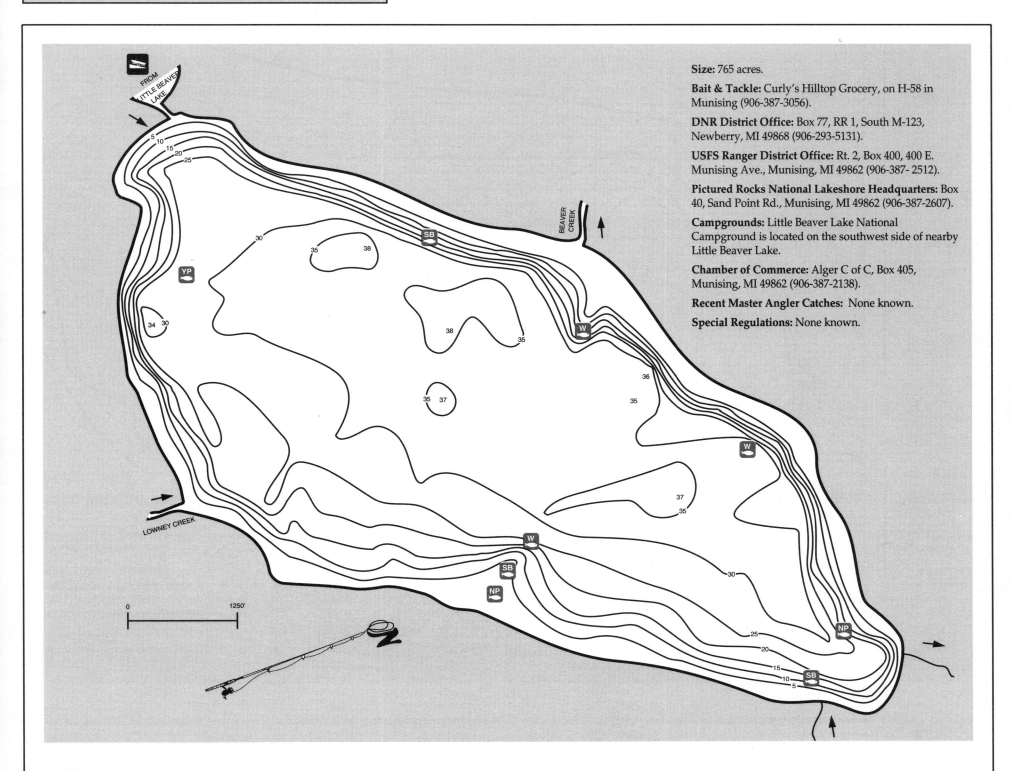

ALGER COUNTY

Size: 765 acres.

Bait & Tackle: Curly's Hilltop Grocery, on H-58 in Munising (906-387-3056).

DNR District Office: Box 77, RR 1, South M-123, Newberry, MI 49868 (906-293-5131).

USFS Ranger District Office: Rt. 2, Box 400, 400 E. Munising Ave., Munising, MI 49862 (906-387- 2512).

Pictured Rocks National Lakeshore Headquarters: Box 40, Sand Point Rd., Munising, MI 49862 (906-387-2607).

Campgrounds: Little Beaver Lake National Campground is located on the southwest side of nearby Little Beaver Lake.

Chamber of Commerce: Alger C of C, Box 405, Munising, MI 49862 (906-387-2138).

Recent Master Angler Catches: None known.

Special Regulations: None known.

Beaver Lake is located in Alger County about 15 miles northeast of Shingleton within the Pictured Rocks National Lakeshore. Surrounding topography of the two-mile-long by one-mile-wide lake is hilly, with mixed pine and hardwoods. The lake connects to Lake Superior a half-mile away via Beaver Creek, which outlets on the west side.

A small flow from Little Beaver Lake enters on the southwest corner, and Lowney Creek flows into the southeast corner. Numerous springs all along the east and south shores contribute more inflow. Bald eagles often nest along the northeast shore.

Surveys/Stocking: Historically, lake trout and splake were stocked, but more recently the DNR has attempted to establish a walleye population. A net survey in May 1988 turned up yellow perch, smallmouth bass,

walleyes, brook trout, steelhead and cohos. Northern pike were also present. At that time small perch were overly abundant and constituted 95 percent of the catch.

Beginning in 1990 fisheries personnel switched over from walleye fry to fingerlings. In 1991 managers released 15,300 walleyes; in 1992 they stocked 30,000; and in 1993 they planted out an estimated 11,000 more.

Tactics to Try: Remnants of brush shelters constructed about 30 years ago exist in various places. They are good locations to try for yellow perch and what few rainbow trout are left. For smallmouth bass, northern pike and walleyes, concentrate efforts first along the east shore over contour breaks from 15 to 30 feet deep.

Another good walleye spot is along the northwest shore in 20 feet of water. Drift or slow-troll an air-injected night crawler pinned to a Junebug Spinner or a Lindy Rig. Copper or sil-

ver blades work best.

The single best spot for smallmouths is at the extreme northeast tip of the lake. Try curly-tailed jigs tipped with leeches, minnows or night crawlers. In low-light conditions choose motor oil or smoke colors. White, blue or yellow tails work best during full light.

The Beaver Creek outlet contains steelhead in spring, but fishing the flow is difficult due to its clear water. A bonus is connecting Little Beaver Lake, which is about 40 acres in size and contains jumbo yellow perch, northern pike, rock bass and pumpkinseed sunfish.

Access: There is no launch site on the lake, but anglers can gain access via the channel connecting to Little Beaver Lake, where there is a federal campground accessible via H-58. However, at times the channel is blocked by a beaver dam. There is no place to rent a boat on Beaver Lake.

FISH LAKE

Fishing Opportunities: Northern Pike—Good to Excellent; Largemouth Bass, Yellow Perch and Bluegills—Fair to Good; Walleyes and Black Crappies—Poor to Fair.

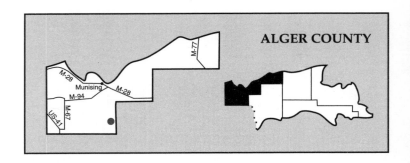

ALGER COUNTY

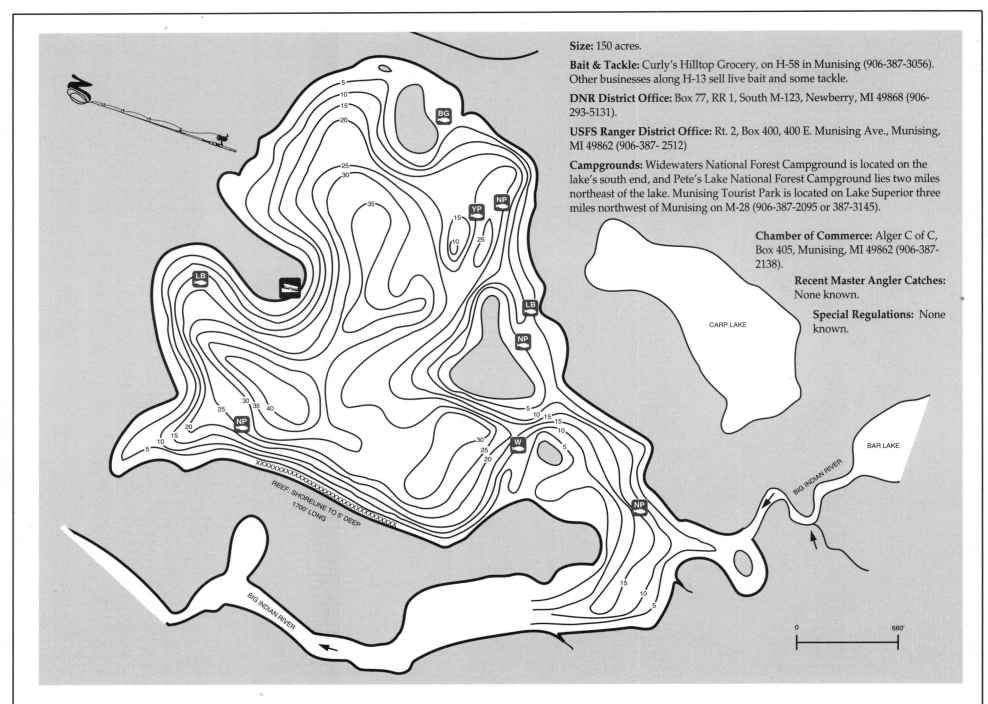

Size: 150 acres.

Bait & Tackle: Curly's Hilltop Grocery, on H-58 in Munising (906-387-3056). Other businesses along H-13 sell live bait and some tackle.

DNR District Office: Box 77, RR 1, South M-123, Newberry, MI 49868 (906-293-5131).

USFS Ranger District Office: Rt. 2, Box 400, 400 E. Munising Ave., Munising, MI 49862 (906-387- 2512)

Campgrounds: Widewaters National Forest Campground is located on the lake's south end, and Pete's Lake National Forest Campground lies two miles northeast of the lake. Munising Tourist Park is located on Lake Superior three miles northwest of Munising on M-28 (906-387-2095 or 387-3145).

Chamber of Commerce: Alger C of C, Box 405, Munising, MI 49862 (906-387-2138).

Recent Master Angler Catches: None known.

Special Regulations: None known.

Fish Lake is located in southcentral Alger County on the Big Indian River, which flows southeasterly to Lake Michigan and the city of Manistique. The lake lies about 13 miles south of Munising. Beech, maple and birch are the predominate hardwoods among the rolling uplands of the Hiawatha National Forest, which surrounds the lake. Jackpines, cherry and aspen are found in brushy openings.

The lake lies about a quarter-mile downstream from Bar Lake (p. 2). The shoreline is highly irregular, and there are three islands along the west side. Shoal waters feature sand with some gravel deposits around the largest island. Offshore material includes pulpy and fibrous peat. Lily pads, pond weeds and bulrushes are important weeds in sheltered bays and shoal areas.

Water clarity of this slightly alkaline lake is a bit stained to mostly clear. A decent amount of fish habitat includes aquatic vegetation, deep water and fallen trees. Fishing pressure is mod-erate to high.

In 1979 the USFS installed a 1,500-foot-long artificial reef along the east shoreline.

Surveys/Stocking: Walleye fry were first intro-duced in 1937, which prob-ably established these fish in the Big Indian River. The DNR first stocked walleye fingerlings in 1979 in the hopes of forming a spawning pop-ulation on the artificial reef. Manual removal and chemical treatments were unsuccessful, however, in removing slow-growing bluegills, sunfish, rock bass and yellow perch.

The lake was last surveyed by the DNR in 1983, and researchers concluded it contained too many small pike. Management effort since has focused on improving the largemouth bass, bluegill, crappie and walleye fisheries while reducing competition from undesirable species.

A USFS survey in April 1990 found northern pike to average nearly 17 inches. The nets pro-duced many bluegills but they averaged only 4 inches; on the other hand, pumpkinseed sunfish averaged 5 inches. Six walleyes averaged 19 inches, and 17 black crappies averaged 8 inches.

Technicians measured plenty of rock bass and bullheads, too.

The lake has not been stocked in recent years.

Tactics to Try: Apparently northern pike are doing better because anglers catch them during midday hours in spring and fall among cabbage weeds and reeds along the north shore between the mainland and the islands. Fall is best for fishing the pockets of reeds along the southeast shore. Rated tactics include trolling with black-and-white Dardevles and various Canadian lake spoons and other hardware, plus backtrolling with night crawlers.

Lily pads among the lake's northwest corner are good for largemouths, rock bass, perch and bluegills. Rainfalls bring food into the lake and improve the fishing.

Access: The USFS maintains a boat launch ramp at its campground on the south point. The launch and lake will accommodate bigger fishing boats, but connection to other lakes in the Big Indian River Chain is possible only by canoe. There is no place to rent a boat on Fish Lake.

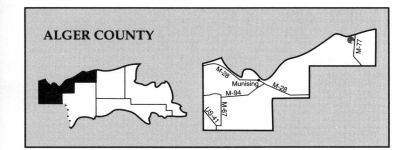

GRAND SABLE LAKE

Fishing Opportunities: Lake Trout—Good; Smallmouth Bass and Northern Pike—Fair; Brook Trout and Yellow Perch—Poor.

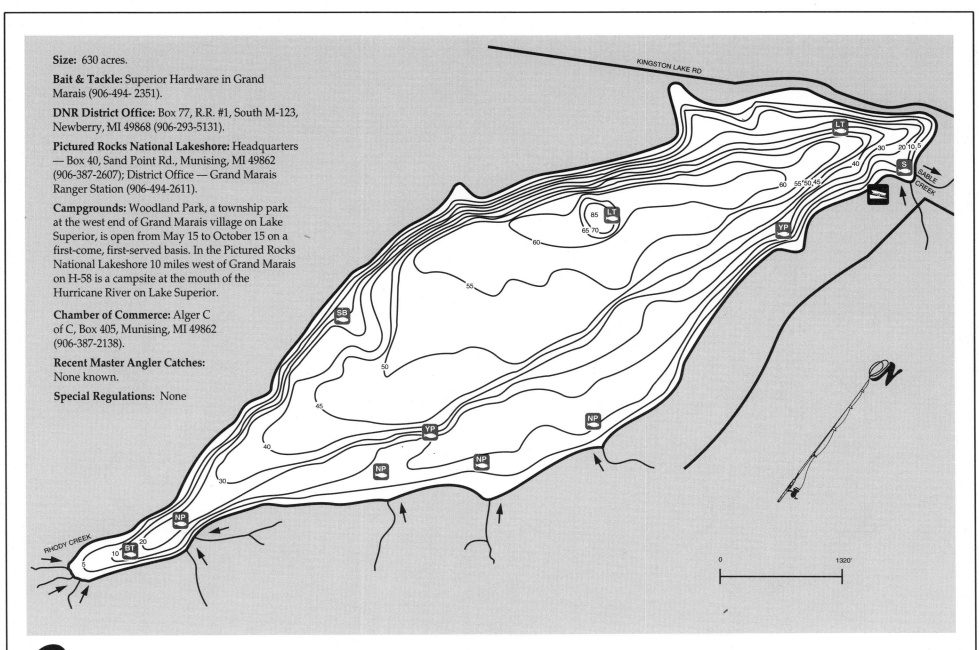

Size: 630 acres.

Bait & Tackle: Superior Hardware in Grand Marais (906-494- 2351).

DNR District Office: Box 77, R.R. #1, South M-123, Newberry, MI 49868 (906-293-5131).

Pictured Rocks National Lakeshore: Headquarters — Box 40, Sand Point Rd., Munising, MI 49862 (906-387-2607); District Office — Grand Marais Ranger Station (906-494-2611).

Campgrounds: Woodland Park, a township park at the west end of Grand Marais village on Lake Superior, is open from May 15 to October 15 on a first-come, first-served basis. In the Pictured Rocks National Lakeshore 10 miles west of Grand Marais on H-58 is a campsite at the mouth of the Hurricane River on Lake Superior.

Chamber of Commerce: Alger C of C, Box 405, Munising, MI 49862 (906-387-2138).

Recent Master Angler Catches: None known.

Special Regulations: None

Grand Sable Lake is a scenic, undeveloped lake within the Pictured Rocks National Lakeshore. The lake is located in Alger County about six miles southwest of Grand Marais. Spectacular 200-foot-high sand dunes rise from the northwest side, and a mixed forest of hardwoods, conifers and cedar abound.

Lake depths of the clear, brown-stained lake average 35 to 40 feet, and the banks drop off quite rapidly. Shoal areas are mostly sand; the deeper bottom is pulpy peat. Several small creeks flow into the lake, the largest of which is Rhody Creek entering from the southwest end. Sable Creek outlets on the northeast end to Lake Superior.

Surveys/Stocking: The lake has a long stocking history of rainbow trout, splake, smelt, smallmouth and largemouth bass, northern pike, bluegills and lake trout. Over the years most of these species have produced good fishing. Today, however, only lake trout are released. Many of the small creeks support spring smelt runs from Lake Superior. Periodically white suckers must be manually removed to reduce competition with more desirable species.

A DNR fisheries crew that surveyed the lake in September 1989 collected lake trout from 10 to 34 inches. The average fish taped a respectable 25.3 inches. Smallmouth bass and northern pike showed up in smaller numbers.

In 1991 managers stocked 12,000 lake trout, in 1992 they released 30,000 lakers, and in 1993 they planted out an estimated 15,000 more. All fish were yearlings.

Tactics to Try: The best lake trout fishing occurs in spring, and fishing pressure is considered light. For spring lakers to 6 lbs., concentrate in 10- to 30-foot deep contours of the northeast region and fish purple Mister Twisters. The deep hole off the northwest shore is productive in midsummer for lakers, plus occasional remnant splake and rainbow trout. Use live minnows or jig dead smelt on a Hopkins Spoon or Swedish Pimple. Another trick is to troll the hole with downriggers and small spoons containing cut bait.

For northern pike and occasional brook trout, time your trip with smelt runs occurring in late April/early May at the lake's extremities. For pike, minnows rigged with bobbers work as do dead smelt fished on bottom. The best single lure for brook trout is a Mepps Comet Spinner in Size 0 or 1.

Other creek mouths along the east shore produce pike and yellow perch in spring. Smallmouths turn up throughout the lake; drift crawler-tipped jigs along fast drop-offs over hard bottom, or seek isolated boulders and deadheads.

Access: The old access site that used to contain a boat launch and was located at the northwest corner off CR-714/710 has been changed to a scenic outlook. To launch a boat, go to the township park at the lake's northeast end. There is no place to rent a boat.

NAWAKWA LAKE

Fishing Opportunities: Walleyes—Good to Excellent;
Northern Pike and Yellow Perch—Fair to Good.

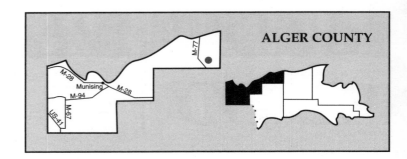

ALGER COUNTY

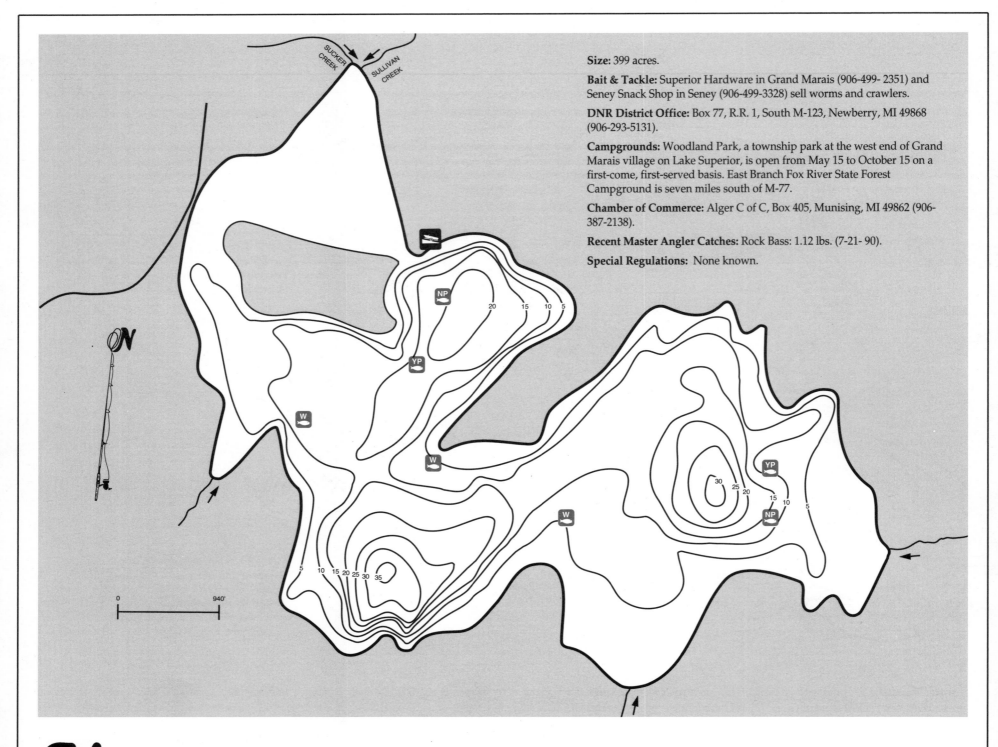

Size: 399 acres.

Bait & Tackle: Superior Hardware in Grand Marais (906-499- 2351) and Seney Snack Shop in Seney (906-499-3328) sell worms and crawlers.

DNR District Office: Box 77, R.R. 1, South M-123, Newberry, MI 49868 (906-293-5131).

Campgrounds: Woodland Park, a township park at the west end of Grand Marais village on Lake Superior, is open from May 15 to October 15 on a first-come, first-served basis. East Branch Fox River State Forest Campground is seven miles south of M-77.

Chamber of Commerce: Alger C of C, Box 405, Munising, MI 49862 (906-387-2138).

Recent Master Angler Catches: Rock Bass: 1.12 lbs. (7-21- 90).

Special Regulations: None known.

Nawakwa Lake, which is sometimes called Sucker Lake because it forms the headwaters for the Sucker River, is located in northeast Alger County about 15 miles north of Seney and nine miles south of Grand Marais. Surrounding forests of the gently rolling hills include birch, maple, beech, hemlock, spruce and cedar. A dozen cottages and the Newton Club are located around the lake. A big island lies across from the access site on the northwest shore.

Sullivan Creek enters in the northwest corner, and the lake is also fed by three smaller, unnamed flows. Nawakwa Lake is fairly shallow: 70 percent features depths less than 15 feet, and the maximum depth is 37 feet. Bottom composition varies from sand to gravel to rocks to pulpy peat in the deeper stretches. The water is brown-stained and slightly turbid. The lake stratifies in summer, and oxygen deficits often occur near bottom.

Bulrushes and cattails are common, along with lily pads and other vegetation, both emergent and submergent. The irregular shoreline supports nine points and nine bays, and there are a number of sand bars and shallow reefs, which occasionally cause problems for boat fishermen trying to access the lake's main portion.

Surveys/Stocking: A June 1989 DNR survey produced 166 walleyes from 10 to 25 inches each. The fish represented nine different age classes, and more than 80 percent of the samples were catchable size of 15 inches or larger. The nets also collected 85 yellow perch, 61 pumpkinseed sunfish (which averaged 7 inches) 344 rock bass, and 141 northern pike. All species were growing near the state average. About 23 percent of the catch by number, however, was brown bullheads.

Nawakwa Lake has good survival and recruitment of walleyes, and some natural reproduction occurs. Managers did not stock the lake during the period 1991-1993.

Tactics to Try: For walleyes, fish the points with jigs containing a fluorescent-colored twister tail. Black, white or pink colors work well too. Another rated tactic for windy days is to drift across the wind-pounded points with a slip bobber and a leech. Winter fishing would probably be good, but because the access road is not plowed, anglers will have to enter via snowmobile or on foot.

The shallow bay off the boat launch is a prime location to catch exceptionally large bullheads (to 16 inches) in the evening.

Access: The DNR maintains an improved access site along a shallow bay on the lake's northwest side. Access is via sand trails off M-77. Facilities include a paved boat launch ramp, toilets, courtesy pier and parking for up to nine vehicles with trailers. There is no place to rent a boat.

CRAIG LAKE

Fishing Opportunities: Northern Muskies and Northern Pike—Good to Excellent; Smallmouth Bass and Black Crappies—Fair to Good; Largemouth Bass and Yellow Perch—Poor to Fair.

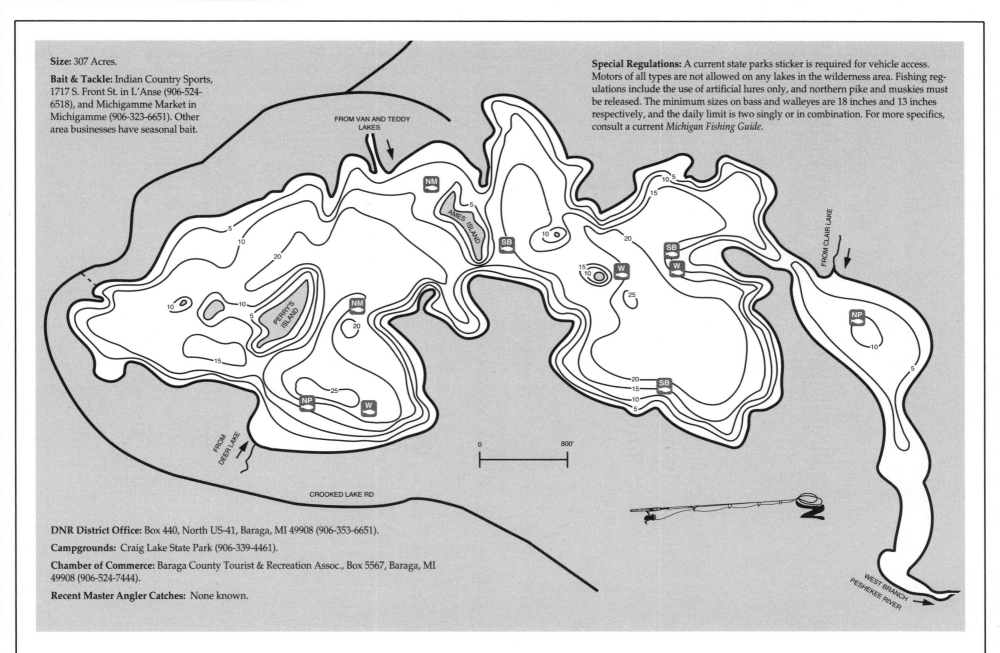

Size: 307 Acres.

Bait & Tackle: Indian Country Sports, 1717 S. Front St. in L'Anse (906-524-6518), and Michigamme Market in Michigamme (906-323-6651). Other area businesses have seasonal bait.

Special Regulations: A current state parks sticker is required for vehicle access. Motors of all types are not allowed on any lakes in the wilderness area. Fishing regulations include the use of artificial lures only, and northern pike and muskies must be released. The minimum sizes on bass and walleyes are 18 inches and 13 inches respectively, and the daily limit is two singly or in combination. For more specifics, consult a current *Michigan Fishing Guide*.

DNR District Office: Box 440, North US-41, Baraga, MI 49908 (906-353-6651).

Campgrounds: Craig Lake State Park (906-339-4461).

Chamber of Commerce: Baraga County Tourist & Recreation Assoc., Box 5567, Baraga, MI 49908 (906-524-7444).

Recent Master Angler Catches: None known.

Craig Lake is located in southeast Baraga County about four miles north of M-28/US-41 and about six miles northwest of Michigamme. The lands comprising Craig Lake State Park were acquired from an estate in 1966. The specially designated Craig Lake Wilderness Area, which is completely forested with species ranging from northern hardwoods to swamp conifers, is one of the most remote in Michigan. It is also among the state's highest land elevations. Rocky outcroppings abound, and the beautiful shoreline of Craig Lake is rock-faced and steep.

A small stream originating at nearby Clair Lake enters the north arm of Craig Lake via a six-foot falls. A west- side inlet brings water from both Van and Teddy lakes. A small stream flowing into the southeast bay comes from Deer Lake, about two miles away. The north arm outlet forms the West Branch of the Peshekee River.

About half of Craig Lake is deeper than 15 feet, maximum depth is 27 feet, and the irregular shoreline is almost 8 miles in length. Much of the bottom composition in the shallows is sand; in the deeper areas it is mostly organic. Vegetation is sparse except for some submergent weeds in the bays. Islands, drowned logs and rocks are common. The water is clear yet stained a dark brown and contains dissolved oxygen to as deep as 23 feet some years. The lake typically develops a thermocline in summer from 10 to 20 feet deep.

Surveys/Stocking: A 1970 DNR survey determined that Craig Lake contained the most diversified gamefish populations of the seven lakes within the special-use area. Restrictive fishing regulations, including a slot limit for bass and catch-and-release protection for muskies, were initiated in 1972. For more than 20 years, managers have tried to keep the highly popular lake productive for trophy smallmouths and muskies with a modest harvest of other species.

In May 1991 a fyke net survey collected 12 northern pike to 25 inches each. All were either ripe males or females with eggs running out of them and provided evidence that the number and average size of pike were improving. The average size of walleyes was small, but fish were fairly abundant. The nets revealed low numbers of smallmouth bass and black crappies.

Researchers returned the next month to net northern muskies. The five they caught averaged 38.7 inches and averaged 13½ pounds.

Walleyes measured from the 46 collected averaged 13 inches, but growth rates were slow. A few largemouth bass were also present.

The stocking record dates to 1947 when largemouth bass were introduced. Walleyes from Big Bay de Noc were first stocked in the 1950s, followed by muskies. The DNR did not stock the lake, however, during the period 1991-1993.

Tactics to Try: The lake is one of Michigan's best for pure-strain muskies. Proof is the fact that walleye anglers report stringered catches being attacked by the toothy predators. Typical muskie lures, including big spinnerbaits and buzzbaits, work well here. However, because of the motor ban, anglers must toss their lures rather than troll them.

Smallmouths will hit jigs and pigs in dark colors. Another good lure is a leadhead jig with a yellow or white curley tail, which walleyes will also take.

Access: The lake is not accessible by vehicle. One mile west of the village of Michigamme, a road leads north from US-41 for about 5 miles to within a quarter mile of Craig Lake. From this point anglers must transport their boat and fishing gear to the lake. There is no place to rent a boat.

CROOKED LAKE

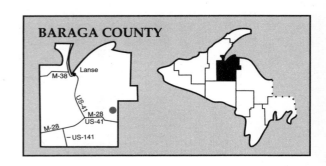
Fishing Opportunities: Largemouth Bass—Good to Excellent; Yellow Perch and Smallmouth Bass—Good; Northern Pike and Northern Muskies—Available.

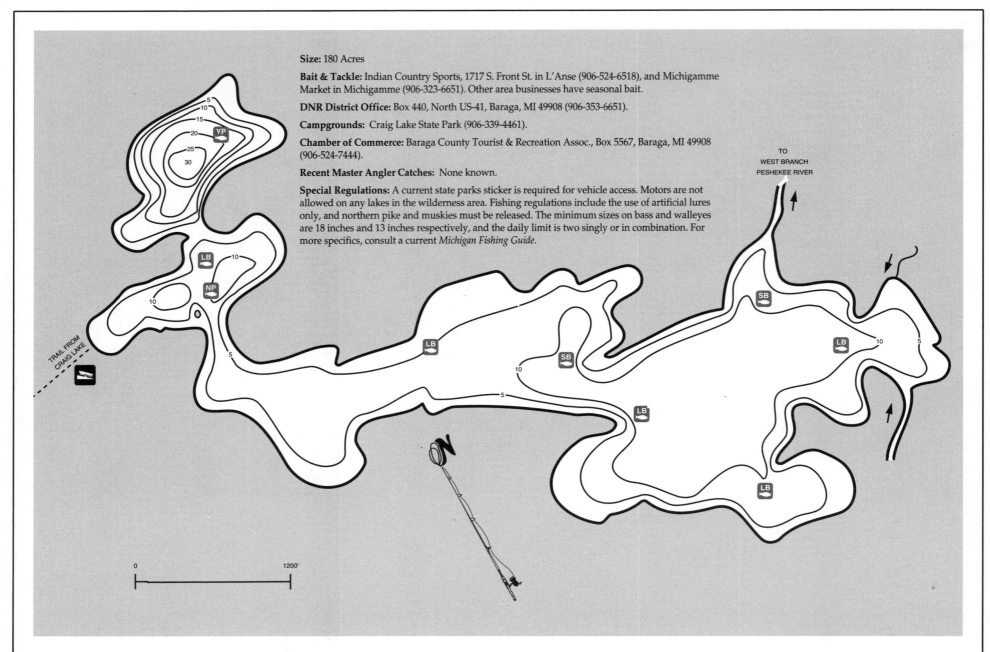

Size: 180 Acres

Bait & Tackle: Indian Country Sports, 1717 S. Front St. in L'Anse (906-524-6518), and Michigamme Market in Michigamme (906-323-6651). Other area businesses have seasonal bait.

DNR District Office: Box 440, North US-41, Baraga, MI 49908 (906-353-6651).

Campgrounds: Craig Lake State Park (906-339-4461).

Chamber of Commerce: Baraga County Tourist & Recreation Assoc., Box 5567, Baraga, MI 49908 (906-524-7444).

Recent Master Angler Catches: None known.

Special Regulations: A current state parks sticker is required for vehicle access. Motors are not allowed on any lakes in the wilderness area. Fishing regulations include the use of artificial lures only, and northern pike and muskies must be released. The minimum sizes on bass and walleyes are 18 inches and 13 inches respectively, and the daily limit is two singly or in combination. For more specifics, consult a current *Michigan Fishing Guide.*

TO WEST BRANCH PESHEKEE RIVER

TRAIL FROM CRAIG LAKE

0   1200'

Crooked Lake is located in southeast Baraga County in the middle of the Craig Lake Wilderness Area about four miles north of M-28/US-41 and 13 miles southeast of L'Anse. The special-use area is remote and rugged, and the entire shoreline of Crooked Lake is heavily forested and rocky. An eagle's nest is located on the northeast shore.

A pair of small, unnamed streams enter from the southeast near where the lake's only outlet, which flows to the West Branch of the Peshekee River, is located.

Crooked Lake is well-named, with several bays and lobes along its approximate two-mile length. Most of the lake is only 5 to 10 feet deep with the exception of the most northerly basin, which has a maximum depth of 30 feet. Although much of the shoreline features a narrow spit of sand, sizable gravel deposits occur throughout the lake. Organic material shows up in deeper stretches, and fibrous peat occurs at the heads of most bays. Floating and submergent vegetation is common, but emergent weeds are sparse. Drowned logs and rocks are everywhere.

Crooked Lake's clear water is stained a dark brown. The northern basin usually develops a thermocline in summer ranging from 10 to 20 feet deep.

Surveys/Stocking: The original fisheries survey in 1937 found only two species of gamefish — yellow perch and green sunfish. Smallmouth bass released in 1947 provided a good fishery, along with largemouths, which were apparently released later, for several years. A 1970 DNR survey determined that Crooked Lake supported the best populations of both smallmouths and largemouths of any lake in the seven- lake special-use area.

A 1984 survey, however, showed that former great fishing for both species had fallen off because of competition from yellow perch, pumpkinseed sunfish and white suckers. To correct the problem, managers partially treated the lake with antimycin in 1987, and fishing began to improve, especially for largemouths. In fact, about 95 percent of the bass caught are now bigmouths.

A June 1991 net survey confirmed that bass populations had responded well. Smallmouths averaged 10.7 inches, and largemouths averaged 13½ inches. The nets collected three northern pike that averaged 27.3 inches, more than 200 yellow perch that averaged 8.2 inches, and a 31½-inch northern muskie.

The DNR did not stock the lake during the period 1991- 1993.

Tactics to Try: Spinnerbaits are the lure of choice for largemouth anglers. Try various combinations of single and double blades in copper, chrome and hammered silver. Blue and white skirts work well, along with black and white, solid white, and yellow with chartreuse.

Grub-bodied ¼-oz. jigs in white are a good lure for perch, but occasional pesky northerns will bite them off. Silver-and-black Rapalas or Dardevle spoons in black and white are rated hardware to toss for pike and the occasional muskie

Access: The lake is not accessible by vehicle. One mile west of the village of Michigamme, a road leads north from US-41 for about five miles to within a quarter mile of Craig Lake. Anglers must carry their canoes down this trail to the south end of Craig Lake and then paddle along its east side to the half-mile-long portage trail leading to Crooked Lake. There is no place to rent a boat.

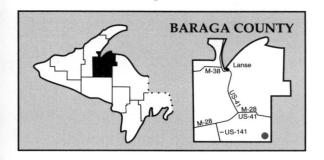

FENCE LAKE

Fishing Opportunities: Rainbow Trout—Good to Excellent; Smallmouth Bass—Fair to Good.

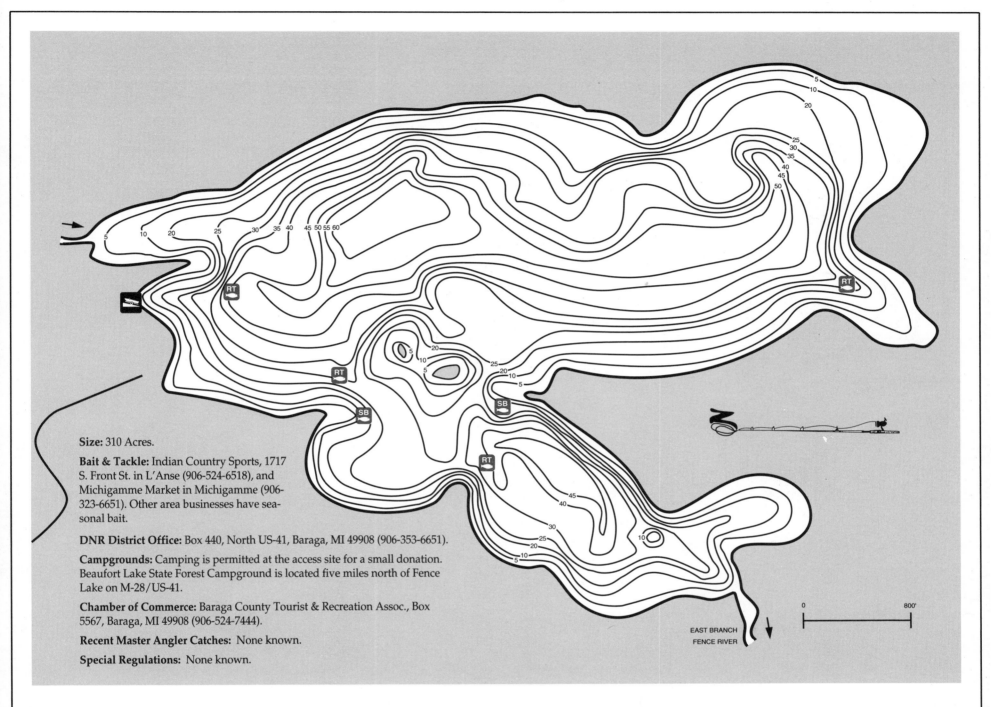

Size: 310 Acres.

Bait & Tackle: Indian Country Sports, 1717 S. Front St. in L'Anse (906-524-6518), and Michigamme Market in Michigamme (906-323-6651). Other area businesses have seasonal bait.

DNR District Office: Box 440, North US-41, Baraga, MI 49908 (906-353-6651).

Campgrounds: Camping is permitted at the access site for a small donation. Beaufort Lake State Forest Campground is located five miles north of Fence Lake on M-28/US-41.

Chamber of Commerce: Baraga County Tourist & Recreation Assoc., Box 5567, Baraga, MI 49908 (906-524-7444).

Recent Master Angler Catches: None known.

Special Regulations: None known.

EAST BRANCH
FENCE RIVER

0   800'

Fence Lake is located in southeast Baraga County about five miles southwest of Michigamme and M-28/U.S.-41. The country surrounding the lake is densely wooded with aspen and some pine, the topography is rolling, and the soil is sand mixed with bedrock. The East Branch of the Fence River, which contains trout and smallmouth bass, exits from the west side. The only inlet is a small stream that enters from the north near the access site.

Counting its three islands, the lake has about 4½ miles of shoreline. Maximum depth of 60 feet occurs in the northcentral portion of the lake's main body, and drops off to 50 or more feet at the south end. A third basin of 45 feet maximum depth is found in the large west bay.

The clear lake is stained a light brown, and it forms a thermocline at 15 to 30 feet deep in the three basins. Shoal areas are mostly rock, rubble and sand, with some decent gravel bars scattered throughout for bass spawning. Deeper areas contain fibrous and marly peat. Vegetative cover is limited to lily pads and bulrushes, but there are plenty of drowned logs in shoreline shallows.

Surveys/Stocking: One hundred years ago, prior to logging in the area, Fence Lake contained a good population of large brook trout. When the woodcutters dammed the lake to float their timber, the brook trout disappeared. During the period 1900 to 1910, smallmouth and possibly largemouth bass were introduced. Rainbow stocking began in 1947 and continues yet today.

An October 1989 DNR net survey indicated a healthy population of trout. Yearlings stocked the previous spring averaged 11 to 12 inches, and fish that had overwintered from the previous year were 16 to 19 inches long. The nets also collected a few smallmouth bass averaging 10.3 inches, along with green sunfish and yellow perch.

In 1991 managers released 10,000 rainbow trout; in 1992 they stocked 15,000 fish; and in 1993 they planted out an estimated 15,000 more. All fish were yearlings.

Tactics to Try: Fishing pressure for trout is moderate to heavy, but the lake appears to be able to withstand it. The best success occurs in midsummer for night-time anglers fishing with lanterns and using whole-kernel corn or pieces of night crawler. Although fish suspend in the thermocline in both basins, many fishermen concentrate in the vicinity of the public access site. Slow trolling by day with Mepps spinners or night crawler harnesses likely would produce also. There is a limited ice fishery.

Apparently few if any anglers target Fence Lake for smallmouths. Based on incidental catches by trout fishermen, bass anglers should enjoy some success.

Access: The lakeshore is entirely owned by the Timber-lee Christian Center in Chicago, but access is assured via a county road access that ends at the lake. The Baraga County Road Commission recently improved the road and enlarged the gravel launch ramp to accommodate boats to 16 feet long. The Timber-lee Christian Center allows parking on its land. There is no place to rent a boat.

KING LAKE

Fishing Opportunities: Smallmouth Bass, Northern Pike and Black Crappies—Good.

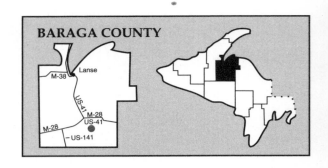

BARAGA COUNTY

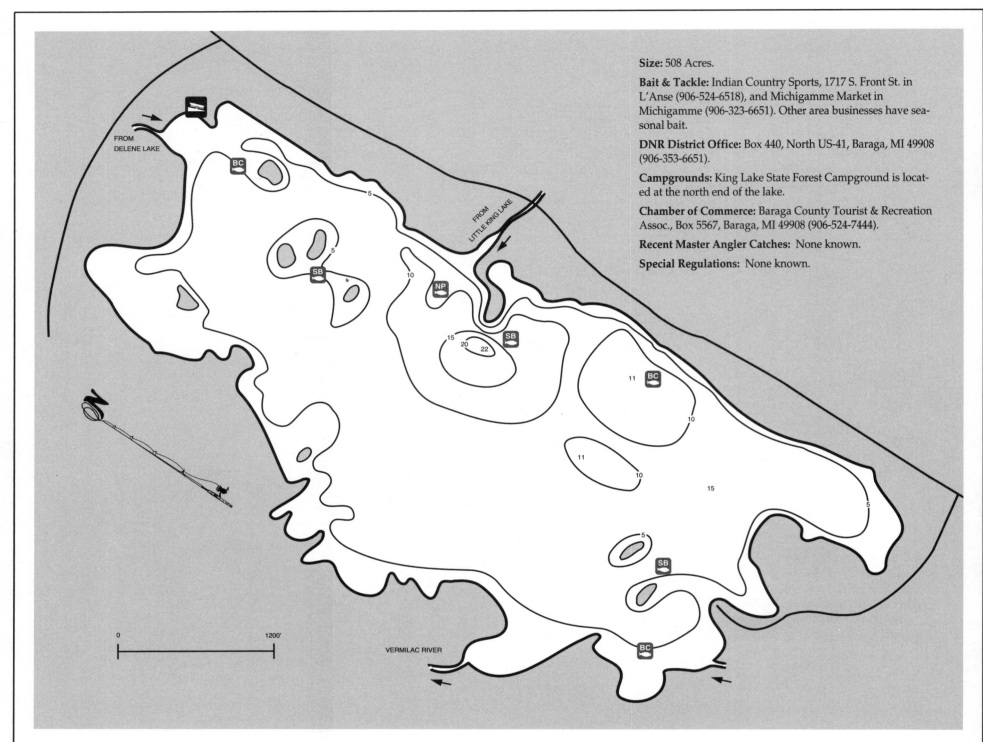

Size: 508 Acres.

Bait & Tackle: Indian Country Sports, 1717 S. Front St. in L'Anse (906-524-6518), and Michigamme Market in Michigamme (906-323-6651). Other area businesses have seasonal bait.

DNR District Office: Box 440, North US-41, Baraga, MI 49908 (906-353-6651).

Campgrounds: King Lake State Forest Campground is located at the north end of the lake.

Chamber of Commerce: Baraga County Tourist & Recreation Assoc., Box 5567, Baraga, MI 49908 (906-524-7444).

Recent Master Angler Catches: None known.

Special Regulations: None known.

King Lake is located in Baraga County about 25 miles south of L'Anse and seven miles southwest of Nestoria. Although the lake is more than 500 acres in size, its maximum depth is only 22 feet. Weeds are scarce and limited mostly to floating and submergent types. The lake's color is a dark brown, cutting lure visibility to only a couple of feet.

Rock reefs and logs provide fish cover in areas less than 5 feet deep, but are a potential hazard to boat fishermen. Bays in the north and south ends occur in swampy areas; shoals in the southeast half are generally steep. Twelve islands feature shores of rock and gravel. The lake's inlets are from Delene and Little King lakes. The outlet is the Vermilac River, which flows from the west side to Vermilac Lake.

Surveys/Stocking: The lake's first survey, conducted in 1929, found north-

ern pike, yellow perch and smallmouth bass along with various rough fish and minnows. Fisheries managers stocked lake trout that year and then added smallmouth bass and bluegills in the 1930s and early 1940s.

Subsequent surveys through 1988 show the lake to contain fishable populations of pike, smallmouths and black crappies. Smallmouths to 18 inches are available, along with fair to good numbers of 25- to 30-inch pike. They averaged 26 inches in the last survey. Although crappies don't run magnum size, there are plenty of them.

Walleyes were introduced in 1985 but were discontinued due to high crappie populations. The DNR did not stock the lake during the period 1991 to 1993.

Tactics to Try: The lake receives moderate fishing pressure in summer, especially when the limited-site campground is full, which is most of the time. Fishing opportunities

shape up throughout King Lake, but one of the best spots for smallmouths is around the north-end islands and their gravel shoals. Fish crawlers or small minnows on a slip bobber for best results.

Crappies tend to wander in King Lake but are nearly always caught over a hard-bottom structure near wood. Look for logs and drowned timber. Tube jigs in pink, white or smoke color work best when mated with small minnows.

Pike will nail bobber-suspended suckers and various plugs and spoons that are cast. Because of the preponderance of rock and the lake's dark color, wholesale trolling is not recommended. Either drift with the wind or still fish for best results.

Access: A paved launch and improved access site are located on the northeast shore at the state forest campground, although parking space is limited. There is no place to rent a boat.

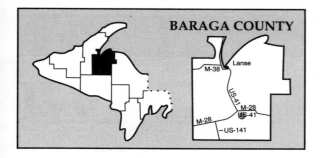

PARENT LAKE

Fishing Opportunities: Yellow Perch and Walleyes—Fair to Good.

Size: 182 Acres.

Bait & Tackle: Indian Country Sports, 1717 S. Front St. in L'Anse (906-524-6518), and Michigamme Market in Michigamme (906-323-6651). Other area businesses have seasonal bait.

DNR District Office: Box 440, North US-41, Baraga, MI 49908 (906-353-6651).

Campgrounds: King Lake State Forest Campground is located about 10 miles west of Parent Lake on King Lake Rd.

Chamber of Commerce: Baraga County Tourist & Recreation Assoc., Box 5567, Baraga, MI 49908 (906-524-7444).

Recent Master Angler Catches: None known.

Special Regulations: None known.

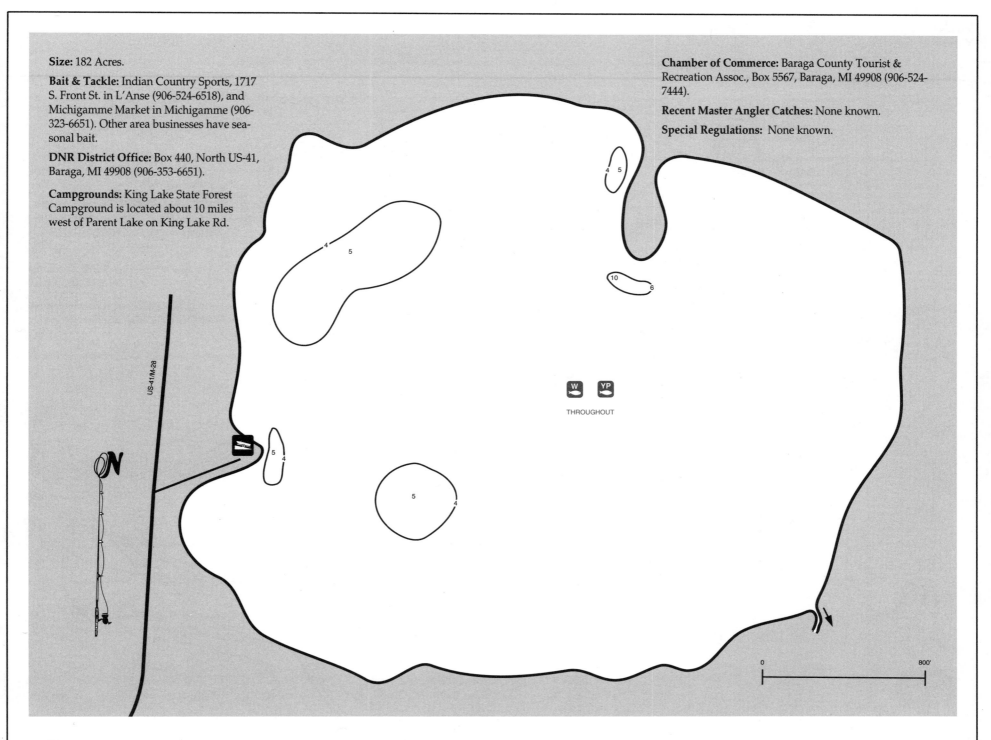

THROUGHOUT

0   800'

arent Lake is located in southcentral Baraga County about 15 miles south of L'Anse and eight miles west of Nestoria right on M-28/US-41 in the middle of a swamp filled with black spruce and white cedar. Surrounding hills are covered with mixed hardwoods and conifers. About 75 percent of the lake frontage is state-owned, with the balance owned by commercial forest interests.

The soft-water, shallow lake averages only 4 feet deep, and its maximum depth is 10 feet. About 90 percent of the lake bottom is silt, with sand, gravel and rock rubble found off the public access site on the north shore and brushy growth along the east side. Weeds are scarce except for scattered beds of water lilies and bulrushes. Logs and large boulders provide most of the shoreline cover. The round-shaped, clear lake is stained a dark brown.

There are no inlets, and the only outlet goes into the Sturgeon River via Watson Creek and the Rock River. Because of its shallow nature, the lake is susceptible to winterkill. Fishing pressure is moderate to heavy.

Surveys/Stocking: Stocking reports date from 1922 when lake trout were released. Survey reports date from 1952 when researchers collected northern pike, along with yellow perch and white suckers. After chemically treating the lake, biologists stocked walleyes about 30 years ago, and the fish appeared to take hold until competition from undesirable species grew. After a 1976 chemical treatment, researchers released tiger muskies and more walleyes, along with black crappies in the 1980s.

A survey in 1987 produced eight-year-old walleyes to 19 inches long, indicating the lake had not suffered from winterkill in recent years. The nets also revealed black crappies, yellow perch, pumpkinseed sunfish and rock bass. A 1988 survey yielded walleyes to 21 inches, along with perch in the 8- to 10-inch class. Each fall a

Michigan Tech biology professor and his students net the lake and report their findings to the DNR. Their most recent efforts collected 45 walleyes to 27 inches long, although the average fish was 15 inches.

Because of walleye natural reproduction, the DNR has not stocked the lake in recent years.

Tactics to Try: Parent Lake is too shallow and rocky to troll safely and effectively. The best technique for walleyes is to row upwind and then drift with Beetle Spins and small minnows or a crawler on a Lindy Rig or other type of harness. When you get bitten by a walleye, toss out your anchor and still-fish or cast and retrieve weedless lures.

Note to fly fishermen: Each June beginning in midmonth, the lake experiences a heavy caddis hatch.

Access: An improved public access site is located on the lake's north shore just south of US-41. There is no place to rent a boat.

PRICKETT DAM BACKWATER

Fishing Opportunities: Largemouth Bass, Bluegills and Black Crappies—Good to Excellent; Walleyes—Good; Yellow Perch and Northern Pike—Fair to Good.

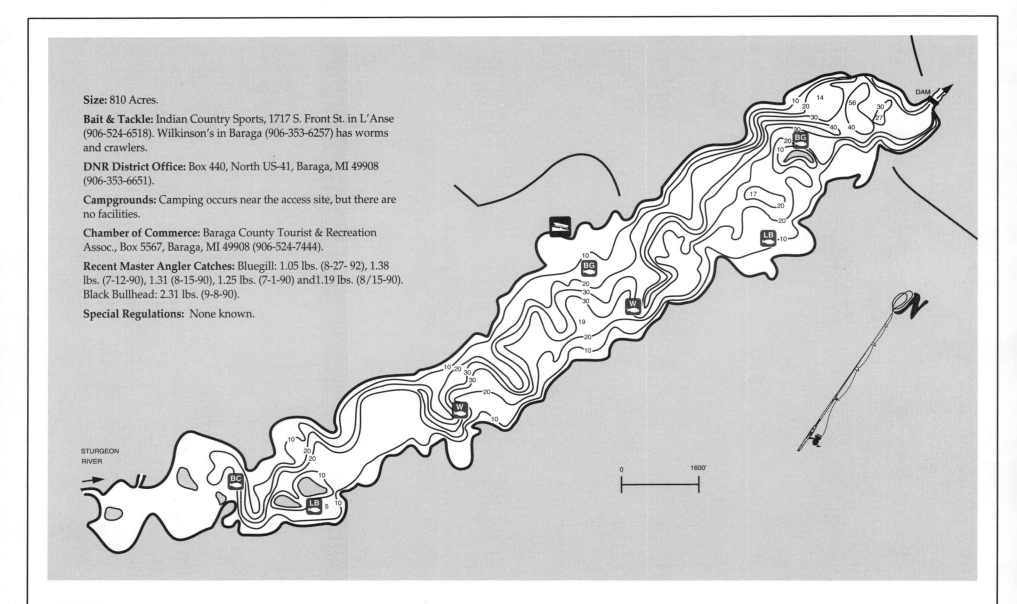

Size: 810 Acres.

Bait & Tackle: Indian Country Sports, 1717 S. Front St. in L'Anse (906-524-6518). Wilkinson's in Baraga (906-353-6257) has worms and crawlers.

DNR District Office: Box 440, North US-41, Baraga, MI 49908 (906-353-6651).

Campgrounds: Camping occurs near the access site, but there are no facilities.

Chamber of Commerce: Baraga County Tourist & Recreation Assoc., Box 5567, Baraga, MI 49908 (906-524-7444).

Recent Master Angler Catches: Bluegill: 1.05 lbs. (8-27- 92), 1.38 lbs. (7-12-90), 1.31 (8-15-90), 1.25 (7-1-90) and 1.19 lbs. (8/15-90). Black Bullhead: 2.31 lbs. (9-8-90).

Special Regulations: None known.

STURGEON RIVER

0   1600'

rickett Dam Backwater is located on the Sturgeon River in westcentral Baraga and eastcentral Houghton counties about 12 miles southwest of Baraga. The reservoir, which is a dark brown in color, was created in 1931. It runs upstream from the dam for about four miles and in some areas of the old stream channel is more than 50 feet deep.

The immediate topography is steep, and the hills are completed forested with maple, birch and hemlock in a relative wilderness setting. The reservoir, which is owned by the Upper Peninsula Power Co., is completely undeveloped.

Stickups, logs and deadheads are abundant throughout the flowage. The bottom composition of the shallows is mostly sand and clay grading to all clay in deeper stretches. Emergent and submergent vegetation occurs in bay and cove areas.

Surveys/Stocking: There is no record of crappies, bluegills and bass ever being stocked in the impoundment. Stocking records date to 1960 when DNR managers released 30,000 brown trout fingerlings. They

added muskies in 1965 and walleyes in 1989. A DNR fyke net survey in June 1990 revealed good fish populations that appeared to be well-balanced. Largemouth bass fishing in the impoundment is better than the survey indicated, but that is because largemouths are hard to catch in nets.

According to the survey, the walleye population was building, black crappies averaged 7 inches but ranged to 12 inches, and bluegills averaged 6 inches with plenty of 7- to 8-inch fish also collected. Northerns averaged 20 inches, walleyes averaged 18½ inches, and yellow perch averaged almost 8 inches.

Over the years, periodic drawdowns in the late spring have helped the DNR to keep the bluegill population in check. The last drawdown occurred in 1982. In 1991 managers stocked 12,000 walleye fingerlings, and in 1992 they released 20,500 more.

Tactics to Try: Golden shiners are now contributing to the forage base, and so bass and walleye anglers might want to approximate these popular baitfish. Sluggos, for example, are effective artificial lures for bass while Rapalas are good for walleyes. Spinnerbaits in chartreuse or white also rate for

bass as do plastic and real night crawlers. Coves and bays are the best places to stick a bucketmouth.

The biggest bluegills are taken in summer but are available year around. Waxworms pinned to an Aberdeen hook or a tiny teardrop spoons are effective. Experiment with colors and presentations until you find a school of biters. Although no one fishes crickets in summer, they should be a good bait, along with small ribbon leeches and red worms.

Crappie fishing is very good in spring for anglers concentrating around stickups over a hard bottom. Use fathead shiners with either a white tube jig or a yellow curley-tailed jig.

Leeches, minnows and crawlers are coming on as preferred walleye baits. From all indications, the impoundment should only improve for this popular gamefish.

Access: The paved, improved public access site is located five miles southeast of Nisula on the westcentral side of the lake. The DNR leases the access site from the Upper Peninsula Power Co. Facilities include a courtesy pier, toilets and parking for 10 vehicles. There is no place to rent a boat.

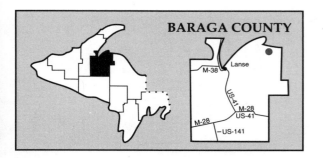

ROLAND LAKE

Fishing Opportunities: Brook Trout—Good to Excellent.

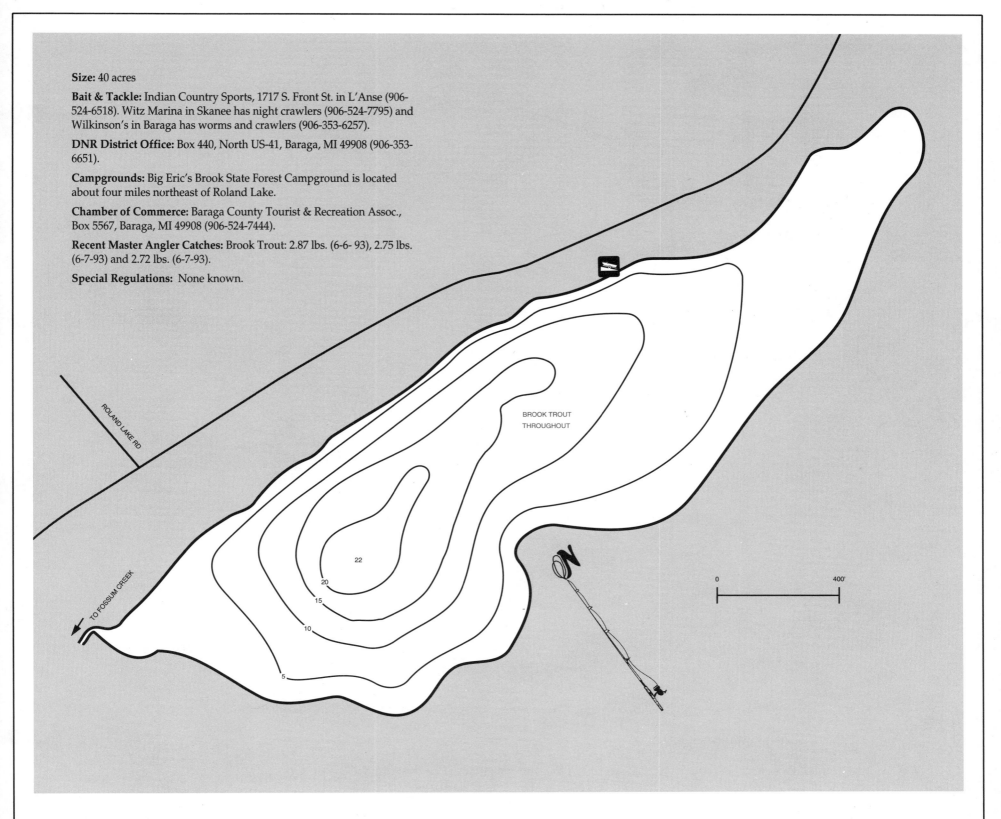

Size: 40 acres

Bait & Tackle: Indian Country Sports, 1717 S. Front St. in L'Anse (906-524-6518). Witz Marina in Skanee has night crawlers (906-524-7795) and Wilkinson's in Baraga has worms and crawlers (906-353-6257).

DNR District Office: Box 440, North US-41, Baraga, MI 49908 (906-353-6651).

Campgrounds: Big Eric's Brook State Forest Campground is located about four miles northeast of Roland Lake.

Chamber of Commerce: Baraga County Tourist & Recreation Assoc., Box 5567, Baraga, MI 49908 (906-524-7444).

Recent Master Angler Catches: Brook Trout: 2.87 lbs. (6-6- 93), 2.75 lbs. (6-7-93) and 2.72 lbs. (6-7-93).

Special Regulations: None known.

BROOK TROUT THROUGHOUT

22
20
15
10
5

ROLAND LAKE RD

TO FOSSUM CREEK

0   400'

Roland Lake is located in northeast Baraga County about four miles southeast of Skanee. This moderately fertile lake is surrounded by forest and a handful of permanent dwellings. There is no inlet. The outlet flows into Fossum Creek, a tributary of the Ravine River, which in turn empties into Lake Superior's Keweenaw Bay.

Vegetation and logs are common throughout Roland Lake. Shoal areas are underlain by sand; deep water contains pulpy peat. White water lily, horsetail and bulrushes are abundant emergent weeds.

Surveys/Stocking: A DNR survey in October 1991 showed that survival and growth of planted brookies was very good. The 155 healthy and robust fish collected averaged 10.3 inches and had grown 4.2 inches in less than six months. The trout apparently feed on creek chubs, which appear to be plentiful.

The lake has received about 3,000 brook trout yearlings each year since 1987. Managers stocked that many in 1992 and 1993 plus they released an estimated 100 adult brookies in 1993.

Tactics to Try: Because Roland is not a designated trout lake, fishing is permitted year-round. The best catches occur in June for anglers who dunk worms while either anchoring or drifting. Most fish taken are suspended from 5 to 15 feet deep.

The lake contains a considerable amount of gravel along both the northcentral and south-central shores. These are good locations to toss or troll small Mepps Spinners. We recommend both the Black Fury and Comet models in sizes 0, 1 and 2. Consider pinching the barbs so as not to harm sublegal trout and those you plan to return to the lake.

In addition to small live minnows, Roland Lake brookies will also hit Muddler Minnows, Wooly Worms and imitation mayfly nymphs. Dry-fly fishermen should also bring Adams and Royal Coachman patterns along with the usual assortment of black ants and mosquito flies.

Access: The DNR maintains a gravel-surfaced boat ramp on the north shore. Toilets are available and there is parking for a dozen vehicles. There is no place to rent a boat.

VERMILAC LAKE

Fishing Opportunities: Walleyes—Good; Black Crappies,
Northern Pike and Yellow Perch—Fair to Good.

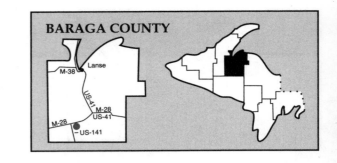

BARAGA COUNTY

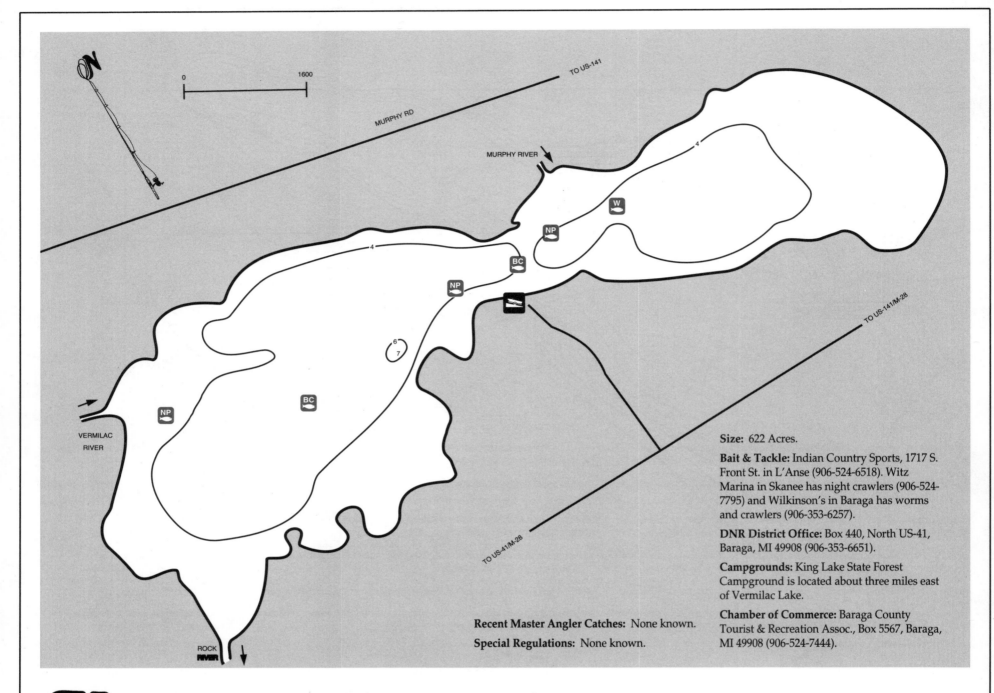

Size: 622 Acres.

Bait & Tackle: Indian Country Sports, 1717 S.
Front St. in L'Anse (906-524-6518). Witz
Marina in Skanee has night crawlers (906-524-
7795) and Wilkinson's in Baraga has worms
and crawlers (906-353-6257).

DNR District Office: Box 440, North US-41,
Baraga, MI 49908 (906-353-6651).

Campgrounds: King Lake State Forest
Campground is located about three miles east
of Vermilac Lake.

Chamber of Commerce: Baraga County
Tourist & Recreation Assoc., Box 5567, Baraga,
MI 49908 (906-524-7444).

Recent Master Angler Catches: None known.
Special Regulations: None known.

Vermilac Lake is located in southcentral
Baraga County about a mile east of
Covington. Although the lake is nearly a square
mile in surface acreage, it has a maximum depth
of only seven feet. Although oxygen levels
become low in winter, surprisingly the lake has
never suffered a winterkill. The water color is a
dark brown, making for poor visibility. Floating
vegetation is abundant and both emergent and
submergent weed types are common.

Additional fish cover includes logs and large
boulders. The gradually sloping shoals are covered with sand, gravel, rubble and peat, and
gravel substrate is available for spawning
walleyes. Northerns target weedbeds for spawning habitat.

The Murphy River inlets along the southcentral shore, and the Vermilac River comes in from
the southeast. The main outlet is the Rock River,
which flows from the northeast corner before
joining the Sturgeon River.

Surveys/Stocking: Vermilac Lake enjoyed relatively balanced fish popula-
tions from 1956 — when it was first surveyed —
to 1977 when a DNR net collection revealed that
49 percent of the biomass consisted of black
bullheads and 21 percent was comprised of
suckers. A 1980 manual removal of these undesirable species was unsuccessful. By 1983 a
comeback of gamefish included walleyes, which
were accidentally stocked, and tiger muskies,
which were deliberately introduced in 1978.

A 1988 survey showed that Vermilac Lake is
now dominated by gamefish. Walleye growth
and survival rates were excellent as evidenced
by the fact that 30 fish — some of which had naturally reproduced — averaged 21 inches and 4.4
pounds each. Crappies averaged a respectable
10½ inches, northern pike averaged 19 inches,
and yellow perch averaged nearly 7 inches.

Researchers returned in the spring of 1993 and
collected 68 crappies that averaged 9½ inches
each. The 23 walleyes examined averaged 22
inches and 4.3 pounds. Pike averaged 21 inches
and yellow perch averaged 7.2 inches. The purpose of the survey was to confirm the presence
of natural reproduction of walleyes; however,
the technicians found little evidence.

Consequently, they stocked an estimated 20,000
walleye fingerlings.

Tactics to Try: The lake's shallow, dark profile
and abundance of weeds make
it difficult to fish. Walleye anglers tend to complain about the lack of fish, a claim that goes
unsubstantiated by the survey results. We recommend black, purple or root-beer-colored
Fuzz-E Grub jigs sweetened with a small minnow. Night crawlers also work when pinned to
Lindy Rigs or fished on a bare hook floated by a
slip bobber. Drift fishing will outproduce
trolling, which is not a good idea because of the
preponderance of hard-to-spot rocks.

The best fishing for northern pike occurs in
winter for tip-up and jig fishermen. Although
most anglers cluster near the access site, the
entire lake is productive. Better crappie fishing
shapes up in summer for tube jig fishermen
using small minnows or crawler bits.

Access: A paved launch and improved access
site is located on the north shore.
Included are toilets and parking for about 15
vehicles. There is no place to rent a boat.

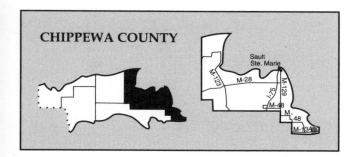

CARIBOU LAKE

Fishing Opportunities: Walleyes—Good; Smallmouth Bass and Northern Pike—Fair to Good; Yellow Perch and Tiger Muskies— Poor to Fair.

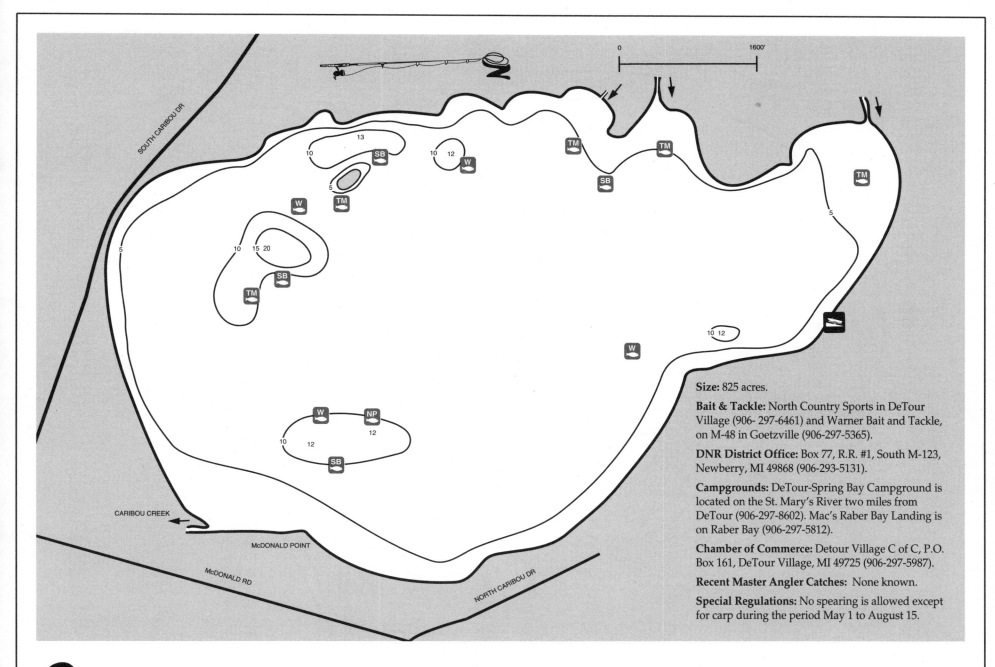

Size: 825 acres.

Bait & Tackle: North Country Sports in DeTour Village (906- 297-6461) and Warner Bait and Tackle, on M-48 in Goetzville (906-297-5365).

DNR District Office: Box 77, R.R. #1, South M-123, Newberry, MI 49868 (906-293-5131).

Campgrounds: DeTour-Spring Bay Campground is located on the St. Mary's River two miles from DeTour (906-297-8602). Mac's Raber Bay Landing is on Raber Bay (906-297-5812).

Chamber of Commerce: Detour Village C of C, P.O. Box 161, DeTour Village, MI 49725 (906-297-5987).

Recent Master Angler Catches: None known.

Special Regulations: No spearing is allowed except for carp during the period May 1 to August 15.

Caribou Lake is located in eastern Chippewa County about four miles west of DeTour Village. The only U.P. walleye lake east of I-75 is surrounded by gently rolling hills covered by birch, aspen, cedar and hemlock. The heaviest cover is along the northwest and south shores. The southeast and north shores are mostly sand with a few bulrushes. The lake has three west-side inlets, and Caribou Creek outlets on the east side to Lake Huron. Fishing pressure is light.

Shoals are covered with sand, gravel, rock rubble or fibrous peat. About 90 percent of the lake is less than 15 feet in depth, and the deepest spot is 20 feet. Downed trees and rocks provide structure, and there is a considerable amount of vegetation including chara, bladder wart, pondweed, water shield, yellow and white lilies, and the bulrushes mentioned.

Gamefish have plenty to eat thanks to moderately abundant numbers of bluntnose minnows, golden shiners, brook stickleback, sculpins, white suckers and shiners. Bottom organisms include crayfish, dragonflies, caddisflies, mayfly larvae, snails and clams.

Surveys/Stocking: A May 1986 survey with boomshocking equipment and trap and fyke nets produced seven year-classes of smallmouth bass to 18 inches, northern pike to 30 inches and tiger muskies to 36 inches.

Since the introduction of walleyes in 1978, the population of yellow perch appears to have fallen off. A May 1991 survey with trap and fyke nets produced 83 walleyes from 12 to 27 inches and proved that natural reproduction was occurring during years when walleyes were not stocked. As a result, the DNR has dropped its walleye release program pending reassessment in 1996.

The more recent survey produced 79 smallmouth bass, but most were under minimum legal size. The nets yielded six pike to 32 inches, 99 small perch, a large quantity of rock bass and white suckers, and a few pumpkinseed sunfish.

In the summer of 1989, a 60-inch sturgeon, which probably entered Caribou Lake from Lake Huron, washed up on the beach. In June 1992, 8,000 to 10,000 bluegills averaging 4 to 4½ inches were transferred into the lake from East Lake in Luce County.

In 1991 managers released 2,500 fingerling tiger muskies and 700,000 walleye fry; in 1992 they stocked 10,000 bluegills.

Tactics to Try: Hotspots for smallmouth bass and tiger muskies shape up around boulders on the south side of the west-shore island and along a submerged gravel spine from MacDonald Point west to a sunken island. Walleyes also gang up here at times, and cabbage weeds in the outer fringes attract muskies and the occasional big northern pike

To catch the toothy predators, at these locations or off inflowing creeks in bays of the northwest shore, troll Pikie Minnows or Rapalas.

It is not uncommon for anglers to stringer a limit of 4- to 6-pound walleyes scattered throughout Caribou Lake. A jig and minnow or harness and crawler works best when wind-drifted or slow-trolled over the points and gravel/rock bars.

Access: The access site is located on the lake's north end. The concrete plank launch is suitable for boats to 19 feet in length. To rent a boat, contact Linger Longer Resort (906- 297-8901), Margaret's Resort (906-297-5532) or Odys' Resort (906-297-ODYS).

CARP LAKE

Fishing Opportunities: Walleyes and Yellow Perch—Fair to Good; Northern Pike, Smallmouth Bass and Pumpkinseed Sunfish—Fair to Good.

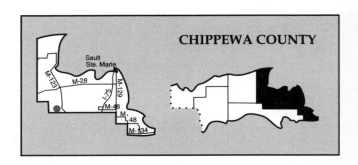

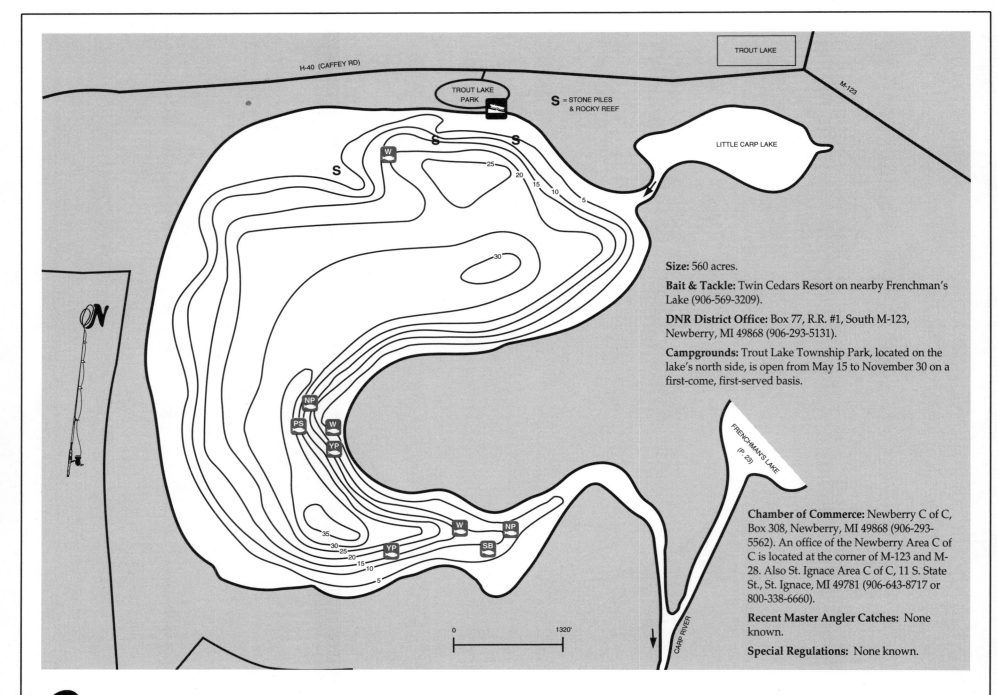

Size: 560 acres.

Bait & Tackle: Twin Cedars Resort on nearby Frenchman's Lake (906-569-3209).

DNR District Office: Box 77, R.R. #1, South M-123, Newberry, MI 49868 (906-293-5131).

Campgrounds: Trout Lake Township Park, located on the lake's north side, is open from May 15 to November 30 on a first-come, first-served basis.

Chamber of Commerce: Newberry C of C, Box 308, Newberry, MI 49868 (906-293-5562). An office of the Newberry Area C of C is located at the corner of M-123 and M-28. Also St. Ignace Area C of C, 11 S. State St., St. Ignace, MI 49781 (906-643-8717 or 800-338-6660).

Recent Master Angler Catches: None known.

Special Regulations: None known.

Carp Lake, which is also known as Trout Lake or Big Trout Lake, is located in southwest Chippewa County a mile west of the village of Trout Lake. The large, shallow lake supports fairly heavy shoreline development with wooded lots and log homes and gets little fishing pressure except during the summer.

The flow from Little Carp Lake enters from the northeast. Both Carp Lake and Frenchman's Lake exit via the Carp River to Lake Michigan.

Structure is limited to a few scattered weedbeds, hard-to-find stone piles that constitute a walleye spawning reef along the 3-foot contour of the north shore, and 36 log cribs constructed in 1973-75. For that reason, as well as the dark tannic acid-stained water, the lake can be difficult to fish. However, those who work at it will be rewarded.

Surveys/Stocking: A spring 1990 manual removal of white suckers eliminated 1,555 fish averaging almost 19 inches and 3½ pounds each. The nets also produced 1,895 walleyes, all of which were returned to the lake. The most recent surveys occurred in the spring of 1983 with boomshocking equipment, various nets and a seine. Walleyes collected averaged 15.6 inches, and northern pike averaged 20.4 inches. Rough fish populations appeared to be low at that time. Smallmouths ranged from 6 to 16 inches, and 10 year-classes of yellow perch, including fish to 13 inches, were represented.

The walleye stocking program dates to 1974, when fry were released in the amount of 750,000 annually for four years. In 1981 the DNR switched to fall fingerlings, and in 1993 they stocked an estimated 11,215 fish. The manmade reefs apparently have failed to trigger natural reproduction among walleyes.

Occasional chinook salmon enter the river due to natural reproduction. Chinooks were last stocked in 1985.

Tactics to Try: Although walleyes and smallmouths can be taken throughout the lake, one good spot to try is the south-end narrows. Another is the rock pile on the west side of the township park near the access site. Leeches are hot bait in the summer, with crawlers and minnows producing in spring and fall. Fluorescent-orange or chartreuse leadhead jigs are favored because of the dark water. Use these same colors or white in crawler harness blades.

Winter is the best time for panfishing — largely because pressure then is slight — and the lake serves up slab pumpkinseed sunfish for teardrop jiggers using larvae. Try the west and south shorelines, especially along the east-side point. For jumbo perch, use crayfish, which have been naturally reproducing on the rock reefs. If crayfish are not available, try wigglers or inch-long shiners.

Northern pike fishing is productive off the east-side point all year and over south-end weedlines in winter.

Access: Trout Lake Township Park maintains an improved launch facility on the lake's north shore with paved ramp, toilets and parking for a dozen or more vehicles. To rent a boat, contact Birch Lodge (906-569-3351). To rent a canoe, contact Carp River Outfitters, which is located near the rivermouth (906-569-3235).

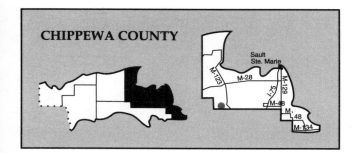

CHIPPEWA COUNTY

FRENCHMAN'S LAKE

Fishing Opportunities: Walleyes—Good; Smallmouth Bass, Largemouth Bass, Bluegills, Yellow Perch and Northern Pike— Fair to Good.

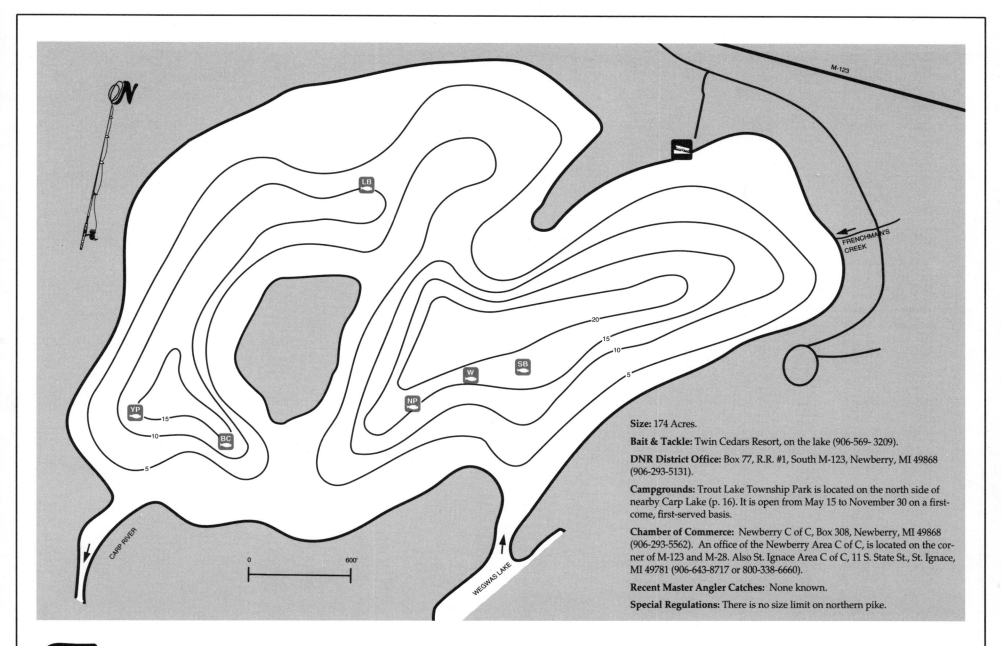

Size: 174 Acres.

Bait & Tackle: Twin Cedars Resort, on the lake (906-569- 3209).

DNR District Office: Box 77, R.R. #1, South M-123, Newberry, MI 49868 (906-293-5131).

Campgrounds: Trout Lake Township Park is located on the north side of nearby Carp Lake (p. 16). It is open from May 15 to November 30 on a first-come, first-served basis.

Chamber of Commerce: Newberry C of C, Box 308, Newberry, MI 49868 (906-293-5562). An office of the Newberry Area C of C, is located on the corner of M-123 and M-28. Also St. Ignace Area C of C, 11 S. State St., St. Ignace, MI 49781 (906-643-8717 or 800-338-6660).

Recent Master Angler Catches: None known.

Special Regulations: There is no size limit on northern pike.

Frenchman's Lake is located in south-west Chippewa County about a mile south of the village of Trout Lake. The shallow lake has an abundance of milfoil, white and yellow lily pads, bulrushes, and curly and broad-leafed pond weed as well as a large island. It is best described as a weedline lake and is typical of U.P. inland waters in that it is clear and stained a light brown due to tannic acid.

The lake is connected to 160-acre Wegwaas Lake, which is privately owned and off limits to anglers because of a barrier between the two bodies of water.

Frenchman's north and southwest shores are somewhat developed; lowland forest constitutes the rest of the shoreline. Eagles, ospreys and herons live in the area, and caddis, mayflies and crayfish are plentiful. The lake's outflow is the Carp River to Lake Michigan, and Frenchman's Creek inlets from the northeast corner.

Surveys/Stocking: A June 1983 net survey produced yellow perch averag-ing about 9 inches, northern pike averaging about 15 inches and walleyes averaging 13½ inches. Rock bass and pumpkinseed sunfish were other species collected along with brown bullheads and white suckers. Although the nets did not yield any bass, the lake has a reputation for producing both largemouths and small-mouths.

Stocking records date from 1921 when managers released yellow perch. Other species introduced over the years include smallmouth and largemouth bass, bluegills, walleyes and northern pike. In 1993 the DNR stocked an estimated 6,700 walleye fingerlings.

Tactics to Try: No special or unusual tactics were turned up as a result of our research. Most fish are caught along weed-lines that encircle the lake or from pockets within the vegetation. There is very little ice-fishing activity, which may be one reason the lake produces so well during the warm- water fishing season.

Largemouth action is best in spring, and we recommend spinnerbaits in chartreuse, lime green or white. In fact, these are good colors for all lures in this lake, along with black, brown and orange. Smallmouth fishing is best in fall. Drift a Lindy-rigged crawler over weeds or toss diving crankbaits along the 15- to 20-foot deep contours.

Bigger yellow perch prefer soft-shelled crayfish if you can get them; if not, fish wigglers in the spring and shiners in the summer and fall.

The lake serves up decent catches of walleyes, especially during low-light days of choppy water. We recommend vertical jigging with minnows or crawlers and slip- bobber fishing with leeches.

Northern pike abound, and although most fish are small, big ones to 10 pounds plus call the lake home. Standard red- and white spoons are as effective as anything else in your tackle box.

Access: The public access site is located on the north shore off M-123. The ramp is hard-surfaced and there is parking for six vehicles. To rent a boat contact Twin Cedars Resort (see Bait & Tackle listing).

CAMP 7 LAKE

Fishing Opportunities: Yellow Perch—Good to Excellent; Smallmouth Bass, Rainbow Trout and Splake—Fair to Good.

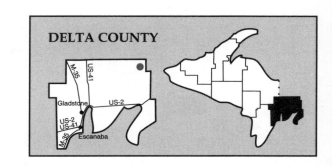

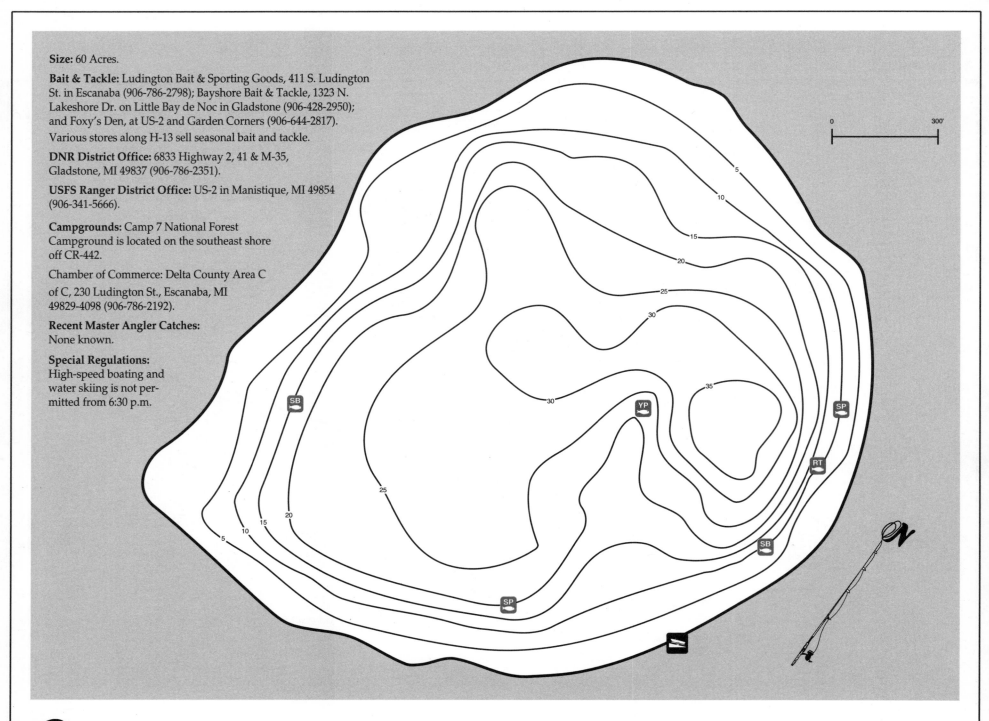

Size: 60 Acres.

Bait & Tackle: Ludington Bait & Sporting Goods, 411 S. Ludington St. in Escanaba (906-786-2798); Bayshore Bait & Tackle, 1323 N. Lakeshore Dr. on Little Bay de Noc in Gladstone (906-428-2950); and Foxy's Den, at US-2 and Garden Corners (906-644-2817). Various stores along H-13 sell seasonal bait and tackle.

DNR District Office: 6833 Highway 2, 41 & M-35, Gladstone, MI 49837 (906-786-2351).

USFS Ranger District Office: US-2 in Manistique, MI 49854 (906-341-5666).

Campgrounds: Camp 7 National Forest Campground is located on the southeast shore off CR-442.

Chamber of Commerce: Delta County Area C of C, 230 Ludington St., Escanaba, MI 49829-4098 (906-786-2192).

Recent Master Angler Catches: None known.

Special Regulations: High-speed boating and water skiing is not permitted from 6:30 p.m.

Camp 7 Lake is located in northeast Delta County about 11 miles northeast of Isabella. Surrounded by woods, the clear, bowl-shaped lake falls within sandy soils of the jack-pine plains country of the Hiawatha National Forest. There is no inlet or outlet. Weeds occur along the south and west shorelines but are limited to bulrushes, lily pads and pondweed. The lake bottom is sandy in shoreline shoal areas and features pulpy peat in deep-water spots.

Over the years, periodic chemical reclamation for stunted panfish and perch has kept the fishery strong. Three years ago USFS technicians used live traps to capture small perch and remove them to other waters.

Surveys/Stocking: Stocking records date from 1936 when fisheries managers released bluegills, yellow perch and smallmouth bass. In 1958 they introduced rainbow trout and continue to stock yearling rainbows today.

An August 1987 DNR net survey produced good numbers of splake and rainbow trout although size was small. Small bluegills and yellow perch were also common. An October 1989 net survey showed that the lake could be managed for both trout and warm-water species. On that lift researchers collected perch to 11 inches and recommended that smallmouth bass be initiated.

In 1991 managers released 1,500 'bows, and in 1992 they planted out 3,000 more along with 4,000 yearling splake and 2,000 smallmouth bass fingerlings. In 1993 they released an estimated 3,490 splake yearlings and 1,800 smallmouth bass fingerlings.

Tactics to Try: The lake is popular with water skiers and other summer recreationists. Consequently, the best fishing in June, July and August occurs after sundown and in early morning. Anglers report fair to good catches of trout while trolling cowbells and small spoons or night crawlers. After dark they jig with small Swedish Pimples or bare Aberdeen hooks tipped with red worms. Most summertime trout are taken in 18 to 28 feet of water. Ice anglers con the rainbows at varying depths with wigglers or waxworms.

The manual thinning project has resulted in bigger yellow-bellied perch, and the best fishing occurs in spring or fall over drop-offs near a hard bottom with some weeds. Use minnows or worms.

The lake produces smallmouth bass for drift, troll and spincast fishermen using leeches or night crawlers. A blue-and-white spinnerbait with silver blade is also an excellent bass producer in this lake. Target drops, logs and any other available structure.

Access: The USFS maintains a hard-surfaced ramp, toilets and parking for eight vehicles on the southeast side of the lake at the campground. A handicapper pier and walk area was recently added. There is no place to rent a boat, but the USFS sponsors a kids fishing derby during National Fishing Week each June.

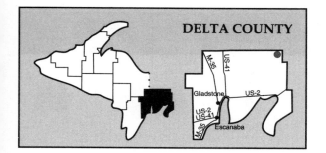

NORWAY LAKE

Fishing Opportunities: Brook Trout—Fair to Excellent.

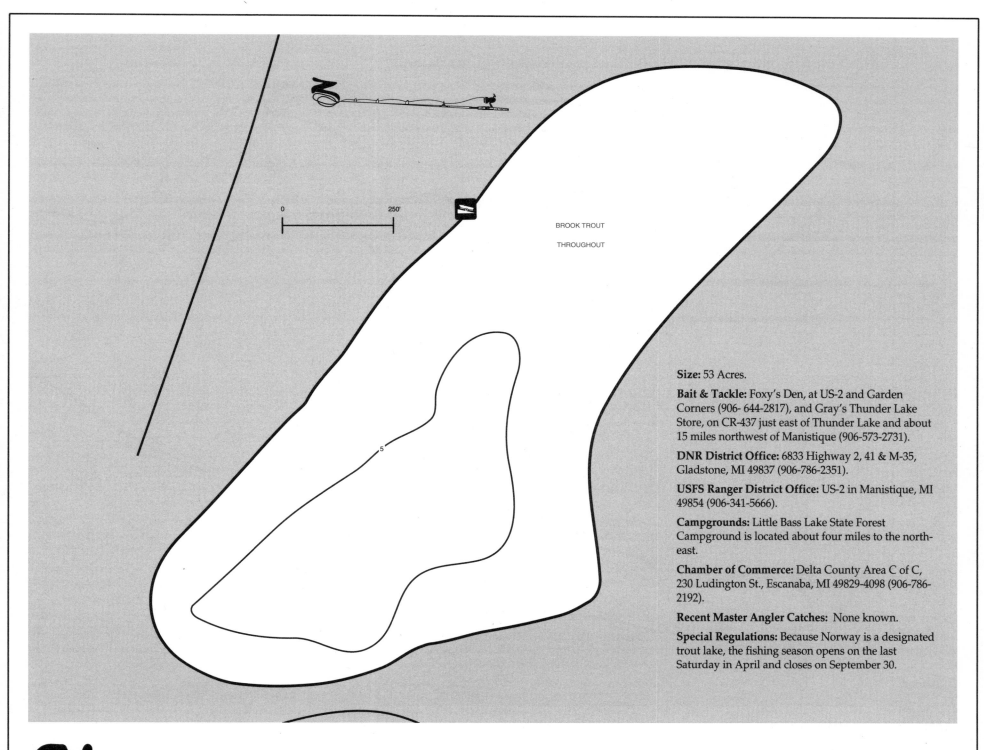

BROOK TROUT

THROUGHOUT

0   250'

Size: 53 Acres.

Bait & Tackle: Foxy's Den, at US-2 and Garden Corners (906- 644-2817), and Gray's Thunder Lake Store, on CR-437 just east of Thunder Lake and about 15 miles northwest of Manistique (906-573-2731).

DNR District Office: 6833 Highway 2, 41 & M-35, Gladstone, MI 49837 (906-786-2351).

USFS Ranger District Office: US-2 in Manistique, MI 49854 (906-341-5666).

Campgrounds: Little Bass Lake State Forest Campground is located about four miles to the north-east.

Chamber of Commerce: Delta County Area C of C, 230 Ludington St., Escanaba, MI 49829-4098 (906-786-2192).

Recent Master Angler Catches: None known.

Special Regulations: Because Norway is a designated trout lake, the fishing season opens on the last Saturday in April and closes on September 30.

Norway Lake is located in extreme northeast Delta County in the Hiawatha National Forest about five miles southwest of Steuben. Much of the shoreline supports tamaracks and is marshy, and the clear lake, which used to be called Arrowhead Lake, is situated in hilly terrain covered with pines. The deepest spot is only about 8 feet.

The spring-fed lake is the source of a tributary to Kilpecker Creek, a good brook trout stream, and, although Norway Lake is shallow, it is better suited to trout and other cold-water species rather than warm-water species. Even so, the lake occasionally throws a 5-pound pike and a few small yellow perch.

Bottom composition is mostly sand encroaching to pulpy peat toward the middle. Plant life is limited to some scattered submerged weedbeds. A few emergent weeds show up along with drowned logs near shore. Fishing pressure is moderate to heavy, and anglers do well on 12- to 14-inch brookies, especially in the spring.

Surveys/Stocking: Managers partially treated Norway Lake with antimycin in the fall of 1985 to thin perch and suckers. A June 1989 gill net survey collected four brook trout from 10 to 14 inches each. The fish had fed on aquatic insect larva and fathead minnows.

The DNR stocked 1,700 Assinica-strain brook trout yearlings in 1991 and again in 1992 and were proposing a similar release in 1993 at our press time.

Tactics to Try: The lake is popular during the trout season opener in late April. Muddler Minnows or various nymph patterns that are flyfished or worms that are spin-fished can be effective then.

By late May and early June, trout turn to surface feeding. Dry fly fishermen using various caddis and mayfly patterns, along with Adams, royal coachman and black ant imitations score in the evening.

Daytime midsummer tactics call for slow trolling a spinner, F-4 Flatfish or small Countdown Rapala. Vertical jigging with a Doll Fly also works. Further, worms or small minnows can be lightly jigged or drifted over deep-water fish, which are harder to catch than in spring and fall.

When water cools in September, the brookies move higher into the water column and will take small spinners and various wet and dry fly patterns.

Tactics to Try: The public access site is located via Thunder Lake Road (CR-437). Go north to USFS-2438, then west about two miles to USFS-2721, and south a quarter-mile to the east side of the lake. The final 150-yard approach is a two-track road with limited parking and turn-around space. The site can accommodate a canoe or cartop boat. There is no place to rent a boat.

ROUND LAKE

Fishing Opportunities: Walleyes and Northern Pike—
Fair to Good; Bluegills and Yellow Perch—Fair; Tiger
Muskies and Largemouth Bass—Available.

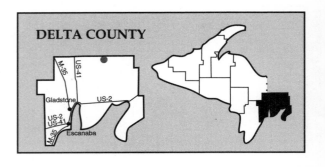

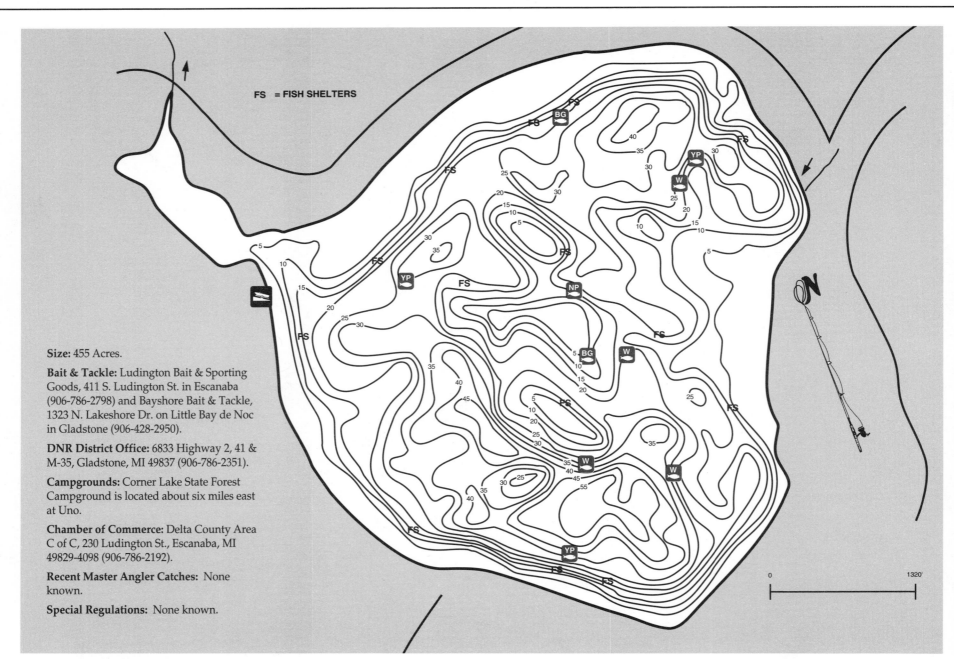

FS = FISH SHELTERS

Size: 455 Acres.

Bait & Tackle: Ludington Bait & Sporting
Goods, 411 S. Ludington St. in Escanaba
(906-786-2798) and Bayshore Bait & Tackle,
1323 N. Lakeshore Dr. on Little Bay de Noc
in Gladstone (906-428-2950).

DNR District Office: 6833 Highway 2, 41 &
M-35, Gladstone, MI 49837 (906-786-2351).

Campgrounds: Corner Lake State Forest
Campground is located about six miles east
at Uno.

Chamber of Commerce: Delta County Area
C of C, 230 Ludington St., Escanaba, MI
49829-4098 (906-786-2192).

Recent Master Angler Catches: None
known.

Special Regulations: None known.

---

ound Lake is located in extreme
northcentral Delta County about six
miles west of Uno. The lake's northern-most tip
extends into Alger County. Northern hardwoods in the form of beech, maple and yellow
birch, along with hemlock and pine, are forest
types along its shores. A little stone and gravel
are found on the southeast side; otherwise the
shore is mostly sandy soils.

Natural springs and a small southeast-shore
inlet from Jones Lake recharge Round Lake's
water. The outlet occurs at the tip of the neck on
the lake's north end, flowing a quarter-mile to
West Branch Lake and eventually to the
Sturgeon River.

Much of the shoreline has extensive shoals
with a gradual drop-off. More abrupt drop-offs
occur along the western shore and off a series of
sandy humps in the central and southcentral
portions of the lake.

The lake supports a large number of seasonal
and permanent dwellings, and it is heavily
impacted by boaters and other recreationists.

Surveys/Stocking: Historically, Round Lake
supported perch, small-
mouth bass, pumpkinseed sunfish, pike,
bluegills and rock bass. Smallmouths and
bluegills were stocked as early as 1937, along
with largemouths, walleyes and perch in later
years. Copper sulphate applied by lakefront
owners in the 1960s to control "swimmer's itch"
sent the fishery into a tailspin.

In 1975 14 clusters of shelters were installed to
improve fishing. Manual removal of rock bass,
bullheads and white suckers began in 1981.

A September 1991 DNR gill net survey produced largemouth bass to 15 inches and
walleyes to 22½ inches. No tiger muskies were
collected. Periodic manual removals of rough
species are necessary to maintain good fishing.
Stocking is essential because, except for the
marshy north- end outlet, the lake does not contain suitable habitat for natural reproduction.

A May 1993 gill and fyke net survey found a
good walleye population that appeared to be
holding up well. Common shiners were the
main forage base. The largemouth bass population was not significant. The nets revealed fair to
good numbers of pike, including several in the

33-inch category. Rock bass were prevalent to
the point of nuisance and could stand another
thinning.

In 1992 DNR managers released 42,400 fall fingerling walleyes.

Tactics to Try: Night fishing is productive for
walleyes, especially when
anglers use Rapalas and other minnow-type
lures to approximate the golden shiner forage.
For best results work the sandy humps.

Northerns and bluegills key along the weedlines and other available structure, including
edges and declines. Along with an occasional
tiger muskie, pike will hit buzzbaits and jerkbaits ripped across the surface. Spinnerbaits are
also productive for those wishing to cast and
interested in trying for bass at the same time.

Best bet for bluegills and perch is to drift or jig
live bait in the form of leeches, worms or small
minnows. Besides fishing near weeds, try the
area around the various fish shelters.

Access: The access site is located in the northwest portion of the lake and features a
hard-surfaced boat launch ramp and space for
parking. There is no place to rent a boat.

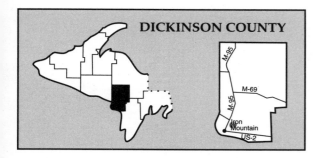

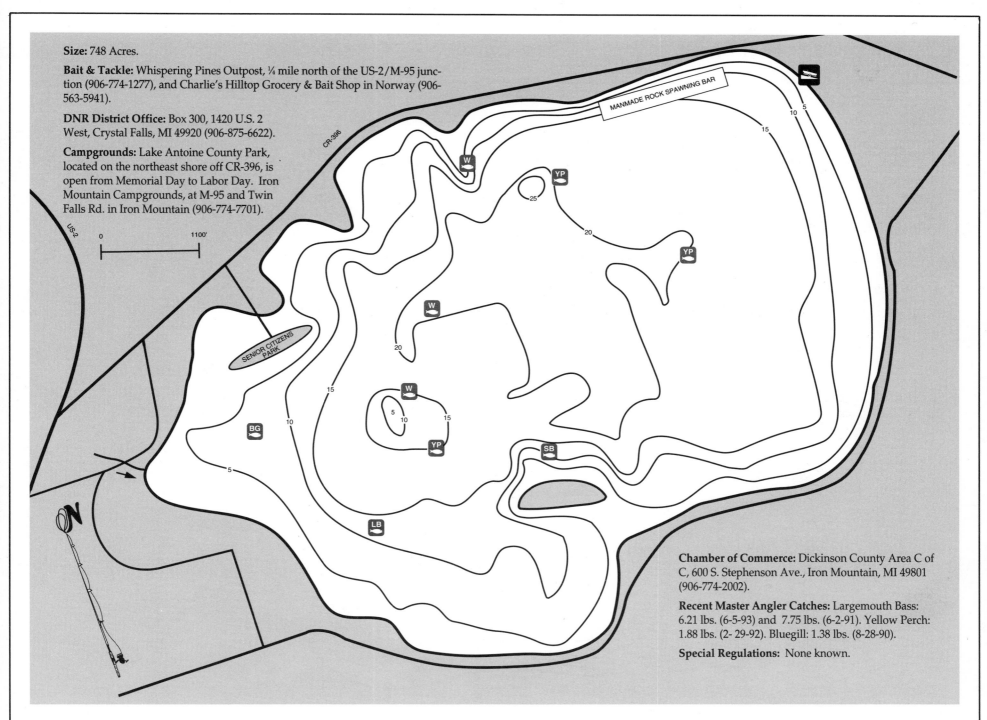

Size: 748 Acres.

Bait & Tackle: Whispering Pines Outpost, ¼ mile north of the US-2/M-95 junction (906-774-1277), and Charlie's Hilltop Grocery & Bait Shop in Norway (906-563-5941).

DNR District Office: Box 300, 1420 U.S. 2 West, Crystal Falls, MI 49920 (906-875-6622).

Campgrounds: Lake Antoine County Park, located on the northeast shore off CR-396, is open from Memorial Day to Labor Day. Iron Mountain Campgrounds, at M-95 and Twin Falls Rd. in Iron Mountain (906-774-7701).

Chamber of Commerce: Dickinson County Area C of C, 600 S. Stephenson Ave., Iron Mountain, MI 49801 (906-774-2002).

Recent Master Angler Catches: Largemouth Bass: 6.21 lbs. (6-5-93) and 7.75 lbs. (6-2-91). Yellow Perch: 1.88 lbs. (2-29-92). Bluegill: 1.38 lbs. (8-28-90).

Special Regulations: None known.

LAKE ANTOINE

Fishing Opportunities: Walleye, Yellow Perch—Good to Excellent; Largemouth Bass and Bluegills—Good; Smallmouth Bass, Black Crappies and Largemouth Bass—Fair to Good.

Lake Antoine is located in extreme southwest Dickinson County a mile north of Iron Mountain. The lake bottom is mostly sand or silt with some rocky areas near shore. Its waters are recharged from springs and mines, and there is no outlet. Weeds and other vegetation are limited to bays of the west end. The water is a light brown in color.

Although the lake is fully developed and fishing pressure is very high, it produces a variety of warm-water species. Some consider it to be one of the best lakes in the western U.P.

Surveys/Stocking: Stocking records date to 1923 when managers released 1,000 bluegills. Through WWII they regularly added smallmouth and largemouth bass, yellow perch and walleyes. A tiger muskie release program was initiated in 1976 but has since been scrapped. Biologists have focused on walleyes since.

An April 1984 DNR net collection produced 234 walleyes from 15 to 24 inches each, indicating a large population of healthy fish. A 1981 trap net survey yielded the following species and their respective average sizes: bluegills, 7.4 inches; pumpkinseed sunfish, 6.2 inches; yellow perch, 6.4 inches; largemouth bass, 15.3 inches; black crappies, 8.1 inches; and northern pike, 21.6 inches.

More recently DNR technicians armed with boomshocking equipment observed a strong year-class of smallmouth bass during an evening of electroshocking. In 1991 they released 30,000 walleye fingerlings and in 1993 stocked an estimated 18,000 more.

Tactics to Try: Fishing pressure is considerable — the most of any lake in the Crystal Falls district — and is especially high during the winter, when it is not unusual to see more than 100 ice shanties on the lake. A February fishing derby held a couple of years ago attracted between 600 and 1,000 anglers.

At all times of year, the west side is better for walleyes; however, the fish do scatter and can be taken over weedlines, humps and breaks throughout the lake and around gravel shoals of the south-side island. The north-side shoreline from an old fountain east to the manmade spawning reef is good habitat for drift fishing. Night crawlers are the preferred bait in summer. In winter, tip-up and jig fishermen rely on minnows. The best bait for perch is minnows in summer and wigglers in winter.

Overall the lake is a steady producer of largemouths, with some decent catches of smallmouths also reported. Try weedlines, docks and moored boats for the former and gravel shoals for the latter.

Access: The county park on the lake's northeast shore off CR-396 features a paved ramp, courtesy pier, toilets and parking for 80 vehicles. Senior Citizen's Park on the northwest shore features shore angling opportunities and a fishing pier with handicapper access. There is no place to rent a boat.

TWIN FALLS FLOWAGE

Fishing Opportunities: Northern Pike and Walleyes—Fair to Good; Bluegills, Yellow Perch and Largemouth Bass—Fair. Yellow Perch and Smallmouth Bass—Fair to Good.

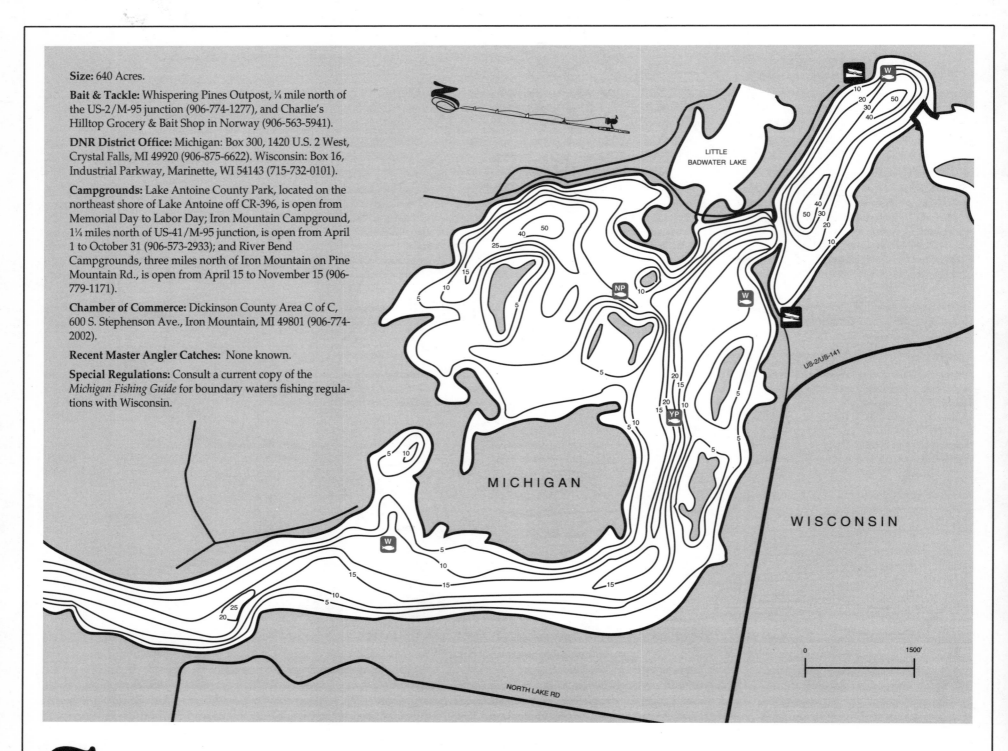

Size: 640 Acres.

Bait & Tackle: Whispering Pines Outpost, ¼ mile north of the US-2/M-95 junction (906-774-1277), and Charlie's Hilltop Grocery & Bait Shop in Norway (906-563-5941).

DNR District Office: Michigan: Box 300, 1420 U.S. 2 West, Crystal Falls, MI 49920 (906-875-6622). Wisconsin: Box 16, Industrial Parkway, Marinette, WI 54143 (715-732-0101).

Campgrounds: Lake Antoine County Park, located on the northeast shore of Lake Antoine off CR-396, is open from Memorial Day to Labor Day; Iron Mountain Campground, 1¼ miles north of US-41/M-95 junction, is open from April 1 to October 31 (906-573-2933); and River Bend Campgrounds, three miles north of Iron Mountain on Pine Mountain Rd., is open from April 15 to November 15 (906-779-1171).

Chamber of Commerce: Dickinson County Area C of C, 600 S. Stephenson Ave., Iron Mountain, MI 49801 (906-774-2002).

Recent Master Angler Catches: None known.

Special Regulations: Consult a current copy of the *Michigan Fishing Guide* for boundary waters fishing regulations with Wisconsin.

Twin Falls Flowage, also known as Big Badwater Lake, is a 640-acre impoundment on the Menominee River about five miles north of Iron Mountain in southwest Dickinson County. The reservoir lies in Wisconsin and Michigan. The sprawling lake with its many bays laps almost 19 miles of shoreline of sand and gravel bluffs. Birch, aspen, cherry and hardwoods comprise the forested, rolling topography.

About 75 percent of the reservoir's shoal waters are less than 15 feet deep, and the slope to the river channel is gradual to steep. Bottom composition in the shallows is sand, gravel and rubble, changing to pulpy peat in deeper areas. The reservoir is brown-stained. Submergent weedbeds are abundant, and there are plenty of deadheads and drowned timber.

Surveys/Stocking: The last complete survey was completed by Wisconsin DNR biologists in 1976 after people feared that the fish population had been wiped out the previous year when the Wisconsin-Michigan Power Company dam broke while being repaired. Researchers' fyke nets produced 506 walleyes. Mature females ranged from 16 to 27 inches, and males ranged from 11.3 to 18.8 inches. Other species collected, their number, and size range include 591 northern pike from 8 to 35 inches, 153 perch from 5½ to 13.8 inches, 88 black crappies from 7.3 to 12.7 inches, 76 bluegills from 5 to 10 inches, 68 smallmouth bass to 19 inches, 58 largemouths to 17.4 inches, and eight muskies to 32 inches.

Managers first stocked walleyes in 1933, adding yellow perch and bluegills a few years later. No fish have been stocked in recent years.

Tactics to Try: Walleyes spread throughout the impoundment soon after spawning. Live bait produces best. Use sonar to find humps, breaks and drops, and jig with yellow or white curly tail leadheads for best results.

Ice fishing is fairly popular for pike and panfishermen, and it is not uncommon to see 12 to 20 shanties on the lake each winter.

Access: There are two public access sites. An older launch is located on CR-607 near the dam. A newer site is just off US-2 about a mile after crossing the bridge into Wisconsin. There is no place to rent a boat.

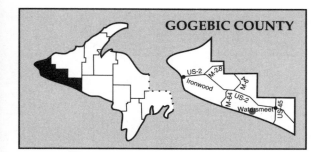

CISCO LAKE

Fishing Opportunities: Walleyes and Bluegills—Good to Excellent; Northern Pike—Good; Yellow Perch and Black Crappies—Fair; Smallmouth Bass and Largemouth Bass— Available.

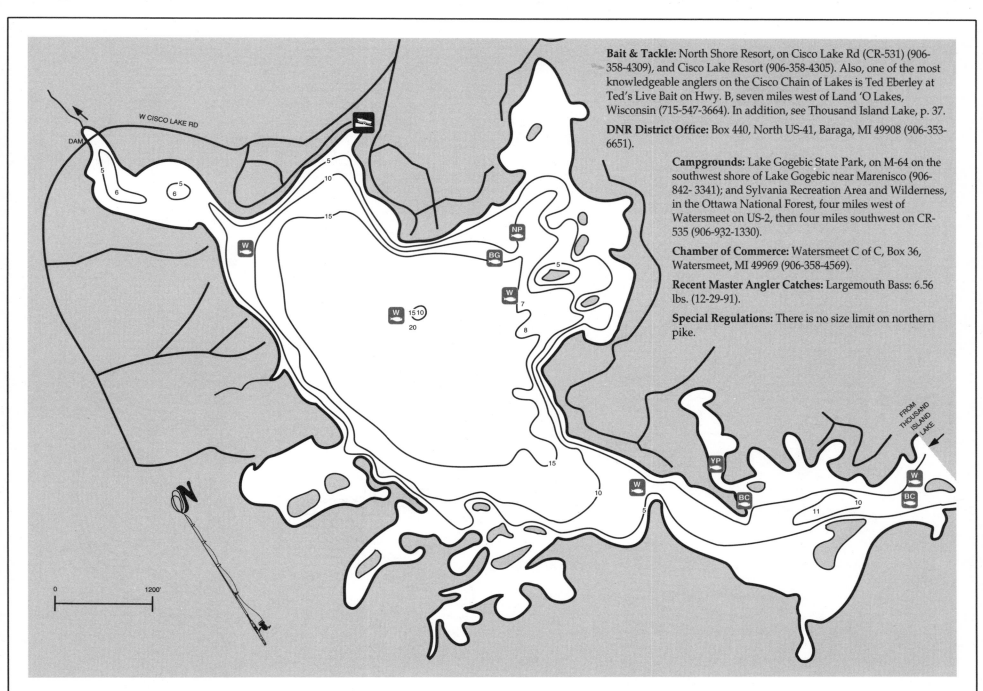

Bait & Tackle: North Shore Resort, on Cisco Lake Rd (CR-531) (906-358-4309), and Cisco Lake Resort (906-358-4305). Also, one of the most knowledgeable anglers on the Cisco Chain of Lakes is Ted Eberley at Ted's Live Bait on Hwy. B, seven miles west of Land 'O Lakes, Wisconsin (715-547-3664). In addition, see Thousand Island Lake, p. 37.

DNR District Office: Box 440, North US-41, Baraga, MI 49908 (906-353-6651).

Campgrounds: Lake Gogebic State Park, on M-64 on the southwest shore of Lake Gogebic near Marenisco (906-842-3341); and Sylvania Recreation Area and Wilderness, in the Ottawa National Forest, four miles west of Watersmeet on US-2, then four miles southwest on CR-535 (906-932-1330).

Chamber of Commerce: Watersmeet C of C, Box 36, Watersmeet, MI 49969 (906-358-4569).

Recent Master Angler Catches: Largemouth Bass: 6.56 lbs. (12-29-91).

Special Regulations: There is no size limit on northern pike.

Cisco Lake is located in Gogebic County about 13 miles southwest of Watersmeet and is one of 15 lakes on the Cisco Lake Chain. Inlets occur from both Thousand Island Lake (p. 37) and Lindsley Lake. The outlet is the Cisco Branch of the Ontonagon River. A lake level control structure is located on the outlet and controls the level for all lakes in the chain.

Both emergent and submergent aquatic vegetation is abundant, and there are plenty of logs and rocks for fish to hide. Although the maximum depth is only 20 feet, shoal areas are fairly steep in the main basin, where the bottom is mostly sand. Elsewhere, it is largely pulpy peat.

Surveys/Stocking: Stocking history dates to the early 1930s and includes yellow perch, walleyes and rainbow trout. A DNR fyke net survey in June 1992 produced walleyes averaging 18.2 inches, higher than any other survey, in spite of a spear fishery by members of the Lac Vieux Desert Indian tribe who have been removing an average of 100 adult fish averaging 16 inches each spring since 1991.

Also in the 1992 survey, northern pike were down slightly in numbers from previous nettings, but their average size of 17 inches was consistent. The lake contains a few smallmouth and largemouth bass along with good numbers of 6- to 7-inch bluegills and pumpkinseed sunfish and 8-inch yellow perch. Black crappies appear to be increasing in number.

The managers' overall conclusion: Cisco Lake continues to have a well-balanced panfish-predator community and provides a good fishery in spite of extensive fishing pressure. Although the pike run small, walleyes are abundant and of good size as are the bluegills and sunfish, which appear to be replacing perch as the dominant panfish species.

The DNR's objective is to maintain good numbers of walleyes in the Cisco Chain in order to keep panfish populations in check. To that end, managers released 28,000 walleye fingerlings in 1992 and an estimated 15,000 more in 1993.

Tactics to Try: The lake is popular with walleye tournament fishermen, who do well with leeches and minnows. Fish them on a bare hook with a slip bobber or lightly jig with 1/8-oz. or 1/16-oz. bald-face jigs in either chartreuse, yellow or pink. If you run out of live bait, bang a yellow Mister Twister along bottom. Try weedlines, drowned timber in the neckdown area at the south end, and a rocky bar 12 feet deep and located off the southwest-side point.

Muskies have been active in the chain of lakes. Hot lures are Buchertails, Suick Plugs, Bobbie Baits and Don Lapp Seekers. The best color is green perch; coal-black is the second choice. If these colors and lures don't produce, try a Panther Martin Muskie Spinner with a brown tail and these color combinations on the propeller: yellow with black spots, black with yellow spots, or red with black spots.

Catch crappies with small minnows pinned to Crappie Killers, Crappie Queens, Beetlespins, or any 1/32-oz. jig. Hot colors are chartreuse or yellow.

Access: The public access site, which includes a paved boat launch ramp, toilets and a minimum amount of parking space, is located on the northeast shore off CR-531. To rent a boat, contact North Shore Resort or Cisco Lake Resort (see Bait & Tackle listings).

CLARK LAKE

Fishing Opportunities: Smallmouth Bass—Good to Excellent; Lake Trout—Fair to Good; Ciscoes and Yellow Perch—Poor to Fair.

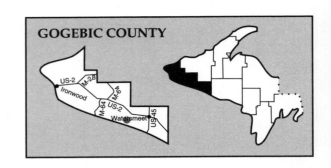

GOGEBIC COUNTY

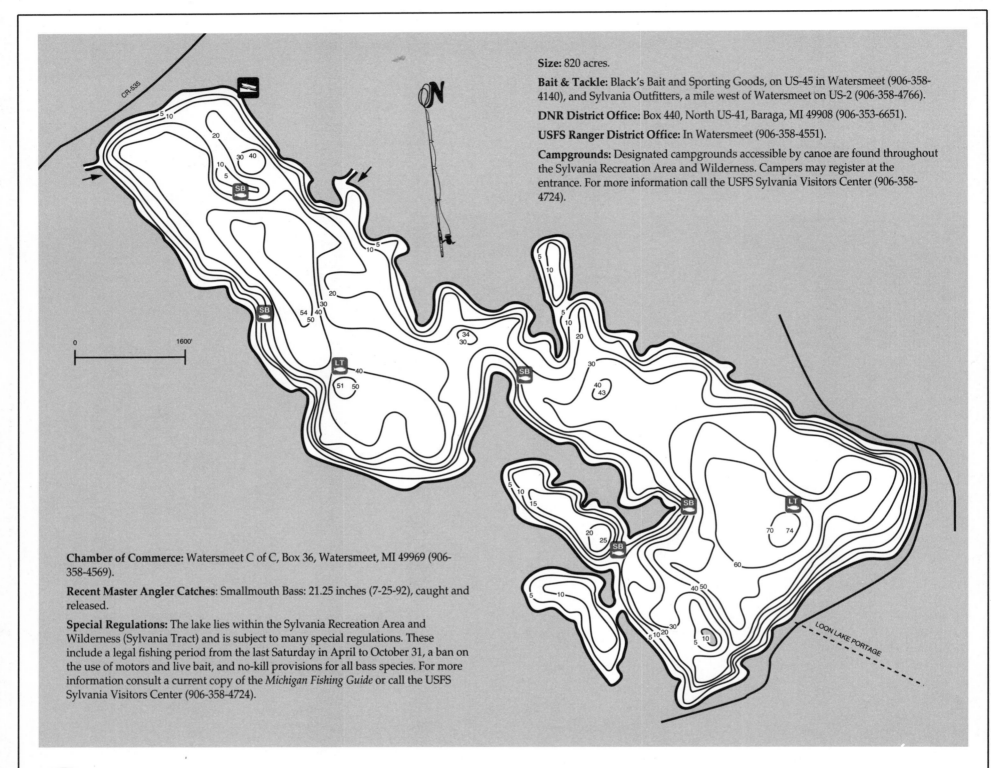

Size: 820 acres.

Bait & Tackle: Black's Bait and Sporting Goods, on US-45 in Watersmeet (906-358-4140), and Sylvania Outfitters, a mile west of Watersmeet on US-2 (906-358-4766).

DNR District Office: Box 440, North US-41, Baraga, MI 49908 (906-353-6651).

USFS Ranger District Office: In Watersmeet (906-358-4551).

Campgrounds: Designated campgrounds accessible by canoe are found throughout the Sylvania Recreation Area and Wilderness. Campers may register at the entrance. For more information call the USFS Sylvania Visitors Center (906-358-4724).

Chamber of Commerce: Watersmeet C of C, Box 36, Watersmeet, MI 49969 (906-358-4569).

Recent Master Angler Catches: Smallmouth Bass: 21.25 inches (7-25-92), caught and released.

Special Regulations: The lake lies within the Sylvania Recreation Area and Wilderness (Sylvania Tract) and is subject to many special regulations. These include a legal fishing period from the last Saturday in April to October 31, a ban on the use of motors and live bait, and no-kill provisions for all bass species. For more information consult a current copy of the *Michigan Fishing Guide* or call the USFS Sylvania Visitors Center (906-358-4724).

Clark Lake is one of two dozen clear, clean lakes nestled in a special wilderness area known as the Sylvania Tract, within the Ottawa National Forest in south Gogebic County about seven miles southwest of Watersmeet.

The biggest lake at 820 acres, Clark is also the gateway lake to the 21,000-acre area, about 4,000 acres of which are water. This beautiful remote area of pristine lakes and climax forest — Michigan's "boundary waters" — is accessible mostly by foot trail and canoe. The area is very popular with visitors from Wisconsin, northern Illinois and even Minnesota. Pressure, including that from anglers, is moderate to heavy, especially in summer, and increasing every year.

Surveys/Stocking: Clark and the other Sylvania lakes are basically self-sustaining, and so the DNR does not stock fish. A

June 1989 DNR fyke and gill net survey turned up several smallmouth bass in the 18-inch range, along with many smaller, sublegal fish. Large numbers of suckers, rock bass and small yellow perch were collected.

Lake trout were first released in 1927, along with whitefish and black bass the following year. The lake still contains lake trout, which must be 30 inches or larger to keep. No lakers turned up in the DNR nets. Collection efforts in 1985 and 1986 did produce lake trout, however, along with 10 year-classes of smallmouth bass, many ciscoes and a couple of largemouth bass.

Tactics to Try: Smallmouths are the key predator species. The no-kill regulations means that many fish have been caught repeatedly. Coupled with the clear water and the fact that live bait is banned, the bass are not always easy to catch.

Fish early or late in the day and paddle along the shoreline off points and drops among the gravel bottom, which covers much of the lake's shoal region. Troll small plugs, spoons or spinners. Black, brown, smoke and other neutral colors work best. During midday hours, anglers will do best by by jigging in deep water.

Deep-water jigging with spoons produces lake trout and ciscoes

Access: An unimproved launch site with gravel ramp and parking for about 35 cars is located on the north shore off CR-535. Crooked (p. 26), Loon (p.33), Deer Island (p. 27) and Whitefish (p.38) lakes, are accessible via well-marked USFS portage trails. The closest lake is Loon, about 400 yards by portage trail from the east end of Clark Lake. To rent a canoe, contact Sylvania Outfitters (see listing under Bait & Tackle).

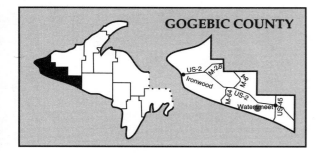

GOGEBIC COUNTY

CLEARWATER LAKE

Fishing Opportunities: Bluegills and Walleyes—Good to Excellent; Northern Pike, Largemouth Bass and Black Crappies—Fair to Good; Smallmouth Bass and Yellow Perch— Fair.

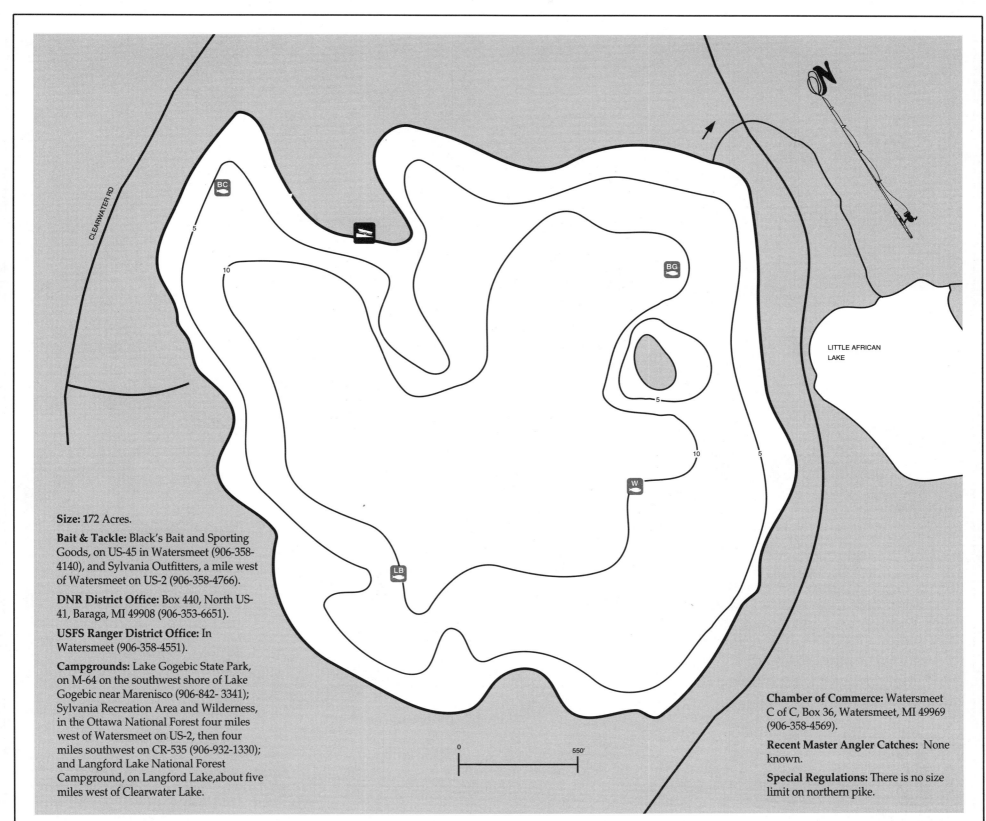

Size: 172 Acres.

Bait & Tackle: Black's Bait and Sporting Goods, on US-45 in Watersmeet (906-358-4140), and Sylvania Outfitters, a mile west of Watersmeet on US-2 (906-358-4766).

DNR District Office: Box 440, North US-41, Baraga, MI 49908 (906-353-6651).

USFS Ranger District Office: In Watersmeet (906-358-4551).

Campgrounds: Lake Gogebic State Park, on M-64 on the southwest shore of Lake Gogebic near Marenisco (906-842- 3341); Sylvania Recreation Area and Wilderness, in the Ottawa National Forest four miles west of Watersmeet on US-2, then four miles southwest on CR-535 (906-932-1330); and Langford Lake National Forest Campground, on Langford Lake,about five miles west of Clearwater Lake.

Chamber of Commerce: Watersmeet C of C, Box 36, Watersmeet, MI 49969 (906-358-4569).

Recent Master Angler Catches: None known.

Special Regulations: There is no size limit on northern pike.

LITTLE AFRICAN LAKE

0   550'

Clearwater Lake is located in southeast Gogebic County in the Ottawa National Forest about 12 miles west of Watersmeet. This clear, clean, lake gets little fishing pressure compared to others in the nearby Cisco Chain of Lakes. It is relatively undiscovered because of its out-of- the-way location on a dead-end road. Clearwater supports about a dozen cottages and contains about 2.3 miles of shoreline. There is no inlet, but a small stream outlets to 18-acre Little African Lake.

Surveys/Stocking: An initial survey in 1974 showed the lake to contain a well-balanced fish population of pumpkinseed sunfish, bluegills, yellow perch, rock bass, largemouth bass, northern pike and brown bullheads. In May 1991 DNR researchers used fyke nets to learn that black crappies had also entered the lake. The perch population was lower, and bluegills had become the dominant panfish species. A total of 666 healthy, robust bluegills collected over seven netting nights averaged 6½ inches.

Pumpkinseeds were also in good shape and only slightly smaller in size than the bluegills. Black crappies averaged 8 inches. Researchers collected and measured good numbers of walleyes, and pike represented many age classes. Walleyes averaged 17.2 inches and ranged from 12 to 24 inches in length. Pike averaged 21 inches, and largemouth bass averaged 7½ inches. Two sublegal smallmouths were also collected.The DNR has not stocked the lake in recent years.

Tactics to Try: No special tactics or lures have evolved among Clearwater Lake anglers. Because of the clear, shallow water, we suggest light line and small lures subdued in color. Natural bait in the form of larvae, worms and minnows should also be effective.

Access: A paved ramp and improved access site is located at the north end of the lake off Clearwater Lake Rd., one mile west of Cisco Lake Rd. (CR-531). Toilets are available and there is parking for about eight vehicles. There is no place to rent a boat.

CROOKED LAKE

Fishing Opportunities: Bluegills and Pumpkinseed Sunfish— Good to Excellent; Black Crappies and Yellow Perch—Fair to Good; Northern Pike, Smallmouth Bass and Largemouth Bass— Poor to Fair.

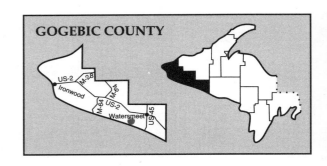

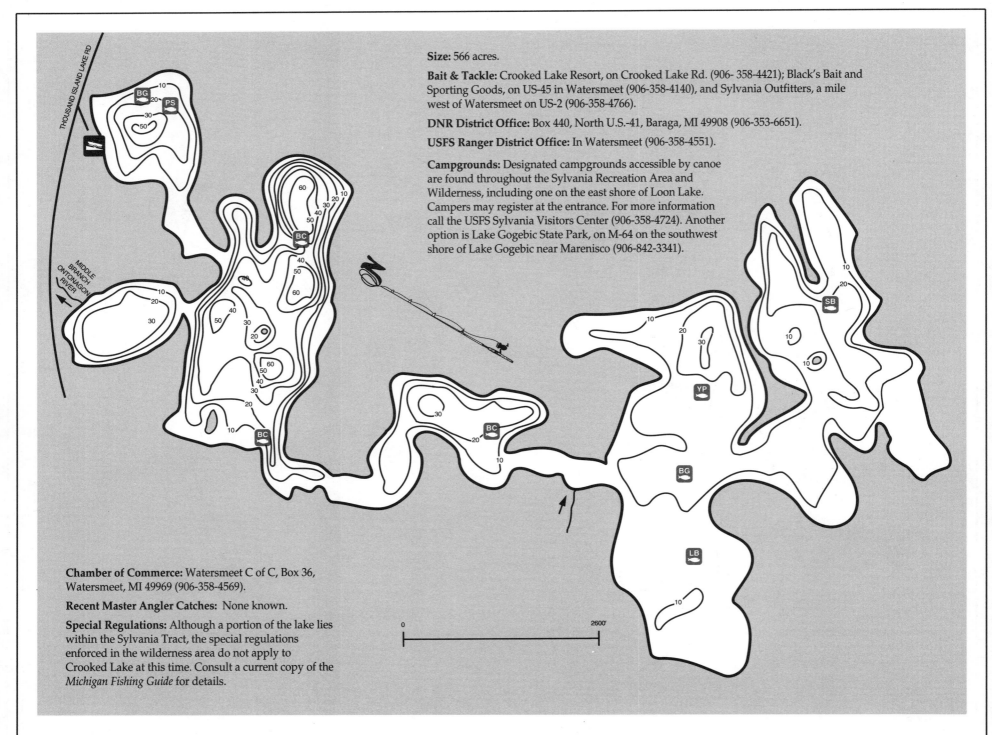

Size: 566 acres.

Bait & Tackle: Crooked Lake Resort, on Crooked Lake Rd. (906- 358-4421); Black's Bait and Sporting Goods, on US-45 in Watersmeet (906-358-4140), and Sylvania Outfitters, a mile west of Watersmeet on US-2 (906-358-4766).

DNR District Office: Box 440, North U.S.-41, Baraga, MI 49908 (906-353-6651).

USFS Ranger District Office: In Watersmeet (906-358-4551).

Campgrounds: Designated campgrounds accessible by canoe are found throughout the Sylvania Recreation Area and Wilderness, including one on the east shore of Loon Lake. Campers may register at the entrance. For more information call the USFS Sylvania Visitors Center (906-358-4724). Another option is Lake Gogebic State Park, on M-64 on the southwest shore of Lake Gogebic near Marenisco (906-842-3341).

Chamber of Commerce: Watersmeet C of C, Box 36, Watersmeet, MI 49969 (906-358-4569).

Recent Master Angler Catches: None known.

Special Regulations: Although a portion of the lake lies within the Sylvania Tract, the special regulations enforced in the wilderness area do not apply to Crooked Lake at this time. Consult a current copy of the *Michigan Fishing Guide* for details.

Except for a small portion of the northeast shore, Crooked Lake lies almost entirely within the Sylvania Recreation Area and Wilderness and is located about six miles southwest of Watersmeet in south Gogebic County. The lake gets its name from the irregular shoreline, which accounts for its many lobes and bays. Unlike most of the others in the Sylvania Tract, Crooked is a murky, muddy lake whose inlet is a small stream on the westcentral shore. The outlet is the headwaters of the Middle Branch of the Ontonagon River. This passage of water through the lake helps provide nutrients and is one reason that Crooked can sustain harvests of fish.

Submerged logs and trees provide fish cover, in addition to many kinds of vegetation. North-end shoals are particularly steep and feature bottom compositions of sand, gravel and some organic material. A midsummer thermocline forms at 12 to 24 feet deep, but there is little oxygen below 20 feet. Although the lake has depths to 60 feet, better fishing occurs in shallower areas.

Surveys/Stocking: During the 1930s fisheries managers stocked largemouth and smallmouth bass, yellow perch and bluegills. Rainbow trout were added for 20 years until the mid-1960s. Surveys date to 1938 when ciscoes were reported as being abundant and bluegills were good-size. A 1988 DNR survey found pumpkinseed sunfish and bluegills to comprise 58 percent of the lake's biomass. The average panfish weighed a quarter-pound and measured six inches. The nets collected yellow perch to 10 inches, largemouth bass to 17 inches, black crappies to 13 inches, northern pike to 27 inches, and smallmouth bass to 14 inches.

The lake has received no fish stockings in recent years.

Tactics to Try: Crooked Lake is a good panfish lake with plenty of 6- to 8-inch bluegills, pumpkinseed sunfish and perch and a decent population of black crappies. For bluegills, concentrate along the weedlines and weedbeds, and fish with waxworms, mealworms or thunder bugs on tiny hooks or tear drop spoons. Crappies and perch nearly always prefer minnows.

The lake grows largemouths and smallmouths to four pounds each, although the typical bass is usually sublegal at less than 14 inches. Try live bait as well as spinnerbaits, Sluggos and jigs and pigs. For largemouths, focus efforts in the weedy bays. Smallmouths frequent rocky points, drops and any hard structure.

Access: The USFS maintains an improved public access site with paved ramp, toilets and parking for 54 cars on the north shore. To rent a boat, contact Crooked Lake Resort (see Bait & Tackle listing). Many other lakes within the Sylvania Tract are accessible from Crooked Lake.

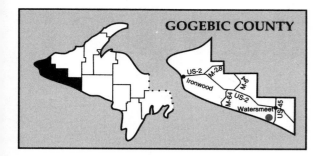

DEER ISLAND LAKE

Fishing Opportunities: Smallmouth Bass—Excellent;
Yellow Perch—Fair to Good.

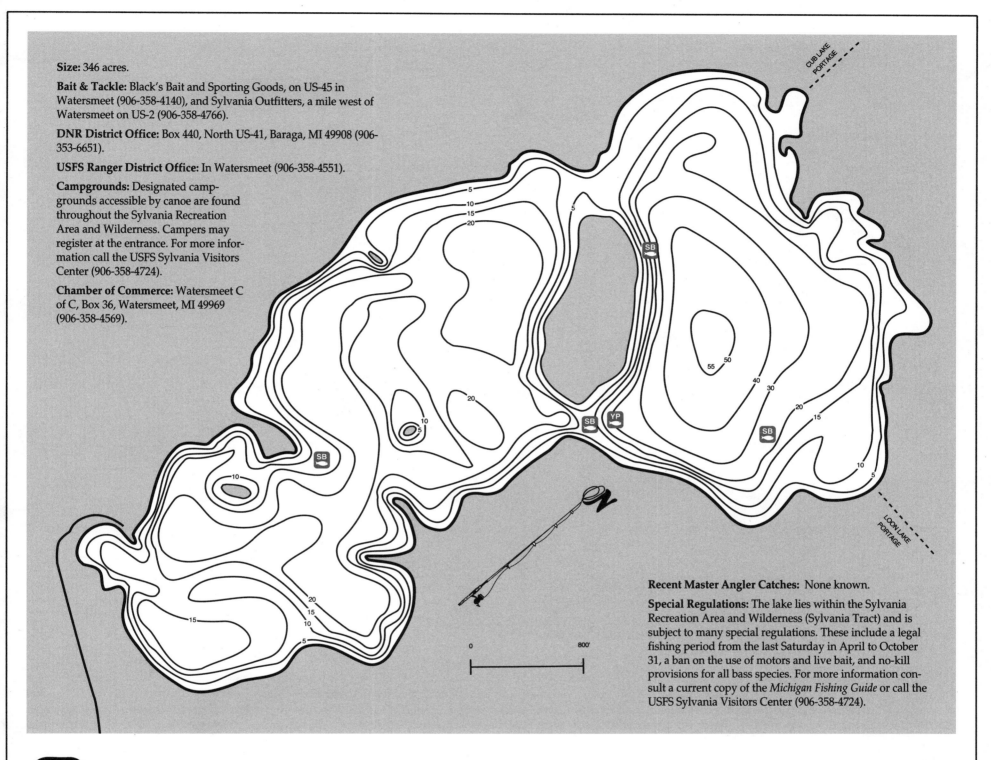

Size: 346 acres.

Bait & Tackle: Black's Bait and Sporting Goods, on US-45 in Watersmeet (906-358-4140), and Sylvania Outfitters, a mile west of Watersmeet on US-2 (906-358-4766).

DNR District Office: Box 440, North US-41, Baraga, MI 49908 (906-353-6651).

USFS Ranger District Office: In Watersmeet (906-358-4551).

Campgrounds: Designated campgrounds accessible by canoe are found throughout the Sylvania Recreation Area and Wilderness. Campers may register at the entrance. For more information call the USFS Sylvania Visitors Center (906-358-4724).

Chamber of Commerce: Watersmeet C of C, Box 36, Watersmeet, MI 49969 (906-358-4569).

Recent Master Angler Catches: None known.

Special Regulations: The lake lies within the Sylvania Recreation Area and Wilderness (Sylvania Tract) and is subject to many special regulations. These include a legal fishing period from the last Saturday in April to October 31, a ban on the use of motors and live bait, and no-kill provisions for all bass species. For more information consult a current copy of the *Michigan Fishing Guide* or call the USFS Sylvania Visitors Center (906-358-4724).

Deer Island Lake is located in the Sylvania Tract of Gogebic County about seven miles southwest of Watersmeet. The crystal-clear lake contains little vegetation, but its drowned logs and rock/rubble shoals drop off steeply and help provide fish habitat. Shallower areas contain mostly a sand bottom, but there are also extensive areas of gravel, which make for good smallmouth spawning habitat.

When the USFS purchased land around the lake in 1966, only white suckers, yellow perch and smallmouth bass were residents. Numbers and sizes have varied considerably since, including some years when perch to 14 inches have turned up in DNR surveys.

Surveys/Stocking: A survey with ¾-inch fyke nets in June 1988 captured only one large perch, however. Suckers, on the other hand, averaged nearly 18½ inches. A total of 161 smallmouths were collected, and they averaged about 13 inches each. Scale samples from various age classes indicated all bass were growing above state averages. The percentage of bass caught by weight and number were the highest recorded since the original survey in 1966.

A June 1993 survey determined that smallmouths remained the dominant species and that 10 percent of them were larger than 18 inches. Only a few suckers and yellow perch were collected. The DNR has not stocked the lake in recent years.

Tactics to Try: The north end of the lake above the big island is the best for smallmouth bass. Look for points, coves and reefs, and experiment with lures and tactics until a pattern emerges. Quarter-ounce crankbaits and topwater lures like the Rebel Pop-R and various poppers have been very successful in this lake when fished with light line and finesse tactics including fly fishing.

Try twister tail jigs and spinners such as Mepps Comets and Blue Fox Vibrax in the flats areas when smallmouths fan out to feed. Two men in a canoe can move quickly throughout the lake's best spots to determine where the bass are. Fishing pressure is usually moderate to high.

Access: There is no boat launch on the lake. Access is through Crooked Lake, from which anglers face a portage of a half-mile or more. Another option is to paddle the length of Clark Lake, then portage to Loon Lake, taking out at the southeast end and lifting the canoe a short distance to Deer Island Lake. The USFS maintains good hiking trails throughout the wilderness area. To rent a canoe, contact Sylvania Outfitters (see listing under Bait & Tackle).

DUCK LAKE

Fishing Opportunities: Walleyes—Good to Excellent; Smallmouth Bass, Black Crappies and Northern Pike— Fair to Good; Largemouth Bass—Available.

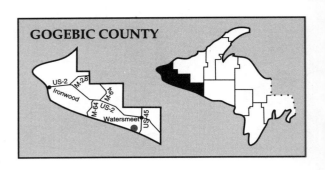

GOGEBIC COUNTY

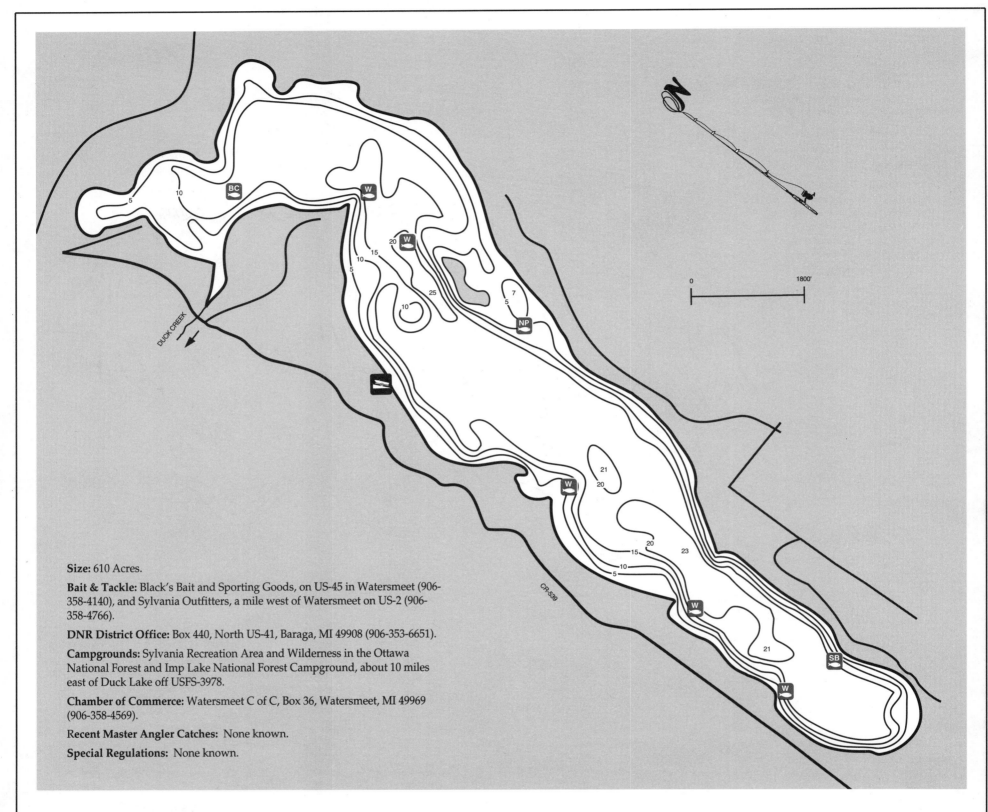

Size: 610 Acres.

Bait & Tackle: Black's Bait and Sporting Goods, on US-45 in Watersmeet (906-358-4140), and Sylvania Outfitters, a mile west of Watersmeet on US-2 (906-358-4766).

DNR District Office: Box 440, North US-41, Baraga, MI 49908 (906-353-6651).

Campgrounds: Sylvania Recreation Area and Wilderness in the Ottawa National Forest and Imp Lake National Forest Campground, about 10 miles east of Duck Lake off USFS-3978.

Chamber of Commerce: Watersmeet C of C, Box 36, Watersmeet, MI 49969 (906-358-4569).

Recent Master Angler Catches: None known.

Special Regulations: None known.

Duck Lake is located about four miles southwest of Watersmeet in south Gogebic County within a couple of miles of the Wisconsin state line. Duck Creek, which drains the lake at its southeast corner, contains brook trout. Duck Lake has a fairly hard bottom featuring sand and gravel over shoals to a depth of 15 to 20 feet and some clay mixed with sand off the west side of the island. Deeper areas and the outlet region contain pulpy peat.

Most of the lake is covered by high hills, and a 3½-acre island lies at the southwest end. Sunken logs are common throughout shallow stretches, and emergent weeds are fairly plentiful in places. The water is clear and colorless.

Surveys/Stocking: A 1986 DNR net survey resulted in the capture of northern pike, pumpkinseed sunfish, black crappies and rock bass. In May 1990 a DNR netting crew found good numbers of walleyes from 11 to 22 inches each, a few smallmouth bass to 14½ inches, and three largemouths to 16 inches.

Researchers were concerned over the absence of young walleyes, and an electroshocking survey that fall did not turn up any young-of-the-year walleyes.

Stocking records date from 1924 when managers began releasing smallmouth bass. Along with largemouths, yellow perch and bluegills, they were stocked regularly through 1938, with brook trout and splake added in the 1960s. In

1991 managers planted out 11,000 walleye fingerlings; in 1992 they released 400 yearling brown trout; and in 1993 they stocked an estimated 47,200 walleye fingerlings.

Tactics to Try: The lake receives fairly high fishing pressure and is popular with anglers from Wisconsin, Illinois and even Minnesota. A west wind drives bait and walleyes to points, drops and gravel spits along the east shore. Try drifting a leech or minnow on a slip bobber. Yellow or white-skirted jigs with half crawlers work well, as do Mister Twisters.

Access: Located on the southeast shore off CR-539, the improved access site includes a paved launch ramp, toilets and parking for four vehicles. There is no place to rent a boat.

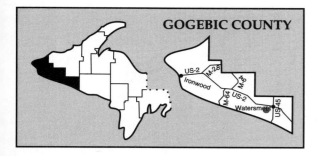
EAST BEAR LAKE

Fishing Opportunities: Largemouth Bass and Bluegills—
Good to Excellent; Yellow Perch—Fair to Good.

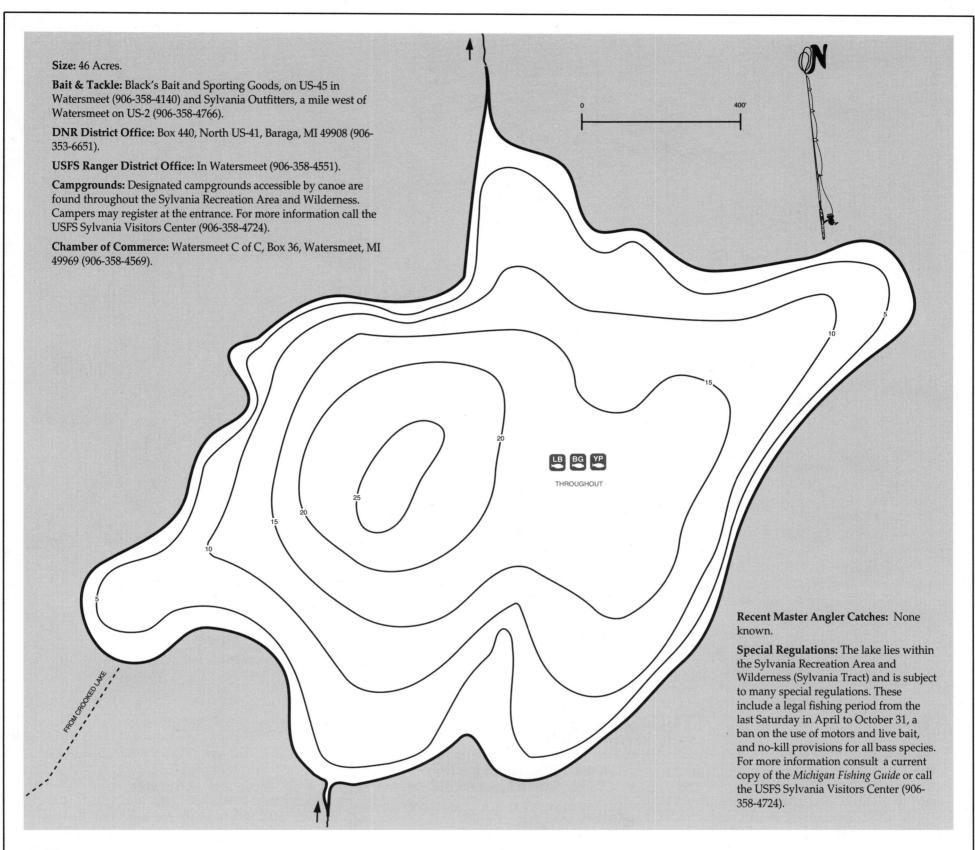

Size: 46 Acres.

Bait & Tackle: Black's Bait and Sporting Goods, on US-45 in Watersmeet (906-358-4140) and Sylvania Outfitters, a mile west of Watersmeet on US-2 (906-358-4766).

DNR District Office: Box 440, North US-41, Baraga, MI 49908 (906-353-6651).

USFS Ranger District Office: In Watersmeet (906-358-4551).

Campgrounds: Designated campgrounds accessible by canoe are found throughout the Sylvania Recreation Area and Wilderness. Campers may register at the entrance. For more information call the USFS Sylvania Visitors Center (906-358-4724).

Chamber of Commerce: Watersmeet C of C, Box 36, Watersmeet, MI 49969 (906-358-4569).

Recent Master Angler Catches: None known.

Special Regulations: The lake lies within the Sylvania Recreation Area and Wilderness (Sylvania Tract) and is subject to many special regulations. These include a legal fishing period from the last Saturday in April to October 31, a ban on the use of motors and live bait, and no-kill provisions for all bass species. For more information consult a current copy of the *Michigan Fishing Guide* or call the USFS Sylvania Visitors Center (906-358-4724).

East Bear Lake is located about three miles southwest of Watersmeet in south Gogebic County within the Sylvania Recreation Area and Wilderness of the Ottawa National Forest. Typical of smaller lakes within the Sylvania Tract, East Bear contains mostly largemouth bass and panfish. Other largemouth lakes to consider include Cub (28 acres), Marsh (65 acres), and West Bear (51 acres).

East Bear Lake contains depths to 25 feet, and its shoal areas are mostly sand with some stretches of gravel.

The lake receives a considerable amount of fishing pressure, especially in June and July. In 1992 the Sylvania Tract hosted an estimated 41,000 visitors, many of whom fished. By comparison, the year before only about 30,000 people came.

Surveys/Stocking: A DNR fyke net survey in June 1991 revealed a modest population of yellow perch with an average size of 9.4 inches. An abundant population of bluegills averaged a whopping 8 inches, and a few pumpkinseed sunfish averaged 7 inches. Although a fair number of largemouths were present, the average size was only 10.3 inches; however, bigger fish are available.

Like others within the Sylvania Tract, the lake is self-sustaining and does not receive hatchery-reared fish.

Tactics to Try: Because live bait is not allowed, anglers should toss crankbaits and spinnerbaits. There is not a lot of weedy habitat in the lake, so concentrate efforts around logs and any other available structure.

Access: The lake is accessed by a portage trail from the east side of Crooked Lake (p. 26), where a public access site is located. Canoeists can also paddle through West Bear Lake, which lies 100 yards or less from East Bear Lake. To rent a canoe, contact Sylvania Outfitters (see Bait & Tackle listing).

IMP LAKE

Fishing Opportunities: Splake—Good to Excellent; Lake Trout and Brown Trout—Available.

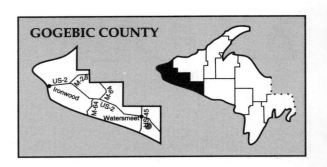

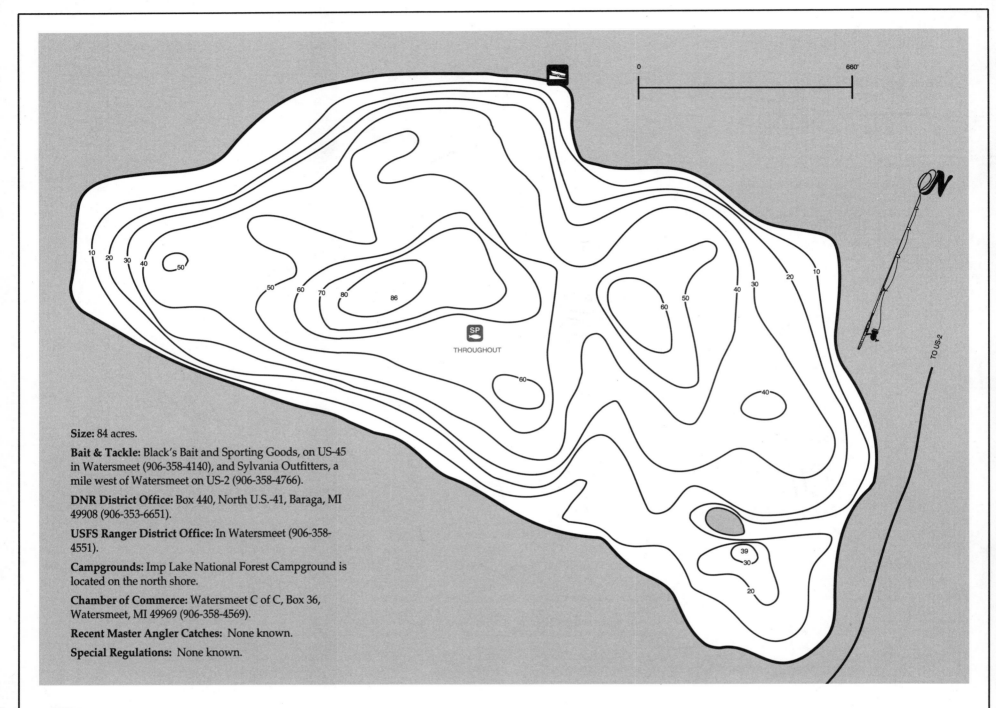

Size: 84 acres.

Bait & Tackle: Black's Bait and Sporting Goods, on US-45 in Watersmeet (906-358-4140), and Sylvania Outfitters, a mile west of Watersmeet on US-2 (906-358-4766).

DNR District Office: Box 440, North U.S.-41, Baraga, MI 49908 (906-353-6651).

USFS Ranger District Office: In Watersmeet (906-358-4551).

Campgrounds: Imp Lake National Forest Campground is located on the north shore.

Chamber of Commerce: Watersmeet C of C, Box 36, Watersmeet, MI 49969 (906-358-4569).

Recent Master Angler Catches: None known.

Special Regulations: None known.

Imp Lake is located in the Ottawa National Forest in Gogebic County about six miles southeast of Watersmeet. The beautiful, undeveloped lake is surrounded by forest. A small, intermittent stream enters from the north, but the lake has no outflow. Structure is limited to snags, deadheads, brush and logs around the perimeter and small stretches of gravel in portions of the narrow, steep shoals. These are found particularly on the east side and around the island in the southeast corner.

Smallmouth bass and bluegills were stocked in 1935, and lake trout were added in 1936. This deep, cold, clear and colorless lake has been under various types of trout management since the 1940s and is popular with both fishermen and campers.

Surveys/Stocking: The DNR introduced splake, brook trout and lake trout in 1961. Splake survived and grew well from these early efforts, but brookies and lakers did not. Management goals since have focused on pro-

viding a good splake fishery. During planting years when splake are not available, the DNR releases other types of yearling trout. For example, in 1989, 2,500 brown trout were introduced, and in 1990, 4,800 brook trout were planted out.

In addition to trout, Imp Lake contains bluegills, pumpkinseed sunfish, yellow perch, smallmouth bass, white suckers, creek chubs and smelt, although none of the latter has been collected in net surveys since 1980. A total of 668 adult smelt were introduced in 1942.

An October 1991 gill net survey collected 38 splake from the previous spring's stocking. The fish averaged 9.7 inches for an average growth rate of 3½ inches, which is considered satisfactory. One splake captured was 25.1 inches. Five browns from the 1989 stocking also showed good growth, ranging in size from 13.6 to 22 inches. Four fish were more than 18½ inches each and averaged 3½ pounds.

Four 12-year-old lake trout collected were each 28 to 31 inches and weighed from about 6½ pounds to nearly 11 pounds.

Tactics to Try: The access road is rarely plowed in winter, but it is only a mile or less from US-2 and therefore accessible to snowmobilers and cross-country skiers who want to try for hardwater trout. Swedish Pimples, Hopkins Spoons and Jigging Rapalas are worthy hardware for big trout. The more abundant, smaller splake are likely to hit ⅟₁₆-oz. jigs, small teardrop spoons, or gold Aberdeen hooks tipped with a single salmon egg, wiggler or kernel of corn. Concentrate on 20- to 40-foot-deep contours on bottom and use portable sonar to locate fish. Then progressively jig, a foot or two at a time, until fish strike.

In summer, jigging tactics also work although worms and crawler pieces are more popular. Early and late in the day are the best times for warm-weather splake, which typically suspend in or near the thermocline. Generally this life band occurs from 18 to 28 feet deep in Imp Lake.

Access: The USFS maintains a paved boat launch ramp, toilets and parking for a half-dozen vehicles at the campground. There is no place to rent a boat.

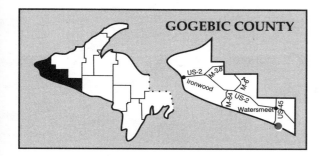

LAC VIEUX DESERT

Fishing Opportunities: Black Crappies and Walleyes—Good to Excellent; Yellow Perch and Northern Muskellunge—Fair to Good.

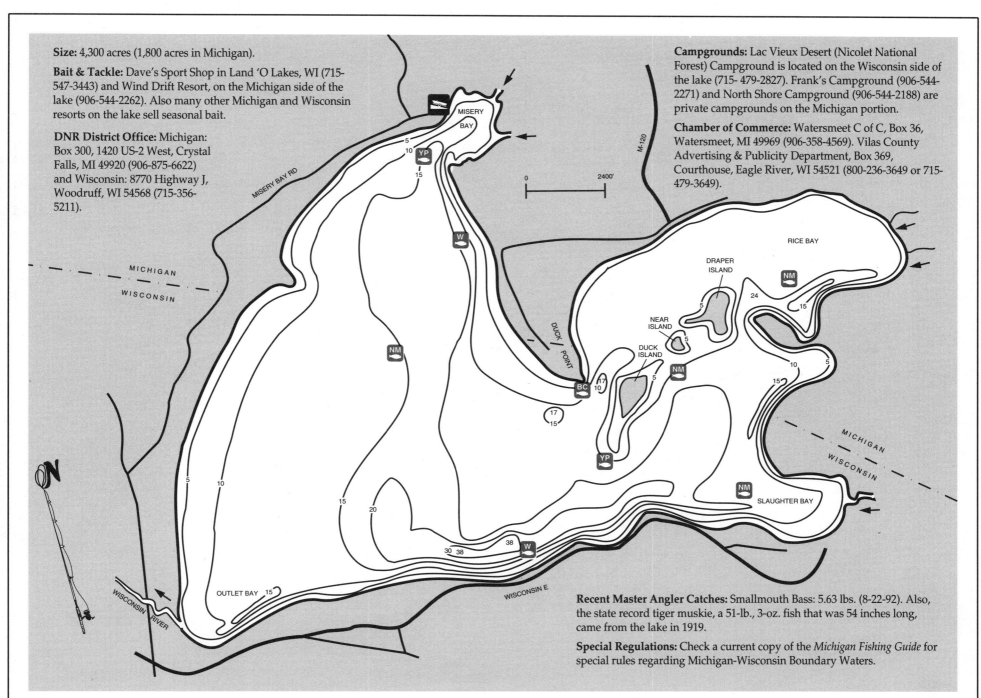

Size: 4,300 acres (1,800 acres in Michigan).

Bait & Tackle: Dave's Sport Shop in Land 'O Lakes, WI (715-547-3443) and Wind Drift Resort, on the Michigan side of the lake (906-544-2262). Also many other Michigan and Wisconsin resorts on the lake sell seasonal bait.

DNR District Office: Michigan: Box 300, 1420 US-2 West, Crystal Falls, MI 49920 (906-875-6622) and Wisconsin: 8770 Highway J, Woodruff, WI 54568 (715-356-5211).

Campgrounds: Lac Vieux Desert (Nicolet National Forest) Campground is located on the Wisconsin side of the lake (715- 479-2827). Frank's Campground (906-544-2271) and North Shore Campground (906-544-2188) are private campgrounds on the Michigan portion.

Chamber of Commerce: Watersmeet C of C, Box 36, Watersmeet, MI 49969 (906-358-4569). Vilas County Advertising & Publicity Department, Box 369, Courthouse, Eagle River, WI 54521 (800-236-3649 or 715-479-3649).

Recent Master Angler Catches: Smallmouth Bass: 5.63 lbs. (8-22-92). Also, the state record tiger muskie, a 51-lb., 3-oz. fish that was 54 inches long, came from the lake in 1919.

Special Regulations: Check a current copy of the *Michigan Fishing Guide* for special rules regarding Michigan-Wisconsin Boundary Waters.

Lac Vieux Desert (Old Desert Lake) is the origin of the Wisconsin River, which flows out from the southwest corner. Roughly one third of the lake lies in Michigan and two thirds in Wisconsin. When all its surface acres are considered, it ranks as Michigan's 23rd largest lake. For years Lac Vieux Desert has been managed for walleyes and muskellunge. Maximum depth is 38 feet, and the lake is quite weedy.

Surveys/Stocking: Stocking dates to 1936 when yellow perch were introduced. Walleyes made their appearance the next year. A Michigan DNR fisheries crew last surveyed the lake in 1975 and found a strong year-class of young perch, along with good numbers of pumpkinseed sunfish. Black crappies, bluegills, rock bass, walleyes and muskies were among other species collected.

A 1986 Wisconsin DNR survey with ¾-inch fyke nets to assess adult walleye stocks captured 2,177 walleyes. Males averaged 15.3 inches, and females averaged 16.2 inches. More than half of the fish collected ranged from 15 to 19 inches each, and less than one percent (13 fish) were longer than 24 inches.

In August 1987 a Wisconsin DNR boomshocking crew collected 181 walleyes to 22.6 inches each. Muskies Inc. reportedly stocks the lake with muskies under DNR supervision.

Tactics to Try: In spite of spearing by members of Wisconsin's Mole Lake band of Chippewas, Lac Vieux Desert is one of the U.P.'s best walleye lakes. Fishing is especially good from the May opener through the first week in June. After that, heavy weeds choke the lake and fishing gets difficult. Silver shiners are the best walleye bait, especially when fished near the big beds of green-leafed muskie weeds. Chubs also produce for drift and jig fishermen.

A good muskie bite occurs each fall, but fish are taken in the summer, too. Some anglers, including area guides, claim the next world record swims in this lake. They can appear anywhere in the lake; start around Duck, Near and Draper islands.

Vieux Desert is also a very good yellow perch and black crappie lake. The best time to catch crappies is from May 15 to 30 when they are spawning among the bulrushes in the several bays. Look for spawning beds, then back off and toss small minnows or bright-colored spinners. Crappies bite again in the fall when they invade shallows to feed. Try Duck Point.

During the summer, panfishermen key on weedbeds throughout the lake. Winter panfishing is very popular, and it is not uncommon to see 200 or more vehicles on the lake on the weekend. As a result, fishing pressure is high.

Access: The public access on the Michigan side is located on Misery Bay in the upper northwest corner. Included are a paved boat launch ramp, courtesy pier, toilets and parking for 17 vehicles. In Wisconsin an access site is located in the national forest campground. To rent a boat, contact the chambers of commerce for names and phone numbers of the many resorts on the lake.

LAKE GOGEBIC

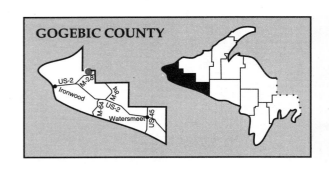
Fishing Opportunities: Walleyes and Yellow Perch—
Good to Excellent; Ciscoes—Good; Smallmouth and
Largemouth Bass— Poor to Fair.

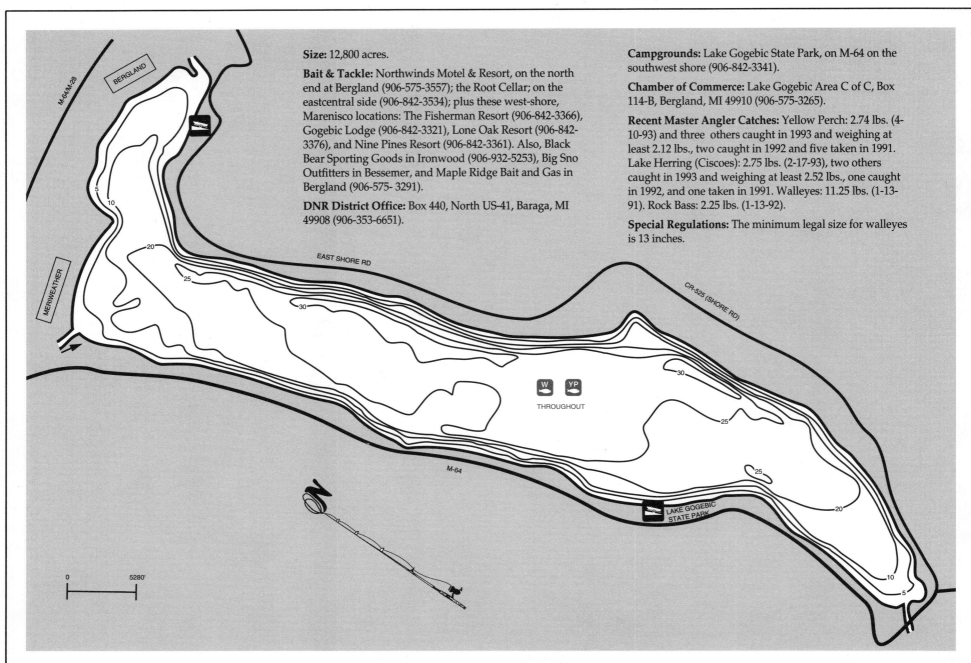

Size: 12,800 acres.

Bait & Tackle: Northwinds Motel & Resort, on the north end at Bergland (906-575-3557); the Root Cellar; on the eastcentral side (906-842-3534); plus these west-shore, Marenisco locations: The Fisherman Resort (906-842-3366), Gogebic Lodge (906-842-3321), Lone Oak Resort (906-842-3376), and Nine Pines Resort (906-842-3361). Also, Black Bear Sporting Goods in Ironwood (906-932-5253), Big Sno Outfitters in Bessemer, and Maple Ridge Bait and Gas in Bergland (906-575- 3291).

DNR District Office: Box 440, North US-41, Baraga, MI 49908 (906-353-6651).

Campgrounds: Lake Gogebic State Park, on M-64 on the southwest shore (906-842-3341).

Chamber of Commerce: Lake Gogebic Area C of C, Box 114-B, Bergland, MI 49910 (906-575-3265).

Recent Master Angler Catches: Yellow Perch: 2.74 lbs. (4-10-93) and three others caught in 1993 and weighing at least 2.12 lbs., two caught in 1992 and five taken in 1991. Lake Herring (Ciscoes): 2.75 lbs. (2-17-93), two others caught in 1993 and weighing at least 2.52 lbs., one caught in 1992, and one taken in 1991. Walleyes: 11.25 lbs. (1-13-91). Rock Bass: 2.25 lbs. (1-13-92).

Special Regulations: The minimum legal size for walleyes is 13 inches.

Lake Gogebic is equally located in west Ontonagon and Gogebic counties. Michigan's sixth-largest inland lake is also the biggest body of water in the Upper Peninsula, with about 20 square miles of surface water and some 33 miles of shoreline. The lake outlet at the north end forms the West Branch of the Ontonagon River.

Average depth is about 18 feet, and the deepest spot is 37 feet. Shoal areas are mostly sand and gravel — particularly along the east side where walleyes spawn—and deeper areas are muck. The lake is clean but fairly dark, and it forms a thermocline from 8 to 18 feet in summer.

Surveys/Stocking: Walleyes, which were shipped to Bergland by train (probably from the hatchery at Sault Ste. Marie), were first introduced in 1904 and have provided the mainstay since, replacing one of the Midwest's finest smallmouth and largemouth fisheries. Early reports of walleyes to 16 pounds being taken were common. Lake Gogebic continues to produce excellent catches of small walleyes and big yellow perch and serves up

occasional good action for smallmouth and largemouth bass.

Lake Gogebic is probably the most heavily researched lake in the Upper Peninsula. During at least the past 20 years, there has been no evidence of a year-class failure or a dominant year-class, and the average size of most walleyes creeled is 13 to 14 inches. Because of the high success of spawning, DNR managers have relied on Lake Gogebic for egg collection, and no fish have been stocked in recent years.

Tactics to Try: The lake has a reputation of producing lots of small walleyes. During the past 25 years, adult male walleyes appear to peak every four years, and tagging studies indicate their number to vary between 38,000 and 63,000 in any given year. Anglers catch an estimated 20 percent each year, and natural mortality claims another 18 percent. Low forage levels keep fish from growing to huge size. Efforts to stock forage minnows have largely failed.

Slip bobbers and live bait score among weedy pockets of the north end. Wolf River rigs are also popular. Anglers typically have to search

for walleyes. The lake's north/south orientation makes for rough water but also pounds the east shore much of the time. Small rock slides here are a tip-off to walleye-holding structure.

Hundreds of fish shelters have been installed over the years, including many in 1989. The shelters are noted by red diamond-shaped signs along the shore and are typically found in 10 to 15 feet of water. Fishing around these shelters is usually good for panfish and occasionally for bass and walleyes.

Ice anglers score on big ciscoes to 19 inches on late ice in March. Use tiny minnows or wigglers.

Access: The state park public access site is located on the southwest shore and includes a paved ramp, courtesy pier, toilets and parking for five vehicles. There is also a boat launch in Bergland at the north end of the lake. To rent a boat, contact Northwinds Motel & Resort, the Fisherman Resort, Gogebic Lodge, Lone Oak Resort or Nine Pines (all under Bait & Tackle listings). Other resorts offering boat rentals include Bailey's Rustic Resort (906-842-3336), Mallard Cove (906-932-1411), The Timber's Resort (906-575- 3542), and Sunset View Cottages (906-842-3589).

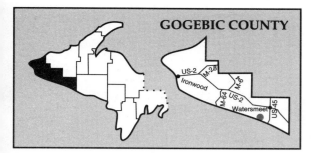

LOON LAKE

Fishing Opportunities: Smallmouth Bass—Good to Excellent.

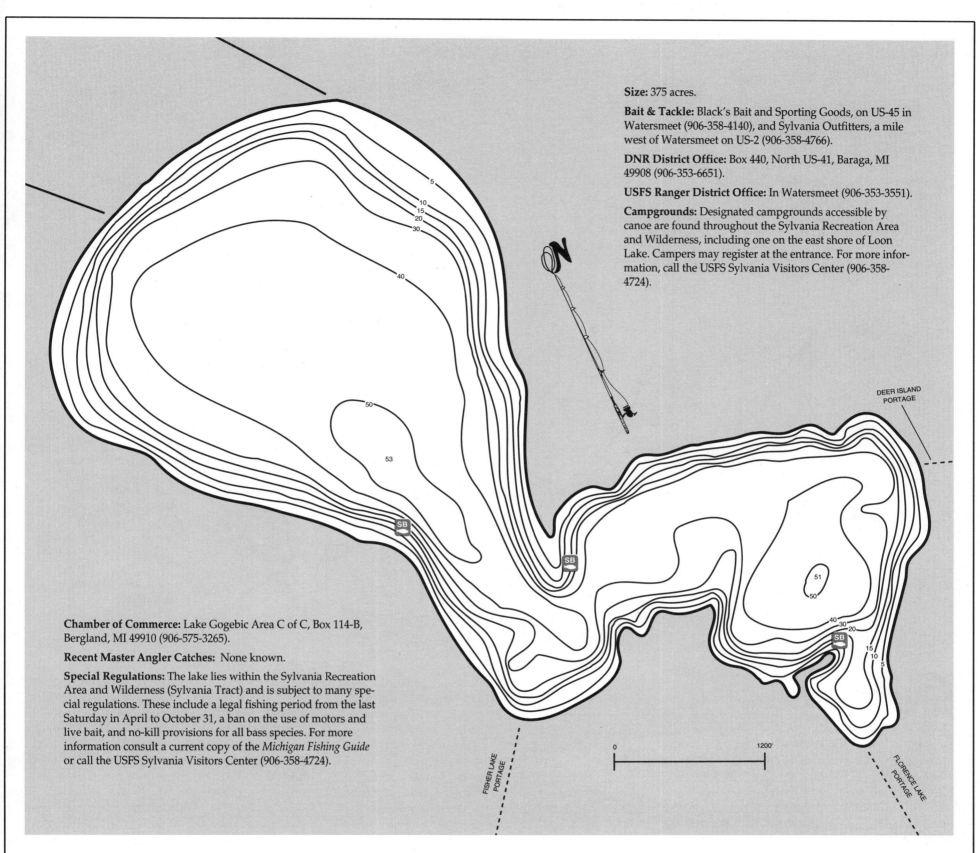

Size: 375 acres.

Bait & Tackle: Black's Bait and Sporting Goods, on US-45 in Watersmeet (906-358-4140), and Sylvania Outfitters, a mile west of Watersmeet on US-2 (906-358-4766).

DNR District Office: Box 440, North US-41, Baraga, MI 49908 (906-353-6651).

USFS Ranger District Office: In Watersmeet (906-353-3551).

Campgrounds: Designated campgrounds accessible by canoe are found throughout the Sylvania Recreation Area and Wilderness, including one on the east shore of Loon Lake. Campers may register at the entrance. For more information, call the USFS Sylvania Visitors Center (906-358-4724).

Chamber of Commerce: Lake Gogebic Area C of C, Box 114-B, Bergland, MI 49910 (906-575-3265).

Recent Master Angler Catches: None known.

Special Regulations: The lake lies within the Sylvania Recreation Area and Wilderness (Sylvania Tract) and is subject to many special regulations. These include a legal fishing period from the last Saturday in April to October 31, a ban on the use of motors and live bait, and no-kill provisions for all bass species. For more information consult a current copy of the *Michigan Fishing Guide* or call the USFS Sylvania Visitors Center (906-358-4724).

Loon Lake is an exceptionally clean, clear lake in the Sylvania Recreation Area of the Ottawa National Forest in south Gogebic County about seven miles southwest of Watersmeet. More than half of the lake bottom and virtually all of its shoal waters are sand mixed with gravel or purely gravel. Deeper areas contain clay.

Surveys/Stocking: A June 1990 DNR fyke net survey found that little had changed from collections three years earlier. Rock bass comprised a little more than half of the biomass lifted, and trophy smallmouth bass

(fish larger than 18 inches) contributed about five percent of the biomass. The bass represented 12 year-classes

Like other lakes within the Sylvania Tract, Loon's fish population is self-sustaining. The DNR has not stocked the lake in recent years.

Tactics to Try: Smallmouths typically spawn along the southeast point where the campground is located on the east shore. Anglers using sonar will often mark fish; looking over the boat side into the clear lake they can actually see the smallmouths. In gin-clear lakes like Loon, the most successful fishermen are those who use specialized tactics like long-lining

small lures on light line behind the canoe while paddling over smallmouth haunts. These include points, breaks, drop-offs and any available structure such as rocks and logs.

Access: There is no boat launch on the lake, which is located in the middle of the wilderness area. Access is through Crooked Lake or Clark Lake to Deer Island. The portage from Deer Island is about a quarter-mile, and like other trails within the wilderness area, is well-marked by the USFS. Florence and Fisher are two small lakes accessible from Loon Lake and which contain panfish and largemouth bass. To rent a canoe, contact Sylvania Outfitters (see listing under Bait & Tackle).

MARION LAKE

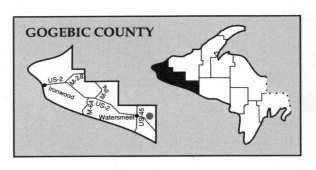
Fishing Opportunities: Smallmouth Bass—Good;
Bluegills, Black Crappies and Walleyes—Fair to Good;
Northern Pike— Available.

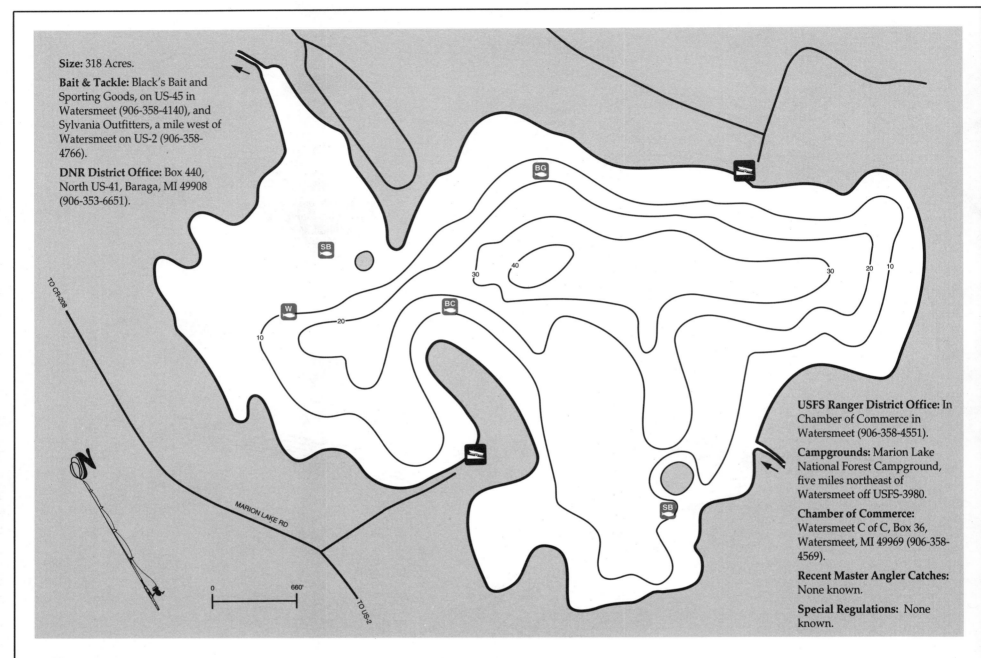

Size: 318 Acres.

Bait & Tackle: Black's Bait and Sporting Goods, on US-45 in Watersmeet (906-358-4140), and Sylvania Outfitters, a mile west of Watersmeet on US-2 (906-358-4766).

DNR District Office: Box 440, North US-41, Baraga, MI 49908 (906-353-6651).

USFS Ranger District Office: In Chamber of Commerce in Watersmeet (906-358-4551).

Campgrounds: Marion Lake National Forest Campground, five miles northeast of Watersmeet off USFS-3980.

Chamber of Commerce: Watersmeet C of C, Box 36, Watersmeet, MI 49969 (906-358-4569).

Recent Master Angler Catches: None known.

Special Regulations: None known.

Marion Lake is located about six miles east of Watersmeet in east Gogebic County. About 75 percent of the lake's shoreline is contained within the Ottawa National Forest. Approximately 20 summer homes are on the lake. A single inlet enters on the southeast side; Marion Creek outlets on the north side and eventually flows into the Middle Branch of the Ontonagon River.

The lake averages about 12½ feet deep with a maximum depth of 40 feet. Bottom composition is mostly sand in the extensive shoals, but there are scattered deposits of gravel and fibrous peat in some areas. The lake is fairly weedy and contains some logs, boulders and recently installed manmade fish structures.

The water is clear but stained a light brown. In summer a thermocline forms at 14 to 27 feet, and oxygen levels below 22 feet during this period will not sustain fish.

Surveys/Stocking: Management records date to 1928 when fisheries biologists released 10,000 lake trout. Through the 1930s they also stocked smallmouth and large-

mouth bass, yellow perch, black crappies and bluegills. In 1941 stocking was discontinued, and during the next 20 years periodic netting and chemical reclamation efforts were introduced to control suckers and other undesirable species. In 1961 biologists released 260 adult walleyes averaging 17 inches. Manual removal of rock bass and the introduction of tiger muskies in 1968 helped restore balance to the lake.

In May 1992 a DNR research crew collected many healthy predators in fyke nets and determined that the lake was the healthiest it had ever been since management began. Many smallmouth bass taken were larger than 12 inches and ranged in size to 16 inches. Walleyes ranged to 27 inches. The nets confirmed that Marion Lake contains trophy, slab-sided bluegills, too. Other species include pumpkinseed sunfish, northern pike, black crappies and rock bass. Bluegills to 10 years of age and walleyes to 14 were confirmed through scale sampling.

Managers stocked 1.1 million walleye fry and 12,400 fingerlings in 1991. In 1992 they transplanted 650 adult bluegills and 3,000 adult perch.

Tactics to Try: The lake receives a fair amount of fishing pressure, including attention from Wisconsin guides. Good spots to try are any of the 20 fish cribs placed into the lake during the winter of 1989-90. Ten are located at the 15-foot-deep contour along the north shore. The other ten went into the 15-foot-deep contour south of the north-shore island. To improve spawning and hiding cover for smallmouth bass, the USFS also installed 20 log structures at various locations around the lake in 1990 and again in 1991.

In front of the access site is a rock bar on the opposite side of the island. Smallmouth bass frequent the 12- to 14-foot-deep structure. To catch them, anchor upwind and drift a mud minnow on a bare hook with the aid of a slip bobber. Leeches also produce for bass and walleyes.

Access: Two public access sites maintained by the USFS serve the lake. The better one is located in the campground on the lake's northeast shore. Included are a paved ramp, toilets and parking for 10 vehicles. The other site, located on the northwest shore, is gravel (also a good launch) and has minimum parking space. To rent a boat or canoe, contact Sylvania Outfitters (see listing under Bait & Tackle).

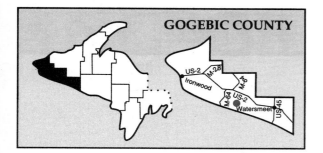

POMEROY LAKE

Fishing Opportunities: Yellow Perch, Bluegills and Black Crappies—Good to Excellent; Walleyes and Largemouth Bass— Good; Northern Pike, Northern Muskies and Smallmouth Bass— Available.

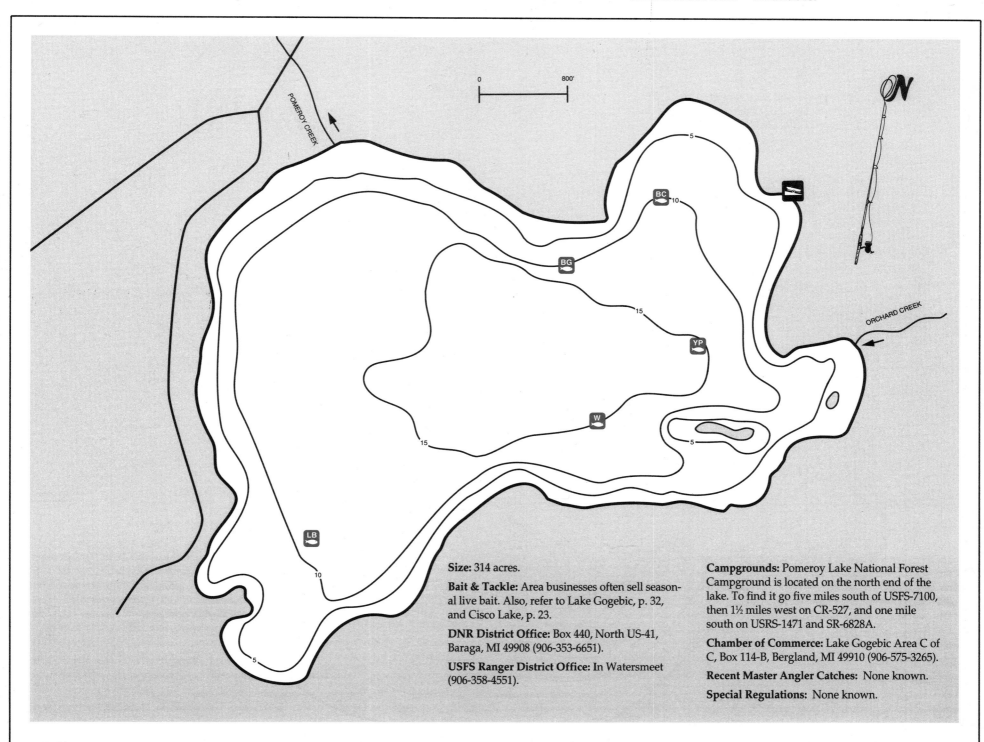

Size: 314 acres.

Bait & Tackle: Area businesses often sell seasonal live bait. Also, refer to Lake Gogebic, p. 32, and Cisco Lake, p. 23.

DNR District Office: Box 440, North US-41, Baraga, MI 49908 (906-353-6651).

USFS Ranger District Office: In Watersmeet (906-358-4551).

Campgrounds: Pomeroy Lake National Forest Campground is located on the north end of the lake. To find it go five miles south of USFS-7100, then 1½ miles west on CR-527, and one mile south on USRS-1471 and SR-6828A.

Chamber of Commerce: Lake Gogebic Area C of C, Box 114-B, Bergland, MI 49910 (906-575-3265).

Recent Master Angler Catches: None known.

Special Regulations: None known.

Pomeroy Lake is located in remote east-central Gogebic County about nine miles southeast of Marenisco and probably 10 miles from the nearest electricity. Because of its relative shallowness (the deepest spot is only 15 feet), Pomeroy features lots of vegetation and wide shoals of mostly gravel and rubble. The lake's inlet is Orchard Creek, and the outlet is Pomeroy Creek, which flows to the East Branch of the Presque Isle River.

Historically, the brown-stained lake has supported a good mix of gamefish with panfish dominating. Walleyes, introduced in 1982, have done well, thanks to apparent natural reproduction keyed to a spawning reef built by the USFS.

Surveys/Stocking: Over the years northern pike, tiger muskies and largemouth bass have thrived here at various times. A 1985 DNR survey showed yellow perch and black crappies to be abundant, with north-ern pike and largemouths common. A boomshocking survey in September 1990 found evidence of a strong year-class of two-year-old pike, with fish from 11 year-classes represented. Fair numbers of largemouth bass were observed. The following autumn the boomshocking crew captured 119 walleyes, including 100 young-of-the-year walleyes from 6 to 8 inches each.

Fishing pressure, which is considered to be moderate to high, might be responsible for the lack of big walleyes, although one 26-incher was collected. The fisheries crew observed good numbers of largemouth bass to 17 inches. Black crappies to 11 inches appeared to be coming on, along with pumpkinseed sunfish.

The DNR has not stocked the lake thus far in the 1990s.

Tactics to Try: Leeches work well for walleyes in Pomeroy Lake, especially when fished with a slip bobber. Drifting and trolling techniques no doubt will work, too.

The lake serves up good panfishing. For best results use a small worm harness or tiny spinner and either troll, drift or chug up and down the lake. Tip the small hardware with a wiggler, waxworm or thunder bug (larvae of the blue dragon fly), which are available from some regional bait shops. The access road is not plowed in winter, necessitating a 10-mile ride by snowmobile.

The lake is underfished for largemouth bass. Although we have no specific catching information to report, live bait is always a good bet. White, yellow or lime-green spinnerbaits would be good lure choices and colors to try in the tannic-acid-stained lake.

Access: The USFS maintains a public access site on the north shore at the end of Pomeroy Lake Road, which is reached via US-2. The boat launch ramp is hard-surfaced, toilets are available, and there is parking for a half-dozen vehicles. There is no place to rent a boat.

TAMARACK LAKE

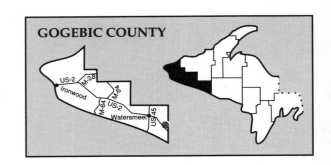
Fishing Opportunities: Walleyes and Northern Pike—
Good to Excellent; Smallmouth Bass and Black
Crappies—Fair to Good; Largemouth Bass, Yellow Perch
and Bluegills—Fair.

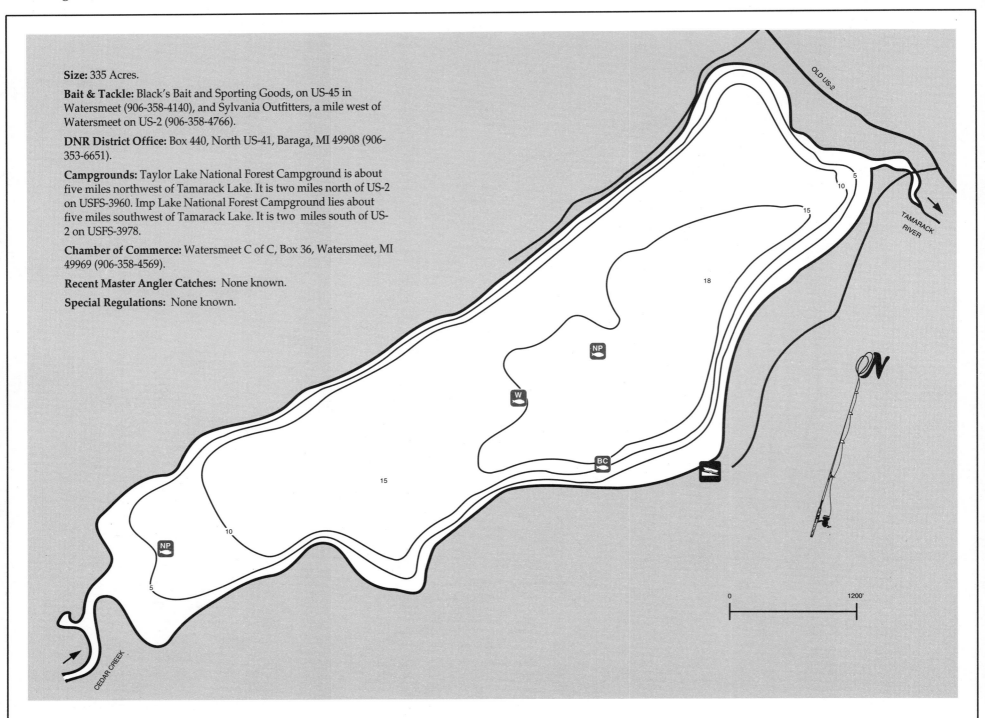

Size: 335 Acres.

Bait & Tackle: Black's Bait and Sporting Goods, on US-45 in
Watersmeet (906-358-4140), and Sylvania Outfitters, a mile west of
Watersmeet on US-2 (906-358-4766).

DNR District Office: Box 440, North US-41, Baraga, MI 49908 (906-
353-6651).

Campgrounds: Taylor Lake National Forest Campground is about
five miles northwest of Tamarack Lake. It is two miles north of US-2
on USFS-3960. Imp Lake National Forest Campground lies about
five miles southwest of Tamarack Lake. It is two miles south of US-
2 on USFS-3978.

Chamber of Commerce: Watersmeet C of C, Box 36, Watersmeet, MI
49969 (906-358-4569).

Recent Master Angler Catches: None known.

Special Regulations: None known.

Tamarack Lake is located 11 miles east of
Watersmeet along the Gogebic/Iron
County line. Cedar Creek inlets from the south,
and the Tamarack River outlets to the north.
Numerous springs contribute inflow as well.
The lake has a maximum depth of 18 feet, and
the water is stained a dark brown. Aquatic vegetation is sparse. Additional fish cover includes
some logs and large rocks. Steep shoals of sand
occupy the west shore, and there are few areas
of rock or gravel that provide spawning habitat
for smallmouth bass.

The lake does not develop a thermocline, and
oxygen levels are sufficient to sustain fish year-
round.

Surveys/Stocking: Smallmouth bass and
bluegills were originally
stocked in 1936, and largemouths went into the
lake in 1937. The DNR planted a total of 6,000
brook trout in 1961.

When the lake was first netted in 1962,

researchers found a large population of big
black crappies, along with some decent yellow
perch. However, white suckers dominated the
biomass at 75 percent. A 1972 survey revealed
that 40 percent of the biomass was still suckers
but that northern pike had increased dramatically. Largemouth and smallmouth bass were present in small numbers.

When a 1981 survey showed that high levels of
undesirable species were dominating the fish
community, managers began conducting a manual removal program. A walleye stocking program began in 1985.

Recent surveys have shown that the lake is
returning to health, in spite of fairly high fishing
pressure. In 1988 biologists netted northern pike
to 37 inches and four-year-old walleyes to 16
inches. Bluegills, although small in number,
were big, and black crappies averaged 10 inches.
Surveys in 1991 and 1992 confirmed that good
fishing occurs in Tamarack Lake in spite of the
fact that the lake has not been stocked during
the 1990s.

In the spring of 1990, members of the Lac
Vieux Desert Indian tribe began spearing
walleyes. That year they took 57 walleyes averaging 17 inches. The following year they speared
27 walleyes.

Tactics to Try: The best technique for catching
walleyes is to drift or troll
down the middle of the lake with a silver- and-
black floating Rapala. Live minnows are good
natural bait as are leeches and crawlers.

Other than bobber fishing with a live minnow,
the best trick for catching northern pike is to toss
or troll a black- and-white spoon, especially one
with a copper-colored underside.

For smallmouth bass, toss yellow or white
Mister Twisters among the shoreline logs. The
best crappie fishing occurs in May when fish are
on the spawning beds. White or pink jigs in ¹⁄₃₂-
to ¹⁄₁₆-oz. size work best.

Access: The DNR maintains an access site
along the eastcentral shore. There is no
place to rent a boat.

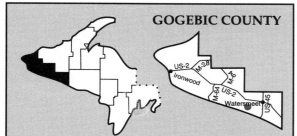

THOUSAND ISLAND LAKE

Fishing Opportunities: Walleyes, Ciscoes, Smallmouth Bass, Northern Muskies and Yellow Perch—Good to Excellent.

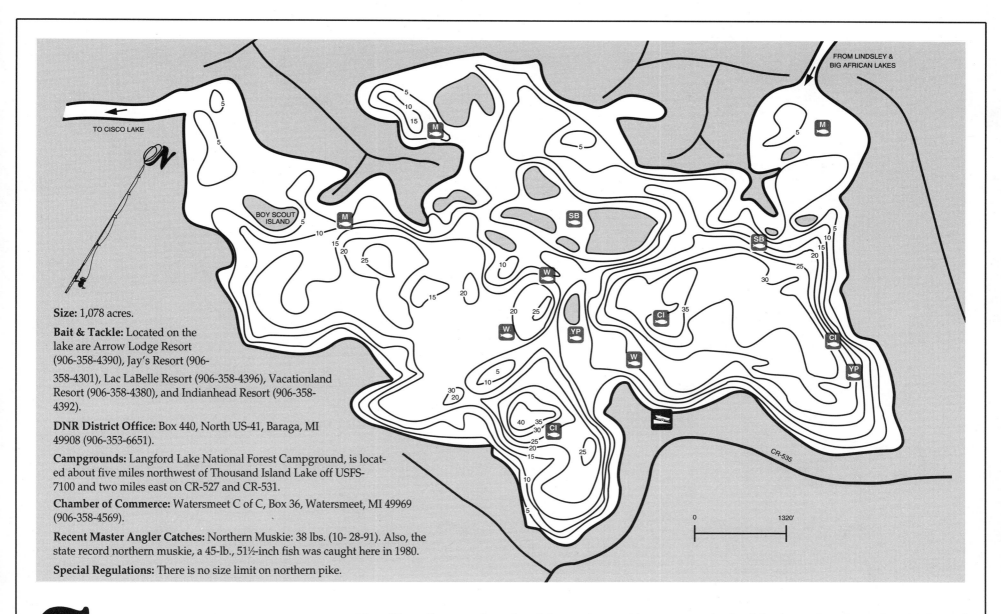

Size: 1,078 acres.

Bait & Tackle: Located on the lake are Arrow Lodge Resort (906-358-4390), Jay's Resort (906-358-4301), Lac LaBelle Resort (906-358-4396), Vacationland Resort (906-358-4380), and Indianhead Resort (906-358-4392).

DNR District Office: Box 440, North US-41, Baraga, MI 49908 (906-353-6651).

Campgrounds: Langford Lake National Forest Campground, is located about five miles northwest of Thousand Island Lake off USFS-7100 and two miles east on CR-527 and CR-531.

Chamber of Commerce: Watersmeet C of C, Box 36, Watersmeet, MI 49969 (906-358-4569).

Recent Master Angler Catches: Northern Muskie: 38 lbs. (10- 28-91). Also, the state record northern muskie, a 45-lb., 51½-inch fish was caught here in 1980.

Special Regulations: There is no size limit on northern pike.

Thousand Island Lake is one of 15 lakes on the Cisco Chain of Lakes located about 13 miles west of Watersmeet in Gegebic County. Four of the lakes, none of which are included in this book, share the Wisconsin border. Cisco Lake (p. 23) is the only other good fishing lake contained within these pages. Area resorts and other businesses often sell detailed maps of the entire chain for those anglers who want to explore all the possibilities.

Logs, sunken islands and plenty of submergent and floating vegetation provide fish habitat, along with fairly steep shoals of sand, gravel and fibrous peat.

Inlets include Big African and Lindsley lakes. The lake outlets through Cisco Lake to the Cisco Branch of the Ontonagon River. A midsummer thermocline forms from 17 to 26 feet. Fishing pressure is considered moderate to heavy.

Surveys/Stocking: The lake has a long history of fish management dating to the early 1930s. Over the years yellow perch, walleye and lake trout were among the species stocked. Surveys since have found good populations of walleyes, smallmouth bass, ciscoes, bluegills, yellow perch and rock bass, along with small northern pike and some muskies and black crappies.

A June 1992 DNR survey with ¾-inch fyke nets indicated that black crappies and bluegills were on the increase while rock and smallmouth bass numbers had slid somewhat. Although fewer walleyes than normal were collected, their average length was 19.4 inches, and the range was 12 to 26 inches. The range of other species included smallmouth bass from 8 to 18 inches, northern pike from 14 to 27 inches, bluegills from 5 to 8 inches, yellow perch from 5 to 10 inches, and black crappies from 5 to 12 inches.

The DNR has not stocked the lake in recent years.

Tactics to Try: About a dozen islands dot the lake and provide excellent gravel and rock bar structure. In addition, Thousand Island Lake features deep water, changing contour breaks and some decent-size weedbeds. Many walleye anglers go deep, especially in summer, when they bounce jigs and Lindy Rig offerings along the rocky bottom.

Although the trend among muskie anglers is also to fish deeper than normal, most of the big ones in the lake are taken from 4 to 12 feet of water. For specific lures and tactics, refer to Cisco Lake, p. 23. Ciscoes in Thousand Island Lake have been known to average four pounds. Best found with sonar, they provide optimum angling opportunities in June, July and August when the fish orientate near bottom in 40 to 50 feet of water. At other times the ciscoes tend to suspend and do not actively feed. Jig with a No. 7 Swedish Pimple, and try tipping it with a single Uncle Josh pink salmon egg, especially if located fish won't bite. Another tip: Tape a sliver of green prism paper along the beveled edge of the Swedish Pimple.

Smallmouths are mostly undersized, given the new Michigan minimum size length of 14 inches. Try Sparkle Tails, Beetlespins, Mepps Spinners and Twisters. An unexpected bonus throughout the Cisco Chain are largemouth bass for anglers casting Johnson Spoons with a trailer of Uncle Josh pork rind or other weedless-type lures.

Access: An improved launch site located on the southeast shore off CR-525 includes a paved ramp, courtesy pier, toilets and parking for 10 vehicles. To rent a boat, contact any of the resorts listed under Bait & Tackle.

WHITEFISH LAKE

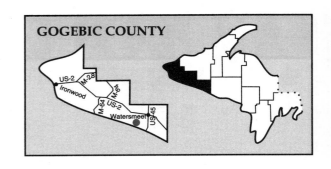

Fishing Opportunities: Smallmouth Bass and Walleyes—
Good to Excellent; Yellow Perch—Fair to Good.

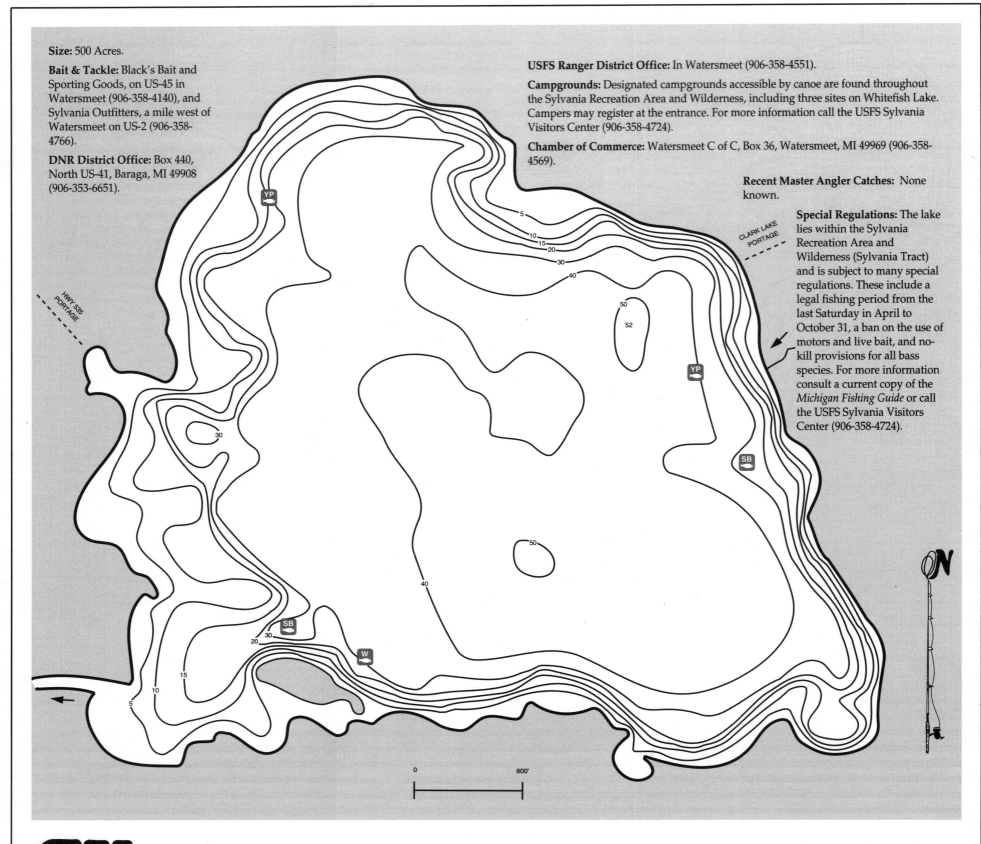

Size: 500 Acres.

Bait & Tackle: Black's Bait and Sporting Goods, on US-45 in Watersmeet (906-358-4140), and Sylvania Outfitters, a mile west of Watersmeet on US-2 (906-358-4766).

DNR District Office: Box 440, North US-41, Baraga, MI 49908 (906-353-6651).

USFS Ranger District Office: In Watersmeet (906-358-4551).

Campgrounds: Designated campgrounds accessible by canoe are found throughout the Sylvania Recreation Area and Wilderness, including three sites on Whitefish Lake. Campers may register at the entrance. For more information call the USFS Sylvania Visitors Center (906-358-4724).

Chamber of Commerce: Watersmeet C of C, Box 36, Watersmeet, MI 49969 (906-358-4569).

Recent Master Angler Catches: None known.

Special Regulations: The lake lies within the Sylvania Recreation Area and Wilderness (Sylvania Tract) and is subject to many special regulations. These include a legal fishing period from the last Saturday in April to October 31, a ban on the use of motors and live bait, and no-kill provisions for all bass species. For more information consult a current copy of the *Michigan Fishing Guide* or call the USFS Sylvania Visitors Center (906-358-4724).

Whitefish Lake is located in south Gogebic County about seven miles southwest of Watersmeet within the Sylvania Wilderness Area of the Ottawa National Forest. Like most of the more than 20 other lakes within the special-use area, Whitefish is a clean, clear lake that is basically sterile and whose shoals are ringed by sand and gravel. It is the only Sylvania Tract lake containing walleyes, which, at this writing, must be larger than 20 inches to keep.

Surveys/Stocking: A June 1989 fyke net survey revealed that yellow perch had increased in number and size since a survey completed in 1982. Smallmouth bass averaged 10.4 inches, and walleyes averaged 12.8 inches. Both predator types were fat and robust, and some females contained eggs. In fact, smallmouths were spawning during the survey; researchers noticed several 14-inch-long males guarding nests.

Like other lakes within the system, Whitefish is self-sustaining and has not been stocked in recent years.

Tactics to Try: The lake hosts big hatches of mayflies, offering flyfishermen unique opportunities. The crystal-clear water and the fact that bigger fish are older and lure shy demand that anglers use finesse tactics and light line. Best times to fish are early and late in the day.

Access: There is no boat launch on the lake. Most anglers drive to within a half-mile of the lake's west side via CR-535. Access is also possible through Clark Lake, but canoeists then face a portage of nearly a mile down a well-marked USFS trail. Although Whitefish Lake lies within a mile of the Wisconsin state line, there is no public access route from Wisconsin anywhere into the Sylvania Tract. To rent a canoe, contact Sylvania Outfitters (see listing under Bait & Tackle).

BOB LAKE

Fishing Opportunities: Walleyes—Good to Excellent.

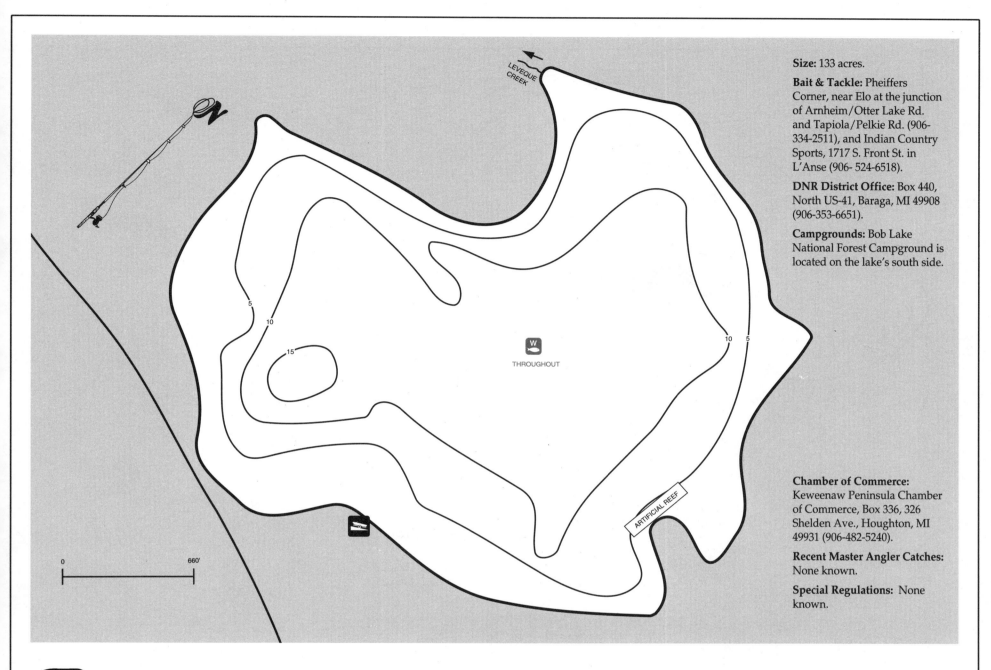
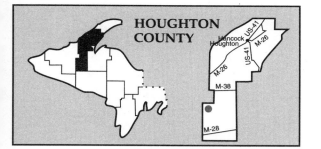

Size: 133 acres.

Bait & Tackle: Pheiffers Corner, near Elo at the junction of Arnheim/Otter Lake Rd. and Tapiola/Pelkie Rd. (906-334-2511), and Indian Country Sports, 1717 S. Front St. in L'Anse (906- 524-6518).

DNR District Office: Box 440, North US-41, Baraga, MI 49908 (906-353-6651).

Campgrounds: Bob Lake National Forest Campground is located on the lake's south side.

Chamber of Commerce: Keweenaw Peninsula Chamber of Commerce, Box 336, 326 Shelden Ave., Houghton, MI 49931 (906-482-5240).

Recent Master Angler Catches: None known.

Special Regulations: None known.

Bob Lake is located in southwest Houghton County between Sidnaw and Mass City and about nine miles southwest of Nisula. The lake has a maximum depth of only 15 feet, and aquatic vegetation is sparse. The water is stained a dark brown, and the bottom is mostly muck or silt. Sandy areas are found on the south and northeast shores.

Submerged logs, and remnants of 60 fish shelters erected in 1949 provide some fish cover. The USFS, which owns about 90 percent of the shoreline, installed an artificial rock reef along a point on the east shore next to the swimming beach. The lake is fed mostly by springs entering from the west shore. Bob Lake's outlet is Leveque Creek, which is a second-quality trout tributary of the East Branch of the Ontonagon River.

The lake has a long history of producing average to good fishing for various species. Prior to 1959, the lake contained a few largemouth and smallmouth bass, bluegills, yellow perch and pumpkinseed sunfish. After chemical reclamation that year, the DNR released brook and rainbow trout, but they stocked too many and Bob

Lake responded poorly. By 1967 the perch were back in force; after reducing them, the DNR tried brown trout, and the lake began to yield an excellent population of hefty, healthy browns for anglers.

By 1975, however, the perch were back, and two years later the DNR stopped stocking trout. Another chemical reclamation occurred in 1979, followed by brook trout releases from 1980 to 1982. More manual removal of perch ensued, and the DNR, in cooperation with the USFS, switched its primary emphasis to walleyes but continued to stock trout.

Surveys/Stocking: Obviously, the lake has a history of overpopulation by small yellow perch. Each spring since 1989, fisheries crews have manually removed little perch, black bullheads and pumpkinseed sunfish. Workers added lime to the lake in 1984 and 1989 to buffer acid content and to make it more productive.

The DNR first stocked walleyes in 1984. In 1989 biologists netted 59 walleyes that averaged 2.2 pounds and 20 inches. During the first day of the manual removal in April 1990, workers captured 13 walleyes averaging 18.9 inches and 2.2 lbs. A large number of 4- to 8-inch walleyes collected in 1992 indicates that fingerlings planted the year before fared well, or that the artificial spawning reef was producing.

In 1991 managers released 5,000 walleye fingerlings, and in 1993 they stocked an estimated 7,600 more.

Tactics to Try: Bob Lake's heavily stained water and shallow nature make it difficult at times to find and catch walleyes. There is no question that the walleye population is expanding, however, and that fishing pressure is on the rise. Air-injected night crawlers attached to Lindy Rigs and drifted throughout the lake produce very well. Crawler harnesses with red or orange blades also work.

Anglers occasionally report catching brook trout, but no releases have been made for at least 10 years. The fish apparently naturally reproduce in Leveque Creek and then enter the lake.

Access: An improved access site is located on the lake's south side at the USFS campground via Rousseau County Rd and USFS-1470 and USFS-1478. The boat launch ramp is gravel, toilets are available, and there is parking for a half-dozen vehicles. There is no place to rent a boat.

CLEAR and BASS LAKES

Fishing Opportunities: Brook Trout—Good to Excellent

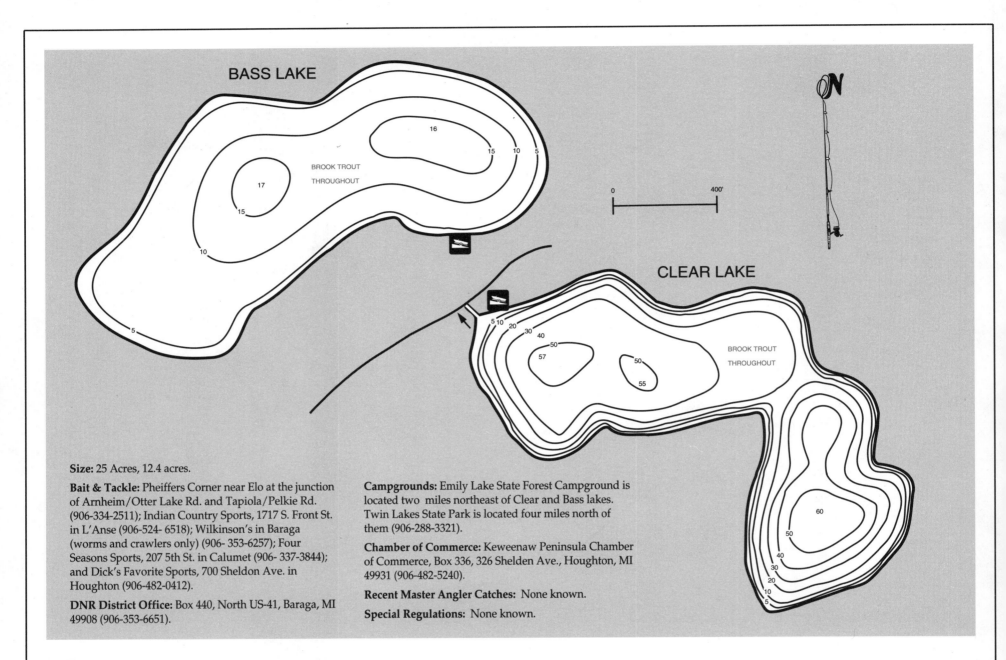

BASS LAKE

BROOK TROUT THROUGHOUT

CLEAR LAKE

BROOK TROUT THROUGHOUT

0   400'

N

Size: 25 Acres, 12.4 acres.

Bait & Tackle: Pheiffers Corner near Elo at the junction of Arnheim/Otter Lake Rd. and Tapiola/Pelkie Rd. (906-334-2511); Indian Country Sports, 1717 S. Front St. in L'Anse (906-524-6518); Wilkinson's in Baraga (worms and crawlers only) (906-353-6257); Four Seasons Sports, 207 5th St. in Calumet (906-337-3844); and Dick's Favorite Sports, 700 Sheldon Ave. in Houghton (906-482-0412).

DNR District Office: Box 440, North US-41, Baraga, MI 49908 (906-353-6651).

Campgrounds: Emily Lake State Forest Campground is located two miles northeast of Clear and Bass lakes. Twin Lakes State Park is located four miles north of them (906-288-3321).

Chamber of Commerce: Keweenaw Peninsula Chamber of Commerce, Box 336, 326 Shelden Ave., Houghton, MI 49931 (906-482-5240).

Recent Master Angler Catches: None known.

Special Regulations: None known.

Clear Lake and Bass Lake are located in Houghton County seven miles north of the village of Nisula and 3½ miles south of M-26 near Winona. Formerly known as the Kratt Lakes, the pair lie next to each other. Clear is only 25 acres in size but features dual basins that plunge to 57 feet and 60 feet respectively. It is possible to see up to 40 feet into this crystalline lake. Bass Lake, on the other hand, is only 17 feet deep.

As might be expected, the sandy shoals of Clear Lake are very steep. Bits of gravel appear here and there along the shoals, and fibrous peat constitutes a portion of the north-side bottom and comprises deep-water areas. Numerous deadheads appear along the shore.

The shoreline is very steep except in the northwest end, where an intermittent stream at one time drained the lake into Bass Lake. The original survey showed evidence of yellow perch and walleye, but since 1948 the DNR has managed the lake for trout, and the best fishing occurs during the few years after chemical reclamation. The lake was treated with rotenone in 1952 and 1976.

Surveys/Stocking: The DNR has historically stocked rainbows, splake and brook trout in both lakes during the past half-century. Splake and brook trout provide the best return when they are released as yearling fish. A 1986 Clear Lake survey found brook trout ranging from 11 to 18½ inches, with the average fish taping more than 14½ inches and weighing 2.1 pounds.

An October 1991 gill net survey produced 37 brook trout from 6 to 17 inches and averaging 9.9 inches. However, many of these were fish stocked six months earlier at an average length of 6.1 inches. Growth rates appear to be slow.

In 1991 managers stocked 1,900 yearling and 660 adult brook trout; in 1992 they released another 1,900 yearling fish; and in 1993 they planted out an estimated 100 adults and 1,900 yearlings.

Because Bass Lake is smaller and more easily fished, anglers tend to crop the brookies down quickly after they reach legal size. A June 1990 survey found fat healthy fish but no individuals larger than 11 inches.

In 1991 the DNR released 900 yearling and 690 adult brook trout in Bass Lake, in 1992 they planted out 900 yearlings, and in 1993 they stocked an estimated 900 yearlings and 75 adults.

Tactics to Try: Clear Lake contains lots of minnows and currently hosts a growing population of bluegills. Because the shoals drop off like a shot, wading is impossible. However, both it and Bass Lake are perfect canoeing lakes for fly fishermen. Just north of Clear and Bass lakes is Sandy Lake, which contains big bluegills.

Because Clear and Bass are not designated trout lakes, the fishing season is open year-round. Best catches occur in early summer, when fish are typically suspended and will take small spinners, worms, minnows and flyfished offerings including nymphs and dries.

Access: The DNR maintains an improved access site on the north shore of Clear Lake. Facilities include a hard-surfaced ramp, toilets and parking for nine vehicles. The access for Bass lake is across the road. There is no place to rent a boat on either lake.

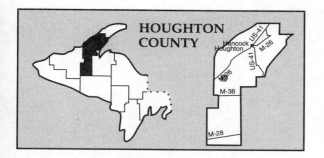

LAKE GERALD

Fishing Opportunities: Rainbow Trout, Yellow Perch and Bluegills—Good to Excellent; Walleyes, Black Crappies and Smallmouth Bass—Fair to Good; Largemouth Bass and Tiger Muskies—Available.

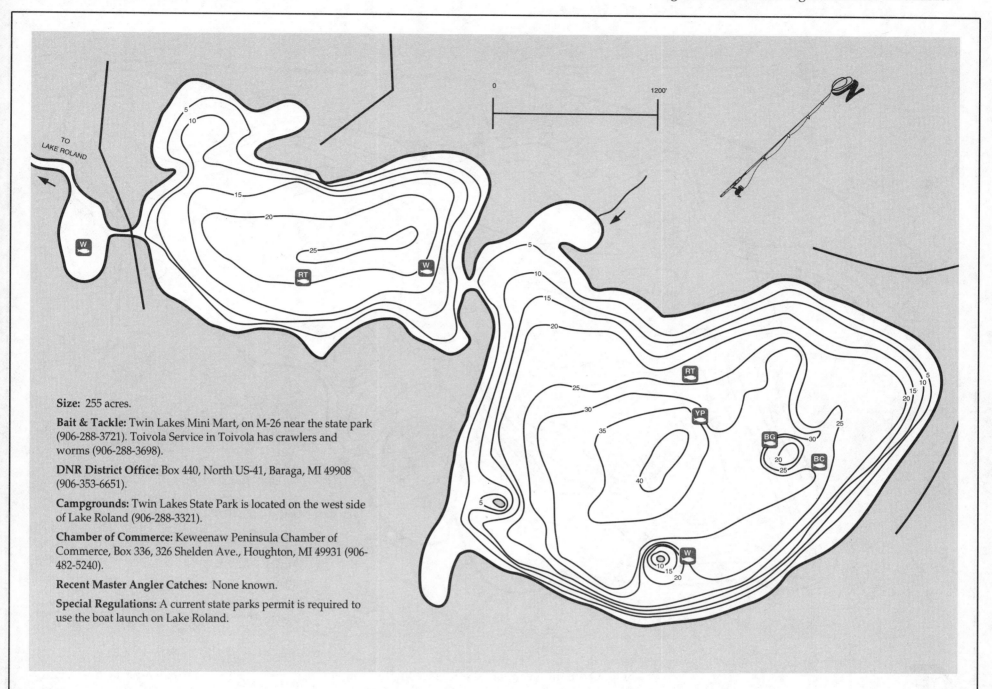

Size: 255 acres.

Bait & Tackle: Twin Lakes Mini Mart, on M-26 near the state park (906-288-3721). Toivola Service in Toivola has crawlers and worms (906-288-3698).

DNR District Office: Box 440, North US-41, Baraga, MI 49908 (906-353-6651).

Campgrounds: Twin Lakes State Park is located on the west side of Lake Roland (906-288-3321).

Chamber of Commerce: Keweenaw Peninsula Chamber of Commerce, Box 336, 326 Shelden Ave., Houghton, MI 49931 (906-482-5240).

Recent Master Angler Catches: None known.

Special Regulations: A current state parks permit is required to use the boat launch on Lake Roland.

Lake Gerald is located at Twin Lakes in central Houghton County. The lightly stained lake is connected to Lake Roland (p. 46) by a small pond and pair of short, navigable channels and is ringed with cottages and year-round homes. At last count the number of dwellings was 72. The lake is popular with water recreationists and receives considerable fishing pressure. On a summer evening it is not uncommon to see 50 to 100 boats on the two lakes.

Gerald features two distinct basins of about 25 and 40 feet deep respectively. Water color is a light brown. Shoals range in width from 75 to 300 feet, and the slope is gradual. Bottom composition of these shoals is mostly sand and gravel with a few pockets of fibrous peat. Deeper stretches feature a basement of muck.

The lake has a long history of producing good smallmouth bass fishing, with occasional bragging catches of black crappies and yellow perch also reported. Fish move freely between lakes Gerald

Surveys/Stocking:

and Roland, and the two bodies of water are similar in size.

The stocking record dates to 1921 when managers released yellow perch. Over the years smallmouth and largemouth bass, along with bluegills, made their way from the hatchery to the lake. Rainbows followed in the 1940s along with splake and, eventually, tiger muskies in 1978. The DNR no longer stocks Lake Gerald, concentrating instead on releasing rainbows in Lake Roland.

Gerald was last surveyed in July 1982, when managers collected smallmouths to 17 inches, pumpkinseed sunfish to 7.8 inches, black crappies to 13.7 inches, yellow perch to 11.4 inches, bluegills to 6.4 inches, tiger muskies to 30.1 inches, and rock bass to 9 inches.

Tactics to Try: For information related to rainbow trout fishing, refer to Lake Roland, p. 46. Most walleye anglers vertical jig in eight or more feet of water. They rely on leadhead jigs with curley tails, and the popular colors are white, yellow and chartreuse.

The pond connecting the two lakes is a good

place to try in spring and fall. Otherwise look for structure, including brushy remnants of old fish shelters around the island on the southwest side and elsewhere on the 10-foot-deep contour.

For yellow perch, bluegills, black crappies and pumpkinseed sunfish, concentrate efforts near weedbeds and off the points in 10 to 30 feet of water. Typical tactics apply.

There are no northern pike in either lakes Roland or Gerald. However, trollings using Rapalas and spoons occasionally are bitten by a huge tiger muskie.

Few people ice fish, and one of the reasons is the large amount of slush the lakes receive in winter. This phenomenon is due to relatively high elevation surrounding the lakes. The region gets a lot of snow, and runoff loads the ice-covered surface. Ice anglers should exercise caution.

Access: The improved public access site is located at Twin Lakes State Park on the west side of Lake Roland. A township access site, which is found about two blocks north of the state park, is also improved. There is no place to rent a boat.

LAKE ROLAND

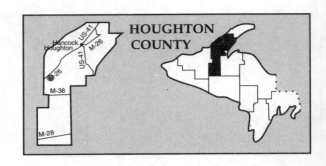

HOUGHTON COUNTY

Fishing Opportunities: Rainbow Trout, Yellow Perch and Bluegills—Good to Excellent; Walleyes, Black Crappies and Smallmouth Bass—Fair to Good; Largemouth Bass and Tiger Muskies—Available.

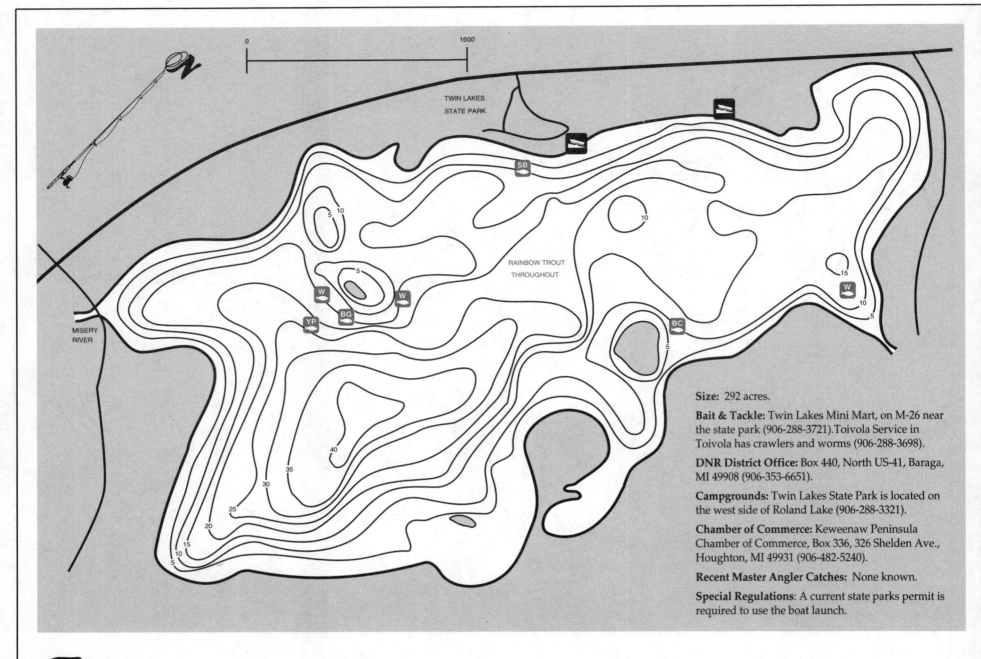

Size: 292 acres.

Bait & Tackle: Twin Lakes Mini Mart, on M-26 near the state park (906-288-3721).Toivola Service in Toivola has crawlers and worms (906-288-3698).

DNR District Office: Box 440, North US-41, Baraga, MI 49908 (906-353-6651).

Campgrounds: Twin Lakes State Park is located on the west side of Roland Lake (906-288-3321).

Chamber of Commerce: Keweenaw Peninsula Chamber of Commerce, Box 336, 326 Shelden Ave., Houghton, MI 49931 (906-482-5240).

Recent Master Angler Catches: None known.

Special Regulations: A current state parks permit is required to use the boat launch.

Lake Roland is located at Twin Lakes in central Houghton County. The lightly stained lake is connected to Lake Gerald (p. 41) by a small pond and pair of channels, which are navigable. Twin Lakes State Park lies on the westcentral shore of Lake Roland.It is popular due to its mostly sand bottom, prime boating water, and good fishing and in summer has the appearance of a southern Michigan lake impacted with water recreationists. At last count 64 cottages ringed the lake.

Surveys/Stocking: Management began in the late 1930s and early 1940s with the introduction of largemouth bass, bluegills and yellow perch. The panfish in particular established themselves early on, but the lack of a predator prompted managers to release walleyes in the late 1950s. The walleyes responded to provide a fair fishery until the early 1970s. Limited spawning habitat and the lack of fingerlings for plant-out brought a slow death to the program.

To compensate, the DNR released tiger muskies until 1981, and in 1987 the lake served up a 23-pounder. A few giant fish are still available. Over the years splake releases failed; on the other hand, rainbow stockings have provided a very good fishery.

The lake contains a large amount of plankton, which provides forage for young trout and other small fish. However, rainbow growth rates appear to have slowed. According to records kept by a local angler, 6- to 7-inch yearlings planted in the spring of 1989 averaged 11½ inches on July 25. The next year on July 25, the average length had slipped to 11¼ inches. On July 25, 1993, it had dropped to 9¾ inches, substantiating angler complaints of not being able to catch legal-size fish. Although growth rates have fallen, they are still acceptable.

And big fish are available. A September 1992 DNR collection produced several older rainbows from 19 to 21½ inches. The fyke nets were most productive, yielding 13 walleyes that averaged 14 inches and 25 smallmouth and four largemouth bass that averaged 8.2 inches and 9 inches respectively. The panfish population was in good shape.

In 1991 managers stocked 11,000 rainbows; in 1992 they planted out 12,200 fish; and in 1993 they released another 12,000. All fish were yearlings.

Tactics to Try: Trout-catching tactics relate to temperature and available oxygen. In the spring the rainbows are scattered, and fishermen catch them just about anywhere on worms or whole-kernel corn. By summer the trout are in the thermocline at 10 to 20 feet deep, and night-time jigging with corn, worms or small minnows aided by lanterns suspended over boat sides works best.

The trout typically disappear by the end of August, perhaps entering shallow water as oxygen is depleted from deep zones. The winter fishery is limited; try tip-ups baited with worms and wigglers (if available) or small minnows. In the spring, trout to 6 pounds have been observed in the vicinity of the Misery River outflow.

See Lake Gerald, p. 41, for more fishing information.

Access: The improved access site at Twin Lakes State Park, along the west shore, includes a paved boat launch ramp, toilets and a limited amount of parking space. A second paved launch is located at Elm River Township Park, two blocks north of the state park. There is no place to rent a boat.

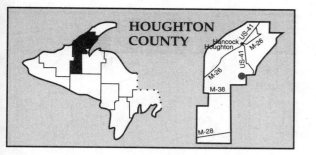

OTTER LAKE

Fishing Opportunities: Northern Pike—Good to
Excellent; Walleyes and Black Crappies—Fair to Good;
Yellow Perch and Smallmouth Bass—Fair.

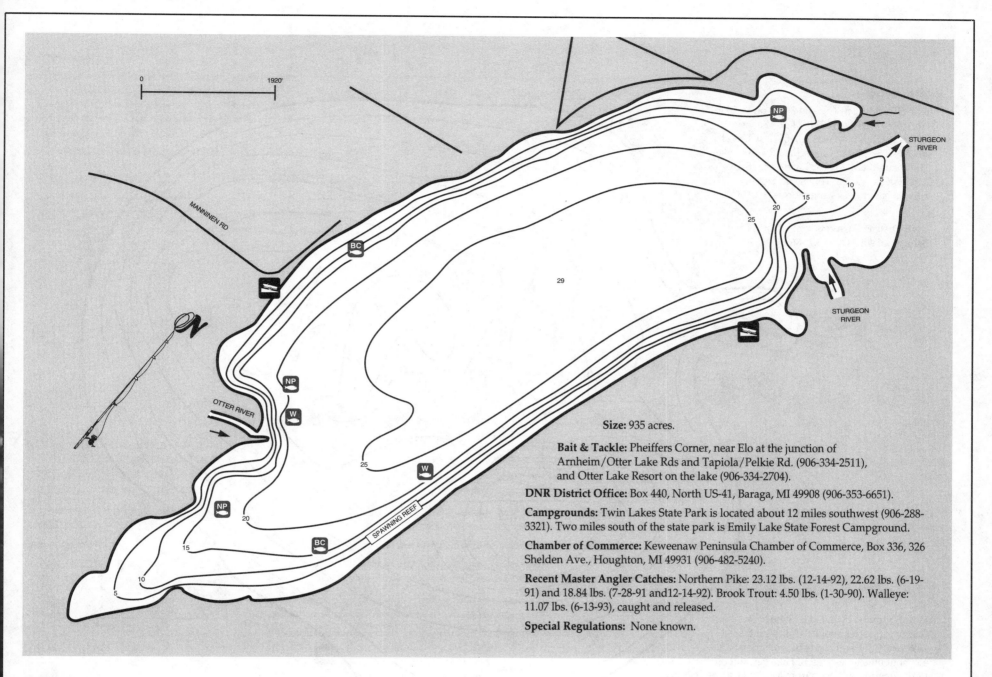

Size: 935 acres.

Bait & Tackle: Pheiffers Corner, near Elo at the junction of
Arnheim/Otter Lake Rds and Tapiola/Pelkie Rd. (906-334-2511),
and Otter Lake Resort on the lake (906-334-2704).

DNR District Office: Box 440, North US-41, Baraga, MI 49908 (906-353-6651).

Campgrounds: Twin Lakes State Park is located about 12 miles southwest (906-288-3321). Two miles south of the state park is Emily Lake State Forest Campground.

Chamber of Commerce: Keweenaw Peninsula Chamber of Commerce, Box 336, 326
Shelden Ave., Houghton, MI 49931 (906-482-5240).

Recent Master Angler Catches: Northern Pike: 23.12 lbs. (12-14-92), 22.62 lbs. (6-19-91) and 18.84 lbs. (7-28-91 and12-14-92). Brook Trout: 4.50 lbs. (1-30-90). Walleye: 11.07 lbs. (6-13-93), caught and released.

Special Regulations: None known.

Otter Lake is located in eastcentral Houghton County about seven miles southwest of Chassell and three miles east of Tapiola on the Baraga County line. The Otter River, home of the last-known native grayling to live in Michigan, flows in from a southwest point. The lake's outflow is the Sturgeon River, which empties into Portage Lake (44).

The Otter River system, which is comprised of some 100 miles of excellent trout water, used to supply the lake with brook trout and steelhead, and the Sturgeon River contributed walleyes. Consequently, Otter Lake earned a tremendous reputation early in the 1900s as an outstanding fishing lake for these species plus big northern pike.

Manmade changes from logging operations and the subsequent building of a dam to control water levels have severely hampered fishing opportunities. However, we include Otter Lake in this book because it continues to produce good fishing for a wide variety of species. Also, its future looks bright. A small artificial spawning reef, located on the southeast side and built by the Otter Lake Sportsman's Club with the aid of DNR funds, should help restore good walleye fishing.

Heavy stockings of fingerlings will also contribute. In addition, the DNR is looking at building specialized fish ladders in the dam to allow walleyes free access from the Sturgeon River, long thought to be the key to strong walleye populations in Otter Lake.

Surveys/Stocking: The last DNR survey, which occurred in August 1983, found low numbers of panfish and gamefish with the exception of black crappies. The nets yielded several 11- to 12-inch-long fish. Pike averaged 16 inches, walleyes averaged 12 inches, yellow perch averaged 6 inches, and smallmouth bass averaged 8 inches. Bullheads made up 74 percent of the catch; walleyes contributed less than one-half percent.

In 1991 managers stocked 15,000 walleyes; in 1992 they released 19,450; and in 1993 they planted out an estimated 10,000 more. All fish were fingerlings.

Tactics to Try: The lake delivers a finned smorgasbord, including sturgeon. In 1988 DNR crews netting bullheads for manual removal caught 12 sturgeon, including several fish from 3½ to 4 feet long. Big northerns are taken from the bays by ice anglers using tip-ups and minnows. In July and August look for pike around any of the many weedbeds, and troll or cast big Dardevles.

The lake is famous for slab crappies, and the best times to catch them are in spring and fall. Move often and key on brush and stickups along the shoreline. Small minnows and ⅟₁₆- to ⅟₃₂-oz. leadhead or tube jigs work best.

Walleye fishing is good in spring off the mouth of the Otter River. Pin minnows to ¼-oz. pink or chartreuse jigs. Walleye action typically drops off by late June but starts again after first frost, usually by mid-September.

Access: An improved access site with paved ramp, toilets and parking for eight vehicles is located at the dam at the lake's north end with access from US-41. An unimproved launch site with gravel ramp, toilets and minimum parking area is located two miles east of Tapiola on the lake's west shore. To rent a boat (no motors available) contact Otter Lake Resort (see Bait & Tackle listing).

PERRAULT LAKE

Fishing Opportunities: Brook Trout—Good to Excellent.

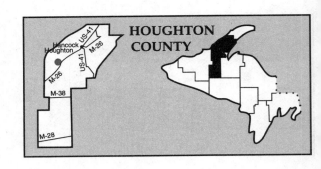

HOUGHTON COUNTY

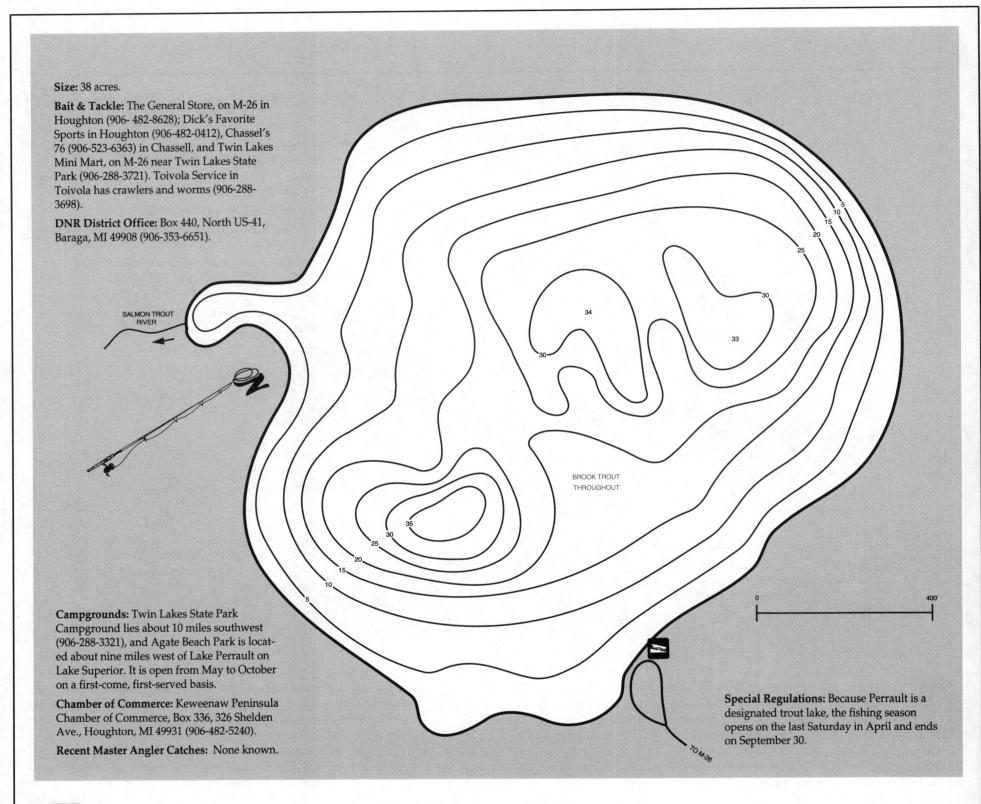

Size: 38 acres.

Bait & Tackle: The General Store, on M-26 in Houghton (906- 482-8628); Dick's Favorite Sports in Houghton (906-482-0412), Chassel's 76 (906-523-6363) in Chassell, and Twin Lakes Mini Mart, on M-26 near Twin Lakes State Park (906-288-3721). Toivola Service in Toivola has crawlers and worms (906-288-3698).

DNR District Office: Box 440, North US-41, Baraga, MI 49908 (906-353-6651).

SALMON TROUT RIVER

BROOK TROUT THROUGHOUT

Campgrounds: Twin Lakes State Park Campground lies about 10 miles southwest (906-288-3321), and Agate Beach Park is located about nine miles west of Lake Perrault on Lake Superior. It is open from May to October on a first-come, first-served basis.

Chamber of Commerce: Keweenaw Peninsula Chamber of Commerce, Box 336, 326 Shelden Ave., Houghton, MI 49931 (906-482-5240).

Recent Master Angler Catches: None known.

TO M-26

Special Regulations: Because Perrault is a designated trout lake, the fishing season opens on the last Saturday in April and ends on September 30.

Perrault Lake, which is also called Lake Perrault, is located in Houghton County about two miles southwest of Painesdale and some seven miles southwest of Houghton. The clear, clean lake, which has a maximum depth of 38 feet, is the only designated trout lake in Houghton County. Fishing pressure is moderate to heavy.

The lake's outlet forms the headwaters of the Salmon Trout River.

Surveys/Stocking: Perrault Lake was first surveyed in 1926 but only minnows were found. Fisheries biologists stocked the lake with smallmouth bass and bluegills for a few years beginning in 1939 and added largemouths in 1943. A 1948 survey showed the lake to be suitable for trout introduction. Managers introduced brook trout in 1949 and continue to stock them today while periodically treating the lake to remove suckers, rock bass and small perch.

A September 1992 survey indicated that stocked trout were growing slower than normal, but this may be due to the Owhi strain the DNR has been releasing. The 38 fish collected were mostly from the spring plant. They averaged 9 inches, ranged to a foot, and disputed claims by some that the lake has poor fishing potential. Biologists recommended that another trout strain be stocked. No other management prescriptions were suggested.

In 1991 the DNR released 1,750 brook trout; in 1992 they stocked 3,000 brookies; and in 1993 they planted out an estimated 3,000 more. All fish were yearlings.

Tactics to Try: The lake has yielded brookies to 4 pounds. The best fishing occurs early in the season. As might be expected, minnows, crawler bits and wigglers are productive, but if you prefer to take your trout on artificial lures, try Colorado or Mepps Black Fury spinners in sizes 0 through 2. Nymph and dryfly fishermen catch trout through mid-June on small mayfly and caddis paterns.

The lake is ideal for fishing from a canoe or float tube. A preponderance of small bluegills and pumpkinseed sunfish means the lake will probably receive another treatment before long.

Access: A township park located on the lake's southeast side contains a gravel launch ramp, toilets and parking for about 10 vehicles. There is no place to rent a boat.

PORTAGE LAKE

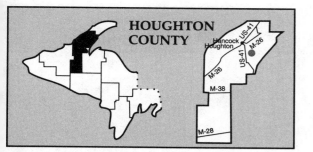

Fishing Opportunities: Walleyes, Northern Pike, Smallmouth Bass and Black Crappies—Good to Excellent; Bluegills and Yellow Perch—Fair to Good; Salmon and Trout—Available.

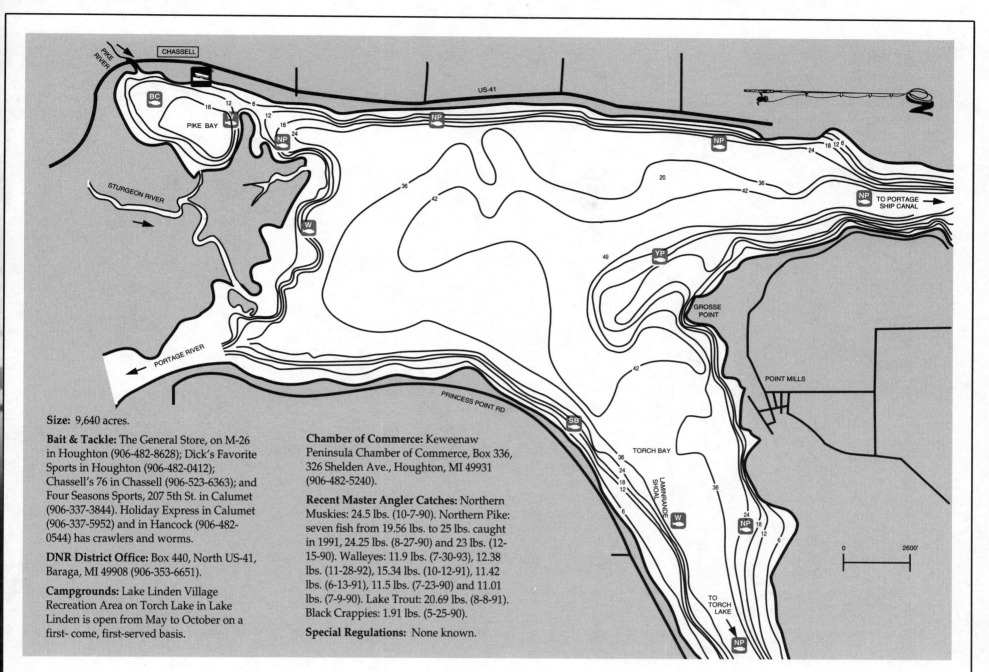

Size: 9,640 acres.

Bait & Tackle: The General Store, on M-26 in Houghton (906-482-8628); Dick's Favorite Sports in Houghton (906-482-0412); Chassell's 76 in Chassell (906-523-6363); and Four Seasons Sports, 207 5th St. in Calumet (906-337-3844). Holiday Express in Calumet (906-337-5952) and in Hancock (906-482-0544) has crawlers and worms.

DNR District Office: Box 440, North US-41, Baraga, MI 49908 (906-353-6651).

Campgrounds: Lake Linden Village Recreation Area on Torch Lake in Lake Linden is open from May to October on a first- come, first-served basis.

Chamber of Commerce: Keweenaw Peninsula Chamber of Commerce, Box 336, 326 Shelden Ave., Houghton, MI 49931 (906-482-5240).

Recent Master Angler Catches: Northern Muskies: 24.5 lbs. (10-7-90). Northern Pike: seven fish from 19.56 lbs. to 25 lbs. caught in 1991, 24.25 lbs. (8-27-90) and 23 lbs. (12-15-90). Walleyes: 11.9 lbs. (7-30-93), 12.38 lbs. (11-28-92), 15.34 lbs. (10-12-91), 11.42 lbs. (6-13-91), 11.5 lbs. (7-23-90) and 11.01 lbs. (7-9-90). Lake Trout: 20.69 lbs. (8-8-91). Black Crappies: 1.91 lbs. (5-25-90).

Special Regulations: None known.

Portage Lake is located in northern Houghton County. The huge lake splits the Keweenaw Peninsula in two, and the Portage Ship Canal canal, which also separates the cities of Houghton and Hancock, connects the northwest arm of Portage Lake to Lake Superior. The Pike and Sturgeon rivers enter Portage Lake from the southwest, and the Portage River leaves the southeast corner of the lake to join Keweenaw Bay a few miles farther. The Torch Bay arm at the northeast corner of Portage Lake leads to Torch Lake, (p. 47).

Surveys/Stocking: An October 1992 fyke net survey caught six cohos, and several walleyes averaging 16 to 18 inches each. Range was 15 to 29 inches. Smallmouths ranged from 14 to 19 inches.

An August 1988 gill net survey completed at four sites found excellent populations of walleyes and northern pike, along with a fair number of yellow perch averaging 8½ inches. A variety of other species were captured, including 30 brown trout averaging 22½ inches each. One 27-incher weighed 10 pounds.

In 1991 the DNR stocked 40,000 coho salmon in the Portage Ship Canal at Lily Pond Harbor and about 60,000 walleyes in Portage Lake itself. In 1992 they planted out 40,000 cohos and 71,000 walleyes, and in 1993 they released 50,000 cohos and 54,800 walleyes. The salmon were yearling fish; the walleyes were fingerlings.

Tactics to Try: For jumbo black crappies try Pike Bay and the Pike River at ice-out with tiny jigs and minnows suspended three feet below clear-plastic bobbers. Tube jigs or Doll Flies, fished clean or pinned with small minnows, also work.

The pike opener sends anglers to Pike Bay and Oscar Bay up the canal from Houghton/Hancock. By late May/early June, northerns show up throughout the Portage Canal near emerging weedbeds along drop-offs. Other good areas include the north end of Torch Bay and all along the west shore from Chassell to Pilgrim Point. For fishing methods, refer to Torch Lake, p. 47.

Smallmouths are largely underfished. Hotspots include the southeast shore of Torch Bay and below Dollar Bay on the east shore of the canal. Be sure to toss Shad Raps and No. 7 Countdown Rapalas here and along any pilings. Leeches and live minnows produce, too, not only for smallmouths but for big walleyes as well.

The lake is fast becoming one of the state's best walleye waters. The Sturgeon River hosts a spring run of spawning walleyes. Fish often disappear by late May, then show up off drop-offs and over weedlines throughout the lake in July and August. Jig fishermen angling from shore at night under the Houghton/Hancock Bridge do well. For more catching details, see Torch Lake, p. 47.

Access: The paved township ramp at Chassell includes a courtesy pier, toilets and parking for 10 vehicles. On the eastcentral side is a hard-surfaced ramp with toilets and parking for a half-dozen vehicles. Additional boat launch ramps are located at the Sturgeon River Sloughs, at the south end of the Portage River, at Hancock Municipal Park on Swedetown Creek on the shipping canal, and at Houghton-Hancock Marina. Resort owners often rent boats with a cabin or cottage.

Houghton County

RICE LAKE

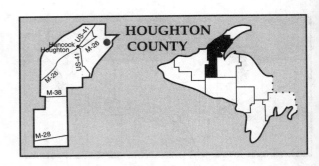
Fishing Opportunities: Walleyes—Good to Excellent; Northern Pike—Fair to Good; Yellow Perch and Bluegills—Fair; Tiger Muskies—Available.

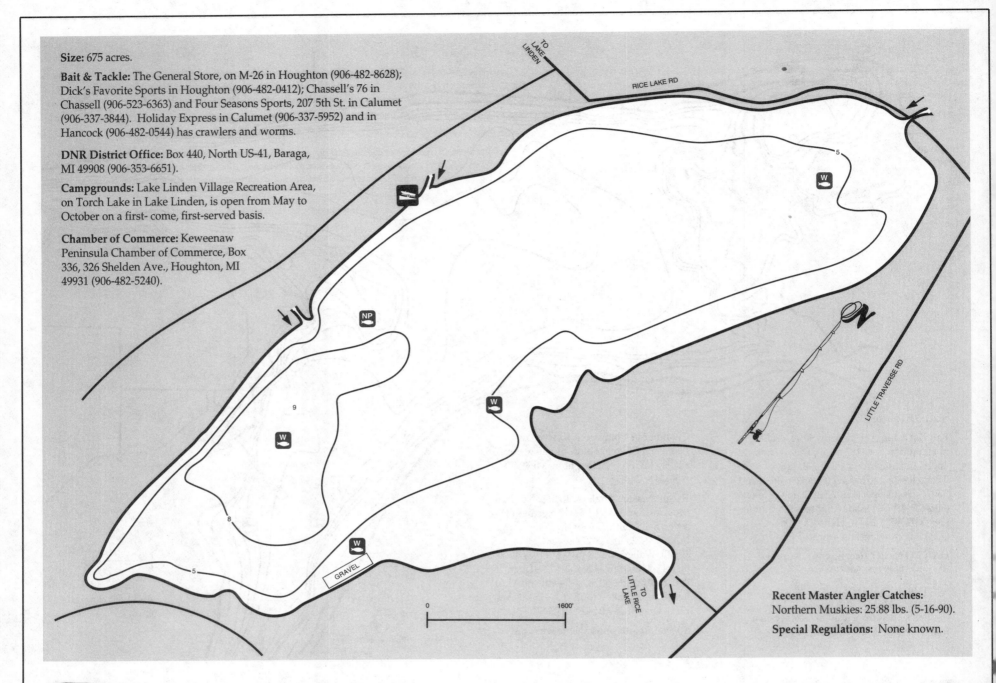

Size: 675 acres.

Bait & Tackle: The General Store, on M-26 in Houghton (906-482-8628); Dick's Favorite Sports in Houghton (906-482-0412); Chassell's 76 in Chassell (906-523-6363) and Four Seasons Sports, 207 5th St. in Calumet (906-337-3844). Holiday Express in Calumet (906-337-5952) and in Hancock (906-482-0544) has crawlers and worms.

DNR District Office: Box 440, North US-41, Baraga, MI 49908 (906-353-6651).

Campgrounds: Lake Linden Village Recreation Area, on Torch Lake in Lake Linden, is open from May to October on a first-come, first-served basis.

Chamber of Commerce: Keweenaw Peninsula Chamber of Commerce, Box 336, 326 Shelden Ave., Houghton, MI 49931 (906-482-5240).

Recent Master Angler Catches: Northern Muskies: 25.88 lbs. (5-16-90).

Special Regulations: None known.

Rice Lake is located in northeast Houghton County about six miles east of Lake Linden and about two miles from Keweenaw Bay. The large, shallow lake has a maximum depth of only 10 feet. Its waters are brown-colored, both submergent and emergent vegetation are abundant, and the bottom is mostly sand although the immediate shoreline is low and swampy.

Less than three dozen dwellings are situated on the lake, which has an inlet stream on the north end and two others on the westcentral shore. The main outlet, however, flows from an eastcentral bay to Lake Superior via Little Rice Lake. A dam on this outlet blocks fish migration, although each fall, local people remove the stop logs in the structure to eliminate shoreline flooding in spring. The lake has no legally established water level, and the annual removal of stop logs allows fish to move into the lake from Lake Superior.

Surveys/Stocking: Nine surveys dating to 1951 consistently turned up walleyes and northern pike. The DNR initially stocked tiger muskies in 1971 to control dominant panfish, bullhead and white sucker populations. In 1975 managers released 900 northern muskies in lieu of tigers, a few of which are caught each year in spite of the fact that they rarely turn up in net surveys.

An April 1991 fyke net survey determined that pike, tiger muskies and walleyes account for nearly half of the biomass collected. The predators represented a wide range of sizes and ages, and the populations appeared to be in good shape. The nets revealed a 44-inch-long northern muskie along with northern pike to 29½ inches and walleyes to 27½ inches. Two walleyes were estimated to be 15 years old and one was about 20 years old.

Brown bullheads represented 16 percent of the biomass compared to 58 percent in the previous survey, which was conducted in 1986. Although white suckers comprised 35 percent of the biomass in 1991, they were spawning in shoal waters where the nets were set. Pumpkinseed sunfish, yellow perch and rock bass were present in small numbers.

In 1991 the DNR stocked 2,700 tiger muskies

Tactics to Try: for their final release of this species.

Walleyes are best sought in May and June and can be found literally anywhere in the lake. A fishing contest each June is centered at the old Boy Scout camp on the west shore. Gravel spits along the southeast shore host some natural reproduction; anglers on the walleye season-opener might want to try there. Most 'eyes range from legal size to 25-inchers, and many anglers seek them with orange or silver jigs treated with minnows. Crawlers and harnesses also score.

Typical trolling and casting tactics work for northern pike. Popular spoons are Little Cleos and Dardevles with bright colors showing up best in the tobacco-colored lake. Occasionally, anglers pick up a tiger muskie

The lake has lots of yellow perch and bluegills although most fish currently run small.

Access: An improved public access site is located on the westcentral side of the lake. Included are a paved boat launch, toilets and parking for about 10 vehicles. To rent a boat, contact Delf's Landing, on the east shore (906-296-0818).

TORCH LAKE

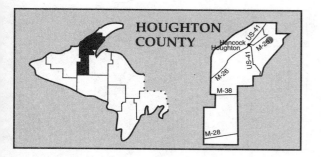

Fishing Opportunities: Walleyes, Northern Pike and Smallmouth Bass—Good to Excellent; Trout and Salmon— Available.

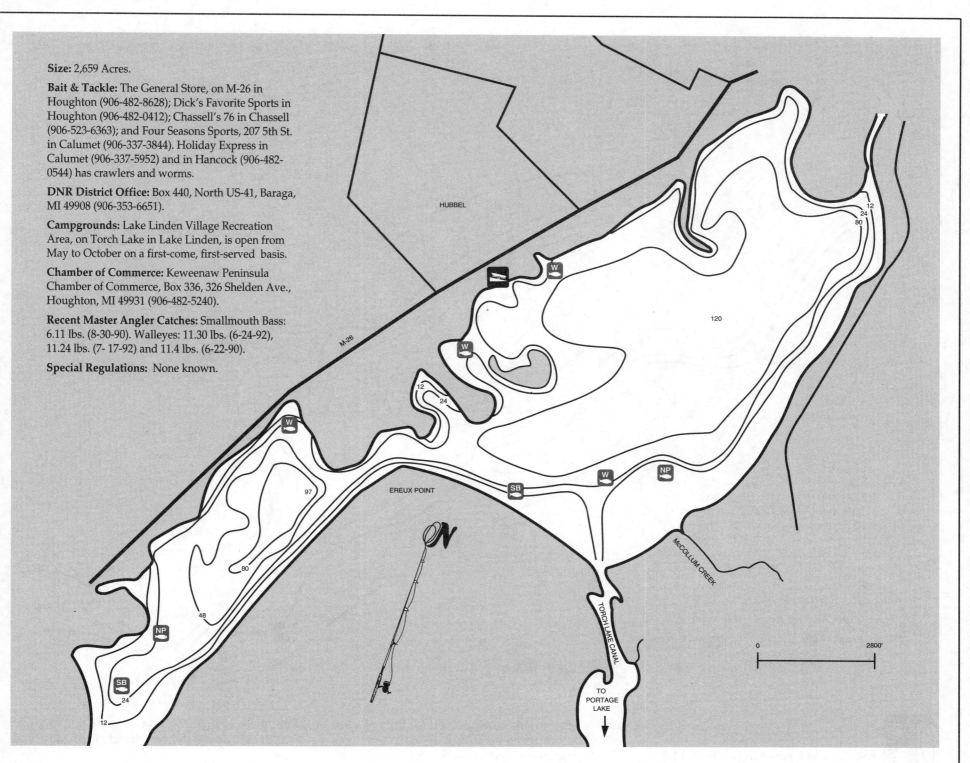

Size: 2,659 Acres.

Bait & Tackle: The General Store, on M-26 in Houghton (906-482-8628); Dick's Favorite Sports in Houghton (906-482-0412); Chassell's 76 in Chassell (906-523-6363); and Four Seasons Sports, 207 5th St. in Calumet (906-337-3844). Holiday Express in Calumet (906-337-5952) and in Hancock (906-482-0544) has crawlers and worms.

DNR District Office: Box 440, North US-41, Baraga, MI 49908 (906-353-6651).

Campgrounds: Lake Linden Village Recreation Area, on Torch Lake in Lake Linden, is open from May to October on a first-come, first-served basis.

Chamber of Commerce: Keweenaw Peninsula Chamber of Commerce, Box 336, 326 Shelden Ave., Houghton, MI 49931 (906-482-5240).

Recent Master Angler Catches: Smallmouth Bass: 6.11 lbs. (8-30-90). Walleyes: 11.30 lbs. (6-24-92), 11.24 lbs. (7- 17-92) and 11.4 lbs. (6-22-90).

Special Regulations: None known.

Torch Lake is located in northern Houghton County. It is connected to Torch Bay and Portage Lake (p. 44) by a shipping canal that is no longer used by the mining companies. The entire west side of Torch Lake was the dumping site for iron ore tailings that were discarded over many years from intensive mining practices in the area. These tailings have created tremendous peak-and-valley structure for walleyes and other fish.

Surveys/Stocking: An August 1988 gill net survey involving six sites on Torch Lake found fair numbers of northern pike, walleyes and yellow perch. Smallmouth bass, in particular, stood out, with a total of 20 fish ranging from 15 to 18 inches each. The nets also collected a few brown trout.

In 1991 the DNR stocked 24,500 walleye fingerlings, and in 1993 they released 25,000 more.

Tactics to Try: Torch Lake is fast coming on as one of the U.P.'s premier walleye waters. One reason is the planting commitment by the DNR. Another is the abundance of great walleye structure comprised of crushed rock tailings. Portions of the lake plunge to more than 100 feet, giving walleyes the deep water they sometimes prefer. As good as connected Portage Lake is, some anglers claim that Torch Lake is twice as good.

Besides the tailings structure, old dock pilings in the Hubbell area also act as a walleye magnet. Many of the pilings are 18 to 24 inches in diameter, creating plenty of surface for algae to grow. The algae, in turn, attracts baitfish, which lure walleyes. Try slow trolling early and late in the day with 2/0 Phelps Floater Jigs or J & D Crawler Harnesses in orange and chartreuse or green and chartreuse. Stand-up jigs in these colors also produce. Another trick is to find 12- to 14-foot-deep weedlines, and slow troll on the outside edge.

The south end and east side of the lake are best for smallmouths, which are largely underfished. For best results, cast with Shad Raps or Mister Twisters in white and chartreuse.

Pike thrive throughout the lake and the entire Portage Lake system. Trollers rely on Rapalas and other minnow-imitating lures along with Dardevle-type spoons. Pike will also hit live suckers fished halfway to bottom below large bobbers, as well as whole dead smelt fished on bottom.

Access: Lake Linden Village Park at the north end of the lake features a paved boat launch township ramp, toilets and parking for 10 vehicles. Resort owners often include a boat with the rental of a cabin or cottage.

BRULE LAKE

Fishing Opportunities: Walleyes—Good to Excellent;
Black Crappies, Northern Pike and Yellow Perch—
Good; Largemouth Bass and Smallmouth Bass—Fair to
Good; Bluegills—Fair; Northern Muskies—Available.

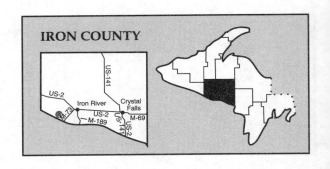

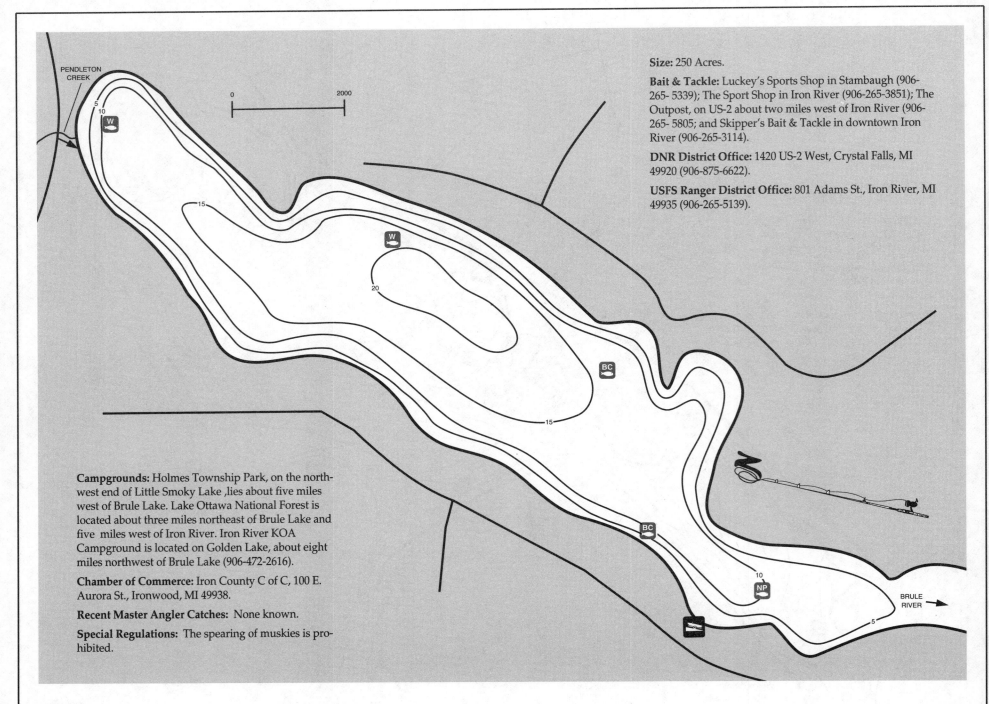

Size: 250 Acres.

Bait & Tackle: Luckey's Sports Shop in Stambaugh (906-
265- 5339); The Sport Shop in Iron River (906-265-3851); The
Outpost, on US-2 about two miles west of Iron River (906-
265- 5805; and Skipper's Bait & Tackle in downtown Iron
River (906-265-3114).

DNR District Office: 1420 US-2 West, Crystal Falls, MI
49920 (906-875-6622).

USFS Ranger District Office: 801 Adams St., Iron River, MI
49935 (906-265-5139).

Campgrounds: Holmes Township Park, on the northwest end of Little Smoky Lake ,lies about five miles
west of Brule Lake. Lake Ottawa National Forest is
located about three miles northeast of Brule Lake and
five miles west of Iron River. Iron River KOA
Campground is located on Golden Lake, about eight
miles northwest of Brule Lake (906-472-2616).

Chamber of Commerce: Iron County C of C, 100 E.
Aurora St., Ironwood, MI 49938.

Recent Master Angler Catches: None known.

Special Regulations: The spearing of muskies is prohibited.

Brule Lake is located in southwest Iron
County about 10 miles southwest of
Iron River in the Ottawa National Forest. The
lake is close to the Wisconsin boundary.
Pendleton Creek, which attracts soon-to-spawn
walleyes in spring, flows in from the north end,
and the Brule River forms the outflow.

The dark-colored, relatively shallow lake experiences algae blooms in spring. Deep spots are
only 16 to 18 feet, and the bottom is mostly sedi-
ment although there is some rock rubble on the
east shore. About 60 percent of the lake is developed with cottages or cabins, mostly along portions of the east and west sides.

Surveys/Stocking: A June 1990 DNR
boomshocking survey
found: (1) a moderate population of largemouth
bass and bluegills with fair size-structures;
(2) adequate growth rates of captured walleyes
including some naturally reproduced fish from
1986 and 1989; (3) a limited number of yellow
perch; (4) a moderate number of pike; (5) availability of northern muskies; and (6) the presence
of black crappies although recruitment was
weak. The overall conclusion was a fairly balanced lake in terms of predators, with no one
species dominating. Forage species populations
appeared to be fair.

Bass ranged from 9 to 17 inches, with most fish
in the 12- to 13-inch category. Most of the
bluegills were 6 to 8 inches, and perch were 7 to
9 inches. Of the nine crappies collected, four
were about a foot long. Only three muskies from
19 to 21 inches each were captured. Pike ranged
to 25½ inches, and walleyes measured to 25
inches.

A more recent survey showed a population
estimate of five adult walleyes per acre, a fairly
good number.

In 1992 managers released 9,000 walleye fingerlings, and in 1993 they stocked another estimated 10,000 fingerlings.

Tactics to Try: Post-spawn walleyes are sometimes still available in or near
Pendleton Creek by the season opener May 15.

The north half of the lake is good for fair-size
walleyes during the hex hatches in May and
June.

There is not a preponderance of big northerns,
but the best place to catch a pike is in the outlet
area. The lake's shallow south end is heavily
vegetated, and boaters have to work their way
up from the public access site through weedy
channels.

Some springs, Brule Lake hosts a hot fishery
for ice-out spawning black crappies. Fish have
been running small in recent years but could
return to 8- to 10-inch size depending on spawning and recruitment success. Some anglers wear
waders or pull boats over the ice to fish at night
with lanterns and small jigging rods. Best bait is
small minnows or plain tube jigs in white,
smoke or pink colors.

Access: The USFS maintains a hard-surface
ramp, toilets and parking for eight
vehicles at an access site located at the southwest end of the lake. There is no place to rent a
boat.

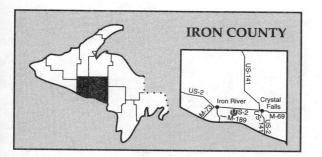

CHICAGON LAKE

Fishing Opportunities: Walleyes—Good to Excellent; Yellow Perch, Northern Muskies and Whitefish—Fair to Good.

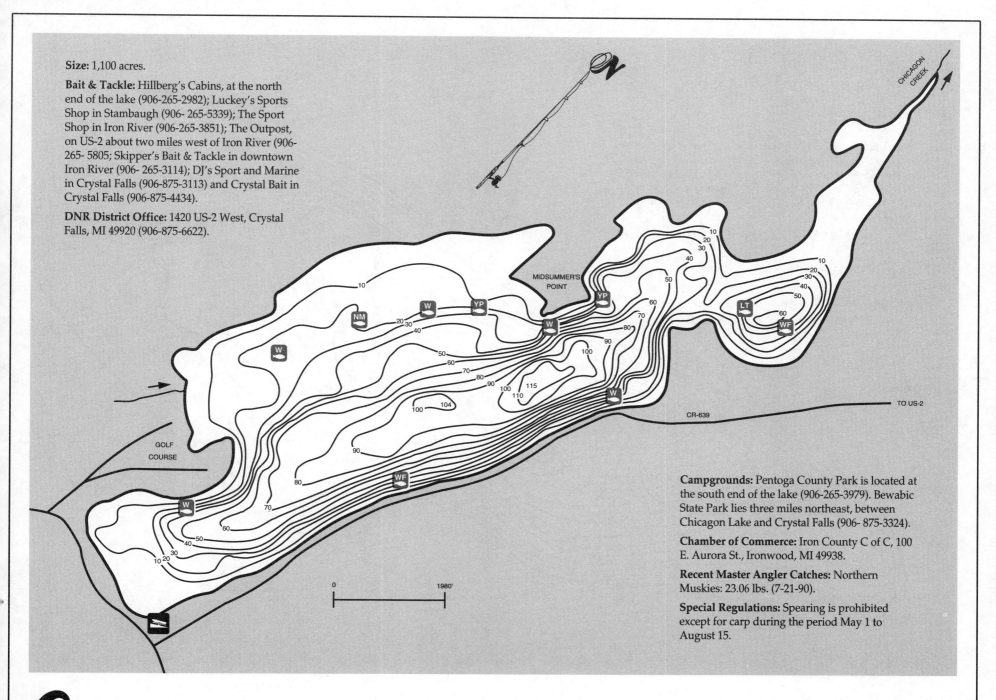

Size: 1,100 acres.

Bait & Tackle: Hillberg's Cabins, at the north end of the lake (906-265-2982); Luckey's Sports Shop in Stambaugh (906- 265-5339); The Sport Shop in Iron River (906-265-3851); The Outpost, on US-2 about two miles west of Iron River (906-265- 5805; Skipper's Bait & Tackle in downtown Iron River (906- 265-3114); DJ's Sport and Marine in Crystal Falls (906-875-3113) and Crystal Bait in Crystal Falls (906-875-4434).

DNR District Office: 1420 US-2 West, Crystal Falls, MI 49920 (906-875-6622).

Campgrounds: Pentoga County Park is located at the south end of the lake (906-265-3979). Bewabic State Park lies three miles northeast, between Chicagon Lake and Crystal Falls (906- 875-3324).

Chamber of Commerce: Iron County C of C, 100 E. Aurora St., Ironwood, MI 49938.

Recent Master Angler Catches: Northern Muskies: 23.06 lbs. (7-21-90).

Special Regulations: Spearing is prohibited except for carp during the period May 1 to August 15.

Chicagon Lake is located in southeast Iron County about 10 miles southwest of Crystal Falls. The lake's major inlet is Wagner Creek, which enters from the southwest, and the outlet is Chicagon Creek, a tributary of the Paint River. The lake lies in an area of steeply rolling hardwood hills. It is a clear, colorless lake with depths to 115 feet. The bottom composition is mostly rock rubble with some sand, muck and marl areas.

Historically, the lake contained northern pike, whitefish and lake trout. The whitefish provided tremendous sport for spear fishermen during WWII. In December 1942, for example, a news report indicated that as many as 200 fishermen and up to 75 cars were on the ice at the peak of the run (spearing is no longer allowed). Periodically, Chicagon Lake has also served up good fishing for brook trout, which ascend Wagner Creek in the fall to spawn.

Surveys/Stocking: Stocking records date to 1921 with the release of lake trout and smallmouth bass. Over the years rainbow trout, bluegills, splake, perch, muskies and walleyes have also gone into the lake. A DNR survey crew first documented walleye natural reproduction in 1987 and also found a good year class of smallmouth bass and plenty of rock bass.

In May 1992 a management team using fyke nets and boomshocking gear collected 2,876 male and 1,450 female walleyes. The number includes about 25 percent of fish that were recaptured after being fin clipped. Most of the fish were 15 to 20 inches long, and a total of 208 mostly females were larger than 20 inches long.

In 1991 managers released 68,500 walleye fingerlings; in 1992 they planted out 40,000 lake trout yearlings; and in 1993 they stocked an estimated 26,500 walleye fingerlings, 947 adult lake trout and 45,000 yearling lakers.

Tactics to Try: The lake has a large amount of prime walleye structure including rock humps and bars and dramatic contour breaks. Most anglers drift or troll minnow rigs and crawler harnesses along the structure from 5 to 40 feet of water. Try copper blades first and then experiment with color if they don't produce. On the lake's west side, Midsummer's Point is especially good. Visibly locate the long ridge with weeds atop that runs south from 2 to 15 feet of water.

June and September are top months for muskies. To take a 20 pounder, slowly drift huge sucker minnows rigged with a three-way swivel and weighted with lead behind the boat or throw/troll jerkbaits or oversized spinners. The grass flats off the south end of Midsummer's Point are a good starting point.

Whitefish spawn in November, and the entire shoreline is productive at times. In winter concentrate on holes to 60 feet deep, and bounce a No. 7 Swedish Pimple off bottom. The tactic will also produce lake trout at times, especially if you tip hooks with a flap of sucker meat. Up to 40 shanties dot the lake in winter.

Access: Pentoga County Park is located on the south shore. Facilities include a boat launch, toilets, parking for boat trailers and vehicles, and a campground. To rent a boat contact Hillberg's Cabins (see listing under Bait & Tackle).

GOLDEN LAKE

Fishing Opportunities: Splake and Lake Trout—Fair to Good; Smallmouth Bass—Available.

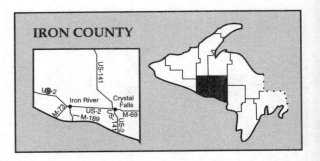

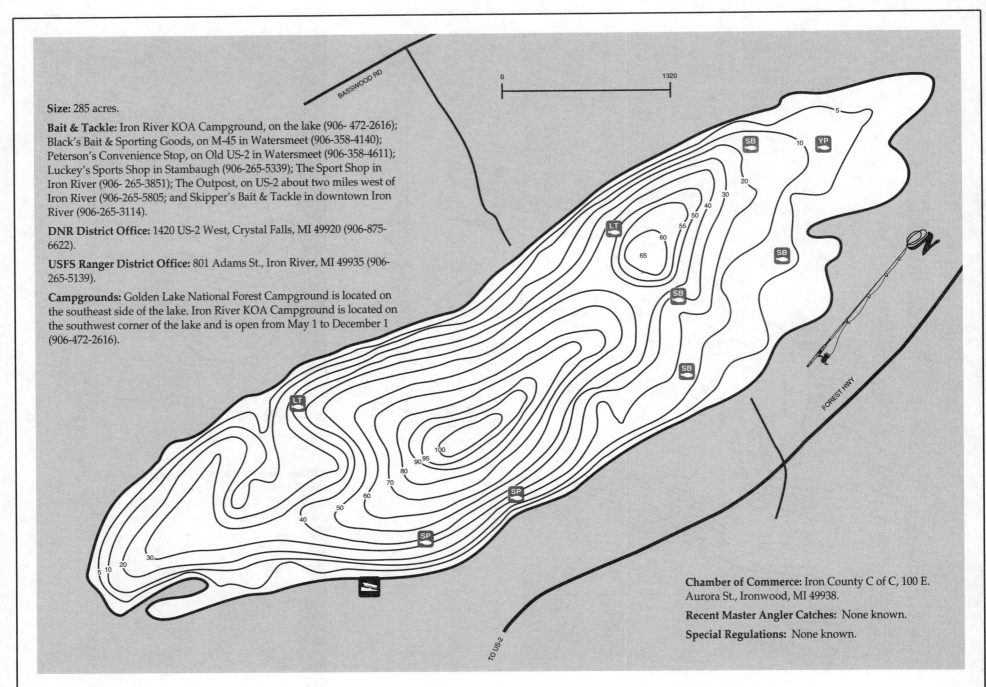

Size: 285 acres.

Bait & Tackle: Iron River KOA Campground, on the lake (906- 472-2616); Black's Bait & Sporting Goods, on M-45 in Watersmeet (906-358-4140); Peterson's Convenience Stop, on Old US-2 in Watersmeet (906-358-4611); Luckey's Sports Shop in Stambaugh (906-265-5339); The Sport Shop in Iron River (906-265-3851); The Outpost, on US-2 about two miles west of Iron River (906-265-5805); and Skipper's Bait & Tackle in downtown Iron River (906-265-3114).

DNR District Office: 1420 US-2 West, Crystal Falls, MI 49920 (906-875-6622).

USFS Ranger District Office: 801 Adams St., Iron River, MI 49935 (906-265-5139).

Campgrounds: Golden Lake National Forest Campground is located on the southeast side of the lake. Iron River KOA Campground is located on the southwest corner of the lake and is open from May 1 to December 1 (906-472-2616).

Chamber of Commerce: Iron County C of C, 100 E. Aurora St., Ironwood, MI 49938.

Recent Master Angler Catches: None known.

Special Regulations: None known.

Golden Lake is located about 12 miles west of Iron River in westcentral Iron County in the Ottawa National Forest. Because the clear lake has no inlets or outlets and is recharged by springs, water levels are constant. At 100 feet maximum depth the lake is one of the deepest in the U.P. Shoal areas are mostly sand with some gravel, rubble and boulders, and deep-water areas contain pulpy peat. Cover is sparse; the immediate shoreline is sand and gravel and cover types are mostly brush and woods.

Fish structures placed years ago in the 10- to 15-foot-deep contour have decayed to the point where they are no longer useful. The east side of the lake along USFS-16 is highly developed.

Surveys/Stocking: Golden lake has a long history of management, beginning with the introduction of lake trout in 1921. Steelhead, yellow perch, whitefish, ciscoes, smallmouth and largemouth bass, brook trout, rainbows, bluegills and smelt all made their hatchery-reared appearance by WWII. Managers continued to stock trout and whitefish through the 1970s and even introduced chinook salmon in 1971 and 1972. The lake was chemically reclaimed with rotenone in 1974.

An October 1987 DNR fyke and gill net survey determined that smallmouth bass were in good condition and that splake survival and growth rates were favorable. Smelt survival appeared to be good, too, and the fish may be naturally reproducing. A total of 66 captured splake ranged to 16 inches, four lake trout ran 13 to 22 inches, 47 smelt measured 5 to 7 inches long, and 18 smallmouths ranged to 18 inches each.

In 1991 managers stocked 7,890 splake and 7,400 lake trout; in 1992 they released 7,500 splake and 10,000 lake trout; and in 1993 they planted out an estimated 6,200 splake and 10,000 lakers. All fish were yearlings.

Tactics to Try: This deep lake with its cold, clear water is not easy to fish. The north half is best for bass, which fishermen often mark with sonar and see with their own eyes but have difficulty catching. Perhaps that is well because the bass fishery in this oligotrophic lake is fragile. Finesse tactics of light line and slow, deliberate presentations are required. Live bait works better than artificial lures.

Splake and rainbows are best fished at night. Hang a lantern over the boat side and chum with corn, then bait a small treble hook with one or two kernels. Most nighttime trout are taken in 12 to 30 feet of water. Wigglers or single salmon eggs produce in winter for jiggers sweetening their Swedish Pimples, small Hopkins Spoons or Jigging Rapalas with the bait.

Golden Lake is capable of throwing big lake trout. Jig for them in winter in 30 to 70 feet of water. In summer troll Great Lakes spoons such as Michigan Stingers and Northport Nailers, and for best results, rig the hardware behind cowbells. Sewn minnows and cowbells should also produce.

Access: The USFS maintains an improved access site at the campground on the southeast side of the lake. Facilities included a paved boat launch ramp, toilets and parking for a dozen vehicles. To rent a boat, contact the Iron River KOA (see listings under Bait & Tackle and Campgrounds).

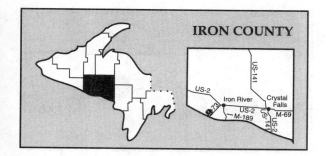

IRON COUNTY

HAGERMAN LAKE

Fishing Opportunities: Bluegills and Walleyes—Good to Excellent; Northern Pike, Smallmouth Bass, Largemouth Bass and Yellow Perch—Good.

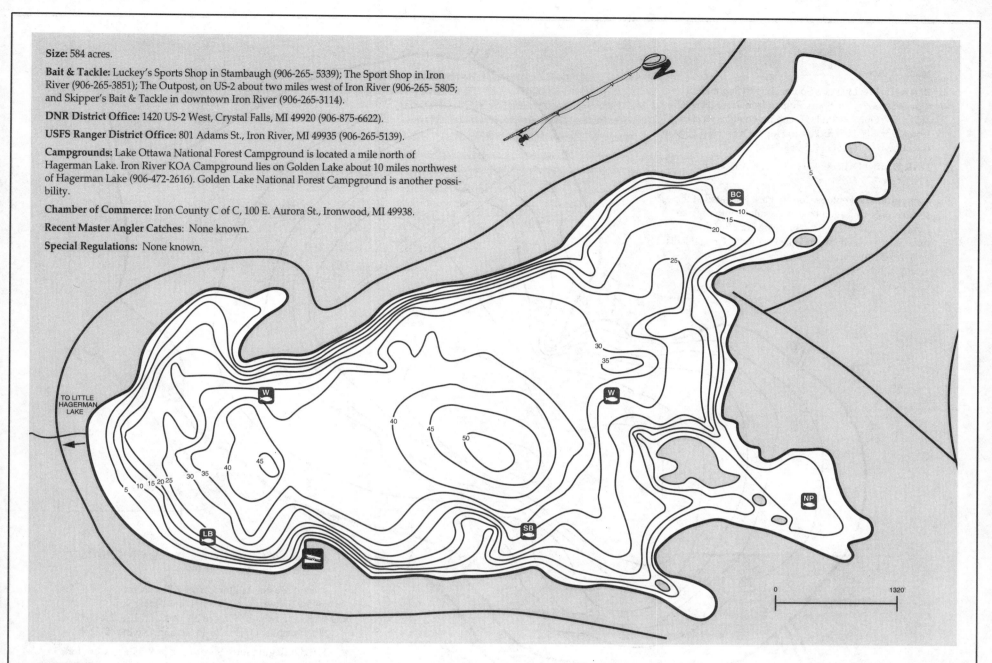

Size: 584 acres.

Bait & Tackle: Luckey's Sports Shop in Stambaugh (906-265- 5339); The Sport Shop in Iron River (906-265-3851); The Outpost, on US-2 about two miles west of Iron River (906-265- 5805; and Skipper's Bait & Tackle in downtown Iron River (906-265-3114).

DNR District Office: 1420 US-2 West, Crystal Falls, MI 49920 (906-875-6622).

USFS Ranger District Office: 801 Adams St., Iron River, MI 49935 (906-265-5139).

Campgrounds: Lake Ottawa National Forest Campground is located a mile north of Hagerman Lake. Iron River KOA Campground lies on Golden Lake about 10 miles northwest of Hagerman Lake (906-472-2616). Golden Lake National Forest Campground is another possibility.

Chamber of Commerce: Iron County C of C, 100 E. Aurora St., Ironwood, MI 49938.

Recent Master Angler Catches: None known.

Special Regulations: None known.

agerman Lake is located five miles southwest of Iron River in southwest Iron County within the Ottawa National Forest about two miles north of the Wisconsin state line. The lake has no major outlet, simply a small, non-navigable stream that connects it to Little Hagerman Lake. The entire west side of Hagerman Lake is developed, and the south end is partly developed with homes and cottages. Fishing pressure is high from lake residents, visitors from Iron River, and Wisconsin anglers.

The clear, clean lake has little vegetation except for the northwest corner, which is relatively shallow and features mostly cabbage weeds. A small island is located in the northeast corner, and there is a considerable amount of downed structure in the form of big trees along the east shore. Fish shelters installed 40 years ago are virtually of no value anymore to anglers.

Surveys/Stocking: Stocking records date to 1921 when Hagerman Lake received 10,000 lake trout. Over the years additional species introduced include smallmouth and largemouth bass, yellow perch, walleyes, bluegills, northern pike and rainbow trout. The DNR introduced walleyes in 1982.

A September 1988 DNR boomshocking survey indicated strong walleye survival from earlier planting and possible evidence of natural reproduction. Managers returned in April 1991 with fyke nets to capture a large number of healthy walleyes representing nine age classes. A total of 178 eight-year-old fish ranged from 17 to 27½ inches. Yellow perch, smallmouth bass and bluegills — including 'gills nearly 10 inches long — were also collected, measured and released.

In 1992 managers released an estimated 40,000 adult yellow perch, and in 1993 they stocked an estimated 9,600 walleye fingerlings.

Tactics to Try: The lake is popular with ice fishermen. A DNR creel survey in January 1986 revealed a total of 82 fishermen with 1,303 perch they had caught between 10:00 A.M. and 2:00 P.M. The average size of the third that were measured was 7.7 inches and included fish to 13 inches. During years of good ice and decent fishing, a dozen or more shanties appear. Perch numbers have fallen off somewhat since the late 80s and early 90s. In the spring of 1992, DNR technicians stocked many 3- to 8-inch-long perch that were thinned from other lakes. The

purpose was to provide forage and to increase sport-fishing opportunities.

To catch walleyes, try the west end of the island, starting deep and working into the shallows with leadhead jigs tipped with crawlers. Very few anglers use minnows and would likely increase their chances if they did.

The lake is underfished for bass, considering that it contains both smallmouths and bigmouths. Docks and moored boats on the west shore and drowned timber along the east shore are good places to try.

The lake throws 7- to 9-inch bluegills in spring for popper fishermen, and are available in deep water in summer to anglers using light line and finesse tactics. There is little winter activity for panfish.

A good winter fishery for northerns exists although most fish are sublegal in size. Try the northeast bay behind the island for jig, spear and tip-up tactics.

Access: The USFS maintains a recently improved access site on the lake's southeast side. The site includes a hard- surface boat launch ramp, toilets and parking for about 40 vehicles. There is no place to rent a boat.

LAKE EMILY

Fishing Opportunities: Largemouth Bass, Walleyes—
Good to Excellent; Yellow Perch, Bluegills and
Smallmouth Bass—Good; Black Crappies—Fair to Good;
Northern Muskies—Available.

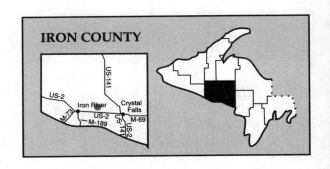
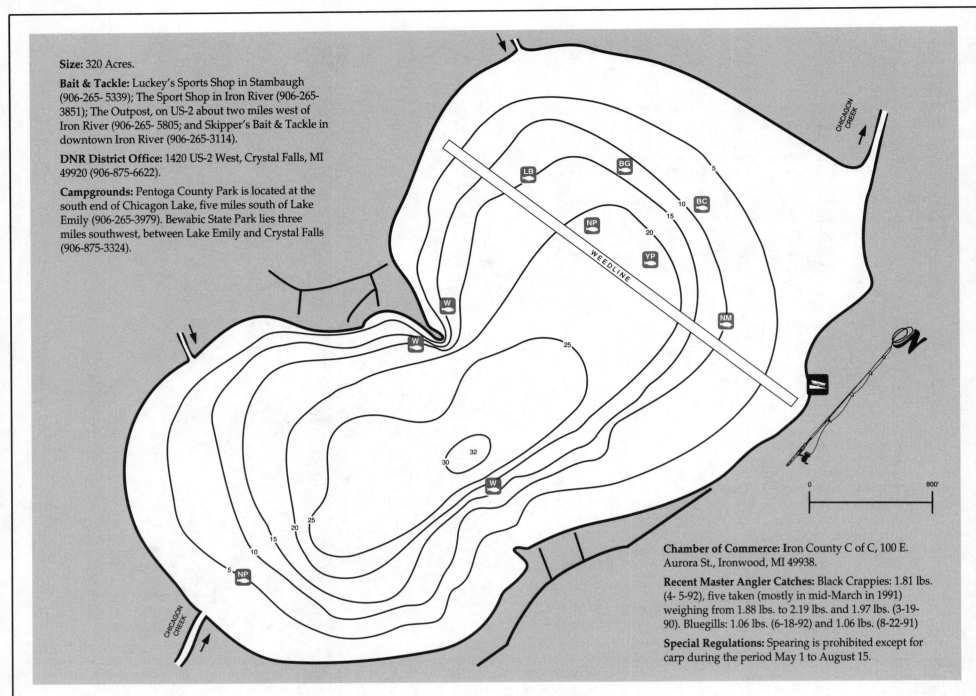

Size: 320 Acres.

Bait & Tackle: Luckey's Sports Shop in Stambaugh
(906-265-5339); The Sport Shop in Iron River (906-265-
3851); The Outpost, on US-2 about two miles west of
Iron River (906-265-5805; and Skipper's Bait & Tackle in
downtown Iron River (906-265-3114).

DNR District Office: 1420 US-2 West, Crystal Falls, MI
49920 (906-875-6622).

Campgrounds: Pentoga County Park is located at the
south end of Chicagon Lake, five miles south of Lake
Emily (906-265-3979). Bewabic State Park lies three
miles southwest, between Lake Emily and Crystal Falls
(906-875-3324).

Chamber of Commerce: Iron County C of C, 100 E.
Aurora St., Ironwood, MI 49938.

Recent Master Angler Catches: Black Crappies: 1.81 lbs.
(4-5-92), five taken (mostly in mid-March in 1991)
weighing from 1.88 lbs. to 2.19 lbs. and 1.97 lbs. (3-19-
90). Bluegills: 1.06 lbs. (6-18-92) and 1.06 lbs. (8-22-91)

Special Regulations: Spearing is prohibited except for
carp during the period May 1 to August 15.

Lake Emily, which is also called Emily
Lake, is located about seven miles east
of Iron River in southcentral Iron County. The
lake's north and south shores are swampy, and
the east and west shores are slightly higher.
Overall, the appearance is low and flat, and the
surrounding terrain is rolling and wooded.
Water color is a light brown. Pondweed, lily
pads and bulrushes are common, especially in
the northern quarter where a distinct vegetation
line forms in six to 10 feet of water.

The bottom is a mixture of sand, gravel, marl,
clay, and some coarse rubble and boulders in the
shallows and pulpy peat in the deeper central
area. About one-fourth of the lake is developed,
especially portions of the southern half, and
fishing pressure is fairly high. Chicagon Creek
enters from the south end and exits from the
northeast corner.

Surveys/Stocking: An April 1988 fyke net survey indicated that walleye

population and size structure were in good condition and that planting survival was good. The
survey also revealed that some natural reproduction was taking place. Yellow perch were
abundant and had a fair size-structure. The nets
collected walleyes to 26 inches, perch to 10 inches, pike to 24 inches, a single 38-inch northern
muskie, and a few rock bass, black crappies and
pumpkinseed sunfish.

Researchers returning in May 1988 with
boomshocking gear determined that yearling
walleye numbers were good and that largemouth bass to 17 inches were plentiful. A remnant population of smallmouth bass exists, and
muskie yearling numbers from the 1987 plant
were fair. Altogether, researchers counted 273
walleyes, 56 largemouth bass, seven muskies, 18
northern pike and five smallmouths. In October
1991 they released 29 tagged northern muskies
ranging from 17 to 20 inches each.

In 1991 managers released 20,387 walleye fingerlings, and in 1993 they stocked an estimated
12,000 more.

Tactics to Try: The vegetated north end is best
for northern pike, panfish,
largemouth bass, and an occasional lunker
muskie — like the 48-inch, 30-pound giant that
was served up about the time we went to press.
A half-dozen shanties dot the lake here in winter, and tip-up fishermen are in evidence.
Summertime pike tactics call for still fishing or
drift fishing with big sucker minnows, tossing
jerkbaits or trolling weedless lures. A good trick
for bass is to hold your boat just off the weedline
and cast plastic night crawlers or spinnerbaits
into it.

Elsewhere the lake drops subtly from 10 feet to
20 or more feet, and leadhead jigs work well for
walleyes. The west-shore point contains cobble
and is a sometimes hotspot for walleyes.
Trolling or drifting with bottom-bumping hardware or crawler rigs from 10 to 20 feet deep also
works.

Access: An improved access site on the east
shore contains a paved boat ramp, toilets and parking for five vehicles. There is no
place to rent a boat.

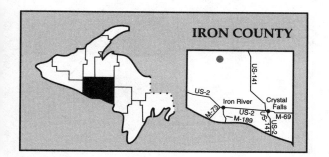

LAKE
STE. KATHRYN

Fishing Opportunities: Walleyes, Largemouth Bass— Good to Excellent; Yellow Perch, Northern Pike and Bluegills—Good; Black Crappies—Available.

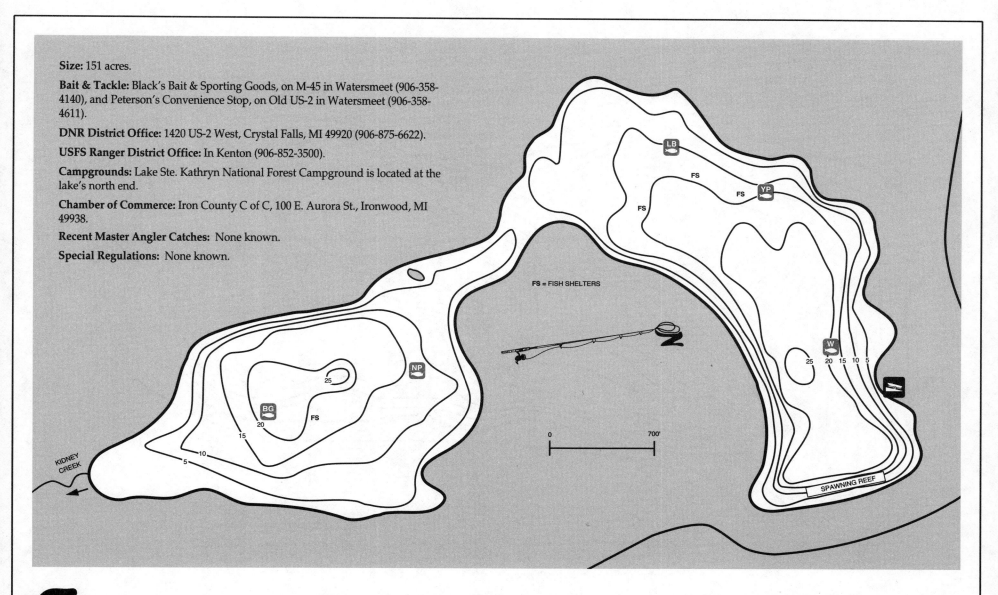

Size: 151 acres.

Bait & Tackle: Black's Bait & Sporting Goods, on M-45 in Watersmeet (906-358-4140), and Peterson's Convenience Stop, on Old US-2 in Watersmeet (906-358-4611).

DNR District Office: 1420 US-2 West, Crystal Falls, MI 49920 (906-875-6622).

USFS Ranger District Office: In Kenton (906-852-3500).

Campgrounds: Lake Ste. Kathryn National Forest Campground is located at the lake's north end.

Chamber of Commerce: Iron County C of C, 100 E. Aurora St., Ironwood, MI 49938.

Recent Master Angler Catches: None known.

Special Regulations: None known.

IRON COUNTY

FS = FISH SHELTERS

KIDNEY CREEK

SPAWNING REEF

Lake Ste. Kathryn, which used to be called Kidney Lake, is located in northcentral Iron County within the Ottawa National Forest about eight miles south of Sidnaw. Water color is a light brown in this fairly clear lake. Bottom areas near shore contain sand; deeper stretches are mostly organic with some gravel. Logs and snags are rare in the north basin but abundant in the south basin. Water lilies and pondweed constitute most of the emergent vegetation, which is found on the west third of the north basin and which nearly covers the south basin.

Kidney Creek exits from the south end enroute to Perch Lake and the Perch and Sturgeon rivers, which eventually reach Lake Superior. There are no inlets. The immediate shoreline is moderately steep and the surrounding wild, undeveloped terrain is slightly rolling and supportive of second-growth hardwoods. Fishing pressure is moderate to heavy in summer because of the campground's popularity.

Surveys/Stocking: The lake was partially treated with the chemical antimycin in October 1978. An April 1990 DNR fyke net survey found good numbers of

walleyes in most age classes, supporting what anglers indicate is a good fishery. The nets revealed a total of 207 walleyes from 12 to 25 inches each. Technicians also removed 313 pounds of white suckers, far from the 3,524 pounds taken out in 1988. They also transplanted 105 netted northern pike averaging 17.2 inches to Tepee Lake (two years earlier they removed 788 pike).

Other species captured, measured and returned to the lake in 1988 included: 25 bluegills to 9 inches, 59 black crappies to 11 inches, 28 pumpkinseed sunfish to 8 inches, 183 yellow perch to 9 inches, and a 14-inch largemouth bass.

An October 1989 boomshocking survey was aimed at determining the extent of walleye natural reproduction from the USFS spawning reef. Apparently natural reproduction was a complete failure, the same as in 1987. On the other hand, the rock reef was responsible for walleyes producing progeny in 1983, soon after it became operative. Survival of stocked walleyes was low, however.

Researchers noted that the lake had a good largemouth bass population with decent growth rates. Sixty-two bigmouths averaged 11.3 inches and ranged to 17 inches. Walleyes averaged 13½

inches and measured to 22 inches.

In 1992 managers released 7,560 walleye fingerlings.

Tactics to Try: This small, beautiful, pristine lake offers decent-size walleyes and yellow perch, especially for anglers who hunt and use light line. The two species school according to age class. Once found, they can be taken with typical lures and bait. Slip bobbers allow for finesse presentations of crawlers or minnows in the clear lake. The best fishing occurs in the north basin.

The lake contains a large population of small northern pike. For best results fish the south basin, which also produces occasional stringers of black crappies and has the best fishing for largemouth bass. Blue-and-white and lime green-and-yellow spinnerbaits with a single silver blade are productive.

Fish shelters and structures added by the USFS to both basins are worth finding and fishing around.

Access: The public access site is located on the north shore near the east end, where the USFS maintains an unimproved gravel boat launch ramp. Included are toilets and parking for 15 vehicles. There is no place to rent a boat.

OTTAWA LAKE

Fishing Opportunities: Smallmouth Bass and Walleyes—
Good to Excellent; Yellow Perch and Northern Pike—
Poor to Fair; Black Crappies and Bluegills—Available.

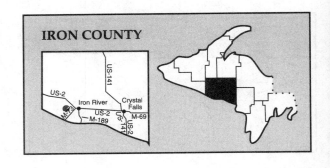
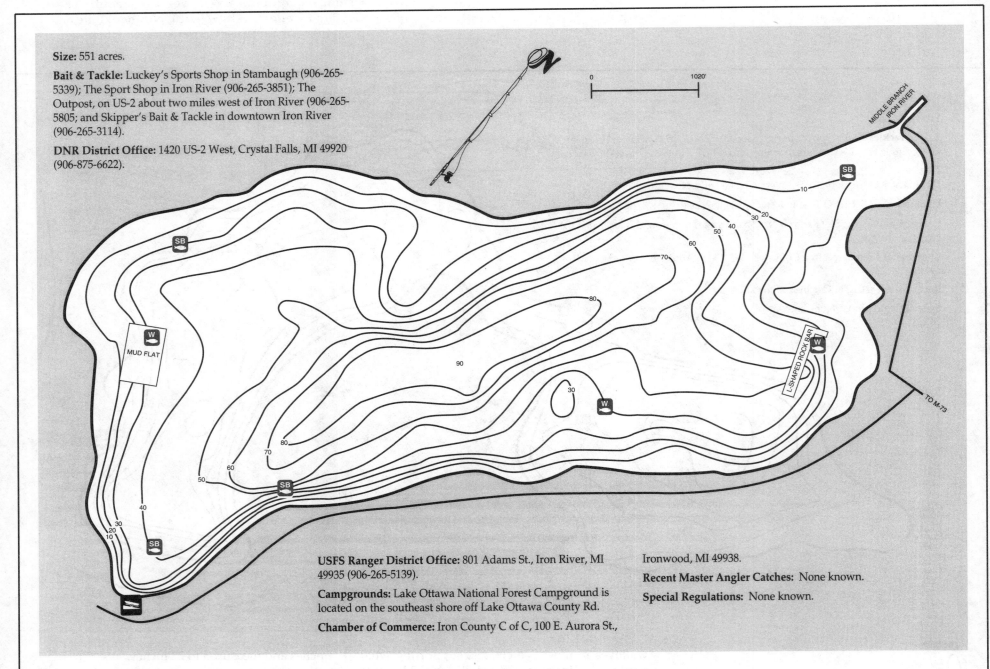

Size: 551 acres.

Bait & Tackle: Luckey's Sports Shop in Stambaugh (906-265-5339); The Sport Shop in Iron River (906-265-3851); The Outpost, on US-2 about two miles west of Iron River (906-265-5805; and Skipper's Bait & Tackle in downtown Iron River (906-265-3114).

DNR District Office: 1420 US-2 West, Crystal Falls, MI 49920 (906-875-6622).

USFS Ranger District Office: 801 Adams St., Iron River, MI 49935 (906-265-5139).

Campgrounds: Lake Ottawa National Forest Campground is located on the southeast shore off Lake Ottawa County Rd.

Chamber of Commerce: Iron County C of C, 100 E. Aurora St.,

Ironwood, MI 49938.

Recent Master Angler Catches: None known.

Special Regulations: None known.

Ottawa Lake, which is sometimes referred to as Lake Ottawa, is located about five miles west of Iron River in southwest Iron County in the Ottawa National Forest. The lake's outlet is the Middle Branch of the Iron River, and there is no inlet. Because the extremely clear lake is oligotrophic, it produces a minimum amount of food for gamefish. This condition requires the occasional introduction of ciscoes and other forage species from hatcheries or other lakes.

Surveys/Stocking: In 1986 DNR fisheries crews manually removed 2,445 pounds of rock bass, along with 30 pounds of suckers and 40 pounds of pumpkinseed sunfish. A spring 1988 DNR survey with fyke and gill nets showed walleyes representing nine year-classes. All the fish were growing well, and 10-year-old fish were 21 to 27 inches long. The survey showed low numbers of perch and northern pike. Both species used to be abundant, and northerns in particular often went 20 pounds or more.

The survey also turned up smallmouth bass to 15 inches, northern pike to 29 inches, bluegills to 10 inches, a pair of 26-inch-long lake trout, and five brook trout to 8 inches each. A boomshocking crew returning in the fall of 1988 determined that walleyes were beginning to reproduce naturally.

In 1991 managers stocked 250 adult lake trout and 2,170 walleye fingerlings. In 1993 they released 400 adult lakers and 11,900 walleye fingerlings.

Tactics to Try: A USFS fisheries crew installed 63 spawning cover logs in January 1986 to improve smallmouth bass reproduction habitat. The logs are located in 5 to 10 feet of water along the southeast, southwest and north shores and are good places to look for fish. Work the shoreline shallows and cast spinnerbaits or crankbaits around the structures and various drowned logs. Leeches and crawlers also produce; in the evening toss a Floating Rapala and twitch it to resemble a wounded minnow.

Two dominant underwater structures concentrate walleyes and some bass. One is an L-shaped rock formation in the northeast corner off the old Iron River Township Park. Surface water over the structure in some places is less than 3 feet deep, and it drops off to 15 to 18 feet on all sides. The second structure of note is a mud bar located directly across the lake from the day-use area and about 1,000 yards off the west shore. The bar is 70 to 75 yards long.

To catch walleyes in Ottawa Lake, cast lead-head jigs skirted with a maribou feather or Mister Twister. Early in the year, tip the jigs with fathead minnows or half night crawlers. In midsummer try a Lindy Rig with an inflated crawler or a leech. Early morning and evening are the best times to troll with single or double-blade spinners on a crawler harness.

The lake is popular with ice anglers, and 10 to 20 shanties typically appear each winter. Heavy fishing pressure leveled the lake for perch and pike in the mid-1980s. Still, it occasionally serves up good catches of both species and could be coming back into health.

Access: The USFS maintains an improved access site at the campground it manages. Included are a paved boat launch ramp, toilets and parking for 20 vehicles. There is no place to rent a boat.

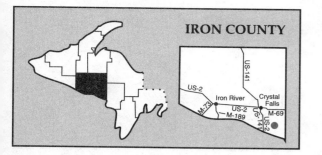

PEAVY RESERVOIR

Fishing Opportunities: Walleyes—Good to Excellent; Yellow Perch, Smallmouth Bass, Black Crappies and Northern Pike— Fair to Good.

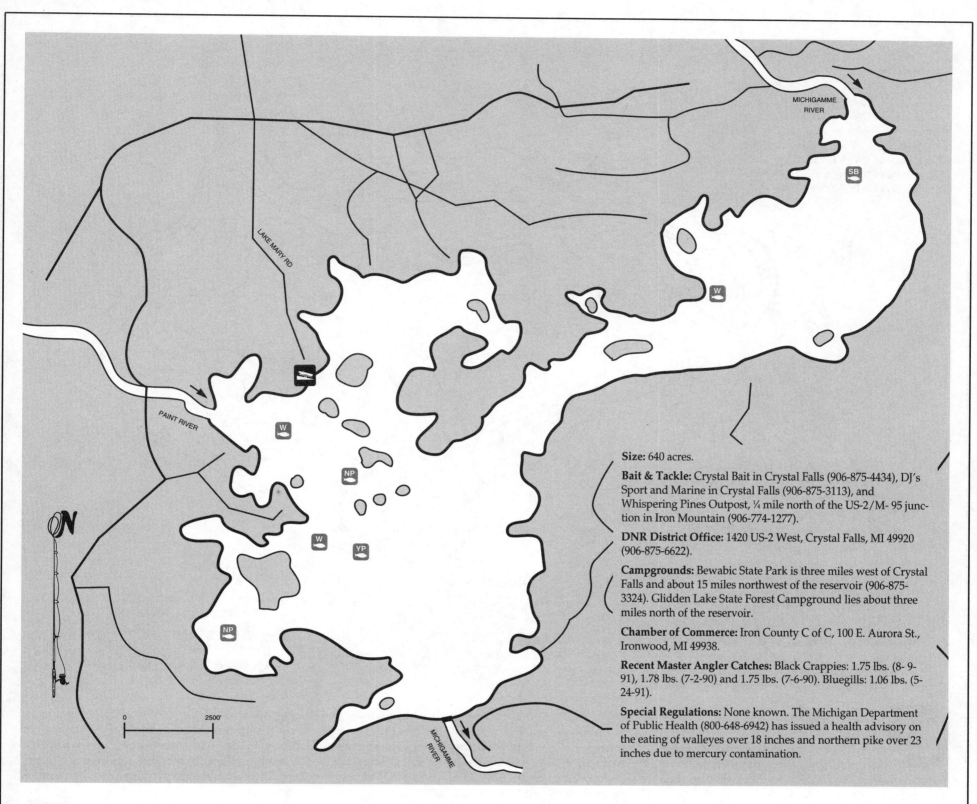

Size: 640 acres.

Bait & Tackle: Crystal Bait in Crystal Falls (906-875-4434), DJ's Sport and Marine in Crystal Falls (906-875-3113), and Whispering Pines Outpost, ¼ mile north of the US-2/M- 95 junction in Iron Mountain (906-774-1277).

DNR District Office: 1420 US-2 West, Crystal Falls, MI 49920 (906-875-6622).

Campgrounds: Bewabic State Park is three miles west of Crystal Falls and about 15 miles northwest of the reservoir (906-875-3324). Glidden Lake State Forest Campground lies about three miles north of the reservoir.

Chamber of Commerce: Iron County C of C, 100 E. Aurora St., Ironwood, MI 49938.

Recent Master Angler Catches: Black Crappies: 1.75 lbs. (8-9-91), 1.78 lbs. (7-2-90) and 1.75 lbs. (7-6-90). Bluegills: 1.06 lbs. (5-24-91).

Special Regulations: None known. The Michigan Department of Public Health (800-648-6942) has issued a health advisory on the eating of walleyes over 18 inches and northern pike over 23 inches due to mercury contamination.

Peavy Reservoir is an impoundment on the Michigamme River and is located in southeast Iron County about 10 miles southeast of Crystal Falls. Its southern portion extends to within a couple miles of the Wisconsin border. The impoundment begins about 15 miles downstream from Way Dam and Michigamme Reservoir. Peavy is the better fishing lake of the two manmade projects.

The impoundment contains lots of weeds, cattails and lily pads, and it tends to support heavy algae growth at times during the summer. The area around the shallow flooding is mostly clearcut aspen regenerating with second growth in varying age classes.

Surveys/Stocking: Recent surveys have been limited to electroshocking, which in the fall at least, is not normally a reliable indicator of big gamefish abundance. A September 1987 sampling to assess walleye year-class strength revealed fair numbers of fingerlings but poor numbers of yearlings. Smallmouth bass, bluegills, black crappies, northern pike to 28 inches, walleyes to 22 inches, and yellow perch to 10 inches were among the species stunned, collected and measured.

Managers returning in September 1988 determined that Station 1, near the center of the reservoir, produced an average year-class of young-of-the-year walleyes. Station 2, toward the north end, yielded a strong young-of-the-year class. Workers observed good numbers of small perch and smallmouth bass. Forage fish appeared to be fairly abundant, and growth rates were average overall.

Tactics to Try: Live bait works best in the dark waters of Peavy Reservoir. Try leeches, minnows and crawlers for bass and walleyes. Insect larvae and small worms are good for panfish. The reservoir gets virtually no fishing pressure in winter, and summer angling activity is light to moderate. Sonar is helpful in finding structure and the river channel.

Access: On the reservoir's northwest shore, the Wisconsin Electric Company maintains a public access site at the end of Lake Mary Rd.,° which runs south for about six miles from M-69 between Crystal Falls and Sagola. Included are toilets and a gravel boat launch ramp. There is no place to rent a boat.

PERCH LAKE

Fishing Opportunities: Walleyes and Yellow Perch—Good
to Excellent; Northern Pike—Fair to Good; Largemouth
Bass, Bluegills and Black Crappies—Poor to Fair.

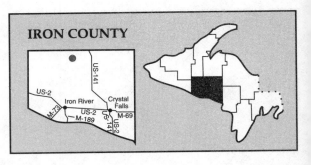

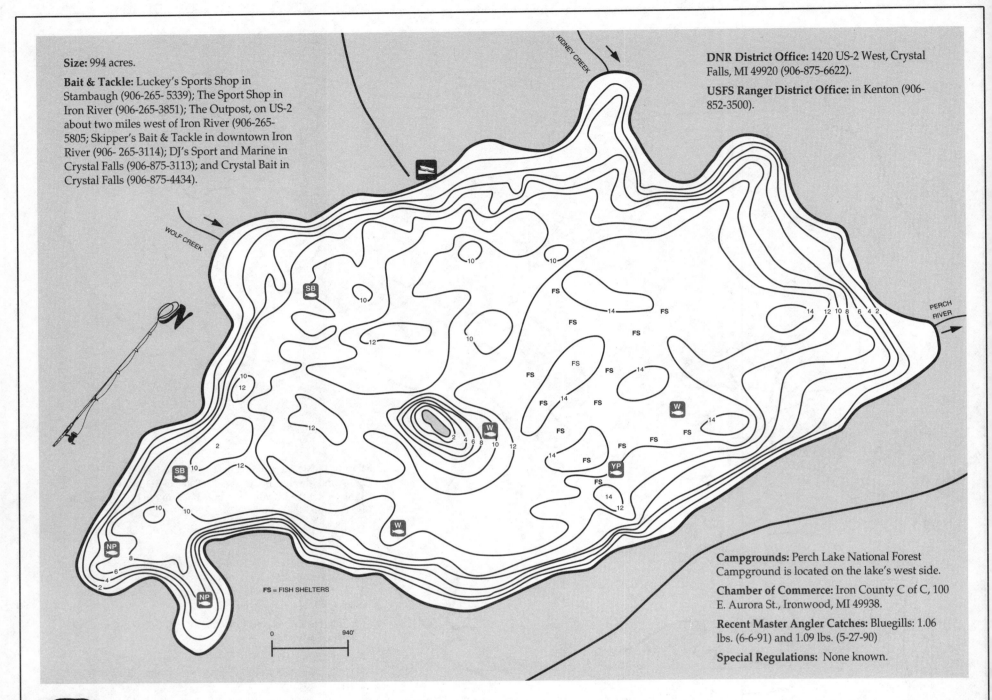

Size: 994 acres.

Bait & Tackle: Luckey's Sports Shop in
Stambaugh (906-265- 5339); The Sport Shop in
Iron River (906-265-3851); The Outpost, on US-2
about two miles west of Iron River (906-265-
5805; Skipper's Bait & Tackle in downtown Iron
River (906- 265-3114); DJ's Sport and Marine in
Crystal Falls (906-875-3113); and Crystal Bait in
Crystal Falls (906-875-4434).

DNR District Office: 1420 US-2 West, Crystal
Falls, MI 49920 (906-875-6622).

USFS Ranger District Office: in Kenton (906-
852-3500).

FS = FISH SHELTERS

Campgrounds: Perch Lake National Forest
Campground is located on the lake's west side.

Chamber of Commerce: Iron County C of C, 100
E. Aurora St., Ironwood, MI 49938.

Recent Master Angler Catches: Bluegills: 1.06
lbs. (6-6-91) and 1.09 lbs. (5-27-90)

Special Regulations: None known.

P erch Lake is located about 10 miles
south of Sidnaw in northcentral Iron
County in the Ottawa National Forest. The shallow lake averages 9 to 12 feet deep, and the
water is brown-stained from tannic acid. Several
cottages appear along the northeast shore, and
new development is occurring along the southeast shore.

The west shoreline has several weedy bays
averaging 3 to 6 feet deep, and the north end is
weedy. A four-acre island in the southcentral
portion of the lake provides excellent fish habitat, plus there is pronounced rock structure
halfway between the island and the northeast
shore where the Perch River outlets. Wolf and
Kidney creeks flow in from the west side.

The lake has held up surprisingly well in spite
of heavy fishing pressure and the fact that it is
not currently being stocked by the DNR. A veri-
table walleye factory some years, Perch Lake
supports natural reproduction. Spawning
walleyes target rock pastures at the north end.

Surveys/Stocking: Fall boomshocking surveys
by DNR fisheries crews
indicate a good population of large walleyes
from mid-1980 year-classes. The last survey,
completed in September 1990, produced several
year-classes, including one 30-inch whopper
that somehow eluded fishermen's hooks for 14
years. Although northern pike and yellow perch
appeared to be in decline, anglers continue to
report good fishing, especially for perch.

As mentioned, DNR managers do not stock
the lake.

Tactics to Try: Perch and walleyes disperse
throughout the lake as they fol-
low young-of-the-year bullheads and other baitfish. Gentle contours around the rocky island
are good places to try, as are structures to the
northeast and southeast indicated on the map.
These include about 20 fish shelters constructed
in 10 to 15 feet of water during the winter of
1991-92. They are located on the lake's east side
due east of the boat launch and join earlier manmade structure in the area.

The lake's shallow nature and tributary influx
allows it to warm more quickly than other area

lakes, giving anglers an early-season headstart.
Drift rigs are popular for walleyes — try copper-
colored blades on harnesses and Lindy Rigs and
sweeten hooks with a crawler, minnow or leech.
Dark days and evenings often produce the most
action.

Minnows fished with jigs, spoons or tip-ups
produce some winter action for walleyes. Perch,
on the other hand, do not provide a solid winter
sport as one might expect.

For northern pike, try the south-end bays
among the cabbage weeds. Smallmouth bass frequent these and other bays around the lake. Try
leadhead jigs tipped with fathead minnows.
Also the mud-bottom bays host mega hex hatches in May and June; flyfishermen can enjoy top
sport for walleyes and smallmouths then.

Access: The USFS maintains an unimproved
access site at the campground it manages on the west shore between the two inflowing creeks. Take USFS-137 to the lake. Included
are a gravel boat launch ramp, toilets and parking for 15 vehicles. On USFS-137 about ¾ mile
from the lake lives a homeowner who keeps
rental boats and motors at the lake itself.

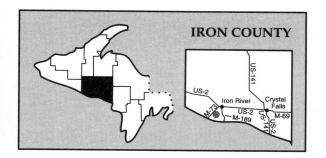

IRON COUNTY

STANLEY LAKE

Fishing Opportunities: Walleyes—Good to Excellent; Largemouth Bass and Smallmouth Bass—Good; Yellow Perch—Fair to Good; Bluegills—Fair; Northern Muskies and Northern Pike—Available.

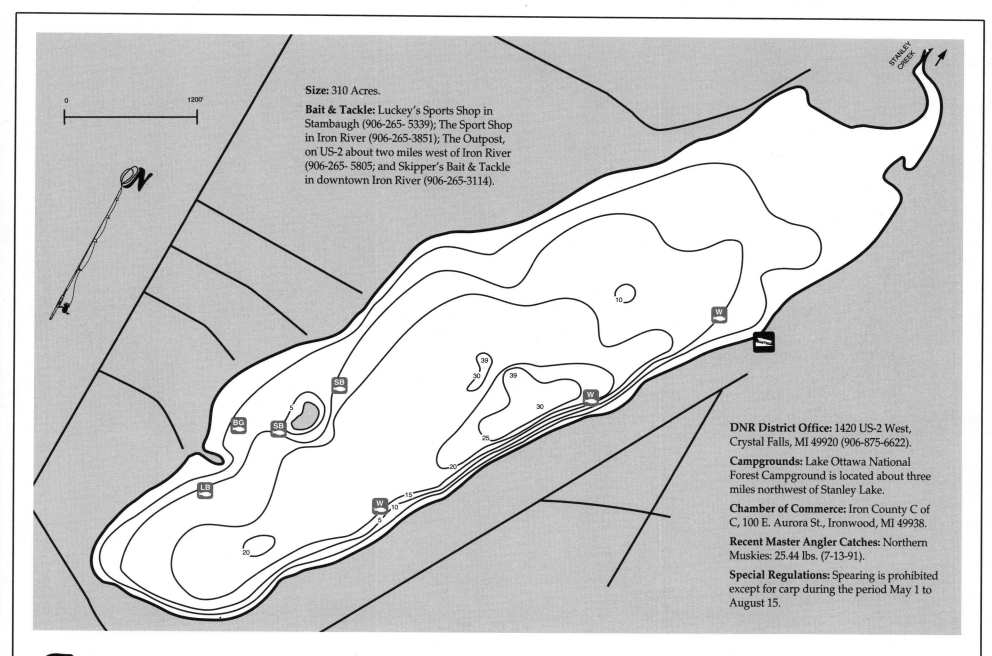

Size: 310 Acres.

Bait & Tackle: Luckey's Sports Shop in Stambaugh (906-265- 5339); The Sport Shop in Iron River (906-265-3851); The Outpost, on US-2 about two miles west of Iron River (906-265- 5805; and Skipper's Bait & Tackle in downtown Iron River (906-265-3114).

DNR District Office: 1420 US-2 West, Crystal Falls, MI 49920 (906-875-6622).

Campgrounds: Lake Ottawa National Forest Campground is located about three miles northwest of Stanley Lake.

Chamber of Commerce: Iron County C of C, 100 E. Aurora St., Ironwood, MI 49938.

Recent Master Angler Catches: Northern Muskies: 25.44 lbs. (7-13-91).

Special Regulations: Spearing is prohibited except for carp during the period May 1 to August 15.

Stanley Lake is located about three miles west of Caspian in southwest Iron County. The north end of the lake is very shallow, only one to 3 feet deep in most places, and the bottom is soft and silty. The south end features a gravel bottom. Shoal areas throughout the lake—except for the north end—contain gravel. Vegetation is fairly abundant. The clear lake's outflow is Stanley Creek, which reportedly contains brook trout. Stanley Creek empties into the Iron River, which is a tributary of the Brule River.

The lake's immediate shoreline is high and steep, containing rubble and boulders. The surrounding wooded countryside is rolling, mostly sandy loam and gravel. About 75 percent of the lake is developed, and fishing pressure is moderate to high.

Surveys/Stocking: Stanley Lake first received stocked fish in 1924 when 8,000 lake trout were introduced. Through the 1930s, managers added smallmouth bass, yellow perch, bluegills, walleyes and largemouth bass. Apparently no releases were made during the 1940s or 50s. In 1962 1,000 walleye fingerlings

were planted out, and in 1969 the first release of 1,000 northern muskie fingerlings was made.

In 1979 a DNR work crew captured and removed about 3,000 pounds of small yellow perch. Further removals in 1980 and 1982 improved fishing.

A May 1990 boomshocking survey indicated that largemouth bass populations were low, supporting an observation made the previous fall. The boomshocker stunned 17 bigmouths from 9 to 18 inches. Smallmouth bass, on the other hand, appeared to be fairly abundant and exhibited a fair size-structure. DNR technicians taped 50 fish to 16 inches long.

Walleyes first reproduced successfully in 1986, and the survey indicated that both stocked and naturally reproduced fish were doing well. A total of 229 walleyes to 25 inches long were shocked, measured and released. The crew observed five muskies to 29 inches each, along with 200 yellow perch from 2 to 10 inches, a few bluegills, pumpkinseed sunfish and black crappies.

The only stocking thus far in the 1990s was a release of 600 northern muskie fingerlings in 1990.

Tactics to Try: The fairly clear lake requires finesse tactics, and fishing can be tough after the sun moves high and the water warms. Best action for walleyes occurs late in the day when hungry fish move from deeper water to shallows. The east shore is better for walleyes due to structure and more pronounced contour breaks. Tip: Keep within casting distance of shore and fancast leadheads or Countdown Rapalas toward shore. A crawler or minnow harness works when slowly drifted along shore. After dark, break out a noodle rod and toss spiders or other surface lures.

The south half of the lake along the east shore features depths to 30 feet. Walleyes go here during the day and can be taken via vertical jigging.

Gravel structure around the island is best for smallmouth bass Bluegills and largemouths show up on the south half of the lake, especially from the island all along the southwest shore. Fish of both species are not large but are fun to catch. Yellow perch tend to wander throughout the lake.

Access: An improved access site located on the northeast shore features a paved boat launch ramp, courtesy pier, toilets and parking for eight vehicles. Boat rentals are available at Lac O'Seasons Resort (906-265-4881).

SUNSET LAKE

Fishing Opportunities: Walleyes and Yellow Perch—Excellent; Bluegills—Good to Excellent; Smallmouth Bass and Largemouth Bass—Fair to Good; Black Crappies and Northern Pike— Available.

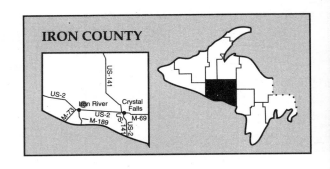

IRON COUNTY

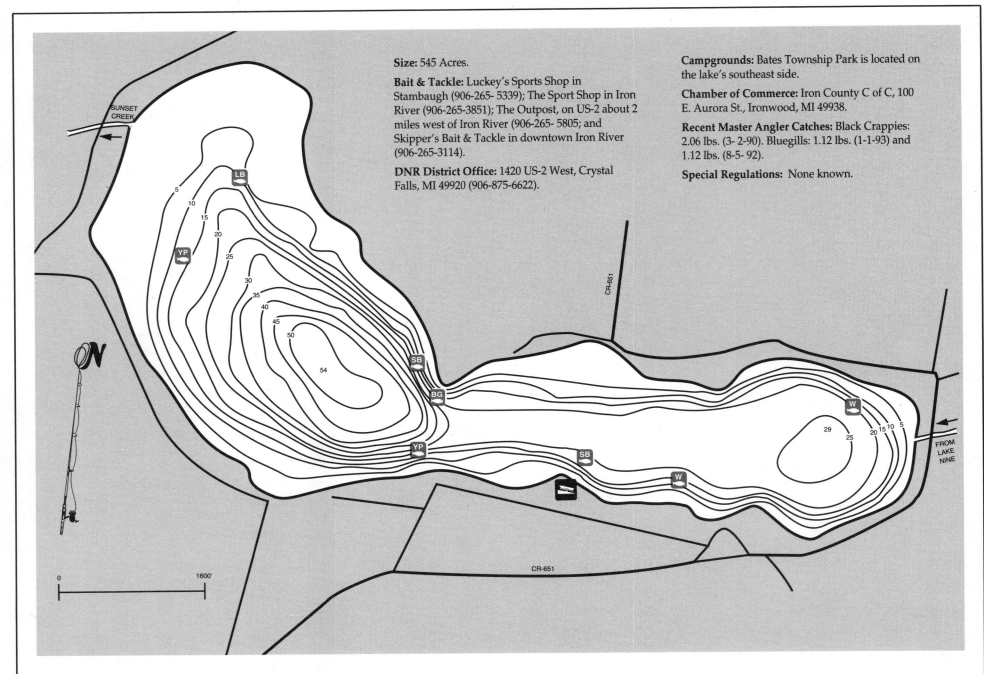

Size: 545 Acres.

Bait & Tackle: Luckey's Sports Shop in Stambaugh (906-265- 5339); The Sport Shop in Iron River (906-265-3851); The Outpost, on US-2 about 2 miles west of Iron River (906-265- 5805; and Skipper's Bait & Tackle in downtown Iron River (906-265-3114).

DNR District Office: 1420 US-2 West, Crystal Falls, MI 49920 (906-875-6622).

Campgrounds: Bates Township Park is located on the lake's southeast side.

Chamber of Commerce: Iron County C of C, 100 E. Aurora St., Ironwood, MI 49938.

Recent Master Angler Catches: Black Crappies: 2.06 lbs. (3- 2-90). Bluegills: 1.12 lbs. (1-1-93) and 1.12 lbs. (8-5- 92).

Special Regulations: None known.

Sunset Lake is located about three miles northeast of Iron River in southcentral Iron County. The lake is popular with resident anglers and visitors alike, and pressure is high. Sand extends to a depth of 20 feet in several places, and deeper stretches support a bottom of mostly pulpy peat. The lake's outlet is Sunset Creek, flowing from the northwest corner and on into the Iron, Brule, Paint, and Menominee rivers respectively. The inlet is a small east-end creek from Lake Nine.

The immediate shoreline of this mostly clear lake is sand and gravel with some scattered marshes. Surrounding terrain is rolling hardwood-covered hills. About 90 percent of the lake is developed with year-round residents. The northwest area has the least development.

Surveys/Stocking: Sunset Lake has a long history of management beginning with the stocking of yellow perch in 1921. Bluegills, largemouth bass, walleyes and lake trout all made their appearance by 1950 when rainbows were introduced. The rainbow stocking program lasted until 1971, when the DNR decided to scrap its two-story lake management approach. The first modern walleye release occurred in 1976, and researchers documented natural reproduction occurring as early as 1981.

An October 1987 boomshocking survey determined that northern pike were also naturally reproducing. An April 1990 fyke net survey indicated that walleyes were abundant although growth rates were poor, a reflection of poor yellow perch and forage minnow populations, which could have been related to a new sewage treatment system installed around the lake. The nets captured 362 walleyes from 11 to 27 inches. Other species included 24 yellow perch to 12 inches, nine northern pike to 24 inches, 22 rock bass, and a couple each of bluegills and pumpkinseed sunfish.

In 1991 managers released 10,000 walleye fingerlings; in 1993 they stocked an estimated 13,500 more.

Tactics to Try: An average of a dozen or more ice shanties dot the lake in winter. Tip-up and jig fishing is popular because of the abundance of year-round residents and the lake's proximity to Iron River. Ice fishing for perch has been very good in recent years. Target the west end and use minnows or wigglers.

Rock rubble on the lake's east end is good for spawning walleyes, with best catches occurring early in the season. Prime conditions are an overcast day with a chop-producing wind, or fish at night. Use leadhead jigs skirted with marabou or plastic, and tip the hooks with cut bait or crawlers.

Bluegills show up in 12 to 14 feet of water off weed edges. Use slip bobbers, light line and small hooks covered with worm or crawler bits. The lake-narrows region along the south shore is a good spot for both bluegills and perch.

The northeast portion flattens out to a muddy bottom and can be good for walleyes at times.

Smallmouths concentrate around logs and hard bottom structure such as drop-offs, humps and points. Largemouths prefer vegetation or manmade structures such as docks. At times the lake delivers good catches of both species.

Access: Bates Township Park, on the southeast shore, features an improved access site that includes a paved boat launch ramp, courtesy pier, toilets and parking for 21 vehicles. There is no place to rent a boat.

GRATIOT LAKE

Fishing Opportunities: Yellow Perch—Good to Excellent; Smallmouth Bass—Good; Walleyes—Fair to Good; Rainbow Trout and Northern Pike—Poor.

Size: 1,438 acres.

Bait & Tackle: Four Seasons Sports, 207 5th St. in Calumet (906-337-3844), and Lac La Belle Resort, on the northwest shore of Lac La Belle (906-289-4293). Holiday Express in Calumet (906-337-5952) has crawlers and worms.

DNR District Office: Box 440, North US-41, Baraga, MI 49908 (906-353-6651).

Campgrounds: Fanny Hooe Resort & Campground, on Manganese Rd. in Copper Harbor about 20 miles northeast of Gratiot Lake, is open all year (906-289-4451). Harbor Heights Campground, near the city, is more primitive and is open from May to October (906-289-4291). Fort Wilkins State Park is located in Copper Harbor (906-289-4215).

Chamber of Commerce: Keweenaw Peninsula C of C, Box 336, 326 Shelden Ave., Houghton, MI 49931 (906-482-5240).

Recent Master Angler Catches: None known.

Special Regulations: None known.

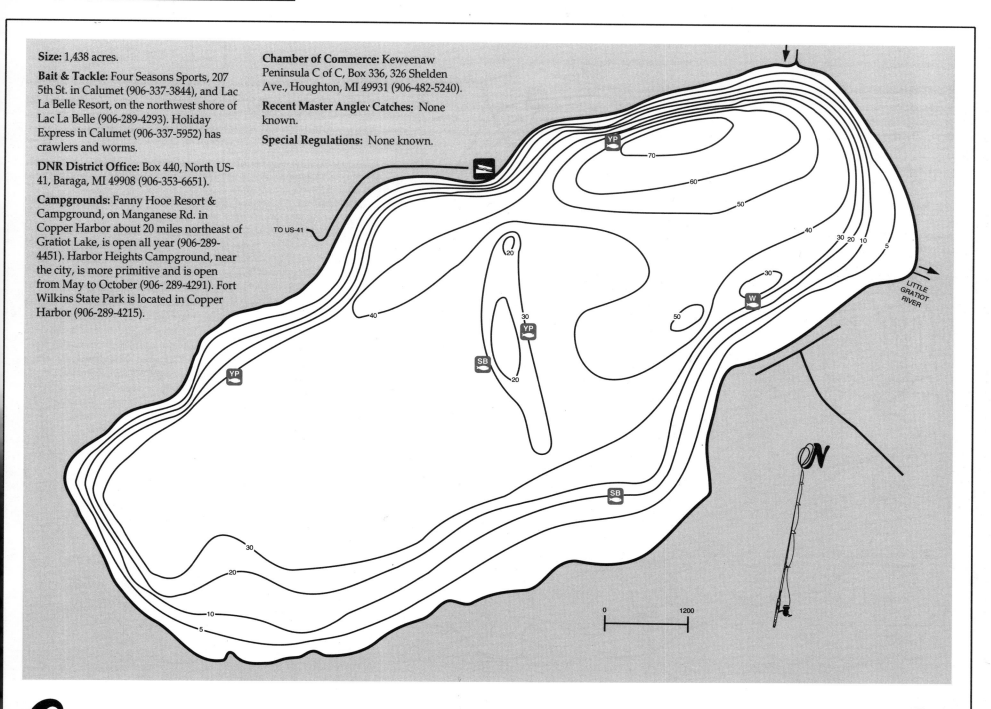

Gratiot Lake, the largest lake in Keweenaw County, is located about two miles southeast of the U.S. Air Force Calumet Radar Base. This clear, clean, beautiful lake is surrounded by northern hardwood forests and is nestled among high hills ranging to the north and west. Several small streams enter the lake. Its outflow is the headwaters of the Little Gratiot River, which flows four miles to Lac La Belle.

The lake's average depth is 25 to 30 feet, about 20 percent exceeds 40 feet, and the deepest spot is 78 feet. Extensive shoal areas, which are mostly sand interspersed with gravel and rubble, range from 75 to 1,200 feet in width. Muck and silt constitute the lake bottom beyond 20 feet of depth.

Vegetation is sparse except for the south and west sides, and there is little log cover throughout the lake. On the other hand, there are plenty of rocks. Ninety brush shelters installed along the 15-foot contour on the north shore are mostly gone. Remnants of another 60 shelters, added along the east shore in 1958, remain.

Surveys/Stocking: The original survey in 1926 found yellow perch and northern pike abundant, rock bass and smallmouth bass in fair numbers, a good supply of white suckers, and a few brook trout. Fifty years ago the lake served up giant northern pike, which were big enough to win national fishing contests sponsored by Field and Stream magazine. Stocking began in 1934 with largemouth bass, followed by walleye fry, northern pike and tiger muskies.

When smelt began showing up in the 1980s, fisheries biologists introduced walleye and rainbow trout fingerlings to take advantage of them.

The lake was last surveyed in 1987 when researchers collected 135 yellow perch that averaged 7.7 inches each. Smallmouth bass to 16 inches were moderately abundant. Suckers and rock bass, however, made up 80 percent of the biomass collected. Pike numbers remain depressed, but the few walleyes and rainbow trout taken then encouraged managers to continue stocking.

In 1991 they released 15,000 rainbow trout fingerlings and 15,000 walleye fingerlings. The rainbow program, however, now appears to be over.

Tactics to Try: Yellow perch are currently the hot item in Gratiot Lake, and ice anglers working the 40-foot contour with small teardrop spoons baited with pieces of smelt catch jumboes. The lake contains smelt, and anglers can try for them, as well as for perch and walleyes after dark by fishing with tiny pieces of worm or small minnows under a lantern's glow.

Perch are available in summer, too, along with dandy smallmouth bass. Cast spinnerbaits or toss jigs and minnows around individual rocks and over gravel spits to 20 feet deep. Light line and finesse tactics work best in the clear lake for both bass and walleyes, which tend to concentrate in water to 35 or even 40 feet deep. Drift night crawlers and ribbon leeches or use a slip bobber to put presentations on target.

Access: A state improved access site on the northwest shore includes a paved boat launch ramp, courtesy pier, toilets and parking for eight vehicles. There is no place to rent a boat.

LAC LA BELLE

Fishing Opportunities: Smallmouth Bass—Good to Excellent; Walleyes, Northern Pike and Black Crappies—Good; Yellow Perch—Fair to Good.

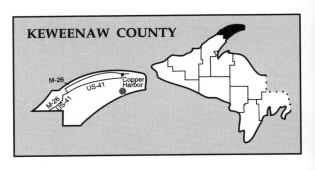

KEWEENAW COUNTY

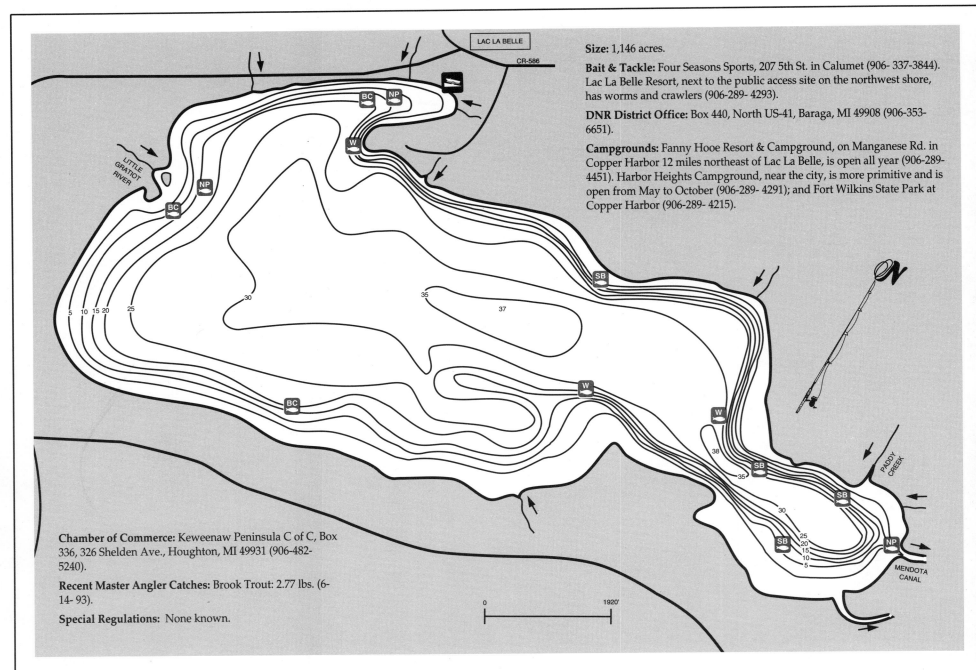

Size: 1,146 acres.

Bait & Tackle: Four Seasons Sports, 207 5th St. in Calumet (906- 337-3844). Lac La Belle Resort, next to the public access site on the northwest shore, has worms and crawlers (906-289- 4293).

DNR District Office: Box 440, North US-41, Baraga, MI 49908 (906-353-6651).

Campgrounds: Fanny Hooe Resort & Campground, on Manganese Rd. in Copper Harbor 12 miles northeast of Lac La Belle, is open all year (906-289-4451). Harbor Heights Campground, near the city, is more primitive and is open from May to October (906-289- 4291); and Fort Wilkins State Park at Copper Harbor (906-289- 4215).

Chamber of Commerce: Keweenaw Peninsula C of C, Box 336, 326 Shelden Ave., Houghton, MI 49931 (906-482-5240).

Recent Master Angler Catches: Brook Trout: 2.77 lbs. (6-14- 93).

Special Regulations: None known.

ac La Belle, which is located in northeast Keweenaw County about a dozen miles southwest of Copper Harbor, is connected to Lake Superior's Bete Grise Bay via the Mendota Ship Canal. Hilly, forested country surrounds the lake, and an extensive cedar swamp lies along the northeast, south and southeast shores. Lac La Belle is fed by the Little Gratiot River, which enters from the east side, and a number of small, intermittent streams.

Shoal areas are mostly sand, even to depths of 25 feet, but deeper portions of the lake bottom are muck-covered with rocky patches showing through. Water clarity is stained a light to medium brown. The lake contains bulrushes and other vegetation in shoreline areas but rock and log cover is scarce.

Fishing pressure has increased considerably the past couple of years, always a sign that fishing is good.

Surveys/Stocking: When the lake was first surveyed in 1926, researchers found northern pike, walleyes, yellow perch and white suckers, along with a few smallmouth bass and saugers. Over the years managers have stocked smallmouth bass, walleyes and tiger muskies.

Although the lake has a reputation for good fishing, a 1987 DNR net survey did not confirm these reports. The nets collected a few large crappies and a fair number of smallmouth bass and pike, but no lunkers. The biggest bass was 18 inches, and the biggest northern taped 28 inches. Average size of the 343 bass netted was 7.1 inches, but rock bass, bullheads and white suckers comprised 70 percent of the fyke net collection by weight. Four walleyes from 8 to 13 inches indicated survival of recent plants.

Each year from 1985 through 1990, the DNR stocked walleye fingerlings for a total release of about 49,000 fish. The lake has not been stocked in recent years.

Tactics to Try: Thanks to the ship canal, Lake Superior salmon, trout and other species have free access to the lake. Smelt runs in spring attract these fish; in August soon-to-spawn salmon begin showing up. Better fishing occurs just into Bete Grise Bay. Most fishermen come for Lac La Belle's warm-water residents anyway.

The lake is tops for smallmouths, and the fishing peaks in late June and early July when spawners spread out over the bulrush-infested shallows on the east end. Perch-colored Shad Raps and white Mister Twisters are hot lures. Minnows are the best live bait.

Lac La Belle has an historic, native population of walleyes, and the big fish are coming back thanks to DNR stockings. Night crawlers and harnesses with bright-colored blades are preferred, although trolling and jig fishing tactics also rate. Most summertime walleyes are taken in 30 feet of water.

Crappie fishing has its peaks and valleys due to annual recruitment or the lack of it. June is the best time, and orange jigs tipped with small minnows is the best method to try. The crappies move around a great deal.

Try the shipping channel for northern pike The lake currently holds lots of perch, but most of them are small.

Access: An improved access site on the lake's north side includes a paved boat launch ramp, courtesy pier, toilets and parking for 44 vehicles. Boats may be rented at Lac La Belle Resort (see Bait & Tackle listing).

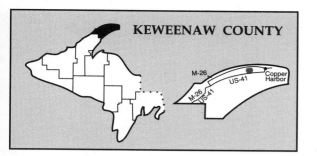
LAKE MEDORA

Fishing Opportunities: Walleyes—Good to Excellent; Yellow Perch and Smallmouth Bass-Fair to Good; Whitefish—Available.

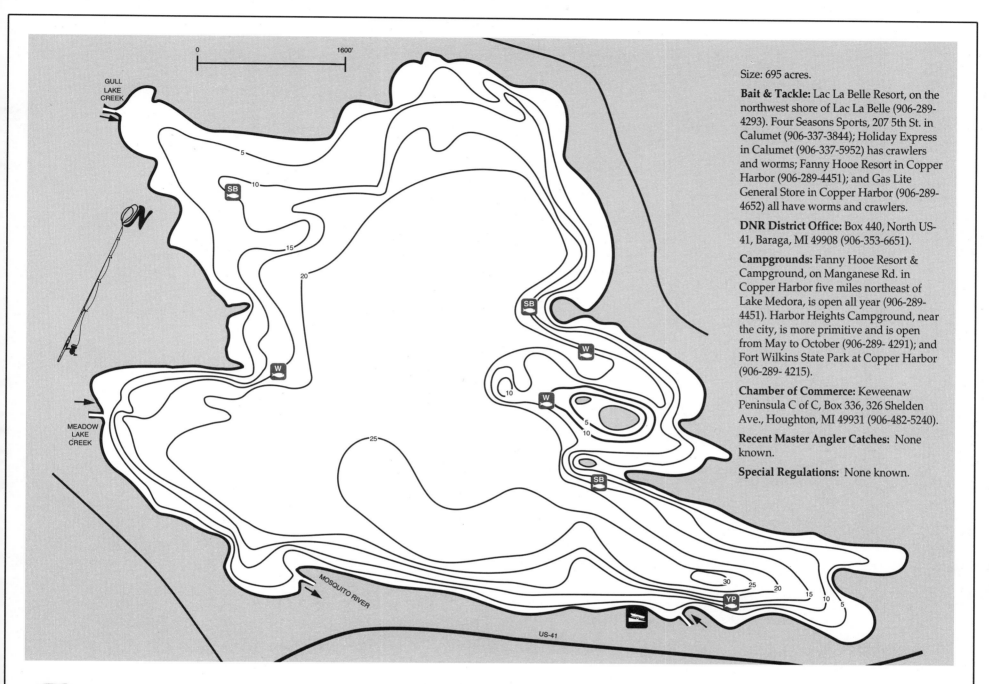

Size: 695 acres.

Bait & Tackle: Lac La Belle Resort, on the northwest shore of Lac La Belle (906-289-4293). Four Seasons Sports, 207 5th St. in Calumet (906-337-3844); Holiday Express in Calumet (906-337-5952) has crawlers and worms; Fanny Hooe Resort in Copper Harbor (906-289-4451); and Gas Lite General Store in Copper Harbor (906-289-4652) all have worms and crawlers.

DNR District Office: Box 440, North US-41, Baraga, MI 49908 (906-353-6651).

Campgrounds: Fanny Hooe Resort & Campground, on Manganese Rd. in Copper Harbor five miles northeast of Lake Medora, is open all year (906-289-4451). Harbor Heights Campground, near the city, is more primitive and is open from May to October (906-289- 4291); and Fort Wilkins State Park at Copper Harbor (906-289- 4215).

Chamber of Commerce: Keweenaw Peninsula C of C, Box 336, 326 Shelden Ave., Houghton, MI 49931 (906-482-5240).

Recent Master Angler Catches: None known.

Special Regulations: None known.

Lake Medora is located about five miles south of Copper Harbor in north Keweenaw County. Formed more than 100 years ago when the Mosquito River was dammed, the brown-stained lake is surrounded by mixed hardwoods and conifers except on the south shore where there are several summer homes. Although the maximum depth of the lake is 30 feet, most of the bottom ranges from 20 to 25 feet deep. The lake's outlet is the Mosquito River, which is a tributary to the Montreal River. Gull Lake Creek and Meadow Lake Creek feed the lake.

Early attempts to provide a fishery beyond the original species of smallmouth bass, yellow perch and whitefish date from 1930 when largemouth bass, bluegills and yellow perch were stocked. Over the years DNR managers have added lake, brook and rainbow trout. Walleyes were introduced to help control an exploding perch population.

Because Lake Medora contains whitefish, which cannot withstand chemical treatment, the DNR began a manual removal program for small perch in 1981. Workers removed more than three tons of perch, which allowed walleye fingerlings to take hold. That program has been so successful that manual removal is no longer needed. In fact, the DNR recently added 4,387 adult perch from Bob Lake to beef up populations and to give walleyes something to eat.

Surveys/Stocking: The DNR scrapped its trout planting program in favor of walleyes, which are now naturally reproducing to preclude the need for stocking. A June 1992 fyke net survey turned up plenty of smallmouth bass, although it appears as though anglers crop them soon after the fish reach legal size. Yellow perch numbers were low, although the 26 collected averaged 12 inches. Walleyes averaged 14.7 inches and included fish to 19 inches. All age classes, however, were growing below the state average, indicating an unbalanced predator-to-prey ratio.

In a 1987 survey the nets yielded only two whitefish, but in the fall of 1983 the lake contained an abundant population of spawners scattered throughout. The DNR has not stocked the lake in recent years.

Tactics to Try: The lake is presently full of small walleyes, which scatter throughout the lake to provide good fishing. Start in the 10-foot-deep contour around the east- side island and drift or troll the shoreline looking for structure. Bright-colored jigs with leeches are very productive, as are Rapalas, perch-colored Shad Raps and Wally Divers.

Good places to start looking for smallmouths are the west-side bays, particularly the more northern bay. White, pink or yellow Fuzz-E Grubs fished clean or with a piece of crawler or small minnow work well.

Lake Medora hosts mega mayfly hatches all summer long. Fly rod fishermen can take bass, walleyes, big perch and even the occasional whitefish at this time. An ice fishery is all but nonexistent on this lake. For anyone wanting to try for big orange-finned yellow perch, we recommend shiner minnows and Russian Spoons or small Swedish Pimples.

Access: A state improved access site on the southeast shore includes a paved boat launch ramp, courtesy pier, toilets and parking for five vehicles. There is no place to rent a boat.

MANGANESE LAKE

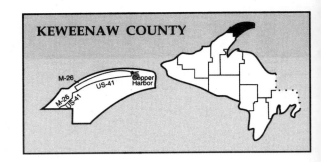
Fishing Opportunities: Brook Trout—Good to Excellent.

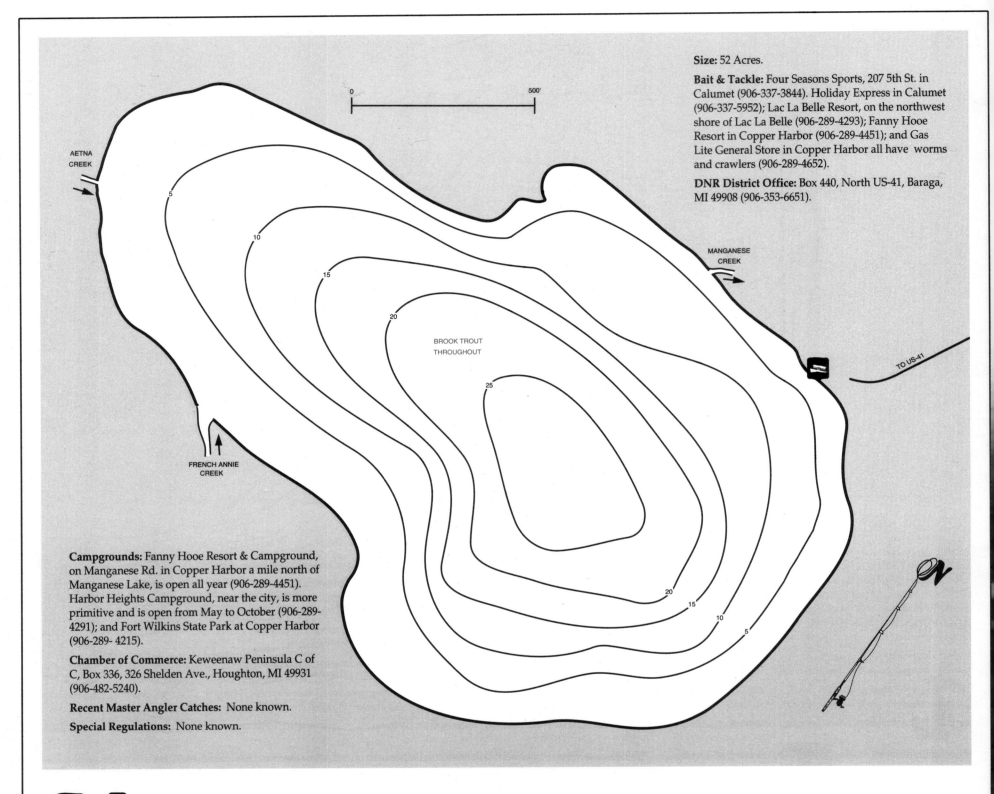

Size: 52 Acres.

Bait & Tackle: Four Seasons Sports, 207 5th St. in Calumet (906-337-3844). Holiday Express in Calumet (906-337-5952); Lac La Belle Resort, on the northwest shore of Lac La Belle (906-289-4293); Fanny Hooe Resort in Copper Harbor (906-289-4451); and Gas Lite General Store in Copper Harbor all have worms and crawlers (906-289-4652).

DNR District Office: Box 440, North US-41, Baraga, MI 49908 (906-353-6651).

Campgrounds: Fanny Hooe Resort & Campground, on Manganese Rd. in Copper Harbor a mile north of Manganese Lake, is open all year (906-289-4451). Harbor Heights Campground, near the city, is more primitive and is open from May to October (906-289-4291); and Fort Wilkins State Park at Copper Harbor (906-289- 4215).

Chamber of Commerce: Keweenaw Peninsula C of C, Box 336, 326 Shelden Ave., Houghton, MI 49931 (906-482-5240).

Recent Master Angler Catches: None known.

Special Regulations: None known.

Manganese Lake is a clear-water trout lake located in north Keweenaw County a mile south of Copper Harbor. The beautiful lake is situated amid hardwood-covered hills with rocky outcroppings. It has a maximum depth of 27 feet, and a gradually sloping shoal of mostly sand with some gravel and pulpy peat in deeper areas. Composition of the shore, which is owned by Lake Superior Land Company, is mostly rock although there is a sandy beach on the north side.

The lake's main inflows are French Annie Creek, which enters from the south side, and Aetna Creek, which comes in from the southwest. The key outlet is Manganese Creek, on the north side, which flows on to Lake Fanny Hooe.

All the tributaries are noted for brook trout.

Surveys/Stocking: Biologists have long managed Manganese Lake for brook trout, and records indicate they first stocked brookies in 1929. Grayling eggs were introduced in 1960, along with smallmouth bass fingerlings in 1968 and largemouth fingerlings the following year. Historically, the lake also contained whitefish.

A May 1990 fyke and gill net survey indicated that white suckers constituted 80 percent of the lake's biomass. Small yellow perch were another problem. Although researchers collected some nice smallmouths, their nets yielded no trout. Manganese Lake was treated with rotenone in October 1991.

In 1992 managers released 1,000 adult and 5,250 yearling brook trout, and in 1993 they stocked an estimated 5,250 more yearling brookies.

Tactics to Try: The lake hosts big hatches of mayflies in early July just before dark. Trout feed on them, along with stoneflies, red-bellied dace, crayfish and other foods. It is a good fly fishing lake, plus it provides good sport through the ice for jig fishermen using waxworms and tiny spoons. Because Manganese is not a designated trout lake, fishing is permitted year around.

Access: There is no public launch site; however, through the courtesy of the Lake Superior Land Company, anglers are permitted to launch their canoes or cartoppers off the sand beach on the lake's north end. The DNR is considering purchasing land from the company on both Manganese Lake and nearby Lake Fanny Hooe. There is no place to rent a boat on Manganese Lake.

BELLE LAKE

Fishing Opportunities: Northern Pike and Walleyes—Good; Splake—Fair to Good; Yellow Perch—Poor.

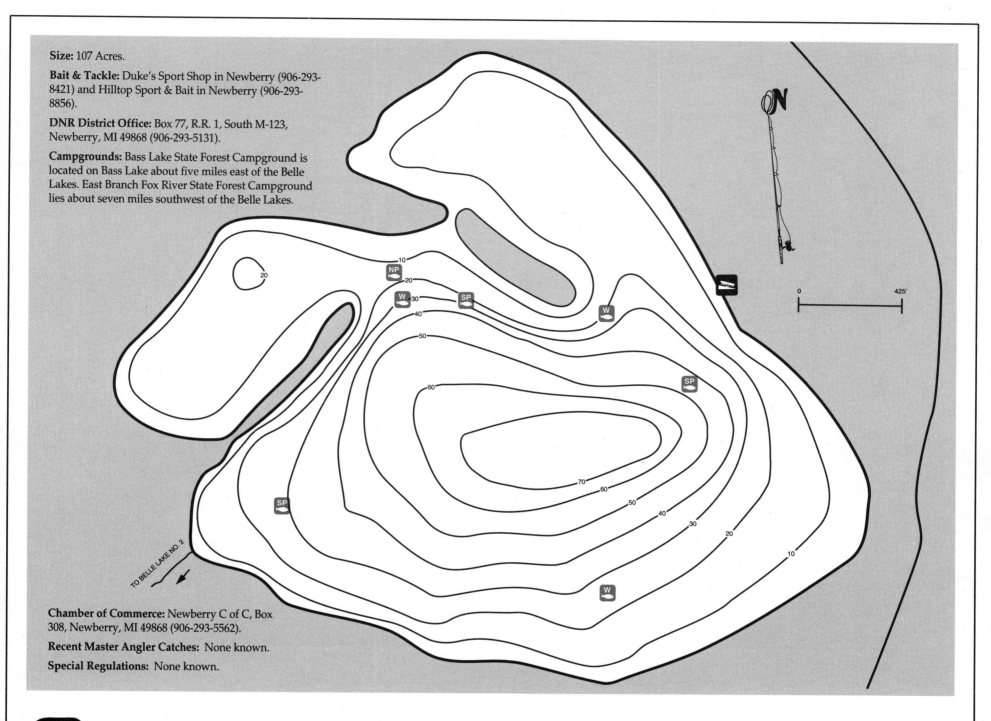

Size: 107 Acres.

Bait & Tackle: Duke's Sport Shop in Newberry (906-293-8421) and Hilltop Sport & Bait in Newberry (906-293-8856).

DNR District Office: Box 77, R.R. 1, South M-123, Newberry, MI 49868 (906-293-5131).

Campgrounds: Bass Lake State Forest Campground is located on Bass Lake about five miles east of the Belle Lakes. East Branch Fox River State Forest Campground lies about seven miles southwest of the Belle Lakes.

Chamber of Commerce: Newberry C of C, Box 308, Newberry, MI 49868 (906-293-5562).

Recent Master Angler Catches: None known.

Special Regulations: None known.

Belle Lake is located in westcentral Luce County about 12 miles northwest of McMillan. Sandy soils and level terrain to moderately rolling hills covered with mixed hardwoods and pine surround the lake. It is often referred to as Belle Lake No. 1 or Upper Belle Lake. The water is clear and well-oxygenated except for the deepest hole, which plunges to 85 feet.

About 40 percent of the clear-water lake is less than 15 feet deep, and shoal areas are a mixture of sand and fibrous peat. Belle Lake No. 1 is is connected to 25-acre Belle Lake No. 2 by a channel that is 4 to 10 feet wide. This lake has a maximum depth of 17 feet and water that is a light-brown color.

Surveys/Stocking: The DNR has managed the resource as a two- story lake and over many years has stocked rainbows, splake and browns. After a manual removal of undesirable species, managers introduced walleyes in 1984.

A June 1991 gill and fyke net survey found that 43 percent of the biomass lifted were northern pike to 36 inches long and that pike and walleyes were the lake's top two predators. There was evidence that some of the fat walleyes, which averaged 13 to 15 inches and ranged in length to 22 inches, had reproduced naturally. Yellow perch comprised 24 percent of the biomass, but very few were larger than 7 inches. This may be the result of competition from young splake. The nets also turned up pumpkinseed sunfish, rock bass and a couple of smallmouths.

In 1991 managers stocked 5,000 splake yearlings, and in 1993 they planted out an estimated 4,490 splake yearlings.

Tactics to Try: The 184 brush shelters erected 40 years ago in 8 to 12 feet of water throughout the southern half of the lake and along both long sides of the island off the northwest point are all but gone. Anglers may find occasional gamefish in these areas.

Deep-diving crankbaits in crayfish or perch color are effective for walleyes when trolled or cast along the 10- to 30-foot-deep inclines. Vertical jigging with stand-up jigs and leeches is also productive in this lake.

The well-marked contours and defined points make for good pike fishing if trollers keep their plugs and spoons near bottom or over weeds. Belle Lake No. 2 is also supposedly good for pike because it serves as a nursery for forage species.

Splake snap at small minnows pinned to Russian hooks or teardrop spoons. Wigglers, red worms and single salmon eggs also produce at times. Fish move off the points in spring and tend to concentrate in deeper water during the summer. Begin jigging near bottom and then move the offering higher, by degrees, until you find biters. Sonar helps tremendously in locating fish in the deep-water lake.

Access: The lake is accessible from M-48 via CR-421 and truck trails. There are two public access sites on the northeast side. One is a camp with an easement. Both feature steep banks and can cause difficulty for boats larger than 18 feet. There is no place to rent a boat.

MOON LAKE

Fishing Opportunities: Brook Trout—Good to Excellent.

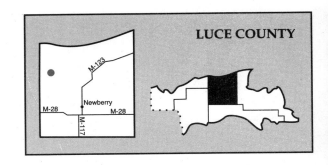
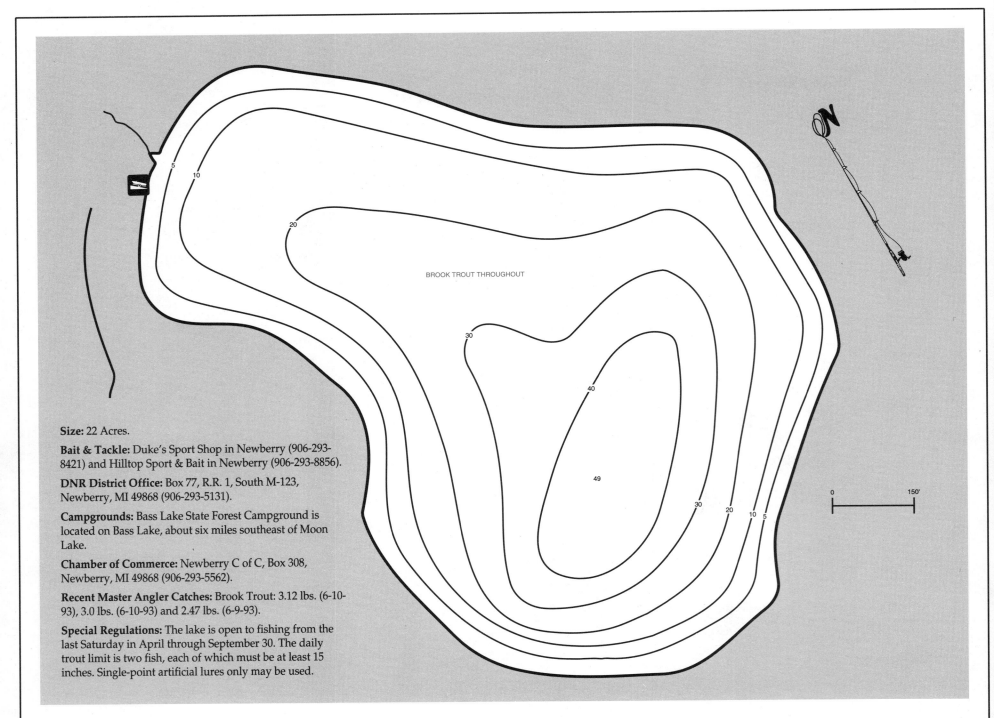

Size: 22 Acres.

Bait & Tackle: Duke's Sport Shop in Newberry (906-293-8421) and Hilltop Sport & Bait in Newberry (906-293-8856).

DNR District Office: Box 77, R.R. 1, South M-123, Newberry, MI 49868 (906-293-5131).

Campgrounds: Bass Lake State Forest Campground is located on Bass Lake, about six miles southeast of Moon Lake.

Chamber of Commerce: Newberry C of C, Box 308, Newberry, MI 49868 (906-293-5562).

Recent Master Angler Catches: Brook Trout: 3.12 lbs. (6-10-93), 3.0 lbs. (6-10-93) and 2.47 lbs. (6-9-93).

Special Regulations: The lake is open to fishing from the last Saturday in April through September 30. The daily trout limit is two fish, each of which must be at least 15 inches. Single-point artificial lures only may be used.

Moon Lake is a pear-shaped lake of 22 clear-water acres located in northwest Luce County about 15 miles northwest of McMillan. The undeveloped lake lies in a deeply wooded pocket of mixed beech and maple with some white pine, spruce and balsam on the fringe. Steep hills of sand and clay loam surround the lake, and bog pockets on the north and south shores indicate an old lake basin that has filled in.

The surrounding land is owned by Cleveland Cliffs Iron Company, but the DNR has an access easement lease with the company.

The lake's shoal areas are mostly sand to 10 or 15 feet deep with pulpy peat constituting the deeper middle portion. Fish find shelter among a few logs in the shoals and overhanging leatherleaf along with a few scattered water lilies. The lake is fairly deep (to 49 feet), with only about 20 percent of the surface acreage less than five feet deep.

Surveys/Stocking: Historically, the DNR has managed the lake for trout, stocking various combinations of brook and rainbow trout from 1940 through 1963, then switching over to splake from 1964 to 1974. Assinica-strain brookies first went into the lake in 1975, and special fishing regulations were imposed the next year to develop a trophy brook trout fishery.

Technicians applied rotenone to Moon Lake in 1979 to chemically reclaim the lake from small yellow perch that dominated the fish population. They then continued to stock brook trout — those collected during a November 1984 fyke net survey ranged from 7½ inches to nearly 22 inches.

In 1991 managers released 100 adult and 1,000 fingerling brook trout; in 1992 they stocked 1,000 fingerlings; and in 1993 they planted out an estimated 1,000 more.

Tactics to Try: Occasional remnants of 240 fish shelters installed in 1957 in the 10- to 20-foot-deep contour around the lake remain. These are good places to try, especially in early June, as well as wading and casting from shore. Clear water, however, makes Moon Lake trout wary, and they can be tough to catch. Best conditions call for a dark sky and a mayfly hatch in progress. Fly fishermen can have a heyday then. Bring both nymph and adult patterns; muddlers are a good streamer choice.

Another worthwhile tactic is to fish Mepps Comet spinners or Black Fury spinners in size 0, 1 or 2, but be sure to clip two hooks of the treble (see Special Regulations above). Recent DNR Master Angler catches came on Mister Twister-type jigs from 20-foot depths or less. Hot jig colors were white, yellow or a brown with a red head.

Access: The access site is off CR-455 and the Grand Marais Truck Trail. The site is undeveloped, but anglers can launch a canoe or cartopper. There is no place to rent a boat.

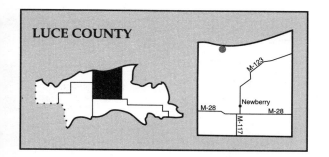

MUSKALLONGE LAKE

Fishing Opportunities: Yellow Perch and Northern Pike—Good to Excellent; Smallmouth Bass and Walleyes—Fair to Good.

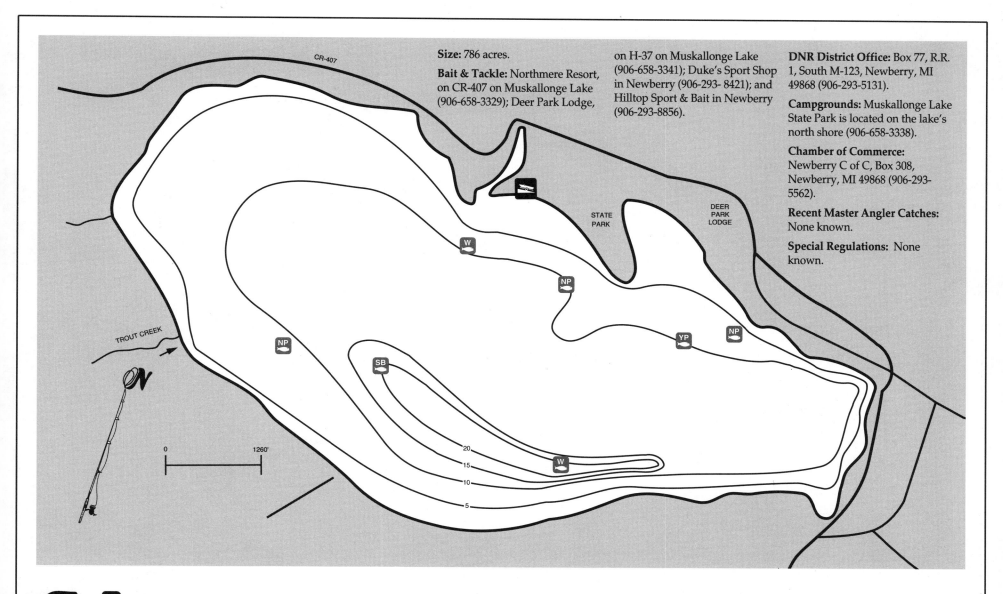

Size: 786 acres.

Bait & Tackle: Northmere Resort, on CR-407 on Muskallonge Lake (906-658-3329); Deer Park Lodge, on H-37 on Muskallonge Lake (906-658-3341); Duke's Sport Shop in Newberry (906-293- 8421); and Hilltop Sport & Bait in Newberry (906-293-8856).

DNR District Office: Box 77, R.R. 1, South M-123, Newberry, MI 49868 (906-293-5131).

Campgrounds: Muskallonge Lake State Park is located on the lake's north shore (906-658-3338).

Chamber of Commerce: Newberry C of C, Box 308, Newberry, MI 49868 (906-293-5562).

Recent Master Angler Catches: None known.

Special Regulations: None known.

Muskallonge Lake is located in northcentral Luce County on Lake Superior about 20 miles east of Grand Marais. The lake supports some development except for the south shoreline which remains mostly natural. It is not an easy lake to fish because of its shallow, weedy nature, and by late summer many anglers give up in frustration.

Trout Creek enters from the southwest corner. The lake is fairly clear but takes on a stained color by late summer due to chopped vegetation from boaters. Fishing pressure is heavy in summer and all but non-existent in winter due to the lake's remoteness and proximity to frigid Lake Superior. Summer visitors include loons and eagles.

Surveys/Stocking: The lake first received hatchery fish in 1925 when 2,400 smallmouth fingerlings were released. Since then fisheries managers have planted out largemouth bass, walleyes, northern pike, northern muskellunge and bluegills. A DNR gill, fyke and trap net survey in August 1992 showed that bullheads continued to dominate the lake, in spite of three manual removals during a 15-year period that resulted in about 1,400 pounds of the species taken out.

In spite of this problem, the lake shows a good balance of sport fish in attractive size ranges. Although northern pike and smallmouth bass appear to have been cropped heavily by anglers, perch, rock bass and walleyes show little sign of fishing pressure. Walleyes collected ranged from 17 to 22 inches, pike from 9 to 31 inches, smallmouths to 17 inches, and perch to 11 inches.

In 1991 managers released 24,165 walleye fingerlings; in 1993 they stocked an estimated 20,500 walleye fingerlings.

Tactics to Try: The lake has been a U.P. perch and pike mainstay for years. Perch run 7 to 13 inches, and the average pike is sub-legal to barely legal at 24 inches, although larger fish are available. For northerns in the 34- to 37-inch range, pick an overcast day when the water is choppy. Sunken islands off the southeast corner of the state park, which is located on the lake's north shore, are good places to try. But northerns (and an occasional muskie from earlier plants) can show up anywhere and are not overly fussy about which lures and bait they'll take.

These same locations produce perch in spring for anglers using worms or minnows and in mid to late summer for those switching to leeches.

The best walleye fishing occurs along developing weedlines paralleling the south shore in spring and summer. Hot hardware includes one- and two-blade bass spinnerbaits in chartreuse or white. Another trick: cast and retrieve over bottom whole night crawlers pinned to weedless sproat hooks. Our source says walleye fishing peaked last year but admitted that successful anglers are those who work at it and know how to fish weeds.

Smallmouth bass action is good in spring over spawning beds. Try beetle spins and spinnerbaits. It picks up again in August and improves through the fall. Fish minnows or crawlers after dark with slip bobbers or burn alphabet cranks over the weeds. Bulrushes on the west side are especially productive at times.

Access: The improved access site at the state park includes a paved boat launch ramp, courtesy pier, toilets and parking for a limited number of vehicles. The launch facility can accommodate larger boats thanks to deep water at the ramp's end. To rent a boat, contact Northmere Resort, Deer Park Lodge (see both under Bait & Tackle Listing), or Superior Four Seasons (906-658-3327).

PERCH LAKE

Fishing Opportunities: Smallmouth Bass—Good; Splake, Bluegills and Yellow Perch—Fair to Good; Northern Pike and Largemouth Bass—Available to Fair.

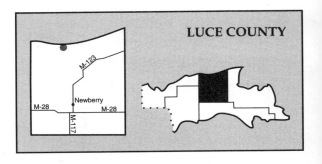

LUCE COUNTY

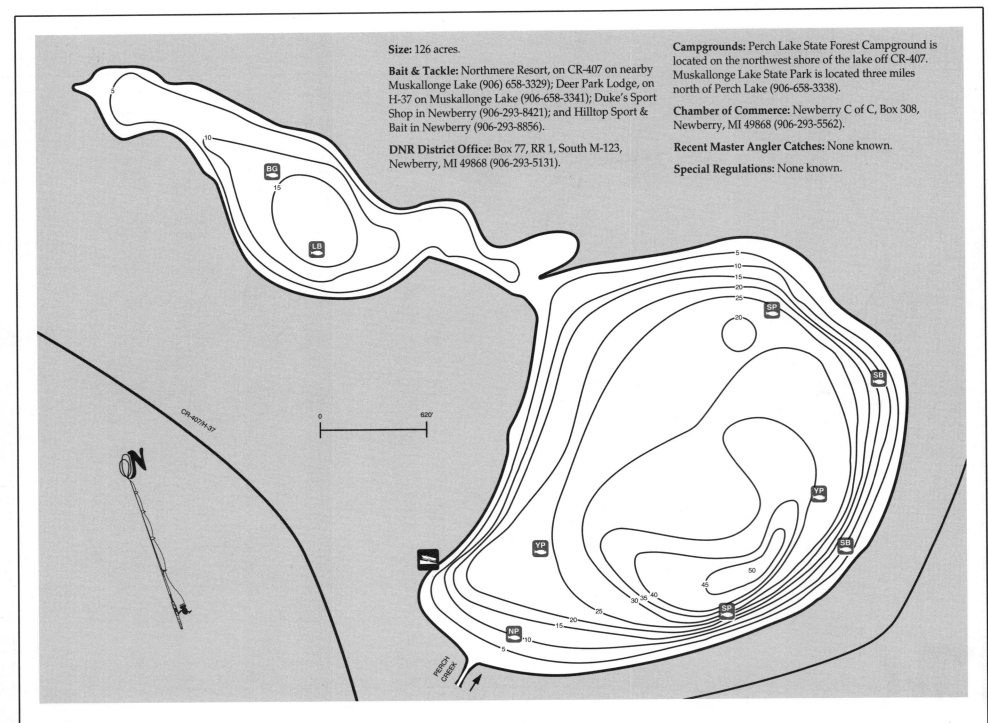

Size: 126 acres.

Bait & Tackle: Northmere Resort, on CR-407 on nearby Muskallonge Lake (906) 658-3329); Deer Park Lodge, on H-37 on Muskallonge Lake (906-658-3341); Duke's Sport Shop in Newberry (906-293-8421); and Hilltop Sport & Bait in Newberry (906-293-8856).

DNR District Office: Box 77, RR 1, South M-123, Newberry, MI 49868 (906-293-5131).

Campgrounds: Perch Lake State Forest Campground is located on the northwest shore of the lake off CR-407. Muskallonge Lake State Park is located three miles north of Perch Lake (906-658-3338).

Chamber of Commerce: Newberry C of C, Box 308, Newberry, MI 49868 (906-293-5562).

Recent Master Angler Catches: None known.

Special Regulations: None known.

Perch Lake is located in northcentral Luce County on Lake Superior about 20 miles north of Newberry. The surrounding shoreline is wooded, with some brush and swampy areas, and there are a few cottages around a big, shallow slough of the north arm. the south shoreline features a high, sandy bluff. Much of the lake averages 25 feet or deeper, and sharp-dropping shoals are evident. Perch Creek enters from the southwest corner.

The bottom composition is mostly sand in shoal areas and peat in deeper spots. Gravel and rubble are sparse, but there is an abundance of logs and some brush. The clear water sometimes takes on a blue-green cast. Vegetation consists of bulrushes, sedges and pondweed and is considered sparse.

Surveys/Stocking: A DNR fyke and gill net survey in June 1988 was dominated by yellow perch (89 percent of the biomass), which averaged 7 inches. Six northern

pike ranged from 19 inches to 29 inches each and averaged 3½ pounds. The nets also collected rock bass to 10 inches and five young splake. An earlier survey produced more than 100 smallmouth bass along with some largemouth bass.

The management goal is for a two-story lake. In 1990 technicians thinned the lake of yellow perch, removing a total of 10,135 fish weighing 692 pounds and transferring them to Blind Sucker Flooding.

In 1991 managers stocked 7,700 splake; in 1992 they planted out 3,000 splake; and in 1993 they released an estimated 3,240 splake. All fish were yearlings.

Tactics to Try: The weedy northern arm is good for bluegills, pumpkin-seed sunfish and largemouth bass.

Tossing Zara Spooks, Torpedoes or Floating Rapalas around individual drowned trees all around the lake produces largemouth and smallmouth bass and northern pike. Black is a hot color along with frog-finished patterns and those lures featuring olive-green with white.

The best smallmouth fishing occurs on the lake's east end over flats areas from 10 to 13 feet deep. Troll with Rapalas or drift a minnow with the aid of a slip bobber.

To catch splake in fall and spring, slow troll ⅛-oz. Dardevles or Little Cleos in silver, blue-and-silver, or orange-and-gold colors. The trick is to keep a tight line and work lures over hard-bottom areas via a quiet electric motor or a deft canoe paddle. In summer, hang a lantern over the boat side in 15 to 20 feet of water and fish with a wiggler, piece of night crawler, or a miniature marshmallow. Slip bobbers make the best presentations.

Since the perch-thinning project, we have reports of good ice fishing for big yellow-bellies. Try wigglers or small minnows attached to a bobber.

Access: The improved access site at the state park includes a paved boat launch ramp, courtesy pier, toilets and parking for a limited number of vehicles. There is no place to rent a boat.

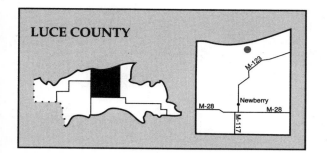

PIKE LAKE

Fishing Opportunities: Northern Pike—Good to Excellent; Walleyes and Yellow Perch—Fair to Good.

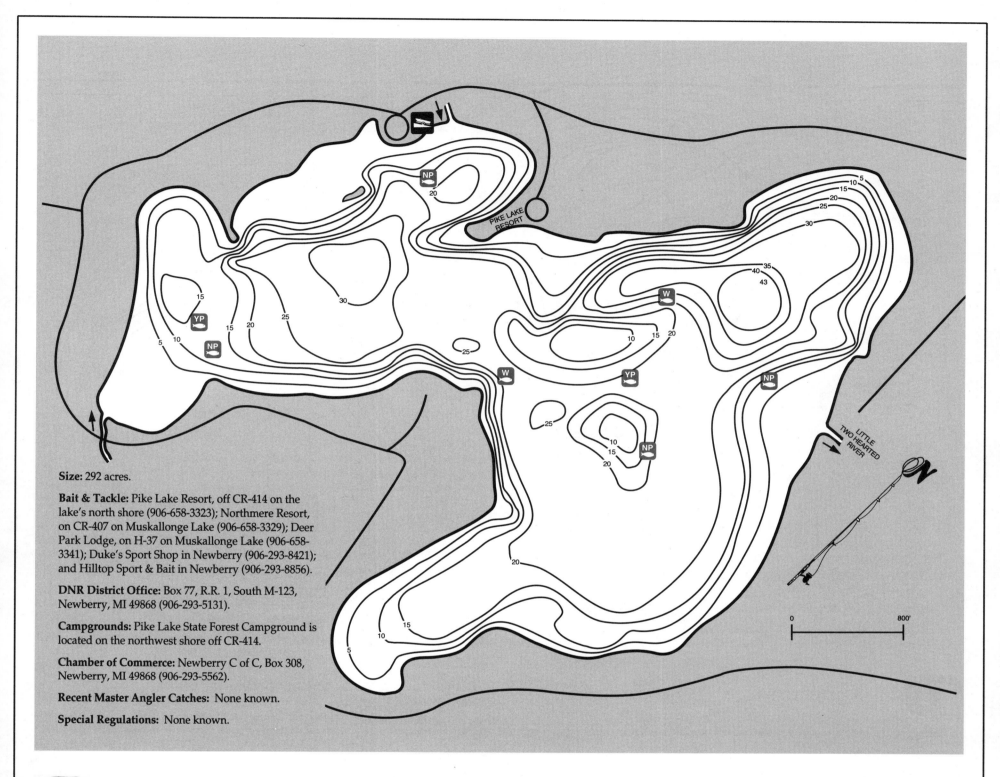

Size: 292 acres.

Bait & Tackle: Pike Lake Resort, off CR-414 on the lake's north shore (906-658-3323); Northmere Resort, on CR-407 on Muskallonge Lake (906-658-3329); Deer Park Lodge, on H-37 on Muskallonge Lake (906-658-3341); Duke's Sport Shop in Newberry (906-293-8421); and Hilltop Sport & Bait in Newberry (906-293-8856).

DNR District Office: Box 77, R.R. 1, South M-123, Newberry, MI 49868 (906-293-5131).

Campgrounds: Pike Lake State Forest Campground is located on the northwest shore off CR-414.

Chamber of Commerce: Newberry C of C, Box 308, Newberry, MI 49868 (906-293-5562).

Recent Master Angler Catches: None known.

Special Regulations: None known.

Pike Lake is located in northeast Luce County roughly halfway between Muskallonge and Tahquamenon state parks and about 25 miles northeast of Newberry. The lake is recharged by a small, unnamed creek that enters from a southwest bay, and it outlets on the east side into the Little Two Hearted River.

The undeveloped lake lies in a remote area of the Lake Superior State Forest but receives a moderate amount of fishing pressure. The north shore has experienced creeping development in recent years. Contour breaks are well-pronounced throughout, and the deepest spot is 50 feet.

Surveys/Stocking: A September 1992 DNR boomshocking survey turned up a large number of yellow perch and young-of-the-year walleyes. In June 1989 a fish-

eries crew using fyke nets found good survival and growth of stocked walleyes. Perch and rock bass had increased in numbers from a 1983 survey. Northern pike were also collected. White suckers and brown bullheads have been periodically removed to give young walleyes a better chance at survival.

Stocking records date to 1930 when largemouth bass were released. In 1992 managers planted out 12,000 walleye fingerlings, and in 1993 they stocked an estimated 12,000 more.

Tactics to Try: The best pike fishing occurs in spring and fall before weed growth takes over much of the lake. Dead smelt fished on bottom or live shiners, suckers and chubs suspended below huge bobbers are good pike bait then. In summer, target weedlines and either troll with Rapalas or cast Mepps Musky Killer spinners or heavy spoons. The average pike is 20 to 25 inches, but there are heavier fish

in the lake. Early and late in the day are the best times to catch a trophy, especially over basin drop-offs and off the river outlet.

These same areas report good yellow perch fishing action. Try minnows or leaf worms in spring, and then switch to leeches as summer's heat bears down. Fall is a good time to return to minnows. We have no reports of ice fishing action, but it should be good for those willing to snowmobile or hike into the lake.

Walleye fishing is just now coming on and holds great promise for the future. Leech fishermen score in summer and early fall; the best springtime technique is to jig with a half crawler.

Access: The improved access site at the state forest campground includes a paved boat launch ramp, toilets and parking for five vehicles. To rent a boat, contact Pike Lake Resort (see Bait & Tackle listing).

PRETTY LAKE QUIET AREA

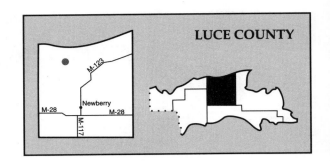

Fishing Opportunities: Pretty Lake: Splake—Good to Excellent.
Long Lake: Largemouth Bass—Fair to Good; Yellow Perch—
Fair.

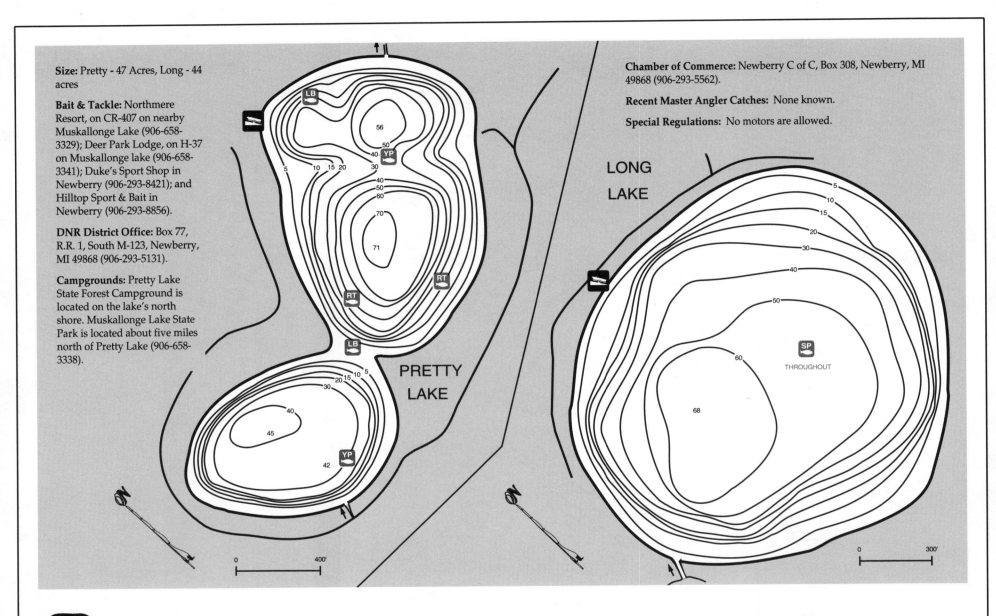

Size: Pretty - 47 Acres, Long - 44 acres

Bait & Tackle: Northmere Resort, on CR-407 on nearby Muskallonge Lake (906-658-3329); Deer Park Lodge, on H-37 on Muskallonge lake (906-658-3341); Duke's Sport Shop in Newberry (906-293-8421); and Hilltop Sport & Bait in Newberry (906-293-8856).

DNR District Office: Box 77, R.R. 1, South M-123, Newberry, MI 49868 (906-293-5131).

Campgrounds: Pretty Lake State Forest Campground is located on the lake's north shore. Muskallonge Lake State Park is located about five miles north of Pretty Lake (906-658-3338).

Chamber of Commerce: Newberry C of C, Box 308, Newberry, MI 49868 (906-293-5562).

Recent Master Angler Catches: None known.

Special Regulations: No motors are allowed.

Pretty and Long lakes are two of several fishing lakes within the Pretty Lake Quiet Area, located in northwest Luce County between Newberry and Grand Marais. The DNR has managed Pretty Lake for rainbow trout and splake since 1960 and successfully rehabilitated it with chemicals to remove undesirable species in 1960, 1963, 1975, 1983 and 1991. These treatments invariably result in good fishing for a few years. Anglers reported catches of splake to 6 pounds during the early 1970s, proving the lake is capable of producing big fish.

Pretty Lake has a fairly steep drop-off and plunges to 68 feet. Shoal areas are sand; deeper water contains pulpy peat. Because little vegetation is present, the DNR installed 111 brush shelters on the north and east shoals in 8 to 10 feet of water. Remnants remain. The lake is fed from an intermittent inlet in the southwest corner.

Long Lake is a light brown in color, and the water is fairly clear. Fish cover consists of shoreline brush, trees, stumps, drowned logs and water lilies. The immediate shoreline of both lakes is mostly flat, and the sandy soils support red and white pine along with maples.

Surveys/Stocking: A June 1990 fyke net survey on Pretty Lake determined that trout survival was poor due to domination by small perch and rock bass—hence the chemical reclamation the following year.

A gill and fyke net survey in August 1985 on Long Lake found poor survival of rainbow trout, possibly because of competition from largemouth bass, which were providing an excellent fishery and showed up in the nets. Researchers' recommendation was to discontinue trout plant and stress bass and perch management.

In 1992 managers stocked Pretty Lake with 1,300 yearling splake, and in 1993 they released an estimated 1,220 more. Long Lake no longer receives hatchery fish.

Tactics to Try: The lakes get virtually no ice-fishing pressure but are worth trying for hardy souls willing to hike in on snowshoes or cross-country skis. In spring, jig and drift anglers on Pretty lake catch splake in water less than 10 feet deep off the southwest corner inlet. Wigglers and small minnows pinned to a teardrop spoon, Russian hook or bare gold hook are effective.

Minnows remain the bait of choice in summer when splake go deeper, but red worms also produce at times. To find out where fish are feeding, start at the bottom in deep water and jig, by degrees, until reaching suspended fish.

In Long Lake, remnants of 50 brush shelters remain off the east, south and north shores of the larger east-side basin in 10 to 15 feet of water. For largemouths, concentrate on lily pads between the basins and along shoreline structure such as logs and the fish shelters themselves. Toss brown or black jigs and pigs, spinnerbaits and rubber worms in blue or purple with metalflake.

Yellow perch, including occasional fish a foot or more in length, can be conned with wigglers or inch-long shiners. Fish will often suspend in 15 to 30 feet of water.

Access: There is no developed boat launch, but fishermen can carry in canoes or lightweight boats and portage through a series of trails to Camp 8, Brush, Otter and Long lakes. To reach Pretty Lake, follow CR-407 north of Newberry, to CR-416 west to Holland Lake, then south to the first lake on the south side. There is no place to rent a boat.

ROUND LAKE

Fishing Opportunities: Walleyes—Good to Excellent; Smallmouth Bass, Yellow Perch and Northern Pike—Fair to Good; Lake Trout—Available.

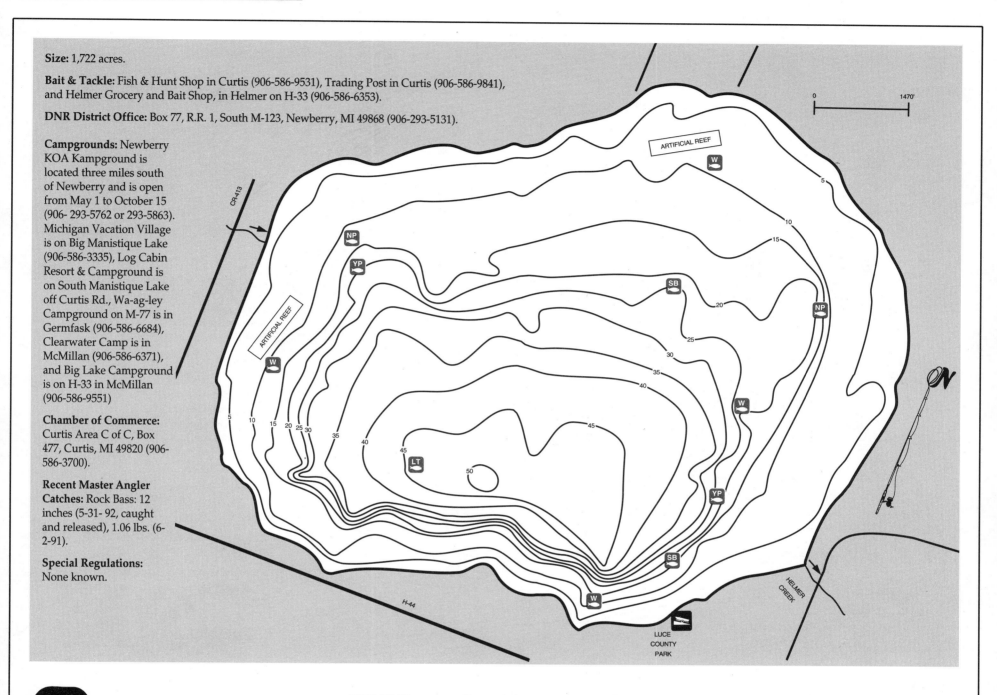

Size: 1,722 acres.

Bait & Tackle: Fish & Hunt Shop in Curtis (906-586-9531), Trading Post in Curtis (906-586-9841), and Helmer Grocery and Bait Shop, in Helmer on H-33 (906-586-6353).

DNR District Office: Box 77, R.R. 1, South M-123, Newberry, MI 49868 (906-293-5131).

Campgrounds: Newberry KOA Kampground is located three miles south of Newberry and is open from May 1 to October 15 (906- 293-5762 or 293-5863). Michigan Vacation Village is on Big Manistique Lake (906-586-3335), Log Cabin Resort & Campground is on South Manistique Lake off Curtis Rd., Wa-ag-ley Campground on M-77 is in Germfask (906-586-6684), Clearwater Camp is in McMillan (906-586-6371), and Big Lake Campground is on H-33 in McMillan (906-586-9551).

Chamber of Commerce: Curtis Area C of C, Box 477, Curtis, MI 49820 (906-586-3700).

Recent Master Angler Catches: Rock Bass: 12 inches (5-31- 92, caught and released), 1.06 lbs. (6-2-91).

Special Regulations: None known.

Round Lake, which is also called North Manistique Lake, is a clear, well-oxygenated lake located in Luce County about 15 miles southwest of Newberry. The bowl-shaped lake averages about 15 feet in depth, and the deepest spot is 50 feet. Many homes and resorts ring the lake. The smallest of the three Manistique Lakes at about two miles across, Round Lake is also the deepest.

Mixed hardwoods and conifers surround the lake along with some cedars on the northeast shore. Helmer Creek outlets from the southeast corner and flows southerly into Big Manistique Lake. Round Lake's bottom is mostly sand, and there are few weedbeds and a limited amount of gravel.

An artificial reef constructed in 1978 and with segments along the west and north shores apparently is too small to prompt walleyes to spawn naturally.

Surveys/Stocking: The manual removal of suckers and perch in 1985 paved the way for subsequent stockings of walleyes, northern pike, lake trout and splake. A 1989 DNR survey showed that 80 percent of the walleyes netted were at least 15 inches long and averaged 19.5 inches. The fish, which were growing above the state average, represented six year-classes and included representatives to 28 inches.

The survey also produced smallmouth bass averaging nearly 10 inches and including fish to 21 inches long. Yellow perch ranged from 4 to 10 inches with the average fish taping 7.6 inches. The few northern pike collected averaged 33 inches. Management prescription calls for continued stocking of pike, lake trout or splake, and walleye. Only smallmouths appear to be capable of sustaining themselves through natural reproduction.

In 1991 managers released 974,000 walleye fry; in 1992 they stocked 1.1 million fry and 64,500 fingerlings; and in 1993 they planted out an estimated 2.1 million fry and 20,000 fingerlings. Also in 1993 the DNR released an estimated 90 adult lake trout and 72 adult northern pike.

Tactics to Try: Fish shelters placed into the lake over the years include 100 jack straw, 148 brush, and two crib-type structures. They help concentrate perch, Master Angler rock bass, panfish and the larger predators.

Walleye anglers drift or jig leeches in spring along drop-offs and over structure throughout the lake. By summer they switch to crawlers or troll Rapalas and Rebels or crankbaits such as Hot 'N Tots and Wiggle Warts.

The lake produces good catches of smallmouth bass using the same tactics and offerings. In addition, spinnerbaits, fake night crawlers, and jigs and pigs are effective.

Bragging-size yellow perch occasionally come from Round Lake, and winter is a good time to catch them on wigglers or shiner minnows. Ice shanties are scattered throughout with jig fishermen and pike spearers. A good tip-up fishery for pike also exists, and each summer the lake serves up northerns to 10 pounds plus.

Access: The public access site in Luce County Park, on the lake's southeast side, has a sandy bottom and is located along a shallow shelf, which makes it difficult for launching big boats. Toilets are provided, and there is parking for about 25 vehicles. To rent a boat, contact Shoreline Resort, on the west side of the lake on CR-413 (906-586-6143).

TWIN LAKES

Fishing Opportunities: Splake—Good; Largemouth Bass and
Bluegills—Fair to Good; Yellow Perch—Fair.

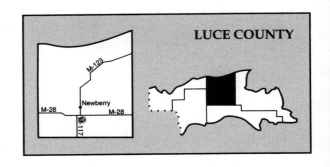
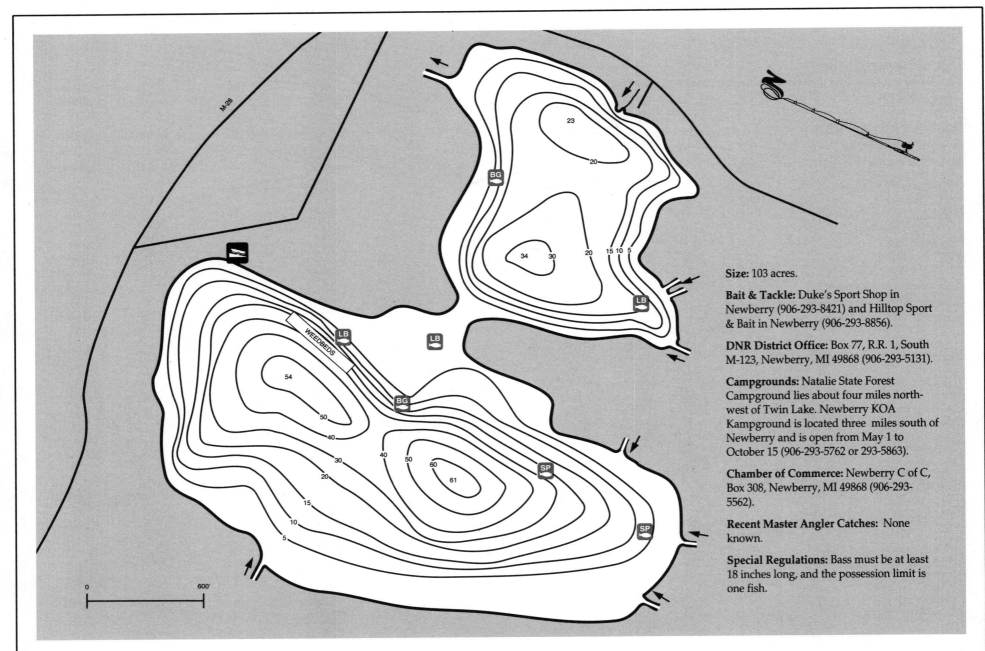

Size: 103 acres.

Bait & Tackle: Duke's Sport Shop in
Newberry (906-293-8421) and Hilltop Sport
& Bait in Newberry (906-293-8856).

DNR District Office: Box 77, R.R. 1, South
M-123, Newberry, MI 49868 (906-293-5131).

Campgrounds: Natalie State Forest
Campground lies about four miles north-
west of Twin Lake. Newberry KOA
Kampground is located three miles south of
Newberry and is open from May 1 to
October 15 (906-293-5762 or 293-5863).

Chamber of Commerce: Newberry C of C,
Box 308, Newberry, MI 49868 (906-293-
5562).

Recent Master Angler Catches: None
known.

Special Regulations: Bass must be at least
18 inches long, and the possession limit is
one fish.

Twin Lakes is located about four miles
southwest of Newberry in southcentral
Luce County. True to its name, the lake has two
personalities: the east basin is fairly shallow, and
the west basin has depths beyond 60 feet. The
immediate shoreline is mostly rolling hills, with
sand, gravel and clay soils. Tag alder, cedar and
spruce are the predominant vegetation types
surrounding the lake.

Although only a couple of homes front the
lake and there are no resorts or cottages, much
of the lakeside property is privately owned.

A small creek on the west side and several
springs serve as inlets. The West Branch of
Teaspoon Creek, a tributary to the
Tahquamenon River, provides the outlet on the
north side of the shallow-water basin. The lake's
water is clear to slightly green-brown, and
weedbeds occupy the shallows. Because of its
closeness to Newberry, Twin Lakes receives fairly heavy fishing pressure, especially in winter.

Surveys/Stocking: The lake received bluegills
in 1938, and currently the
DNR manages it for largemouth bass and panfish in the shallows and splake in the deeper

reaches.

A September 1988 trap, gill and fyke net survey produced the following types and numbers
of game fish (average size in parentheses): six
splake (11.2 inches), nine yellow perch (7.7 inches), 99 bluegills (6.3 inches), 28 pumpkinseed
sunfish (5.8 inches), and 27 largemouth bass (7.2
inches). Researchers believed that splake survival and growth were satisfactory. Although
manual removals have resulted in fewer small
perch, the number of white suckers had
increased considerably. Largemouth bass had
declined from earlier surveys.

In 1991 managers stocked 3,990 splake; in 1992
they released another 3,900 splake; and in 1993
they planted out an estimated 3,690 more. All
fish were yearlings.

Tactics to Try: The lake used to be a premier
largemouth water but overfish-
ing caused its demise. Consequently, special
regulations were adopted, and now the lake
appears to be coming back, but ever so slowly,
to trophy status. We include it for this reason
and because it is a showcase lake for catch-and-
release fishing.

The best spot for bass is the weedbed just
south of the access site, but other good places

shape up throughout the east side in particular.
Live bait is always effective, but using spinnerbaits or crankbaits is more fun. Anglers report
success on black or purple rubber crawlers, too.

The best panfishing occurs in winter for jig
fishermen using teardrop spoons tipped with
waxworms or other larvae. Perch tend to hang
out near weeds over a sandy bottom, and sunfish and bluegills prefer denser vegetation. Try
¼-oz. jigs with mallard-wing tails, and cover the
hook barb with a bit of worm or piece of larvae.
Spring is another good time, when bluegills are
preparing to spawn.

Winter is the hot time for splake and remnant
rainbow trout. Although whole-kernel corn,
waxworms and wigglers produce, the ticket on
Twin Lakes is a Russian hook with a shiner minnow. Sometimes fish are caught in water from 2
to 4 feet deep, especially on early and late ice.
Otherwise, fish the bottom to 50 feet deep and
work your bait toward the surface, stopping to
jig at 3-foot intervals.

Access: The improved public access site on the
lake's northwest corner includes a
paved boat launch ramp, courtesy pier, toilets
and parking for 14 vehicles. There is no place to
rent a boat.

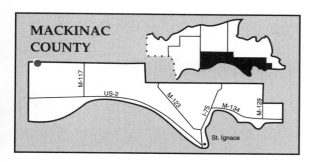

BIG MANISTIQUE LAKE

Fishing Opportunities: Walleyes and Yellow Perch—Good to Excellent; Largemouth Bass, Smallmouth Bass, Bluegills and Northern Pike—Fair to Good; Northern Muskies and

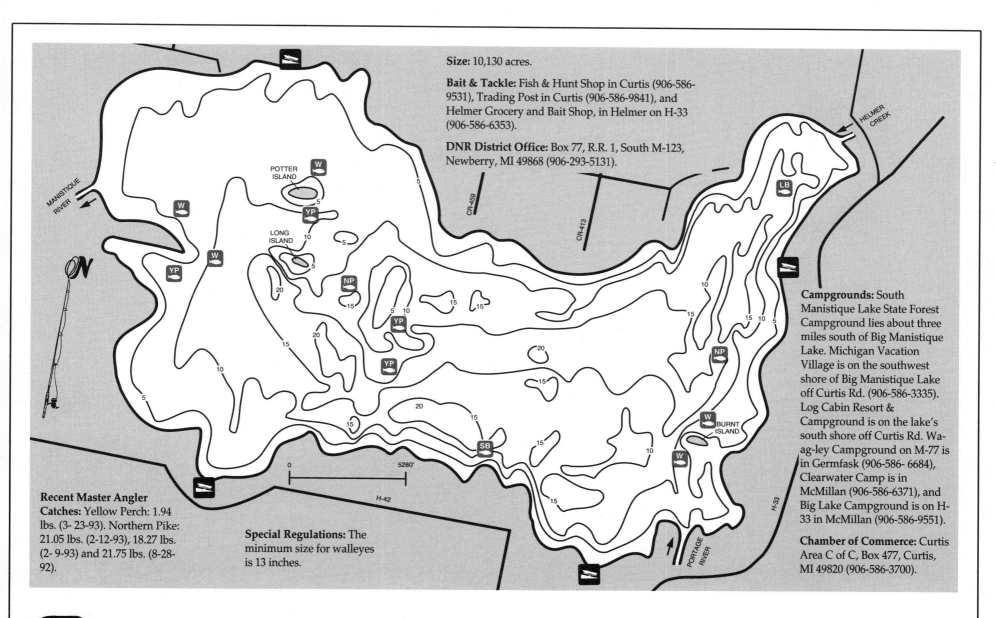

Size: 10,130 acres.

Bait & Tackle: Fish & Hunt Shop in Curtis (906-586-9531), Trading Post in Curtis (906-586-9841), and Helmer Grocery and Bait Shop, in Helmer on H-33 (906-586-6353).

DNR District Office: Box 77, R.R. 1, South M-123, Newberry, MI 49868 (906-293-5131).

Campgrounds: South Manistique Lake State Forest Campground lies about three miles south of Big Manistique Lake. Michigan Vacation Village is on the southwest shore of Big Manistique Lake off Curtis Rd. (906-586-3335). Log Cabin Resort & Campground is on the lake's south shore off Curtis Rd. Wa-ag-ley Campground on M-77 is in Germfask (906-586- 6684), Clearwater Camp is in McMillan (906-586-6371), and Big Lake Campground is on H-33 in McMillan (906-586-9551).

Chamber of Commerce: Curtis Area C of C, Box 477, Curtis, MI 49820 (906-586-3700).

Recent Master Angler Catches: Yellow Perch: 1.94 lbs. (3- 23-93). Northern Pike: 21.05 lbs. (2-12-93), 18.27 lbs. (2- 9-93) and 21.75 lbs. (8-28-92).

Special Regulations: The minimum size for walleyes is 13 inches.

Big Manistique Lake is located in the northwest corner of Mackinac County and the southwest corner of Luce County about 20 miles southwest of Newberry. Michigan's eighth- largest inland lake is about 7 miles long by 3½ miles wide. Popular with cottagers, it is surrounded by forests and farms. East-side inlets include Portage, Helmer and Mud creeks, along with several springs. Outletting from the west shore is the Manistique River, and the lake's central location means that both South (p. 76) and North Manistique (Round Lake, p. 69) flow into it.

Average depth is only 10 feet, and the lake's deepest spot is only 20 feet. Bottom composition ranges from sand to gravel, with mixtures of the two types common. Plenty of submergent vegetation shapes up throughout.

The lake is popular with perch and walleye fishermen. An intensive creel census conducted about 15 years ago indicated that most walleyes were taken through the ice, but that anglers also caught three times more yellow perch then. During the 1978-79 season an estimated 6,435 walleyes were taken compared to a total of 5,335

caught in 1979-80. Angling pressure has since increased.

Surveys/Stocking: A fall 1992 boomshocking survey designed to evaluate young-of-the-year walleyes indicated that the lake, which does not receive hatchery-reared walleyes, was healthy and productive.

A 1987 survey determined that walleyes, representing seven age- classes and measuring 11 to 26 inches, were in good shape. Those nets also yielded largemouth bass to 16½ inches, smallmouths to 18½ inches, a large population of 7- to 12-inch yellow perch, northern pike to 40 inches, and bluegills and pumpkinseed sunfish to 7 inches.

Over the years managers have stocked walleyes, yellow perch, northern pike, largemouth bass and lake sturgeon. However, they have released no fish in recent years. Walleyes are plentiful enough for the DNR to rely on Big Manistique lake for hatchery brood stock.

Tactics to Try: Five- to 6-pound walleyes are not uncommon, although summer is traditionally the hardest time to catch them. A good spring and fall tactic is to drift slowly over weeds with a floating jig head and leech, small minnow or half crawler.

Midsummer walleyes hit mayflies flyfished over the mud flats around Greenfield Island. Also troll Rapalas or crankbaits over sunken islands and along weedlines. Once located, walleyes will hit vertically jigged leeches, too.

Perch fishing has been down but is reportedly coming back. Leeches produce the biggest yellow-bellies in summer, and wigglers or shiners score in winter. The lake serves up decent largemouth and smallmouth bass, bluegills, northern pike (to 20 pounds) and muskies — all with typical tactics and lures. Occasionally a sturgeon rips the rod from an unsuspecting angler.

Access: Boat fishermen may choose from four access sites: (1) east side off H-33 on the Luce/Mackinac County line; (2) north side off CR-98; (3) an improved southwest facility off Curtis Rd. (H-42) includes a paved boat launch ramp, courtesy pier, toilets and parking for 40 vehicles; and (4) Cooks Bay three miles farther east features a hard-surfaced ramp, courtesy pier, toilets and parking for 15 vehicles. In addition, there are many county road endings that provide access, and cartoppers can also reach the lake via the Portage Creek inlet. Lakeside resorts rent boats (contact the Curtis Area C of C listed above).

BREVOORT LAKE

Fishing Opportunities: Walleyes, Smallmouth Bass and Ciscoes—Good to Excellent; Bluegills, Black Crappies and Largemouth Bass—Fair to Good; Yellow Perch, Northern Pike

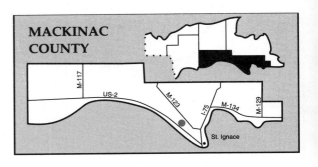

MACKINAC COUNTY

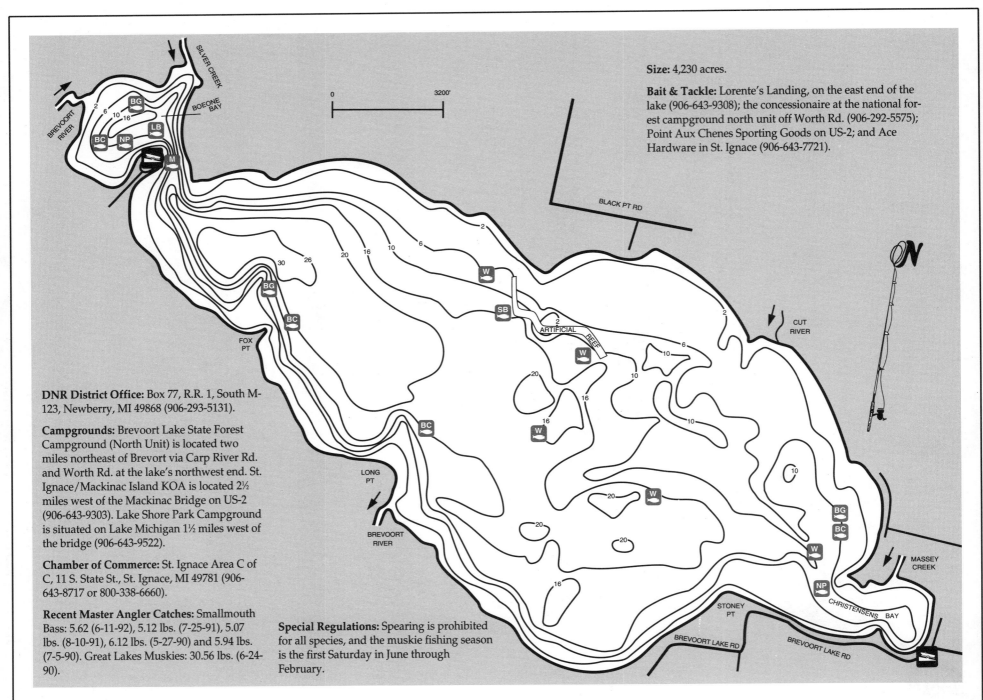

Size: 4,230 acres.

Bait & Tackle: Lorente's Landing, on the east end of the lake (906-643-9308); the concessionaire at the national forest campground north unit off Worth Rd. (906-292-5575); Point Aux Chenes Sporting Goods on US-2; and Ace Hardware in St. Ignace (906-643-7721).

DNR District Office: Box 77, R.R. 1, South M-123, Newberry, MI 49868 (906-293-5131).

Campgrounds: Brevoort Lake State Forest Campground (North Unit) is located two miles northeast of Brevort via Carp River Rd. and Worth Rd. at the lake's northwest end. St. Ignace/Mackinac Island KOA is located 2½ miles west of the Mackinac Bridge on US-2 (906-643-9303). Lake Shore Park Campground is situated on Lake Michigan 1½ miles west of the bridge (906-643-9522).

Chamber of Commerce: St. Ignace Area C of C, 11 S. State St., St. Ignace, MI 49781 (906-643-8717 or 800-338-6660).

Recent Master Angler Catches: Smallmouth Bass: 5.62 (6-11-92), 5.12 lbs. (7-25-91), 5.07 lbs. (8-10-91), 6.12 lbs. (5-27-90) and 5.94 lbs. (7-5-90). Great Lakes Muskies: 30.56 lbs. (6-24-90).

Special Regulations: Spearing is prohibited for all species, and the muskie fishing season is the first Saturday in June through February.

Brevoort Lake (also spelled Brevort) is Michigan's 25th-largest inland lake and is located in eastern Mackinac County about 15 miles northwest of St. Ignace. The area is home to old beach dunes on the south end and flat to gently rolling sand plains to the north. Forest types are mostly upland hardwoods with some scattered white pine and hemlock. About 30 percent of the lake is developed, and the heaviest growth is on the east end at Christensens Bay.

The Little Brevoort River, Silver Creek, Cut River and Massey Creek all serve to recharge Brevoort Lake. The drainplug is the Brevort River, which exits on the southcentral shore and flows directly into Lake Michigan.

Brevoort's shoal areas are comprised of loose organic material in Boedne Bay, mixed sand/organics in Chirstensens Bay, and scattered rock along the north shore. The remainder is mostly sand in the form of shallow rippled flats caused from extensive erosion of the dunes.

The best fish habitat is located in the bays and in north-shore bulrush beds.

A long history of management practices include the installation of 277 fish shelters, operation of a northern pike spawning marsh on Massey Creek (since discontinued), creation in 1985 of a 2,000-foot-long artificial spawning reef, and a smorgasbord of gamefish stocking. In addition to those rated above, the lake contains smelt and sturgeon and occasional migrating trout and salmon.

Surveys/Stocking: A fall 1991 boomshocking survey designed to evaluate the impact of natural spawning resulted in solid evidence that both walleyes and smallmouth bass were successfully using the reef.

Managers currently release rainbow trout and steelhead in the Brevoort River just south of the lake but have not stocked the lake itself in recent years.

Tactics to Try: Most walleye anglers key on rock piles and submerged islands in the lake's central region. Hot tactics include slip bobber fishing with leeches, trolling

with crawler harnesses and jigging minnows pinned to chartruese leadheads. The reef, portions of which can be seen along the 5-foot-deep contour off Black Point, concentrates walleyes and smallmouths in spring.

Good fishing for bluegills and black crappies occurs in the bays, off south-side points, and over fish shelter remnants. Use tube jigs and small minnows in summer and waxworm-tipped teardrops in winter.

The best spot for pike, muskies and panfish is Boedne Bay because it offers both structure and weeds. Christensens Bay is another good place for general fishing.

Access: The USFS campground at Boedne Bay on the lake's northwest corner features unimproved access with a boat launch ramp. Better access is available at the extreme east end of the lake, where the ramp is paved and there are a courtesy pier, toilets and parking space. To rent a boat, contact Dunn's Resort, (906-643-9542), Lorente's Landing, and the north unit campground concessionaire (see both listings under Bait & Tackle).

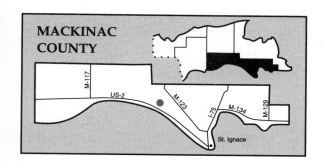
LITTLE BREVOORT LAKE

Fishing Opportunities: Bluegills—Good; Walleyes and Black Crappies—Fair to Good; Northern Pike, Yellow Perch and Pumpkinseed Sunfish—Fair, Largemouth Bass—Poor to Fair.

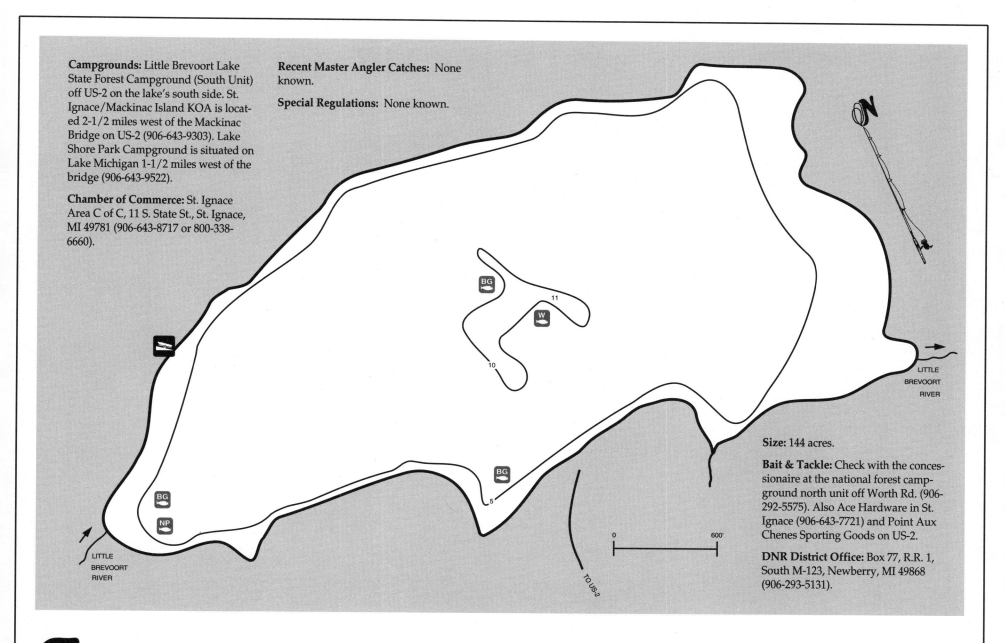

Campgrounds: Little Brevoort Lake State Forest Campground (South Unit) off US-2 on the lake's south side. St. Ignace/Mackinac Island KOA is located 2-1/2 miles west of the Mackinac Bridge on US-2 (906-643-9303). Lake Shore Park Campground is situated on Lake Michigan 1-1/2 miles west of the bridge (906-643-9522).

Chamber of Commerce: St. Ignace Area C of C, 11 S. State St., St. Ignace, MI 49781 (906-643-8717 or 800-338-6660).

Recent Master Angler Catches: None known.

Special Regulations: None known.

Size: 144 acres.

Bait & Tackle: Check with the concessionaire at the national forest campground north unit off Worth Rd. (906-292-5575). Also Ace Hardware in St. Ignace (906-643-7721) and Point Aux Chenes Sporting Goods on US-2.

DNR District Office: Box 77, R.R. 1, South M-123, Newberry, MI 49868 (906-293-5131).

L ittle Brevoort Lake (also spelled Brevort) is located in southcentral Mackinac County about 25 miles west of St. Ignace and only a half-mile from Lake Michigan. This shallow, clear, lightly brown-stained lake features a submerged ridge running throughout its middle section from east to west. Shoreline structure runs heavily to logs and fallen trees, and the lake bottom is mostly fibrous peat except for the north and south shores, portions of which are sandy. Tag alder swamps are located on the west and east shores, and northern hardwoods line the north and south shores.

The undeveloped lake's inlet is the Little Brevoort River. After entering from the southwest, the river exits in the northeast corner enroute to Big Brevoort Lake and Lake Michigan.

Surveys/Stocking: An August 1985 fyke net survey indicated that brown bullheads and panfish dominated the fish population. The nets also revealed northern pike to 26 inches, walleyes to 19 inches, black crappies to 11 inches, bluegills to 10 inches, and pumpkinseed sunfish to 8 inches. Yellow perch were small in size.

Like most lakes, Little Brevoort hosts good and poor fishing years for its various denizens. A 1983 net survey, for example, showed these species and average sizes: perch, 10 inches; crappies, 8½ inches; pike 18½ inches; walleyes, 13½ inches; and smallmouths, 9 inches.

In 1988 DNR technicians manually removed suckers, bullheads and bowfin. In 1991 they released 5,000 largemouth bass fingerlings, and in 1992 they stocked 5,000 walleye fingerlings.

Tactics to Try: Because of its small size and easy accessibility, Little Brevoort Lake can't take heavy fishing pressure. Although there is a catchable population of walleyes, they can be easily fished out, and so anglers should practice catch and release. No real hotspots develop; simply work the edges and shorelines with live bait for best results.

At times the lake throws magnum bluegills, along with good-size crappies and occasional jumbo perch and pumpkinseed sunfish. Although these fish are available year-round,

few ice anglers venture onto the lake because of poor winter access.

Small ribbon leeches produce the biggest panfish in spring and summer. Wigglers are also good in summer, and we have one report of a July jig fishermen catching big bluegills on waxworms and a chartreuse teardrop with black dot. Excellent flyfishing opportunities exist.

Bullheads currently dominate the lake, but if the DNR follows through on a manual removal as planned, fishing for all species should improve. That prospect prompts us to include the lake in this book.

Northern pike and largemouth bass offer incidental action.

Access: An unimproved access site with gravel ramp and parking for campers only is located at the south unit of the state forest campground and can be accessed via US-2. In the north unit off Worth Rd. anglers will find a gravel boat launch ramp with a minimum amount of parking. To rent a boat (no motors are available), contact the north unit campground concessionaire (see listing under bait and tackle).

MILAKOKIA LAKE

Fishing Opportunities: Northern Pike and Walleyes—Good;
Yellow Perch and Smallmouth Bass—Fair to Good.

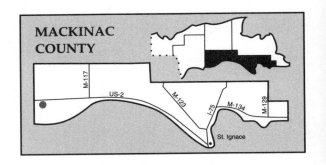

MACKINAC
COUNTY

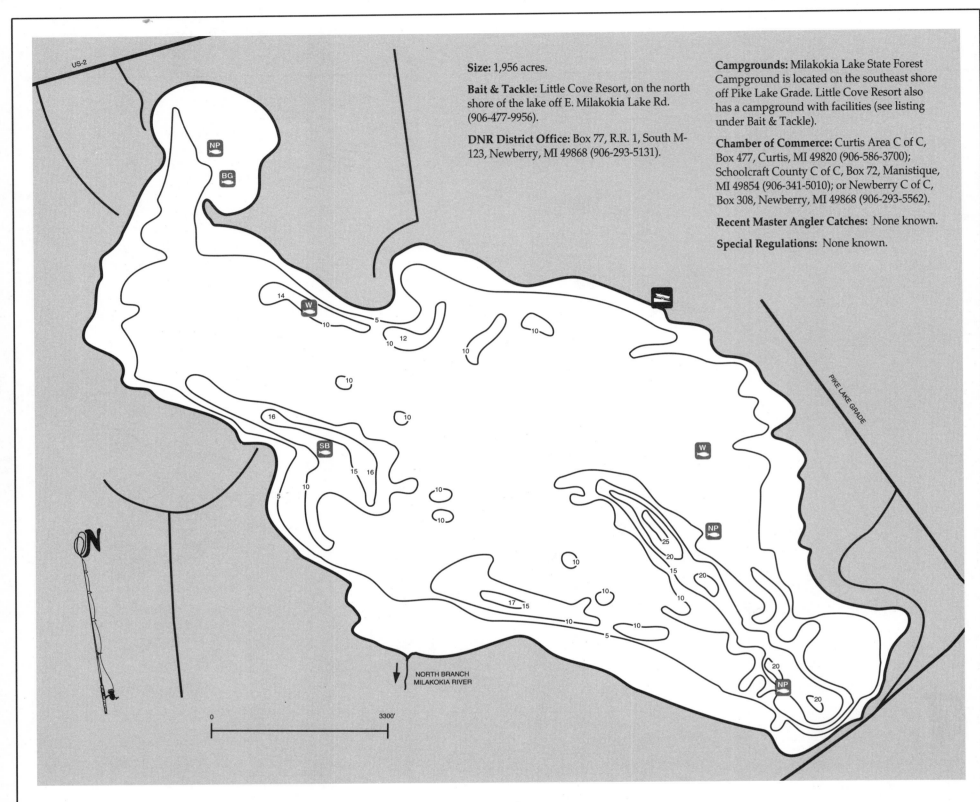

Size: 1,956 acres.

Bait & Tackle: Little Cove Resort, on the north shore of the lake off E. Milakokia Lake Rd. (906-477-9956).

DNR District Office: Box 77, R.R. 1, South M-123, Newberry, MI 49868 (906-293-5131).

Campgrounds: Milakokia Lake State Forest Campground is located on the southeast shore off Pike Lake Grade. Little Cove Resort also has a campground with facilities (see listing under Bait & Tackle).

Chamber of Commerce: Curtis Area C of C, Box 477, Curtis, MI 49820 (906-586-3700); Schoolcraft County C of C, Box 72, Manistique, MI 49854 (906-341-5010); or Newberry C of C, Box 308, Newberry, MI 49868 (906-293-5562).

Recent Master Angler Catches: None known.

Special Regulations: None known.

Milakokia Lake is located in southwest Mackinac County about five miles west of Gould City. No permanent tributaries enter the lake, but the North Branch of the Milakokia River exits from the southcentral shore. Most of the lake is less than 15 feet deep, and the maximum depth is 26 feet.

Shoal areas are sand and gravel, and deeper spots exhibit an organic bottom. Vegetation types include pondweed, water lilies, milfoil and bulrushes and are present throughout the lake except for the rocky northeast and along the west-shore point.

Surveys/Stocking: Between 1938 and 1957, fisheries biologists stocked walleyes, bluegills, smallmouth bass, pike and perch. A June 1985 survey indicated that walleyes, including fish that had naturally reproduced, comprised 34 percent of the overall biomass. Northern pike, although down in numbers, continue to provide good fishing opportunities.

The DNR has been planting out walleyes at regular intervals during the past 15 years. In 1993 managers stocked an estimated 750,000 walleye fry.

Tactics to Try: The lake produces walleyes to 6 pounds. Summer catches occur in deeper holes, off the points, and along the well-defined contour breaks. Most fishermen troll with leech-sweetened Lindy Rigs or drift fish with night crawlers. Jigging works, too, as does trolling with orange- and-gold Hot 'N Tots.

Big bucktail spinners with orange, chartreuse or hot- green skirts are good hardware for northern pike, along with standard spoons. Again, most fishermen troll. For Master Angler-size northerns, try bobber fishing the cabbage weeds with 5- to 8-inch suckers.

Walleye anglers occasionally luck into keeper perch, including tiger-striped jumbos a foot or more in length. Leeches are good summertime bait for yellow bellies; in winter use wigglers or shiner minnows.

Access: The access site at Milakokia Lake State Forest Campground,. on the northeast shore off Pike Lake Grade, includes a hard-surfaced boat launch ramp, toilets and parking for 14 vehicles. To rent a boat, contact Little Cove Resort (see listing under Bait & Tackle). Green Gables Resort furnishes a boat with each of its six rental cottages (906-477-6207).

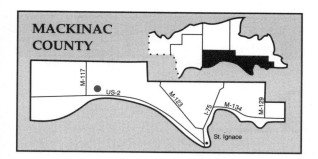

MILLECOQUIN LAKE

Fishing Opportunities: Bluegills, Walleyes and Northern Pike—Good; Smallmouth Bass, Largemouth Bass, and Yellow Perch—Fair to Good.

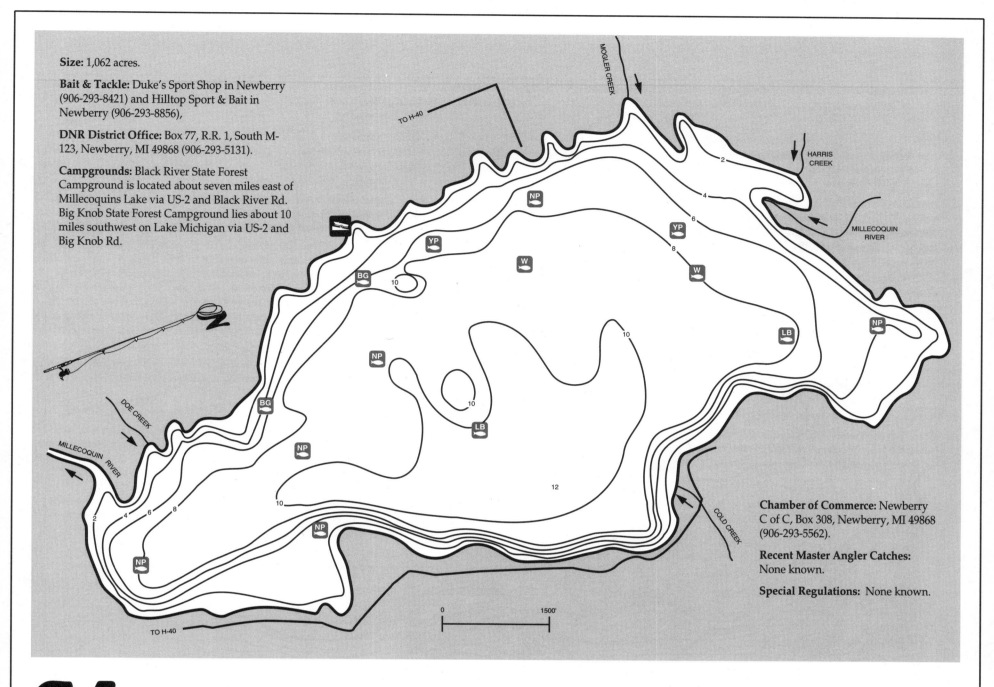

Size: 1,062 acres.

Bait & Tackle: Duke's Sport Shop in Newberry (906-293-8421) and Hilltop Sport & Bait in Newberry (906-293-8856),

DNR District Office: Box 77, R.R. 1, South M-123, Newberry, MI 49868 (906-293-5131).

Campgrounds: Black River State Forest Campground is located about seven miles east of Millecoquins Lake via US-2 and Black River Rd. Big Knob State Forest Campground lies about 10 miles southwest on Lake Michigan via US-2 and Big Knob Rd.

Chamber of Commerce: Newberry C of C, Box 308, Newberry, MI 49868 (906-293-5562).

Recent Master Angler Catches: None known.

Special Regulations: None known.

Millecoquin Lake is located in west-central Mackinac County about six miles northwest of Naubinway. The mostly wooded, brown-stained lake is centered in the Millecoquin River drainage, which originates from spring-fed trout ponds near the Luce-Mackinac county line. The Millecoquin River enters from the north end, along with Hogler and Harris creeks, and exits on the south end heading for Lake Michigan.

Three permanent dams impede the upstream progress of lake sturgeon, channel catfish, rainbow trout and other Lake Michigan anadromous species. The Hiawatha Sportsman Club owns about 80 percent of the shoreline. Fishing pressure is low to moderate. Several eagles reside in the region.

The large, shallow, weedy lake is fairly productive even though maximum and average depths are only about 12 and 4 feet respectively. Sand comprises most of the lake bottom except for deeper areas, which also include organic material. There is some rock and gravel along the west shore. Plenty of bulrushes and surface weeds surround the lake, and the northeast shore features cabbage weeds.

Surveys/Stocking: A May 1989 net survey found that northern pike had increased an average of five inches since a 1982 survey and that 88 percent were considered of catchable size. The walleye stocking program appeared to be successful, and although not many yellow perch were taken, they averaged 11½ inches. Both largemouth and smallmouth bass appeared to be increasing in number.

Besides evaluation, the purpose of the netting effort was to remove undesirable species. Workers took out nearly 11,000 pounds of white suckers that averaged 19 inches each and another 945 pounds of brown bullheads.

In 1991 managers released 20,200 walleyes; in 1992 they stocked 33,400 walleyes; and in 1993 they planted out an estimated 20,000 more. All fish were fingerlings.

Tactics to Try: The lake tosses walleyes to 6 pounds, although most stringers contain 15- to 18-inch-long fish. Summer catches occur in deeper holes, off the points, and along the clean contour breaks of the east shore. Most fishermen troll with Rapalas or vertical jig with leadheads and worms.

Most pike are 18 to 22 inches, but bigger fish — including Master Angler candidates — swim here. Anglers troll Rapalas or cast spinners and spoons. An occasional lunker pike falls for a bobber-fished sucker or decoy tantalized by a spearing shack fisherman.

Bass anglers occasionally luck into a 4- or 5-pound bucketmouth, but the average fish is barely legal. Surface baits work around the weedbeds; earlier in the season toss crankbaits or spinnerbaits.

Bluegill fishing has improved since the thinning project. Try the area around the access site and all along shore to the south. Waxworms in winter, flies in spring and drifting in summer with worms are all hot tactics. Crickets could be dynamite, but no one fishes them.

Perch fishing is good in winter from the access site all along the north shore.

Access: An improved access site on the north-central shore features a paved boat launch ramp, toilets and parking for 20 vehicles. Boats are available with cabin and resort rentals on the lake.

SOUTH MANISTIQUE LAKE

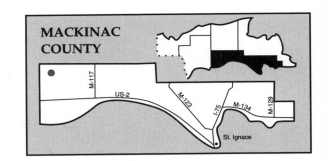

MACKINAC COUNTY

Fishing Opportunities: Walleyes—Good to Excellent; Yellow Perch, Bluegills, Northern Pike, Largemouth Bass and Smallmouth Bass—Fair to Good; Northern Muskies and Tiger Muskies—Poor to Fair.

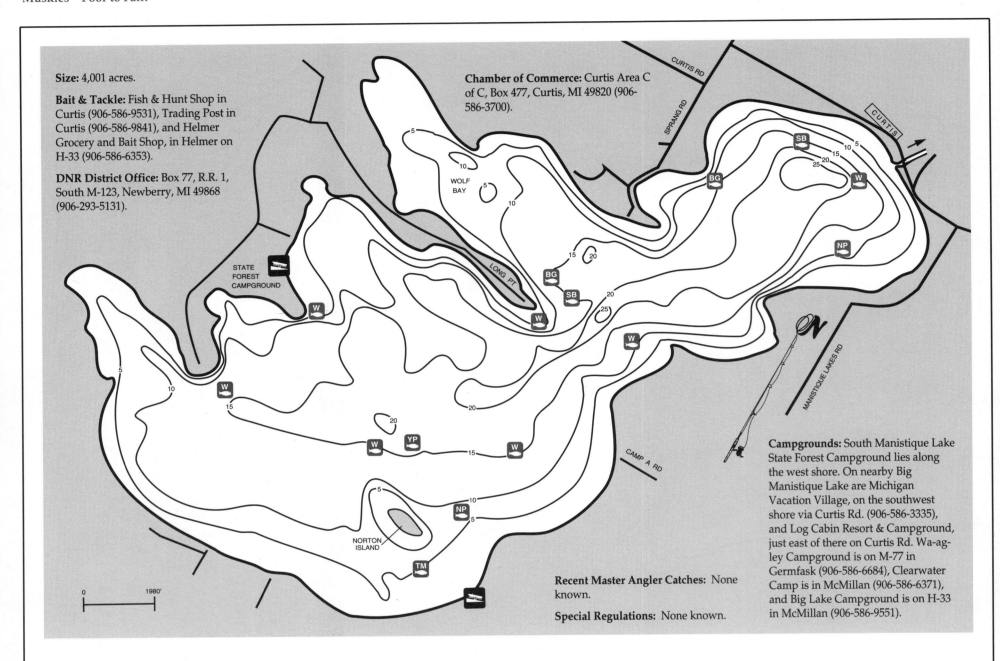

Size: 4,001 acres.

Bait & Tackle: Fish & Hunt Shop in Curtis (906-586-9531), Trading Post in Curtis (906-586-9841), and Helmer Grocery and Bait Shop, in Helmer on H-33 (906-586-6353).

DNR District Office: Box 77, R.R. 1, South M-123, Newberry, MI 49868 (906-293-5131).

Chamber of Commerce: Curtis Area C of C, Box 477, Curtis, MI 49820 (906-586-3700).

Campgrounds: South Manistique Lake State Forest Campground lies along the west shore. On nearby Big Manistique Lake are Michigan Vacation Village, on the southwest shore via Curtis Rd. (906-586-3335), and Log Cabin Resort & Campground, just east of there on Curtis Rd. Wa-ag-ley Campground is on M-77 in Germfask (906-586-6684), Clearwater Camp is in McMillan (906-586-6371), and Big Lake Campground is on H-33 in McMillan (906-586-9551).

Recent Master Angler Catches: None known.

Special Regulations: None known.

Shis managed for walleyes. A creel survey in 1978-79 indicated that anglers caught more than 14,000 'eyes in a single year.

South Manistique Lake, also called Whitefish Lake, is located in west Mackinac County at Curtis. About 25 percent of the lake features depths of less than 20 feet, and the maximum depth is 29 feet. The bottom is sand, muck and fibrous peat in the bays and marl/peat in deeper reaches. Water color is light brown. Inleting is a creek from Shoepack Lake as well as several east-side small streams, which reportedly contain brook trout.

The east shore winds about in broad curves, but the west side is irregular, consisting of long points and narrow intervening bays. The lake empties on its north end through Portage Creek, which in turn flows into Big Manistique Lake (p. 71).

Surveys/Stocking: A long stocking history dates to 1925 when 40,000 lake trout were released. Over the years biologists have also released smallmouth and largemouth bass, walleyes, perch, bluegills, pike, and both tiger and northern muskies. Today, the lake

A fall 1988 net survey produced northern pike to 33 inches, largemouth bass to 11½ inches, smallmouths to 19 inches, ciscoes to almost 19 inches, walleyes to 28 inches, yellow perch to almost 11 inches, pumpkinseed sunfish to 8½ inches, and bluegills to 9½ inches. Walleyes collected represented 11 year-classes. A fall 1992 boomshocking survey turned up several largemouth bass and plenty of young-of-the-year walleyes.

In 1991 managers planted out 1.4 million walleye fry and 1,700 northern muskie fingerlings. In 1992 they stocked 1.5 million walleye fry, and in 1993 they released another estimated 2.1 million fry.

Tactics to Try: West-side points (especially Long Point) and bays start up spring walleye action and are good spots to try again in fall — the two best times to fish. Lindy Rigs with crawlers or leeches are good baits to drift across these points. Hot colors in lures,

leadheads and spinner blades show up best in the dark water.

Bluegills pop up throughout the lake, but the bays are most productive during spawning seasons, and the two northwest points furnish summer hotspots. Drift or slowly jig small ribbon leeches off bottom in summer.

A good spot for northerns and muskies is on the lake's southeast side between the access site and Norton Island. For bass, locate weedlines and toss blue-and-white spinnerbaits.

Access: Several options: (1) two miles southwest of Curtis at Wolfe Bay off Wolfe Rd. is a paved boat launch ramp with toilets and parking for five vehicles; (2) three miles south of Curtis off Norton Rd. (via Manistique Lakes Rd.) is another improved site with paved ramp, courtesy pier, toilets and parking for 10 vehicles; (3) an unimproved site with gravel slope, toilets and parking for 12 vehicles is located within the state forest campground on the west shore; (4) several county road endings where cartoppers and canoes can be launched. To rent a boat, contact the Curtis Area C of C (see listing above).

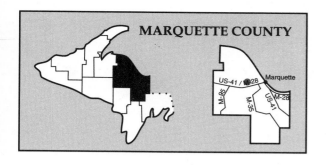

DEER LAKE BASIN

Fishing Opportunities: Walleyes and Northern Pike—Good to Excellent; Yellow Perch—Poor to Fair.

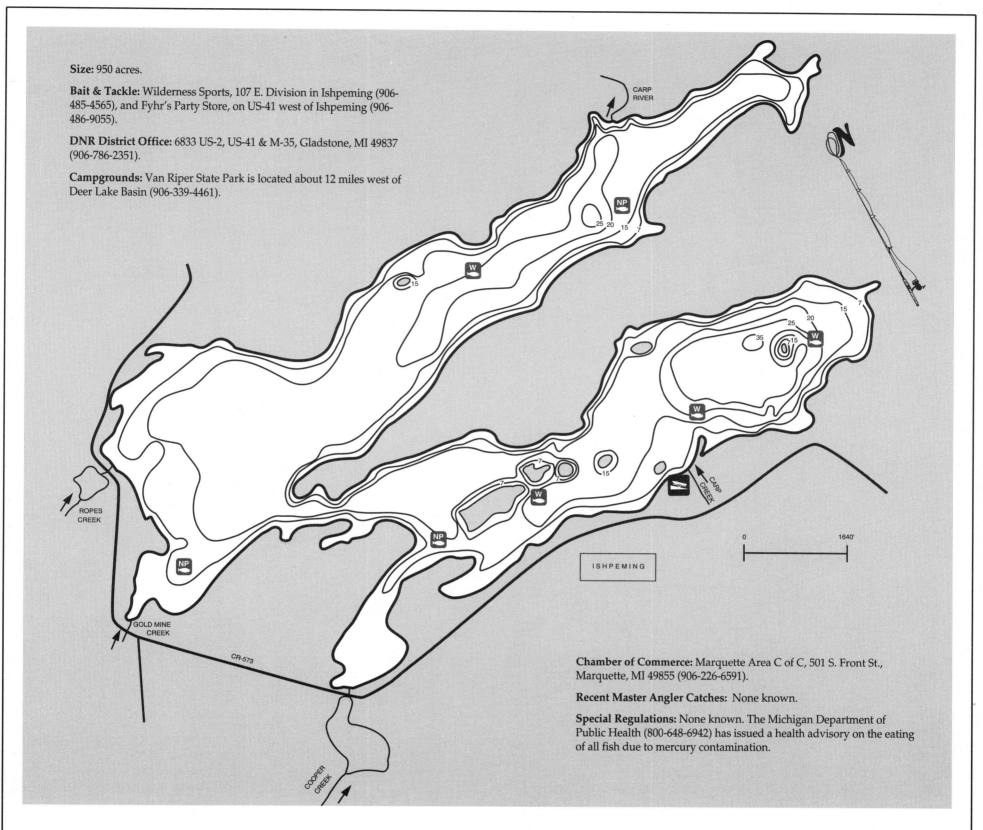

Size: 950 acres.

Bait & Tackle: Wilderness Sports, 107 E. Division in Ishpeming (906-485-4565), and Fyhr's Party Store, on US-41 west of Ishpeming (906-486-9055).

DNR District Office: 6833 US-2, US-41 & M-35, Gladstone, MI 49837 (906-786-2351).

Campgrounds: Van Riper State Park is located about 12 miles west of Deer Lake Basin (906-339-4461).

Chamber of Commerce: Marquette Area C of C, 501 S. Front St., Marquette, MI 49855 (906-226-6591).

Recent Master Angler Catches: None known.

Special Regulations: None known. The Michigan Department of Public Health (800-648-6942) has issued a health advisory on the eating of all fish due to mercury contamination.

Deer Lake Basin is located in northcentral Marquette County off US-41/M-28 just north of Ishpeming. Ropes, Gold Mine and Cooper creeks flow in to west-end arms, and Carp Creek comes in from the southcentral shore. The Carp River outlets from the northeast.

The lake was badly contaminated with mercury, and part of the litigated recovery plan with the responsible company was to restore the fishery and to provide annual monitoring by the DNR.

Drop-offs, broken rocks and weedbeds provide good fish cover. The water is the color of root beer.

Surveys/Stocking: A DNR gill net survey in October 1992 was designed to evaluate walleyes, northern pike and yellow perch. Northerns averaged 26 to 28 inches, and walleyes averaged 13 to 14 inches. Only a small number of perch were collected, probably because walleyes and pike tend to graze them down heavily in this lake. Researchers noted that the shallows contained a large number of bullheads.

Age and growth data from this survey were not available at our press time. However, young walleyes and northerns from a 1991 survey were growing above state averages, indicating a healthy forage population.

The DNR stocked the lake with walleye fry in the mid 1980s and then released more in 1990. The lake has received no hatchery-reared fish since.

Tactics to Try: Deer Lake produces consistent catches of 18- to 25-inch walleyes. Anglers drift fish, troll and jig with whole night crawlers. For best results, use chartreuse, orange or white blades on spinners. Skirt ¼-oz. stand-up jigs with double curly tails in those colors. Northerns tend to steal lures and break leaderless lines. Most anglers are after walleyes and catch the pike incidentally.

Access: The public access site is located at the mouth of Carp Creek, off CR-573. There is no place to rent a boat.

GOOSE LAKE

Fishing Opportunities: Walleyes, Northern Pike and Yellow Perch—Fair to Good.

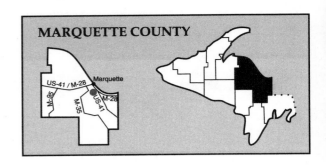
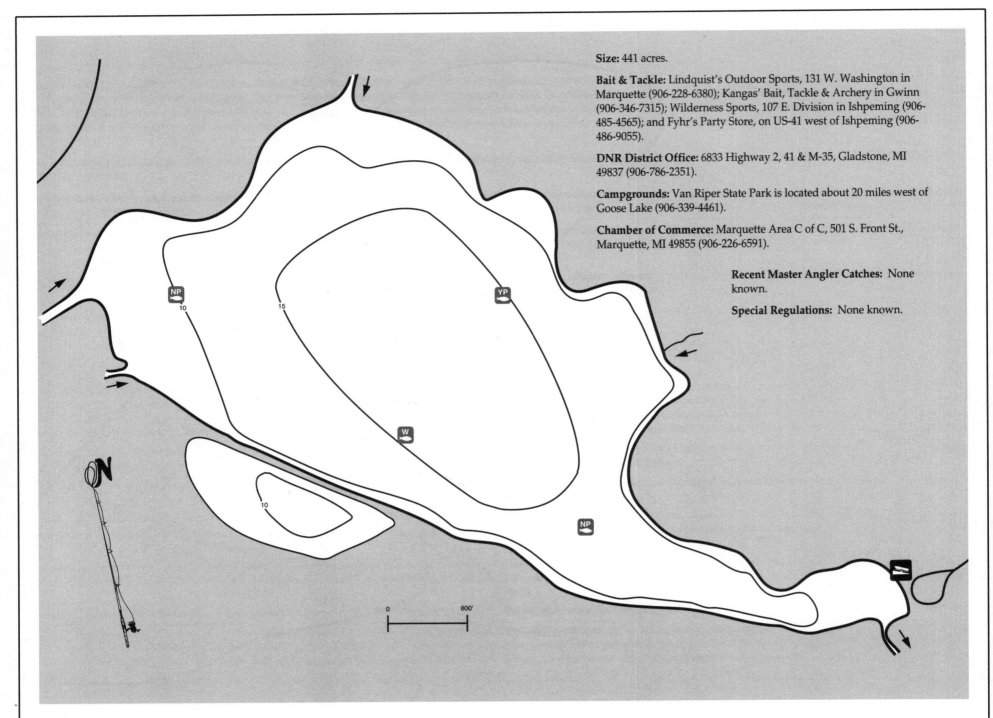

Size: 441 acres.

Bait & Tackle: Lindquist's Outdoor Sports, 131 W. Washington in Marquette (906-228-6380); Kangas' Bait, Tackle & Archery in Gwinn (906-346-7315); Wilderness Sports, 107 E. Division in Ishpeming (906-485-4565); and Fyhr's Party Store, on US-41 west of Ishpeming (906-486-9055).

DNR District Office: 6833 Highway 2, 41 & M-35, Gladstone, MI 49837 (906-786-2351).

Campgrounds: Van Riper State Park is located about 20 miles west of Goose Lake (906-339-4461).

Chamber of Commerce: Marquette Area C of C, 501 S. Front St., Marquette, MI 49855 (906-226-6591).

Recent Master Angler Catches: None known.

Special Regulations: None known.

Goose Lake is located in northcentral Marquette County about three miles southeast of Negaunee. Its major tributary is the Goose Lake inlet, also known as Partridge Creek, which enters from the northwest corner. Several small flows also contribute from picturesque hills to 300 feet high that surround the lake. Goose Lake outlet leaves the lake on the southeast end.

Although sewage discharge from the City of Negaunee ended many years ago, the shallow, bowl-shaped lake continues to be nutrient-loaded and therefore productive of much weed growth. Maximum depth is 12 to 15 feet throughout, and the bottom is mostly mud and peat over a shoal substrate of gravel and rock. North-shore bays contain the most sand, and the shoreline itself is largely rock and gravel.

Surveys/Stocking: Lake populations swing back and forth between pike and perch, although netting surveys have also turned up largemouth bass (which were introduced in 1925), pumpkinseed sunfish and brook trout (introduced in 1924) and white suckers and black bullheads.

The DNR conducted a fyke net survey during a week in late May 1993. Researchers found healthy, fat populations of walleyes, northern pike and pumpkinseed sunfish. Many walleyes ranged in the 16- to 23-inch category, and about half of the 15 northerns netted were larger than 24 inches. Pumpkinseeds ran 7 to 9 inches, and plenty of 9- to 11-inch perch were captured along with many golden shiners, the principle forage.

In 1992 DNR managers stocked 40,200 walleye fingerlings.

Tactics to Try: Despite the numbers of fish in the lake, anglers complain that it is tough to fish, a condition probably due to the abundance of forage. Typically, the best fishing for pike occurs in summer and for perch in winter and spring.

Fish tend to scatter throughout the lake, and so anglers should move often to maximize their effort. Weedless lures work best for pike, which will also nail minnows hooked below the dorsal fin and fished halfway to bottom below a bobber. Dead smelt fished on bottom also produce.

Small minnows are the bait of choice for perch fishermen. Both drift and jig tactics work. Leeches or night crawlers fished with these presentations are the ticket for walleyes.

We have reports of recent brook trout catches from the outlet.

Access: Nearly all the lake's frontage is owned by Cleveland Cliffs Iron Company, with whom the state has a lease for the public access site on the extreme southwest side. The site consists of a parking lot and trail to Goose Lake and is mostly used by ice fishermen. Open-water anglers either fish from the causeway or access the lake at an undeveloped site on the extreme southeast end. To reach it, turn down the forest trail directly across from Lindberg's Gravel Pit on CR-480. There is no place to rent a boat.

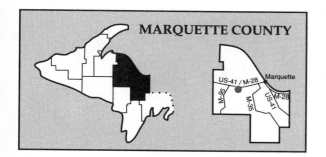

GREENWOOD RESERVOIR

Fishing Opportunities: Black Crappies—Good to Excellent; Northern Pike—Good; Smallmouth Bass, Yellow Perch and Walleyes—Fair to Good.

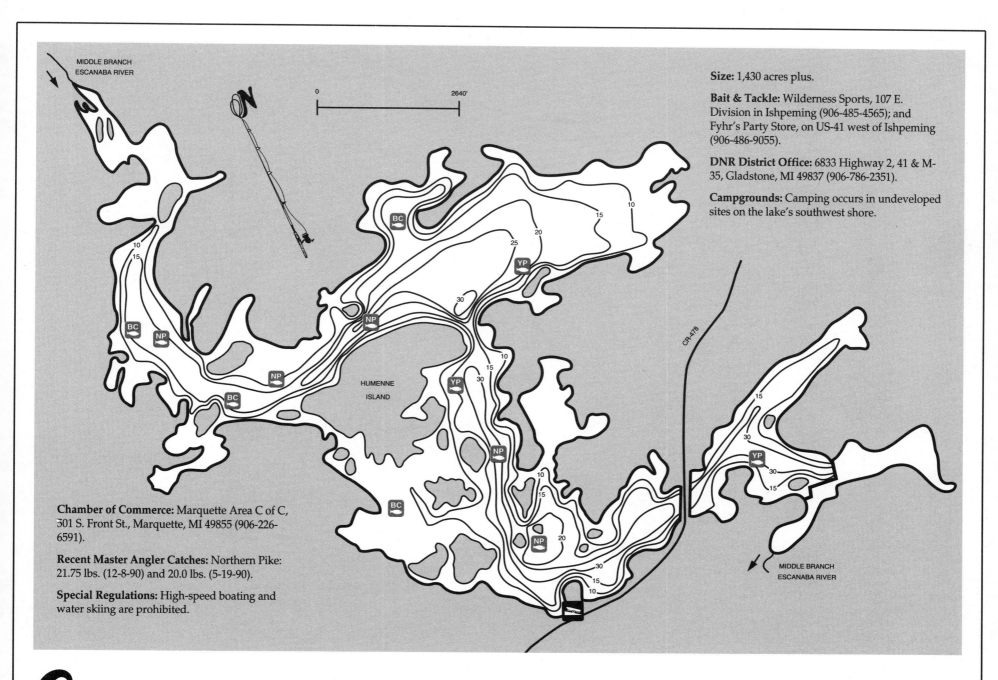

MIDDLE BRANCH ESCANABA RIVER

N

0   2640'

BC

15

10

20

25

YP

30

NP

10

15

BC

NP

BC

HUMENNE ISLAND

YP

15
30

CR-478

NP

10
15

10
15

NP

20

30

15
10

MIDDLE BRANCH ESCANABA RIVER

15

30

YP

15

Size: 1,430 acres plus.

Bait & Tackle: Wilderness Sports, 107 E. Division in Ishpeming (906-485-4565); and Fyhr's Party Store, on US-41 west of Ishpeming (906-486-9055).

DNR District Office: 6833 Highway 2, 41 & M-35, Gladstone, MI 49837 (906-786-2351).

Campgrounds: Camping occurs in undeveloped sites on the lake's southwest shore.

Chamber of Commerce: Marquette Area C of C, 301 S. Front St., Marquette, MI 49855 (906-226-6591).

Recent Master Angler Catches: Northern Pike: 21.75 lbs. (12-8-90) and 20.0 lbs. (5-19-90).

Special Regulations: High-speed boating and water skiing are prohibited.

Greenwood Reservoir is located in west-central Marquette County about six miles southwest of Ishpeming. The reservoir, which was constructed in 1973 by damming the Middle Branch of the Escanaba River, contains some two dozen islands and nearly 30 irregular miles of wooded shoreline. Built and operated by the Cleveland Cliffs Iron Co., the impoundment provides water for the Tilden and Empire Mines pelletizing plants.

Most of the reservoir is fairly shallow with a maximum depth of 35 feet. The bottom is predominately rock and gravel with some sand. Logs, drop-offs and scattered weedbeds provide excellent cover. Water color is moderately stained. Forage species include white suckers, small perch and various minnows.

Surveys/Stocking: An August 1988 DNR net survey showed a decline in the average size of northern pike from 27½ inches in 1976 to 21.2 inches. The nets collected yel-low perch to 9 inches, largemouth bass to 16 inches, black crappies to 8 inches, and pumpkinseed sunfish to 7 inches. Most fish were growing above state averages, indicating a healthy, productive lake.

During the reservoir's infancy, the DNR stocked rainbow trout in 1975 but discontinued them in favor of warm-water management. In 1991 technicians released 39,260 walleye fingerlings; in 1992 they planted out 1.7 million walleye fry; and in 1993 they stocked an estimated 51,800 more fingerlings.

Tactics to Try: For crappies, fish yellow grub-bodied jigs or yellow Fuzz-E Grubs at varying depths, moving frequently until finding a school of papermouths. The reservoir features good cover for crappies in the form of woody vegetation — scattered fallen trees throughout the lake and stickups in the backwaters.

In 1978 an angler and his wife caught more than 100 northern pike that were at least 24 inch-es or larger. Both crappies and yellow perch were plentiful that year, and although the pike fishing has fallen off, it is still respectable. Weedy areas, rocks, contour breaks, island points and shelves, and drowned logs produce for Dardevle fishermen as well as those tossing or trolling Mepps bucktail spinners or green Cleos.

An active winter fishery is also productive for pike, crappies and perch, but use caution because snow and river current conditions make for tricky, often unsafe ice.

Biologists expect the walleye fishery to take off soon. After initial stocking nearly 20 years ago, the DNR stopped releases until recently. Greenwood Reservoir has the potential to become one of the U.P.'s better walleye lakes.

Access: Located on the reservoir's southcentral shore at Nob Point off CR-478, the DNR access site includes a paved boat launch ramp, toilets and parking for 17 vehicles. There is no place to rent a boat.

LAKE INDEPENDENCE

Fishing Opportunities: Northern Pike—Good to Excellent;
Walleyes and Smallmouth Bass—Good; Ciscoes—Fair to Good;
Yellow Perch—Fair.

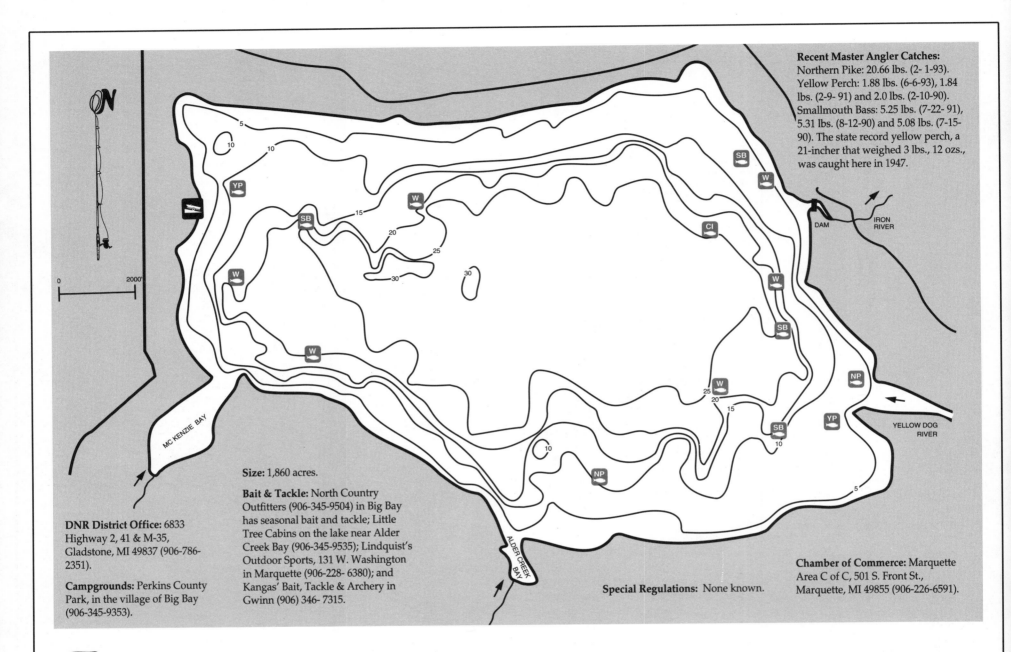

Recent Master Angler Catches:
Northern Pike: 20.66 lbs. (2- 1-93).
Yellow Perch: 1.88 lbs. (6-6-93), 1.84
lbs. (2-9- 91) and 2.0 lbs. (2-10-90).
Smallmouth Bass: 5.25 lbs. (7-22- 91),
5.31 lbs. (8-12-90) and 5.08 lbs. (7-15-
90). The state record yellow perch, a
21-incher that weighed 3 lbs., 12 ozs.,
was caught here in 1947.

Size: 1,860 acres.

Bait & Tackle: North Country
Outfitters (906-345-9504) in Big Bay
has seasonal bait and tackle; Little
Tree Cabins on the lake near Alder
Creek Bay (906-345-9535); Lindquist's
Outdoor Sports, 131 W. Washington
in Marquette (906-228- 6380); and
Kangas' Bait, Tackle & Archery in
Gwinn (906) 346- 7315.

DNR District Office: 6833
Highway 2, 41 & M-35,
Gladstone, MI 49837 (906-786-
2351).

Campgrounds: Perkins County
Park, in the village of Big Bay
(906-345-9353).

Special Regulations: None known.

Chamber of Commerce: Marquette
Area C of C, 501 S. Front St.,
Marquette, MI 49855 (906-226-6591).

Lake Independence is located in northwest Marquette County at Big Bay near Big Bay Point on Lake Superior. The entire east end of the lake is low, with sand bluffs beyond covered with white birch, oak and maple. A firm sand bottom is found on the south shore off the Yellow Dog River among the stumps.

Surveys/Stocking: A DNR boomshocking survey in June 1988 produced yellow perch to 10 years of age and 12 inches along with walleyes to 18 inches. Most of the perch, which represented seven age classes, were growing above state averages.

The net collection and a survey that fall yielded brown trout to 19½ inches, ciscoes to 16 inches, northern pike to 34½ inches, yellow perch to 13 inches, smallmouth bass to 15½ inches, and walleyes to 23½ inches. Walleyes, pike and ciscoes were especially abundant, and the lake appeared to be healthy overall. A manual removal of 7,580 pounds of white suckers in the spring of 1989 resulted in the capture of several

40-inch-plus pike.

The lake has not been stocked in recent years.

Tactics to Try: In spite of heavy angling pressure, Lake Independence continues to produce good to excellent fishing for most species. Great walleye spawning habitat in the form of cobble and gravel bars occurs on the northeast point and are good spots in the early season. Also, try these locations: (1) the small gravel point just north of the dam at the Iron River outlet on the east side, (2) the old Alder Creek bed, (3) contour breaks off McKenzie Bay, and (4) drop- offs from 18 to 25 feet deep elsewhere in the lake.

Although McKenzie Bay is privately-owned, plenty of food enters the lake through a connecting culvert. Anglers drift fish or troll off bottom near the culvert with minnows and night crawlers pinned to snelled hooks.

The lake's weedy east end — particularly flooded brush, grass and stumps at the mouth of the inflowing Yellow Dog River — produce northern pike year-round. Another good spot is a big weedbed just east of Alder Creek Bay. Toss or troll Mepps bucktail spinners and red-and-

white spoons, or bobber fish with a sucker minnow.

Walleye hotspots, along with the west-end rocky beach, produce yellow perch. In spring and fall look to the mouth of the Yellow Dog for good perching. Know, however, that a recent abundance of rusty crayfish appear to be impacting perch populations.

Smallmouths show up off the rocky west shore, the north-shore gravel bars, and the east-end contour breaks. Surface plugs and poppers rate along with slow-trolled crawlers or minnows.

The best ciscoe fishing occurs in winter for jig fishermen working the 20- to 30-foot depth region near the dam. Use a wiggler or single salmon egg on a tiny hook.

Access: The public access site at Perkins County Park in the village of Big Bay on the lake's west side features a boat launch ramp, toilets and parking (906-345-9353). To rent a boat and motor, contact North Country Outfitters (906) 345-9504 or Little Tree Cabins (906) 345-9535.

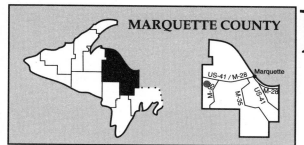
LAKE MICHIGAMME

Fishing Opportunities: Walleyes and Smallmouth Bass—Good to Excellent; Northern Pike, Yellow Perch and Whitefish—Good; Northern Muskies—Fair to Good.

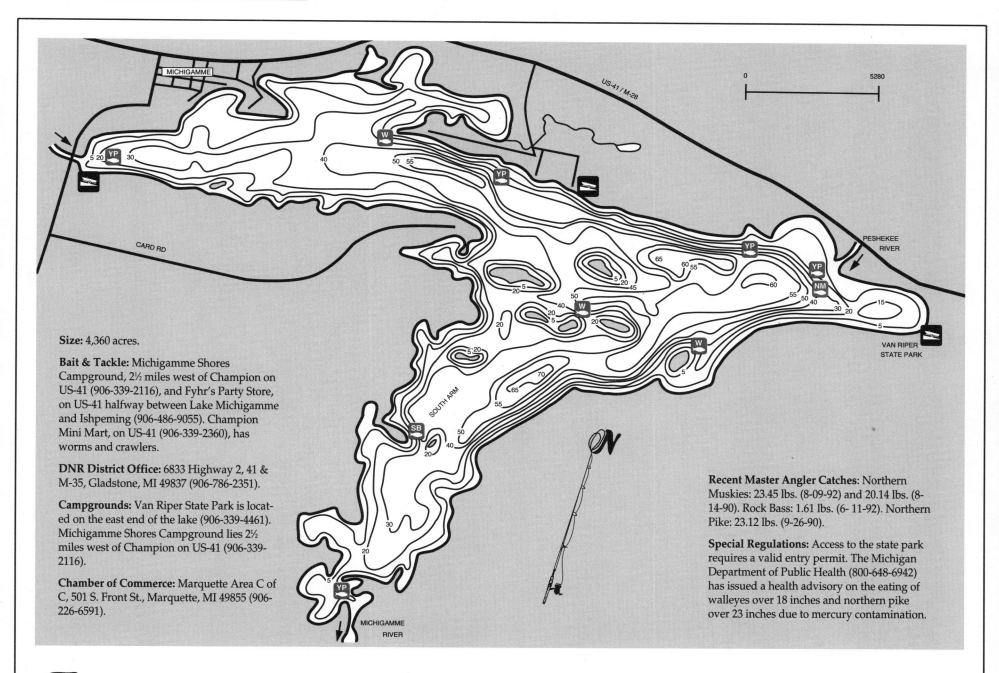

Size: 4,360 acres.

Bait & Tackle: Michigamme Shores Campground, 2½ miles west of Champion on US-41 (906-339-2116), and Fyhr's Party Store, on US-41 halfway between Lake Michigamme and Ishpeming (906-486-9055). Champion Mini Mart, on US-41 (906-339-2360), has worms and crawlers.

DNR District Office: 6833 Highway 2, 41 & M-35, Gladstone, MI 49837 (906-786-2351).

Campgrounds: Van Riper State Park is located on the east end of the lake (906-339-4461). Michigamme Shores Campground lies 2½ miles west of Champion on US-41 (906-339-2116).

Chamber of Commerce: Marquette Area C of C, 501 S. Front St., Marquette, MI 49855 (906-226-6591).

Recent Master Angler Catches: Northern Muskies: 23.45 lbs. (8-09-92) and 20.14 lbs. (8-14-90). Rock Bass: 1.61 lbs. (6-11-92). Northern Pike: 23.12 lbs. (9-26-90).

Special Regulations: Access to the state park requires a valid entry permit. The Michigan Department of Public Health (800-648-6942) has issued a health advisory on the eating of walleyes over 18 inches and northern pike over 23 inches due to mercury contamination.

Lake Michigamme is located in west-central Marquette County a mile west of Champion. It is one of Michigan's top 25 lakes in size. Much of the bottom of the dark, tannic acid-stained lake is rock and gravel, and the shoreline is mostly rocky. These conditions, plus the inflowing Peshekee River, which enters from the northeast corner, make for excellent habitat and good angling. The Michigamme River exits from the South Arm.

Anglers want to exercise caution when running motors because occasional rock piles may not be marked. Also, strong west winds tend to produce dangerous waves.

Surveys/Stocking: Complaints about poor walleye fishing prompted the DNR to schedule a fall 1993 survey, which had not been completed at our press time. The lake has a long history of good fishing; however, its great size, abundance of structure, and dark color make it difficult to fish. Another reason may be the large numbers of suckers and whitefish, which provide excellent forage for the bigger predators.

An October 1982 survey produced muskies to 43 inches, and one the following June yielded 143 whitefish that averaged about 11½ inches. In the fall of 1985 researchers found muskies ranging in size from 30 to 34 inches and also netted walleyes, yellow perch, whitefish and rock bass. When technicians returned in the spring of 1988 to remove about 4,000 pounds of nuisance suckers, they found that walleyes, smallmouths, muskies and pike all looked good.

Stocking records date to 1937 when lake trout were introduced. Biologists added smelt in 1942 and currently stock the lake with fingerlings during even-numbered years. In 1990 they released 40,000 walleyes and in 1992 planted out 28,000 walleyes and 10,500 smallmouth bass.

Tactics to Try: Michigamme is one of the U.P.'s premier native muskie lakes, and one of the best spots to catch a big muskie or pike is along the drop-off below the mouth of the Peshekee River, which has formed a delta of sand over the years. Big spoons, bucktail spinners and jerkbaits produce at any given time. In 1976 the lake yielded a former state record muskie, a 40-lb., 15-oz. brute.

Sometimes anglers retrieving a hooked walleye witness a big pike or muskie maul their catch. Most 'eyes are 12 to 14 inches although the lake throws occasional 7-pounders. A hot tactic is to slow troll an F4 or F5 Flatfish in fluorescent green after weighting it with a ⅜-oz. sinker to get the lure down 15 to 20 feet. Bounce the lure along the rocky bottom around the many islands and throughout the lake.

First discovered in 1950, whitefish can best be caught in summer by jigging worms or single salmon eggs on small hooks in water over 25 feet deep. In October, whitefish spawn in the shallows and anglers can wade for them. Fish are available on the surface during mayfly hatches in May and June.

The best places for perch are around remnant north-shore fish shelters, above the old dam at the terminus of the South Arm, and along the extreme west end.

Access: An improved access site three miles east of Michigamme on the north shore includes a paved boat launch ramp, courtesy pier, toilets and parking for 20 vehicles. There is also a boat launch in Van Riper State Park and another at the lake's extreme west end on Card Rd. just into Baraga County. To rent a boat, contact Michigamme Shores Campground (906-339-2116) (see listing under Campgrounds, Bait & Tackle).

SQUAW LAKE

Fishing Opportunities: Rainbow Trout and Splake—Fair to Good; Smallmouth Bass, Bluegills and Yellow Perch—Fair; Northern Pike—Poor.

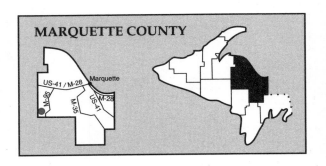
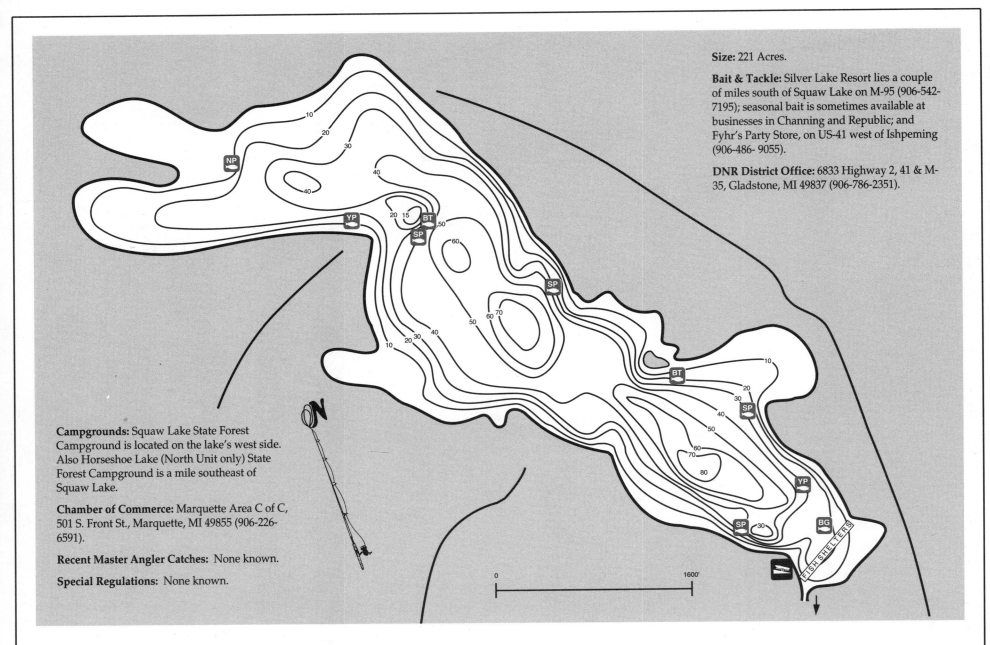

Size: 221 Acres.

Bait & Tackle: Silver Lake Resort lies a couple of miles south of Squaw Lake on M-95 (906-542-7195); seasonal bait is sometimes available at businesses in Channing and Republic; and Fyhr's Party Store, on US-41 west of Ishpeming (906-486- 9055).

DNR District Office: 6833 Highway 2, 41 & M-35, Gladstone, MI 49837 (906-786-2351).

Campgrounds: Squaw Lake State Forest Campground is located on the lake's west side. Also Horseshoe Lake (North Unit only) State Forest Campground is a mile southeast of Squaw Lake.

Chamber of Commerce: Marquette Area C of C, 501 S. Front St., Marquette, MI 49855 (906-226-6591).

Recent Master Angler Catches: None known.

Special Regulations: None known.

Squaw Lake, which acts as a tributary to the Fence River, is located in extreme westcentral Marquette County a couple of miles west of M-95 between Channing and Republic. The scenic surrounding countryside is mostly hardwood-covered hills, and the soil is light, with rocky outcroppings. Squaw Lake, which also goes by the name of Long Lake, is connected to 30-acre Little Squaw Lake by a 300-foot-long navigable channel. Deeper waters of both lakes contain organic deposits, while gravel, rubble, boulders and sand occur in shoal areas. This structure, along with drop-offs, are good places to fish.

Most of Squaw Lake's beautiful shoreline is undeveloped, and weeds and other vegetation are scarce. Besides stocked trout, the lake occasionally serves up a few northern pike, small yellow perch and smallmouth bass.

The DNR has managed the lake as a two-story trout lake for rainbows, lakers and splake since 1942. Fishing quality typically runs from good to poor depending upon how large the trout are when planted out and how often undesirable species like suckers and small yellow perch are removed manually or chemically.

Surveys/Stocking: A September 1985 gill net survey yielded nine year-classes of yellow perch to 13 inches, all of which were growing above respective state averages. A few bluegills ranged to 8½ inches and smallmouth bass measured to 19 inches. A single northern pike taped 33 inches, rainbows ran to 21½ inches, and splake measured to a bragging 37 inches.

A spring/summer 1993 net survey produced a large number of 13- and 14-inch rainbow trout along with fair numbers of 9- to 10-inch yellow perch. Largemouth and smallmouth bass, rock bass, pumpkinseed sunfish and bluegills were also collected. Overall, the fish population looked very healthy.

In 1991 managers released 10,260 rainbow trout; in 1992 they stocked 12,260 rainbows and 9,000 splake; and in 1993 they planted out an estimated 11,300 rainbows and 7,350 splake. All fish were fingerlings.

Tactics to Try: Although most trout taken are barely legal in length, the lake has served up splake and rainbows to 10 pounds and lake trout to 20 pounds. A good wintertime technique is to bait tip-ups with chubs or dead smelt. Oxygen levels fall off fast below 30 feet,

indicating that anglers will have most success in the shallower stretches.

Mepps spinners, Rapalas and small Flatfish are effective for trout during the open-water fishing season because the lures resemble the lake's main forage species — spottail and bluntnose shiners and small suckers in 3- to 4-inch lengths. A good tactic is to troll slowly over drop-offs, shelves and humps, of which there are plenty. Pull the lures clean or fish them behind small cowbell strings.

A good trick to nail big perch, along with trout, is to drift a small minnow through the 20- to 30-foot depths on a tight line, especially when bottom or structure is nearby.

We know of no one targeting bluegills but because the lake can be easily accessed in winter, recommend that anglers carry a few small teardrop spoons and a container of waxworms. If 'gills don't hit, the splake and perch will. Best spot: remnants of fish shelters in the 10- to 20-foot- deep contour at the boat launch site.

Access: The state forest campground on the west shore features a paved boat launch ramp, toilets and parking for seven vehicles in the extreme southwest corner. There is no place to rent a boat.

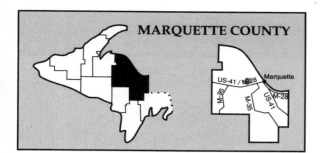

TEAL LAKE

Fishing Opportunities: Yellow Perch and Walleyes—Good to Excellent; Smallmouth Bass, Pumpkinseed Sunfish and Black Crappies—Available.

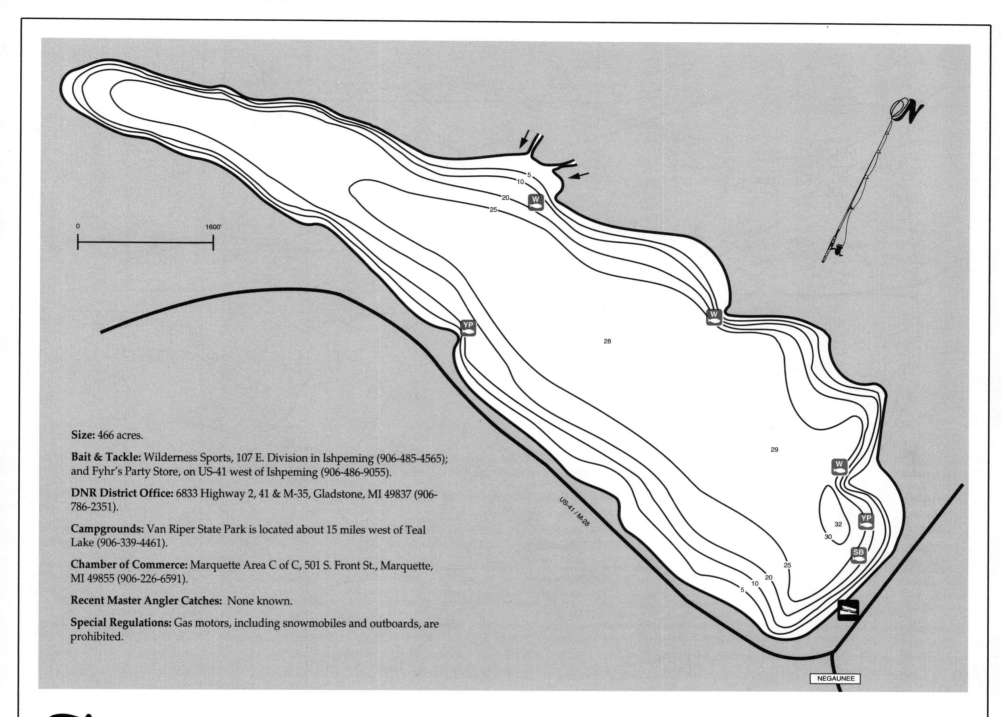

Size: 466 acres.

Bait & Tackle: Wilderness Sports, 107 E. Division in Ishpeming (906-485-4565); and Fyhr's Party Store, on US-41 west of Ishpeming (906-486-9055).

DNR District Office: 6833 Highway 2, 41 & M-35, Gladstone, MI 49837 (906-786-2351).

Campgrounds: Van Riper State Park is located about 15 miles west of Teal Lake (906-339-4461).

Chamber of Commerce: Marquette Area C of C, 501 S. Front St., Marquette, MI 49855 (906-226-6591).

Recent Master Angler Catches: None known.

Special Regulations: Gas motors, including snowmobiles and outboards, are prohibited.

eal Lake is located in northcentral Marquette County off US-41/M-28 between Negaunee and Ishpeming. The lake lies in the vicinity of rocky soils and rolling hills forested by aspen and red and white pine. The north and west shores remain in a wild state and are characterized by large granite outcroppings and mixed hardwoods and pine timber. Cottages and homes dot the east end along with undeveloped frontage owned by the City of Negaunee.

Water color is green due to algae growth, and weeds are common along the south shore to depths of 8 feet and are also scattered elsewhere throughout the lake. Two unnamed inlets fuel the lake, whose outlet is the water treatment plant for the city. Water fluctuations of three to four feet occur annually. The lake features a limited amount of shoreline shallows, with most of its bottom at least 15 feet deep.

Surveys/Stocking: A May 1988 DNR net survey showed all ages of yellow perch, pumpkinseed sunfish and smallmouth bass to be growing above respective state averages. A large number of 9- to 12½-inch perch were collected along with walleyes to 19 inches and sunfish to 7½ inches. The lake should continue to improve due to a spring 1992 workers' removal of 38,189 pounds of white suckers, which averaged nearly 18 inches in length. A 1982 removal, which resulted in a similar amount of suckers taken out, contributed to an improved fishery for a few years.

Smallmouth bass were released as early as 1922, and lake trout first went into the lake in 1927. Species stocked in later years include largemouths, pike, perch and bluegills. In recent years managers have focused on walleyes.

In 1992 they stocked 19,400 walleye fingerlings and 600,000 walleye fry, and in 1993 they released an estimated one million fry. Teal is one of the few U.P. lakes where walleyes naturally reproduce as well.

Tactics to Try: Rock and gravel shoals along the north shore and points on the northwest end are always good spots for walleyes, and anglers recently reported plenty of young fish from 11 to 12 inches long, which should just be coming into the fishery.

Drift fishing with leeches, minnows or air-injected night crawlers is a rated tactic, but walleyes will also hit crankbaits and vertical jigs with curley tails. White, chartreuse, yellow or green are good colors to try.

Walleye fishermen report catching smallmouths and perch with these lures, baits and methods. Spinnerbaits or plastic crawlers are good artificials to toss for smallmouths, and small minnows work well on big perch, especially in winter.

Fishing pressure is moderate then — compared to heavier activity in summer — and the northwest points get the most attention.

Access: The City of Negaunee owns an unimproved access site, including a boat launch, at the lake's east end off US-41. The ramp is soft sand and can cause problems for anglers with larger boats. The DNR is working with a local sportsmen's club to improve the launch site. There is no place to rent a boat.

WITCH LAKE

Fishing Opportunities: Walleyes, Bluegills, Smallmouth Bass and Walleyes—Good; Northern Pike—Fair.

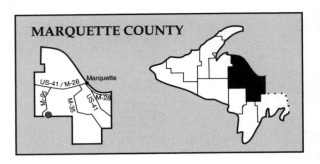

MARQUETTE COUNTY

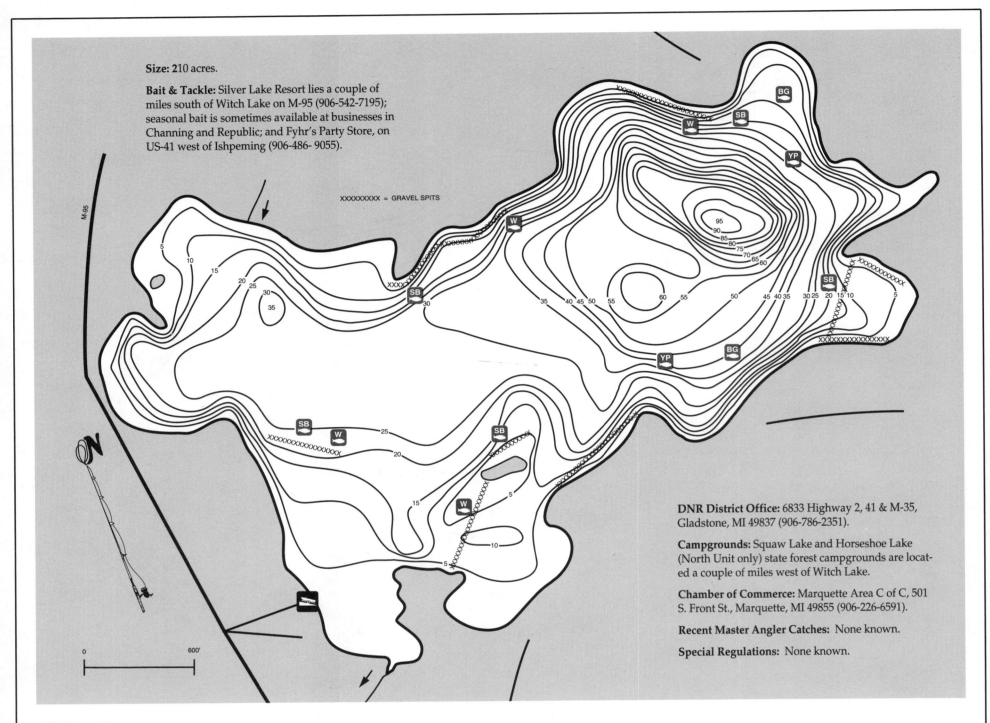

Size: 210 acres.

Bait & Tackle: Silver Lake Resort lies a couple of miles south of Witch Lake on M-95 (906-542-7195); seasonal bait is sometimes available at businesses in Channing and Republic; and Fyhr's Party Store, on US-41 west of Ishpeming (906-486- 9055).

XXXXXXXXX = GRAVEL SPITS

DNR District Office: 6833 Highway 2, 41 & M-35, Gladstone, MI 49837 (906-786-2351).

Campgrounds: Squaw Lake and Horseshoe Lake (North Unit only) state forest campgrounds are located a couple of miles west of Witch Lake.

Chamber of Commerce: Marquette Area C of C, 501 S. Front St., Marquette, MI 49855 (906-226-6591).

Recent Master Angler Catches: None known.

Special Regulations: None known.

Witch Lake is located in extreme southwest Marquette County between Channing and Republic and is visible from Highway M-95, which connects the two communities. The lake is fairly well- developed with cottages and year-round homes, but it also supports heavy growths of white birch, spruce, poplar and Norway pine in upland areas and balsam, hemlock and even some tamarack in lowland areas along the west side.

The clear, clean lake is lightly stained due to moderate amounts of weed growth in shallow areas. Gravel spits in several locations provide good spawning habitat for smallmouth bass and walleyes. Twin deep-water basins in the east third of the lake plunge to 80 and 95 feet respectively. Points, shoals and a small island provide habitat diversity.

The soft bottom in the northwest corner of the lake along M-95 allegedly claimed a bulldozer years ago. According to local legend, the dozer is still buried somewhere deep in the muck, and it is clearly a poor place for wading fishermen to visit.

Surveys/Stocking: A September 1989 DNR gill net survey collected walleyes to 20 inches, yellow perch to 13 inches, smallmouth bass to 4½ pounds, bluegills and pumpkinseed sunfish to 7 inches, and several small northern pike. Nearly all fish collected were growing above respective state averages for species and age.

The survey further revealed that biannual walleye fingerling plants were succeeding and that yellow perch were in good shape, thanks to a manual removal of white suckers in the early 1980s.

In 1991 managers released 21,000 walleye fingerlings.

Tactics to Try: The rock and gravel bottom along the north shore produces smallmouth bass and walleyes for drift fishermen using Lindy Rigs and jiggers relying on Fuzz-E Grubs in purple or smoke colors. Leeches are the hands-down favorite for these lures, but crawlers and minnows also produce. Further, Hot 'N Tots, Storm Thundersticks, Ratt-L- Traps and other crankbaits are productive here and along gravel seams elsewhere in the lake.

Weedlines produce good catches of bluegills and yellow perch for anglers who row slowly or stillfish with small ribbon leeches. A good technique is to pin the leech to a bare hook and weight it slightly with a small barrel sinker. The slip bobber approach to live-bait fishing is also productive. Good spots include the bays and around the small island. The best times are low-light conditions of early morning and evening.

Fishing pressure is moderate in summer and light in winter.

Access: The public access site is located on the lake's south side and features a paved boat launch ramp, toilets and parking for eight vehicles. There is no place to rent a boat.

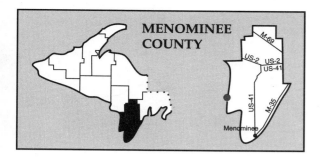

MENOMINEE COUNTY

CHALK HILLS FLOWAGE

Fishing Opportunities: Walleyes, Northern Pike and Yellow Perch—Good to Excellent; Black Crappies, Bluegills, Largemouth Bass and Smallmouth Bass—Poor to Fair.

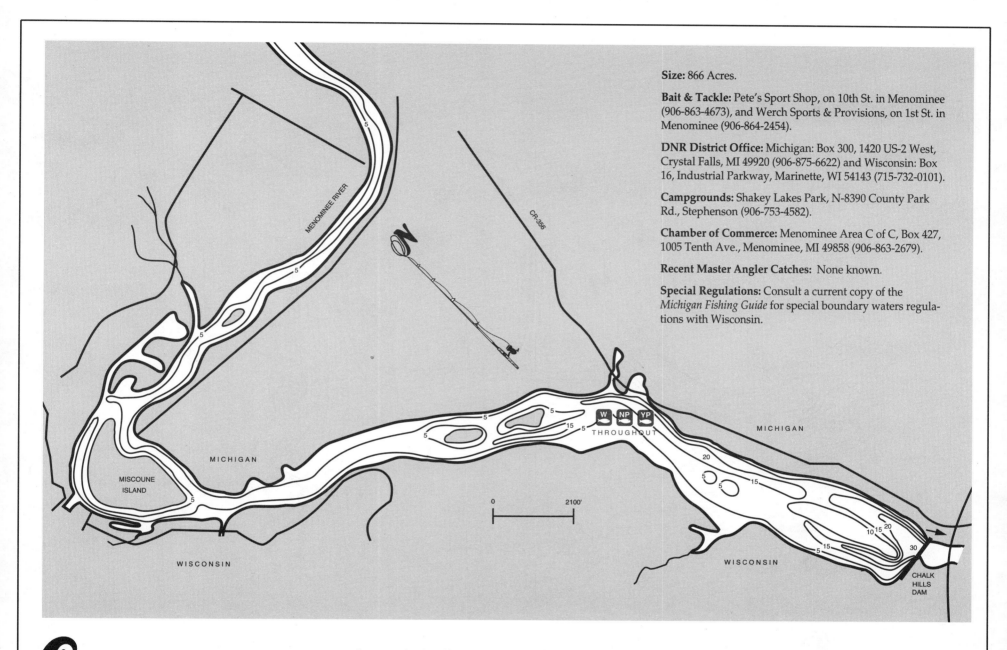

Size: 866 Acres.

Bait & Tackle: Pete's Sport Shop, on 10th St. in Menominee (906-863-4673), and Werch Sports & Provisions, on 1st St. in Menominee (906-864-2454).

DNR District Office: Michigan: Box 300, 1420 US-2 West, Crystal Falls, MI 49920 (906-875-6622) and Wisconsin: Box 16, Industrial Parkway, Marinette, WI 54143 (715-732-0101).

Campgrounds: Shakey Lakes Park, N-8390 County Park Rd., Stephenson (906-753-4582).

Chamber of Commerce: Menominee Area C of C, Box 427, 1005 Tenth Ave., Menominee, MI 49858 (906-863-2679).

Recent Master Angler Catches: None known.

Special Regulations: Consult a current copy of the *Michigan Fishing Guide* for special boundary waters regulations with Wisconsin.

Chalk Hills Rapids Flowage is the fifth upstream impoundment on the Menominee River in central Menominee County. The huge river, which is formed from the Michigamme and Brule rivers near Florence, Wisconsin, flows southerly for 118 miles, separating Wisconsin from Michigan, before emptying into Green Bay at Marinette, Wisconsin and Menominee, Michigan.

A detailed Menominee River Fisheries Plan defines a number of objectives that, if enacted, will improve fishing on the many impoundments for years to come. These objectives include restoring the population of lake sturgeon to historic levels of 20,000 to 25,000 fish (currently sturgeon numbers are at only 30 percent) and to restore historic runs of pike, smallmouths, muskies, walleyes and whitefish from Green Bay. Blocking lampreys from the lower river and improving water quality will improve trout and salmon populations.

Chalk Hills Flowage has a maximum depth of 30 feet and features several islands and shallow bays, which offer good habitat diversity. The 20 miles of river between the impoundment and Sturgeon Falls Dam is mostly undeveloped and includes two natural water falls, numerous rock outcroppings, rapids and deep pools, all of which make for one of the Menominee's most scenic sections.

Surveys/Stocking: A 1991 fall boomshocking survey by the Wisconsin DNR indicated that walleyes were sustaining good natural reproduction. Earlier that year researchers surveyed the impoundment with fyke nets and learned that northern pike showed good size distribution although big fish were rare. The dominant panfish was yellow perch, carp were present in moderate numbers, and bullheads were the dominant species.

The number of gamefish and their maximum respective lengths included 248 walleyes to 29 inches, 216 pike to 42 inches, five largemouths to 15.2 inches, 10 smallmouths to 17 inches, 508 yellow perch to 13.4 inches, and a few crappies, pumpkinseed sunfish and bluegills.

The Wisconsin DNR has been stocking sturgeon below the Sturgeon Falls Dam, and from 1978 to 1987, an average of 3,000 tiger or northern muskies were also released. No releases were made during the period 1991 to 1993.

Tactics to Try: Fishing pressure is light, with only 98 shore anglers and 270 boat fishermen using the impoundment during the period July to October 1991. This usage amounts to about two anglers per day.

In addition to fishing the flowage, walleye anglers should know that spawners congregate below the dam in spring and, along with occasional smallmouths, make for a good summer fishery as well. No special tactics work better than others, but those anglers with sonar have a decided advantage due to their ability to find structure and fish in the discolored water.

Sturgeon fishermen score in the fall by fishing worm gobs or dead minnows on bottom.

Access: At Gerald Welling Memorial Park, four miles west of Nathan, is a paved boat launch ramp, toilets and parking for two dozen vehicles. Power company campgrounds also permit access to the lake. There is no place to rent a boat.

Menominee County

WHITE RAPIDS FLOWAGE

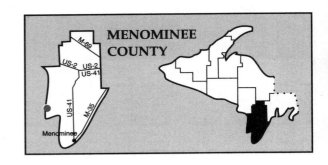

MENOMINEE COUNTY

Fishing Opportunities: Walleyes, Northern Pike and Largemouth Bass—Fair to Good; Smallmouth Bass, Yellow Perch, and Bluegills—Fair.

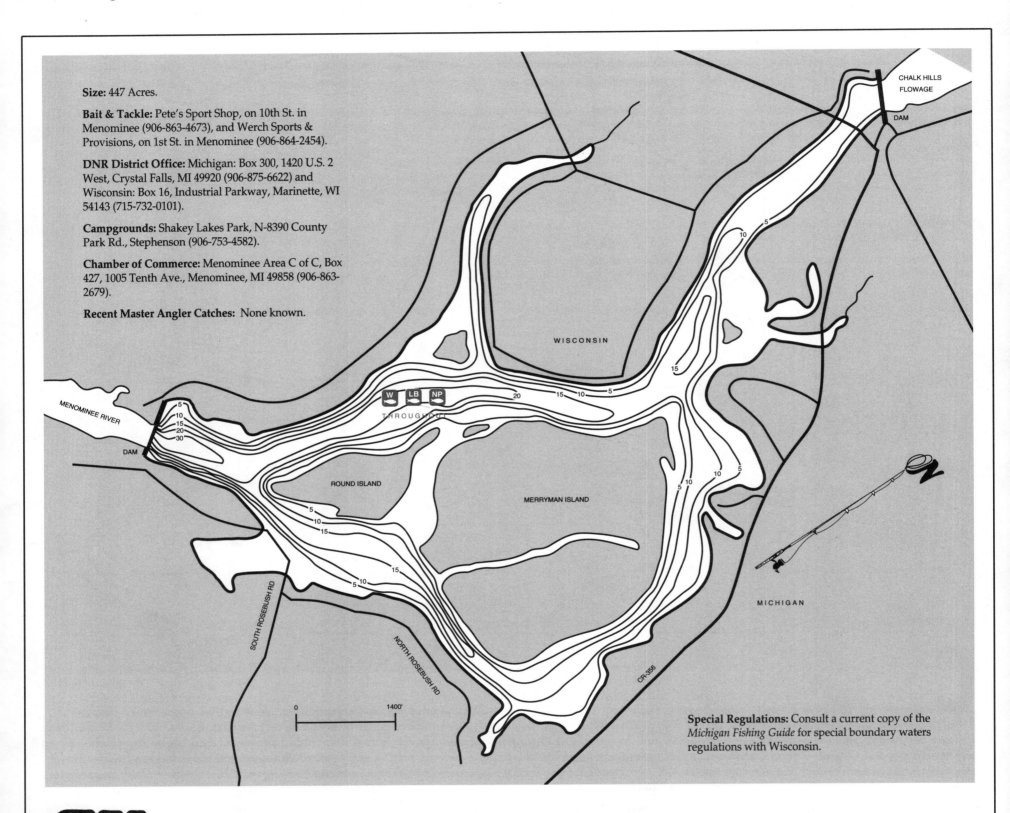

Size: 447 Acres.

Bait & Tackle: Pete's Sport Shop, on 10th St. in Menominee (906-863-4673), and Werch Sports & Provisions, on 1st St. in Menominee (906-864-2454).

DNR District Office: Michigan: Box 300, 1420 U.S. 2 West, Crystal Falls, MI 49920 (906-875-6622) and Wisconsin: Box 16, Industrial Parkway, Marinette, WI 54143 (715-732-0101).

Campgrounds: Shakey Lakes Park, N-8390 County Park Rd., Stephenson (906-753-4582).

Chamber of Commerce: Menominee Area C of C, Box 427, 1005 Tenth Ave., Menominee, MI 49858 (906-863-2679).

Recent Master Angler Catches: None known.

Special Regulations: Consult a current copy of the *Michigan Fishing Guide* for special boundary waters regulations with Wisconsin.

White Rapids Flowage is the fourth upstream impoundment on the Menominee River in central Menominee County. Fishing pressure is considered to be light, with only 271 shore anglers and 381 boat fishermen noted during a July to October 1991 survey. This figures out to an average use of less than two anglers per day.

Surveys/Stocking: Current fish populations are generally stable but at lower levels than before 10 hydro dams blocked access from Green Bay to the upper river. A 1991 fyke net survey by the Wisconsin DNR resulted in a catch similar to the last survey conducted in 1977. Although there were more northern pike in 1991, they ran smaller in size.

Walleye populations were unchanged, with plenty young-of-the-year fish present. Some muskies were captured, and there was an increased number of bluegills plus a shift from domination of smallmouth bass to largemouth bass. Black crappies and yellow perch are also available. Although historically present, lake sturgeon no longer live in the impoundment.

The number of gamefish and respective maximum lengths included 162 walleyes to 29½ inches, 383 pike to 42 inches, six muskies to 37 inches, 33 largemouths to 19½ inches, one smallmouth at 13.3 inches, 342 yellow perch to 12.2 inches, 186 bluegills to 8.3 inches, and 108 crappies to 13.8 inches. Neither the Wisconsin nor Michigan DNRs stock the reservoir.

Tactics to Try: Live bait is best for all species, but northern fishermen can also score on various spoons, plugs and spinners. Hot lures for largemouths include bass-colored diving Rebels, chrome Tadpollies and crayfish-colored Shad Raps.

Access: Access is available at the White Rapids Dam tailwater, but the site is not improved. There is no place to rent a boat.

ONTONAGON COUNTY

COURTNEY LAKE

Fishing Opportunities: Brook Trout—Good to Excellent.

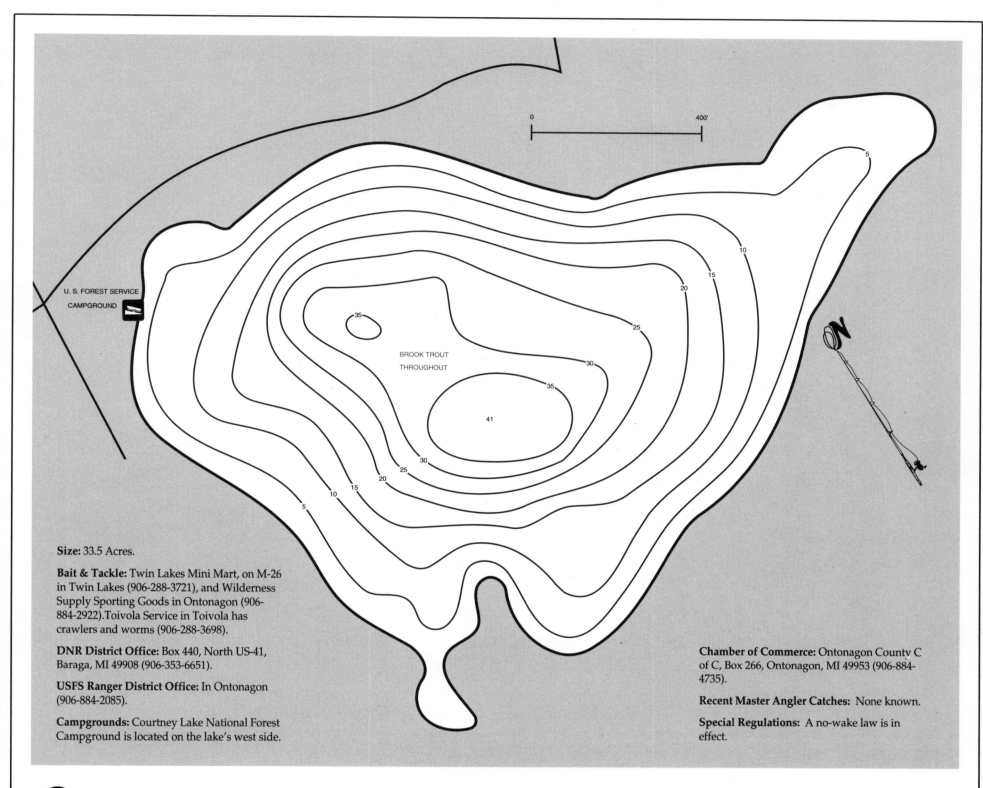

U. S. FOREST SERVICE CAMPGROUND

BROOK TROUT THROUGHOUT

Size: 33.5 Acres.

Bait & Tackle: Twin Lakes Mini Mart, on M-26 in Twin Lakes (906-288-3721), and Wilderness Supply Sporting Goods in Ontonagon (906-884-2922).Toivola Service in Toivola has crawlers and worms (906-288-3698).

DNR District Office: Box 440, North US-41, Baraga, MI 49908 (906-353-6651).

USFS Ranger District Office: In Ontonagon (906-884-2085).

Campgrounds: Courtney Lake National Forest Campground is located on the lake's west side.

Chamber of Commerce: Ontonagon County C of C, Box 266, Ontonagon, MI 49953 (906-884-4735).

Recent Master Angler Catches: None known.

Special Regulations: A no-wake law is in effect.

Courtney Lake is located in the Ottawa National Forest in northeast Ontonagon County about 7½ miles east of Mass and seven miles west of Nisula. It is southeast of the junction of Highways M-38 and M-28. The pretty, green lake is surrounded by mixed hardwoods and conifers and consists of a single basin with a depth of 41 feet.

The immediate shoreline is fairly steep. Shoal areas contain a mixture of sand and pulpy peat, and deeper areas are peat-bottomed. Vegetation is limited to scattered water lilies and a few submerged weedbeds.

Surveys/Stocking: In the late 1930s and early 1940s, biologists stocked bluegills and smallmouth and largemouth bass. By 1948, however, a survey indicated that the lake was suitable for cold-water species, and so managers began stocking rainbows in 1951. Before long, yellow perch and sunfish took over the lake, and the first of several chemical treatments was initiated.

At various times between subsequent treatments, the DNR has released rainbows, splake and brook trout. Good fishing resulted after each chemical reclamation and restocking. A July 1990 fyke net survey indicated that the lake was again being taken over by golden shiners and stunted perch. The lake was subsequently treated in the fall of 1991.

In 1992 managers released 600 adult brook trout and 3,500 yearlings, and in 1993 they stocked an estimated 2,865 additional yearling fish. Some of these adult fish are large enough to qualify for a DNR Master Angler Award at 18 inches or 2 pounds.

Tactics to Try: The lake hosts big hatches of mayflies in early July just before dark. Trout feed on them, along with stoneflies, red-bellied dace, crayfish and other foods. Besides providing fly fishing opportunities, the lake offers ice anglers the chance to catch a trophy brook trout. For best results, use tiny teardrop spoons and waxworms or wigglers. A portable sonar unit will help you locate fish.

Because Courtney is not a designated trout lake, fishing is permitted year around.

Access: The USFS maintains an unimproved access site at its campground on the northwest shore that includes a gravel boat launch ramp, toilets and parking for a half-dozen vehicles. There is no place to rent a boat.

MIRROR LAKE

Fishing Opportunities: Brook Trout—Good to Excellent.

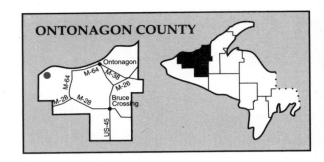
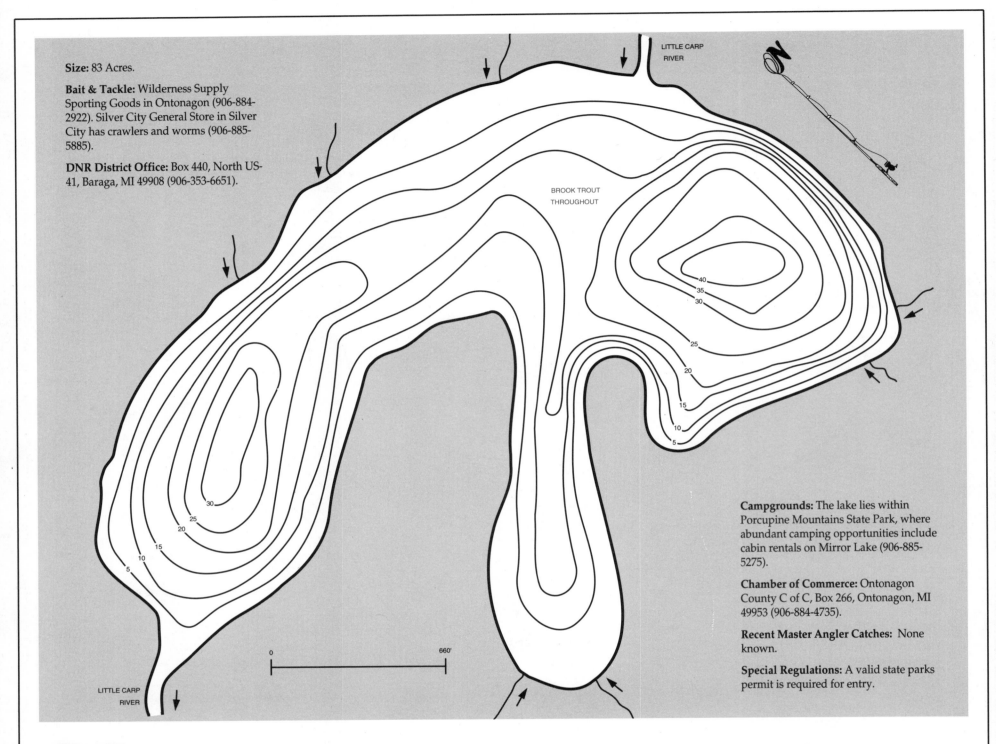

Size: 83 Acres.

Bait & Tackle: Wilderness Supply Sporting Goods in Ontonagon (906-884-2922). Silver City General Store in Silver City has crawlers and worms (906-885-5885).

DNR District Office: Box 440, North US-41, Baraga, MI 49908 (906-353-6651).

BROOK TROUT THROUGHOUT

LITTLE CARP RIVER

Campgrounds: The lake lies within Porcupine Mountains State Park, where abundant camping opportunities include cabin rentals on Mirror Lake (906-885-5275).

Chamber of Commerce: Ontonagon County C of C, Box 266, Ontonagon, MI 49953 (906-884-4735).

Recent Master Angler Catches: None known.

Special Regulations: A valid state parks permit is required for entry.

LITTLE CARP RIVER

0   660'

Mirror Lake is located in extreme westcentral Ontonagon County about 10 miles west of White Pine and lies entirely within Porcupine Mountains State Park. Surrounding terrain is rolling to hilly and is largely wooded. Lake depths slide to 40 feet, water color is a light brown, and vegetation is mostly scarce except for water lilies, water shield and musk grass. Bottom composition along the inclines is mostly sand and gravel.

The lake's main inlet and outlet is the Little Carp River, which comes in on the eastcentral side and exits from the west side of the north basin. Other small inlets provide a source of water as well as spawning habitat for brook trout.

In spite of its remoteness, Mirror Lake sustains moderate to high fishing pressure. It is an ideal place to hike in and relax, and the fishing at times can be very good for small brookies.

Surveys/Stocking: The lake has a long history of producing decent brook trout fishing except for periods when large chubs dominated the biomass. The first survey, conducted in 1941, found brook trout and white suckers along with creek chubs, fathead minnows, sticklebacks and black-nosed dace. An initial chemical treatment occurred in 1964 for the purpose of removing suckers, but a subsequent gill net survey showed both the sucker and chub population to be unchanged.

The DNR annually stocked rainbows and splake from 1965 to 1971. More recently, hybrid brook trout have been released. In 1993 managers planted out an estimated 6,300 yearlings.

An October 1988 gill net survey found good numbers of splake plus one brook trout. About 15 percent of the biomass was trout; the rest was suckers, chubs and shiners. Because of connection to the Little Carp River, the lake can never be completely rid of suckers and chubs, which, as adults, compete for food with brook trout.

Tactics to Try: The midsummer thermocline in Mirror Lake is reportedly at only 12 to 24 feet, and so trout fishermen will do well to concentrate efforts there. Oxygen levels are too low to support fish deeper than this, especially in summer. The best fishing occurs in the spring or until mid-June. Although fish bite year around, including in the winter, they can be difficult to induce to bite.

Live bait helps, and waxworms, wigglers, worms, pieces of crawler and whole salmon eggs will occasionally work. Fly fishermen seem to do better on nymph patterns in this lake.

Because Mirror is not a designated trout lake, fishing is permitted year around.

Access: The DNR maintains 2½ miles of foot trails to the lake. Three wilderness cabins along the north shore can be rented through Porcupine Mountain State Park, which is open year around. The fee includes a rowboat (906-885-5275).

ONTONAGON COUNTY

SUDDEN LAKE

Fishing Opportunities: Walleyes—Good to Excellent; Yellow Perch and Northern Pike—Fair.

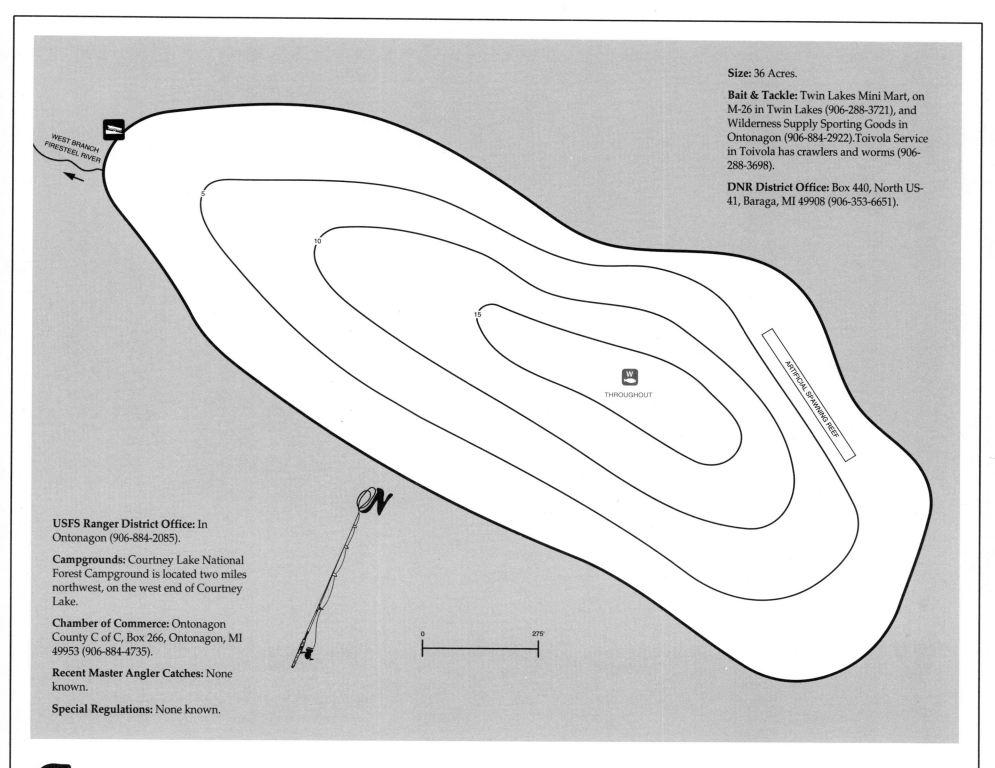

Size: 36 Acres.

Bait & Tackle: Twin Lakes Mini Mart, on M-26 in Twin Lakes (906-288-3721), and Wilderness Supply Sporting Goods in Ontonagon (906-884-2922). Toivola Service in Toivola has crawlers and worms (906-288-3698).

DNR District Office: Box 440, North US-41, Baraga, MI 49908 (906-353-6651).

USFS Ranger District Office: In Ontonagon (906-884-2085).

Campgrounds: Courtney Lake National Forest Campground is located two miles northwest, on the west end of Courtney Lake.

Chamber of Commerce: Ontonagon County C of C, Box 266, Ontonagon, MI 49953 (906-884-4735).

Recent Master Angler Catches: None known.

Special Regulations: None known.

WEST BRANCH FIRESTEEL RIVER

THROUGHOUT

ARTIFICIAL SPAWNING REEF

0   275'

S udden Lake is located in northeast Ontonagon County in the Ottawa National Forest about six miles southwest of Nisula. This shallow, weedy lake is often encircled with pondweed and is dark brown in color. Maximum depth is 15 feet. The south and west shores are especially marshy, and surrounding terrain is mostly level and covered with pine. An outlet on the west side is the West Branch of the Firesteel River.

Surveys/Stocking: After an initial release of 450,000 walleye fry in 1940, and 400 smallmouth bass and 170 largemouth bass in 1942, the lake was not stocked for several years due to its supposed unsuitability for gamefish. In the 1950s managers released bluegills, largemouth bass and northern pike. They also began a periodic manual removal of small yellow perch. Tiger muskies made their

appearance in 1982.

In June 1990 DNR researchers surveyed the lake with fyke nets and collected 70 walleyes that averaged 1½ pounds and ranged to 3 pounds each. These healthy fish were apparently from the 1986 stocking, although fingerlings were also released in 1988 and 1989. Other species collected were northern pike and yellow perch, the latter of which provides forage for the predators. The number and size of pike are not large, and perch tend to run small.

The lake was treated with 4,850 pounds of lime in 1990 to improve pH levels for fish, and USFS workers created a rock reef that winter. An October 1991 boomshocking survey turned up 24 young-of-the-year walleyes, an indication that the reef was working to naturally reproduce fish. A few other walleyes that were stunned measured up to 20 inches each.

The DNR has not stocked the lake in recent

years.

Tactics to Try: The spawning reef is located on the northeast shore straight across from the boat landing. The reef is 200 feet long and lies along the 5-foot-deep contour. It is sometimes a good spot to find walleyes at the season opener. Otherwise, the walleyes wander freely throughout the lake.

Finding them can be difficult, however, due to weeds and the lake's shallow nature. Getting them to bite depends on a subtle presentation. Use orange, gold or silver-colored lures because of the dark water. Minnows, leeches and crawlers will all work on various delivery systems including jigs, Lindy Rigs and crawler harnesses.

Access: An unimproved access site is located off USFS-16 on the lake's west side. Included are a gravel boat launch ramp, and parking for a half-dozen vehicles. There is no place to rent a boat.

VICTORIA DAM BACKWATER

Fishing Opportunities: Smallmouth Bass, Black Crappies and Yellow Perch—Good to Excellent; Northern Pike and Walleyes— Good.

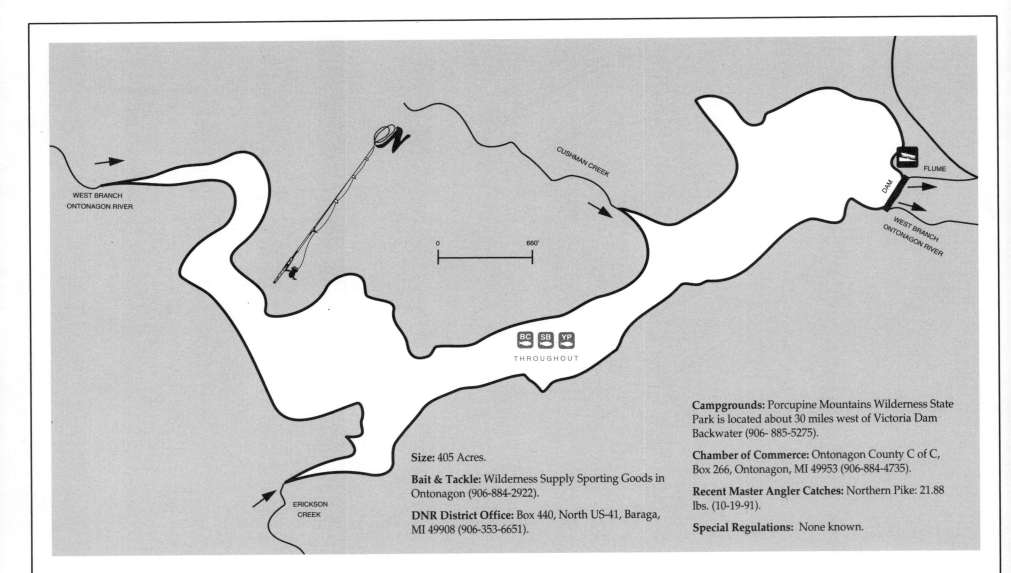

Size: 405 Acres.

Bait & Tackle: Wilderness Supply Sporting Goods in Ontonagon (906-884-2922).

DNR District Office: Box 440, North US-41, Baraga, MI 49908 (906-353-6651).

Campgrounds: Porcupine Mountains Wilderness State Park is located about 30 miles west of Victoria Dam Backwater (906- 885-5275).

Chamber of Commerce: Ontonagon County C of C, Box 266, Ontonagon, MI 49953 (906-884-4735).

Recent Master Angler Catches: Northern Pike: 21.88 lbs. (10-19-91).

Special Regulations: None known.

Victoria Dam Backwater is located in remote eastcentral Ontonagon County about 15 miles south of Ontonagon and five miles southwest of Rockland. The impoundment dates to 1930 when the original dam on the West Branch of the Ontonagon River was completed. Upper Peninsula Power Company, which owns the land around the backwater, recently rebuilt the dam.

Cushman Creek enters the northwest portion of the forested, undeveloped reservoir; Erickson Creek flows in on the southeast corner. The impoundment's water color is often turbid due to clay soils upstream and the general dark nature of rivers and lakes in this region. Aquatic vegetation is sparse, and fish cover is mostly limited to logs and rocks. Steep shoals are made up mostly of gravel, rock and a mixture of silt and clay.

Smallmouth bass and walleyes successfully spawn on some of the gravel substrate. Perhaps because of the river, the backwater does not sustain a thermocline in summer. Oxygen levels, however, are sufficient for gamefish throughout the water column. Fishing pressure is moderate to high except in winter, when only a few hardy anglers venture onto the ice.

Surveys/Stocking: A DNR survey in 1977 found an overall healthy population of gamefish. Yellow perch and black crappies were large and abundant. The nets yielded good numbers of smallmouth bass and northern pike. Fewer walleyes were found in spite of the lake having a good angling reputation for these fish.

A 1988 DNR survey revealed that walleye numbers were about the same but that pike and smallmouths had increased in both size and quantity. Yellow perch, which averaged 7.7 inches, had doubled in number to 91. Crappie abundance also doubled. All totaled, gamefish constituted more than 96 percent of the biomass collected. White suckers and rock bass were few in number.

The only fish ever planted were 2.3 million walleye fry in 1972.

Tactics to Try: The impoundment serves up good yellow perch fishing year-round for anglers willing to hunt bigger fish. At times they report catches of yellow bellies to 15 inches each. The overall best time is from the second week of July to well into the fall. Use minnows, worms or small ribbon leeches on a leadhead jig or a bare hook weighted with a slip sinker. Then drift in 25 feet of water until you find structure and fish.

The key to catching smallmouths, northerns, walleyes, crappies and even the occasional tiger muskie, according to our source, is to find the fish first. For smallmouths, start at the rocky headwaters in 15 to 20 feet of water and bounce a worm pinned to a jig off bottom. Fall is the best time. Mister Twisters and Beetle Spins also rate.

It is not uncommon for perch anglers to witness toothy northerns chase their catch to the boat. The impoundment is capable of throwing 10- to 20-pound pike. During the drawdown when the new dam was built, some anglers reported pike success while trolling and casting near the headwaters with spoon and plug hardware.

To catch slab crappies, which tend to suspend over woody structure along shore, tip a rubbertailed jig with a worm or small minnow. July is the best month.

Walleyes smack live bait skewered to a No. 4 hook weighted with a split shot or small bell sinker. Anchor or drift. Trolling coves and inlets with Shad Raps or jointed Rapalas in gold and black is also effective.

Access: Upper Peninsula Power Company maintains a public access site on the west side of the dam along the north shore. There is no place to rent a boat.

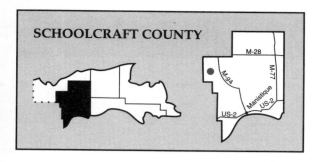

BIG ISLAND LAKE COMPLEX

Fishing Opportunities: Largemouth Bass, Smallmouth Bass, Bluegills, Yellow Perch and Northern Pike—Fair to Excellent.

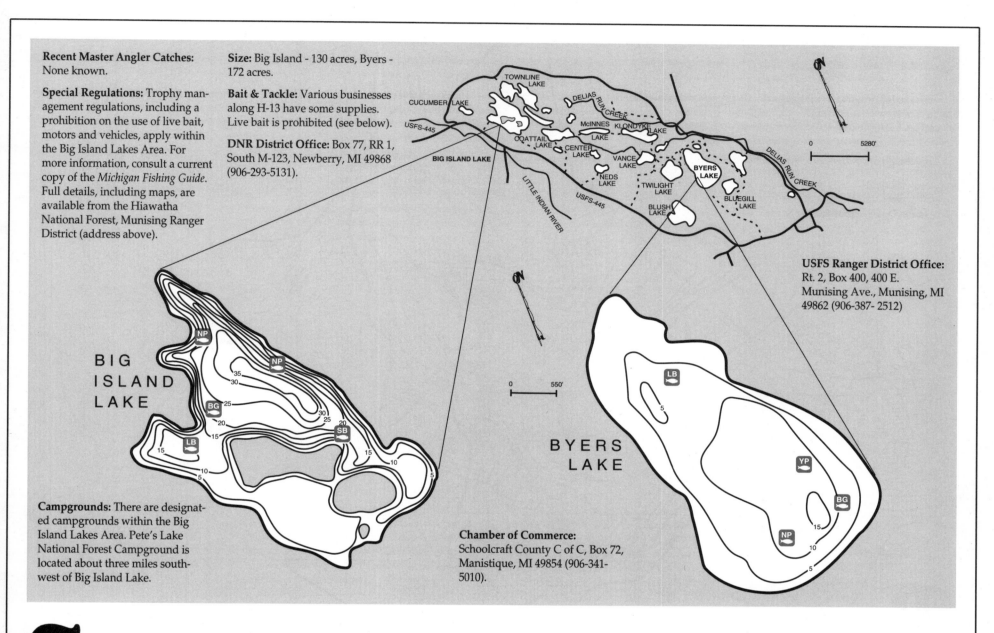

Recent Master Angler Catches: None known.

Special Regulations: Trophy management regulations, including a prohibition on the use of live bait, motors and vehicles, apply within the Big Island Lakes Area. For more information, consult a current copy of the *Michigan Fishing Guide*. Full details, including maps, are available from the Hiawatha National Forest, Munising Ranger District (address above).

Size: Big Island - 130 acres, Byers - 172 acres.

Bait & Tackle: Various businesses along H-13 have some supplies. Live bait is prohibited (see below).

DNR District Office: Box 77, RR 1, South M-123, Newberry, MI 49868 (906-293-5131).

USFS Ranger District Office: Rt. 2, Box 400, 400 E. Munising Ave., Munising, MI 49862 (906-387- 2512)

Campgrounds: There are designated campgrounds within the Big Island Lakes Area. Pete's Lake National Forest Campground is located about three miles southwest of Big Island Lake.

Chamber of Commerce: Schoolcraft County C of C, Box 72, Manistique, MI 49854 (906-341-5010).

The Big Island Lake Complex is comprises 13 lakes in a special-use area of west-central Schoolcraft County near the corner with Delta and Alger counties. It is also referred to as the Big Island Lakes Canoeing Area. This federally- dedicated wilderness region is part of the Hiawatha National Forest and is managed by the U.S. Forest Service out of Munising.

We have included Big Island and Byers lakes in this book. The others are Klondyke, Mid (also called Cucumber), McInnes, Bluegill, Twilight, Blush, Neds, Vance, Coattail, Townline and Center. Neds, Bluegill, Twilight and Mid lakes are being managed for brook trout, and the others for warm-water species.

The Big Island Lake Complex is bounded on USFS-445 on the west, USFS-2257 on the south, Delias Run Creek on the east, and an unnamed east-west trail on the north. Drainage from the complex is to Lake Michigan via Delias Run Creek and the Indian River. The lakes are being managed under a 10- year program to be completed in 1994. A draft plan was being evaluated as we went to press.

Surveys/Stocking: The last DNR survey on Big Island Lake — in June 1992 — indicated that bluegills, pumpkinseed sunfish and largemouth bass were experiencing heavy harvest pressure. Even so, the nets revealed a fairly large number of 9- to 10-inch bluegills. Northern pike and rock bass were other species taken.

Byers Lake was last surveyed in 1984. Both largemouth bass and northern pike showed up in sufficient quantity and quality to make the lake a candidate as a trophy fishery. The nets revealed pike to 35 inches and largemouths to 19 inches, along with bluegills to 11 inches and pumpkinseed sunfish to 8 inches. Perch averaged 7 inches.

The DNR has not stocked the lakes in recent years with the exception of 198 tiger muskie yearlings released in Big Island in 1990.

Tactics to Try: The lakes serve up good northern pike fishing for spincasters tossing various spoons, plugs and spinners. Lunker pike are available, but the use of live bait is illegal and all artificial lures must feature only a single hook point.

Big Island Lake also produces trophy bluegills at times for flyrod fishermen and those using small tube jigs and tiny spinners. White, pink or yellow are usually the best colors. A good place for bedding bluegills on Byers Lake is among bulrushes along the east and south shoals. The fish are especially fun on a flyrod and popper or spider.

Largemouth bass redds show up along the east and west shoals. Both largemouth and smallmouth bass are available on Big Island. For best results, troll floating Rapalas or Beetlespins or toss spinnerbaits, Zara Spooks and Torpedoes.

Access: There are two ways to access the wilderness area. The more popular access site leads to Big Island Lake off USFS-445. Parking space is ample, and fishermen will have a quarter-mile hike to the lake. The other entrance is located at the Byers Lake end of the complex and involves a mile hike off a two-track road. That entrance is located about one mile west of Steuben, and there is limited parking. Personnel with the USFS expect to improve signage and mark trails in the near future. There is no place to rent a boat.

DODGE LAKE

Fishing Opportunities: Largemouth Bass, Northern Pike, Yellow Perch and Bluegills—Good; Rainbow Trout and Splake— Fair.

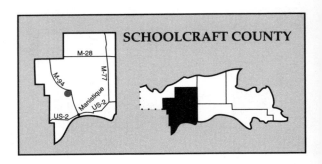

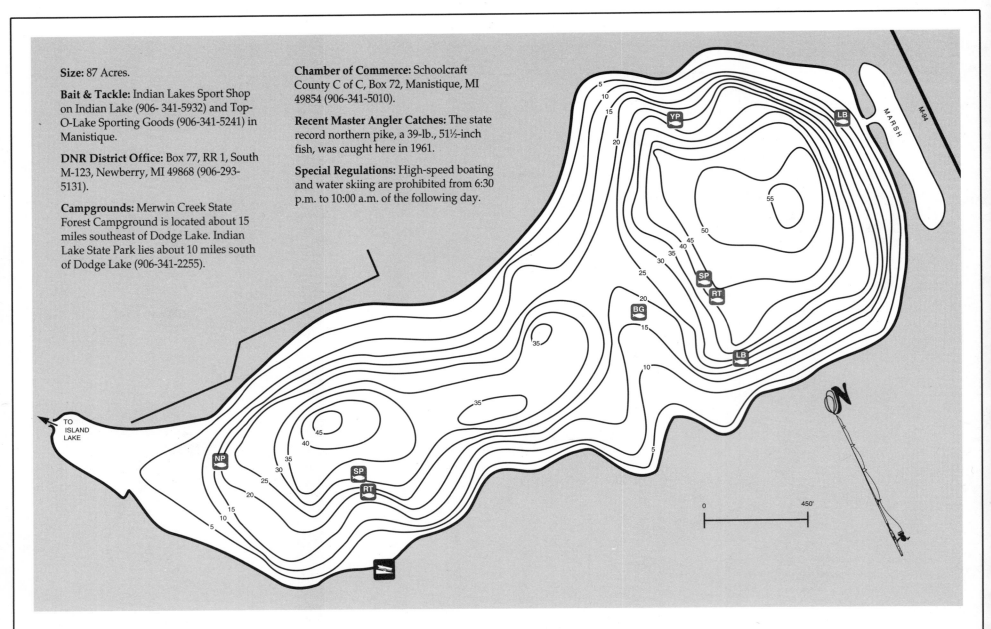

Size: 87 Acres.

Bait & Tackle: Indian Lakes Sport Shop on Indian Lake (906- 341-5932) and Top-O-Lake Sporting Goods (906-341-5241) in Manistique.

DNR District Office: Box 77, RR 1, South M-123, Newberry, MI 49868 (906-293-5131).

Campgrounds: Merwin Creek State Forest Campground is located about 15 miles southeast of Dodge Lake. Indian Lake State Park lies about 10 miles south of Dodge Lake (906-341-2255).

Chamber of Commerce: Schoolcraft County C of C, Box 72, Manistique, MI 49854 (906-341-5010).

Recent Master Angler Catches: The state record northern pike, a 39-lb., 51½-inch fish, was caught here in 1961.

Special Regulations: High-speed boating and water skiing are prohibited from 6:30 p.m. to 10:00 a.m. of the following day.

Dodge Lake is located in southwest Schoolcraft County about 11 miles north of Manistique. Mixed hardwoods cover the hills that surround the lake, which is experiencing rapid development and, consequently, increased fishing pressure.

Years ago, Dodge and connecting Island Lake produced outstanding northern pike catches and still throw the occasional lunker, but fishing pressure has cropped off most of the bigger pike and bass. Still, it is a pretty lake that affords good fishing for both warm-water species as well as splake and rainbows.

Fishing prospects appear to be picking up, and the future looks good, especially if DNR technicians replace some of the fish cover such as trees and stumps that have disappeared in recent years due to development and removal by water skiers and other boating activists.

Surveys/Stocking: The lake was first stocked in 1926 with yellow perch and in subsequent years received plantings of largemouth and smallmouth bass, bluegills and walleyes. Rainbow trout made their introduction in 1942 and have been planted at regular intervals since.

A June 1992 fyke, trap and gill net survey was hampered by severe thunderstorms. Like Island Lake, to which Dodge is connected by a short channel, the lake is experiencing heavy fishing pressure, as evidenced by the fact that only 15 percent of the largemouth bass netted were 12 or more inches long. Even so the nets revealed nine 9-inch bluegills; scale sampling proved that the bigger fish were growing faster than the state average. Bluegill stunting appeared to be imminent, however, and a manual thinning or partial chemical reclamation was suggested.

Technicians treated the lake with antimyicyn in the spring of 1993, but the effort failed and it was not clear at our press time if the DNR planned to try again. Larger statewide minimum-size limits on bass (12 inches) and pike (24 inches) that were recently enacted should improve overall fishing and could correct the stunted bluegill problem by providing larger predators.

The 1992 nets also produced northern pike, yellow perch, pumpkinseed sunfish, rock bass, and a single splake. One yellow perch older than 10 years was 14.2 inches long. An earlier survey (1985) produced a few small rainbow trout.

Some local opposition to trout releases in Dodge Lake has not daunted the DNR from wanting to manage the resource as a two-story lake. In 1991 technicians released 2,250 splake and 1,600 rainbow trout; in 1992 they stocked 2,250 of each species; and in 1993 they planted out an estimated 2,250 rainbows and 1,600 splake. All fish were yearlings.

Tactics to Try: Bass fishing is especially productive after sundown and early in the morning around docks, swimming rafts and moored boats. Try spinnerbaits in various colors during daylight hours and surface poppers, plugs and buzzbaits after dark.

Trollers and bobber fishermen using suckers or shiners catch northerns in summer, but the bigger fish typically come through the ice via tip-up or spear. This is also a good time to try for bluegills with light line and larvae pinned to a tiny gold hook or small teardrop.

Occasionally, a 10- to 15-inch splake or rainbow will hit the bluegill offerings. To concentrate solely on trout, use wigglers in winter or red worms in summer and concentrate in the 20- to 30-foot depths. Particularly in winter, trout may be deeper and often closer to the bottom. Small minnows are also worth trying.

Access: The public access site, which is located on the southwest shore, includes a paved boat launch ramp, toilets and parking for eight vehicles. To rent a boat, contact Brady's Resort on connecting Island Lake (906-341-6400).

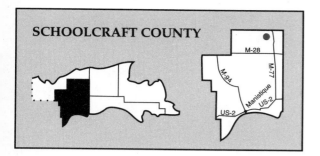

DUTCH FRED LAKE

Fishing Opportunities: Brook Trout—Good to Excellent.

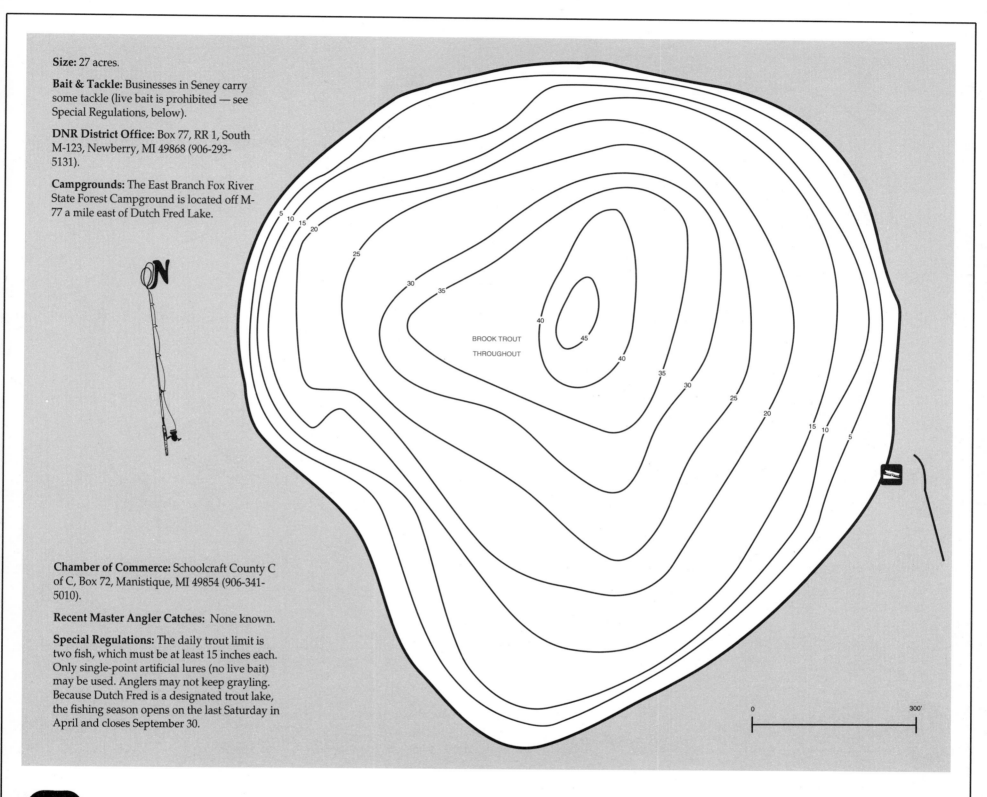

Size: 27 acres.

Bait & Tackle: Businesses in Seney carry some tackle (live bait is prohibited — see Special Regulations, below).

DNR District Office: Box 77, RR 1, South M-123, Newberry, MI 49868 (906-293-5131).

Campgrounds: The East Branch Fox River State Forest Campground is located off M-77 a mile east of Dutch Fred Lake.

Chamber of Commerce: Schoolcraft County C of C, Box 72, Manistique, MI 49854 (906-341-5010).

Recent Master Angler Catches: None known.

Special Regulations: The daily trout limit is two fish, which must be at least 15 inches each. Only single-point artificial lures (no live bait) may be used. Anglers may not keep grayling. Because Dutch Fred is a designated trout lake, the fishing season opens on the last Saturday in April and closes September 30.

BROOK TROUT THROUGHOUT

0   300'

utch Fred Lake is located in northeast Schoolcraft County about 10 miles north of Seney. Only two or three cottages dot the lake, which has no inlets nor outlets. The immediate shoreline is heavily wooded with cutover pine and some hardwoods among hilly terrain. Soil types are mostly sand, and a sandy beach surrounds most of the lake.

The lake is clear, with a maximum depth of 45 feet. Bottom composition in the shallows is mostly sand with some gravel; deeper areas feature pulpy peat. Water lilies, pondweed and smartweed occur in the 5- to 10-foot deep contour, and there are some deadheads scattered throughout.

Surveys/Stocking: Since 1949, fisheries managers have fought an ongoing battle in this lake with yellow perch and brown bullheads. After periodic chemical reclamation, biologists typically restock with brook or rainbow trout. The latest reclamation occurred in 1989 following a 1988 DNR net survey that proved yellow perch were back in force. Although no brook trout were netted— possibly due to warm weather, which limited movement of fish — arctic grayling survival was good. If any grayling currently exist, they are remnants of 1,000 surplus fish stocked in 1987 and that might have survived the latest chemical reclamation.

The DNR estimates that Dutch Fred Lake can support a harvest rate of 15 to 25 pounds of brook trout per acre. In 1991 managers stocked 100 adult and 500 yearling fish, and in 1993 they released an estimated 140 adults and 1,140 yearlings. The adult fish may qualify for Master Angler Award status.

Tactics to Try: Fishing pressure is light to moderate. Dutch Fred is capable of growing big Assinica-strain brook trout, and the best fishing typically occurs on the late-April opener and again in early summer.

Hot lure is a Black Roostertail spinner with all hooks but one removed (see Special Regulations). Work the shallows near weeds for best results, or try for suspended fish. The lake is also conducive to fishing with dry flies and nymphs. Mayfly and caddis patterns work best.

Access: A sand boat launch ramp surrounded by steep hills is located on the lake's south side off Resident Dam Rd. Toilets are provided and there is parking for a half-dozen vehicles. There is no place to rent a boat.

GULLIVER LAKE

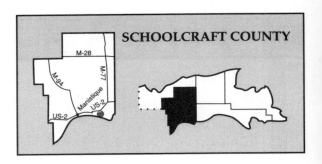
Fishing Opportunities: Smallmouth Bass—Good; Northern Pike and Walleyes—Fair to Good; Bluegills and Yellow Perch—Fair.

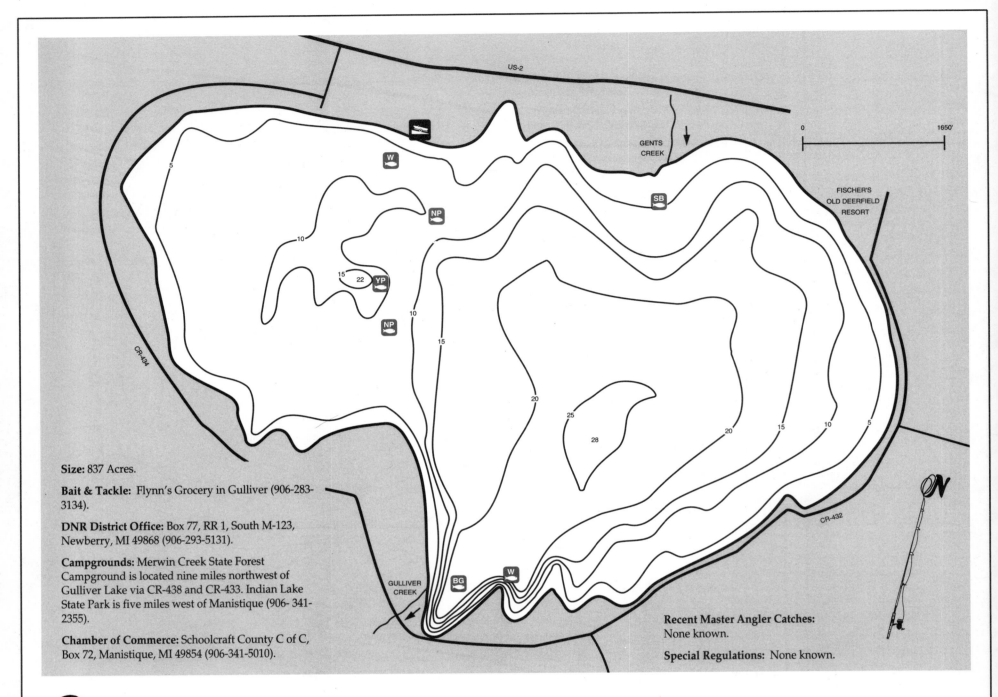

Size: 837 Acres.

Bait & Tackle: Flynn's Grocery in Gulliver (906-283-3134).

DNR District Office: Box 77, RR 1, South M-123, Newberry, MI 49868 (906-293-5131).

Campgrounds: Merwin Creek State Forest Campground is located nine miles northwest of Gulliver Lake via CR-438 and CR-433. Indian Lake State Park is five miles west of Manistique (906- 341-2355).

Chamber of Commerce: Schoolcraft County C of C, Box 72, Manistique, MI 49854 (906-341-5010).

Recent Master Angler Catches: None known.

Special Regulations: None known.

Gulliver Lake lies in southeast Schoolcraft County off US-2 about 11 miles east of Manistique. Many cottages surround the lake, whose sandy and rock rubble shoreline is mostly level and forested. Gents Creek inlets from the northeast corner. The outlet is Gulliver Creek, which flows from a southcentral bay for about one mile before emptying into Lake Michigan.

The lake is fairly shallow, most of it less than 15 feet deep. The maximum depth is only 28 feet, and much of the lake supports abundant weedy vegetation in the form of pondweed and milfoil. This open-bottom lake doesn't have much cover. Areas of rocky rubble, some of which support natural reproduction by walleyes, are scattered throughout the lake but are somewhat concentrated along the north-shore shallows and east of the west-side basin in 10 to 15 feet of water. The bottom composition of deeper water is mostly organic.

Remnants of brush shelters installed 40 years ago may be found along the east shore in 10 to 15 feet of water and in the lake's westcentral area around the deep-water basin there.

Surveys/Stocking: Historically, Gulliver Lake contained yellow perch, walleyes, northern pike, smallmouth bass, rock bass and ciscoes. Stockings include walleyes and yellow perch from 1933 to 1939, northerns in 1941, bluegills in 1950 and 1954, and tiger muskies from 1966 to 1974. In recent years DNR managers have focused on walleye releases.

A May 1990 fyke and trap net survey produced smallmouth bass to 17 inches, walleyes to 26 inches, northern pike to 26 inches, bluegills to 8½ inches, and several small yellow perch and pumpkinseed sunfish.

In 1991 managers released 26,500 walleye fingerlings, and in 1993 they stocked an estimated 20,000 more.

Tactics to Try: The lake serves up good northern pike fishing all year, with brutes to 16 pounds coming via the spearing shack in winter. Activity centers in the area between the south-side point and the public access site on the north shore. Summer tactics include bobber fishing with pike minnows in summer, casting gold (dark day) and silver (bright day) No. 4 Mepps spinners, and trolling or drifting with Dardevle spoons. Black and white is the best color.

Smallmouths to 5 pounds-plus are available, but typical fish run barely legal size. The lake's close proximity to US-2 and the Mackinac Bridge make it vulnerable to overfishing anytime the word about good catches gets out. Casting crankbaits and Mepps spinners along rocks and weeds of the north shore works best.

Forty years ago Gulliver was one of the best walleye lakes in the U.P., and it is coming back thanks to hefty plants. Fish from 6 to 8 pounds are taken every summer on jigs and crawlers and Wolf River rigs tipped with minnows or leeches. Work the south-side points and gravel beds.

Access: Doyle Township Park, which includes a boat launch ramp, is located on the lake's north side off US-2. Facilities include a paved launch, toilets and parking for 11 vehicles. To rent a boat, contact Fischer's Old Deerfield Resort on the lake's north shore (906-283-3169).

INDIAN LAKE

Fishing Opportunities: Walleyes, Smallmouth Bass and Yellow Perch—Good to Excellent; Black Crappies and Northern Pike—Fair to Good; Tiger Muskies—Fair; Lake Sturgeon—Available.

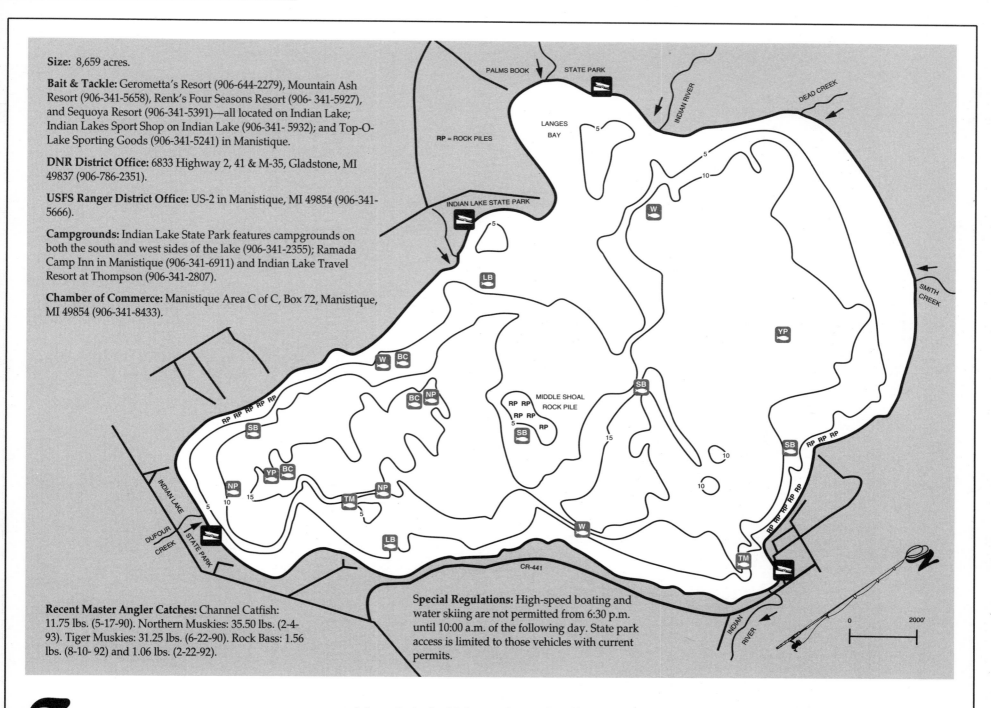

Size: 8,659 acres.

Bait & Tackle: Gerometta's Resort (906-644-2279), Mountain Ash Resort (906-341-5658), Renk's Four Seasons Resort (906- 341-5927), and Sequoya Resort (906-341-5391)—all located on Indian Lake; Indian Lakes Sport Shop on Indian Lake (906-341- 5932); and Top-O-Lake Sporting Goods (906-341-5241) in Manistique.

DNR District Office: 6833 Highway 2, 41 & M-35, Gladstone, MI 49837 (906-786-2351).

USFS Ranger District Office: US-2 in Manistique, MI 49854 (906-341-5666).

Campgrounds: Indian Lake State Park features campgrounds on both the south and west sides of the lake (906-341-2355); Ramada Camp Inn in Manistique (906-341-6911) and Indian Lake Travel Resort at Thompson (906-341-2807).

Chamber of Commerce: Manistique Area C of C, Box 72, Manistique, MI 49854 (906-341-8433).

Recent Master Angler Catches: Channel Catfish: 11.75 lbs. (5-17-90). Northern Muskies: 35.50 lbs. (2-4-93). Tiger Muskies: 31.25 lbs. (6-22-90). Rock Bass: 1.56 lbs. (8-10- 92) and 1.06 lbs. (2-22-92).

Special Regulations: High-speed boating and water skiing are not permitted from 6:30 p.m. until 10:00 a.m. of the following day. State park access is limited to those vehicles with current permits.

Indian Lake is located in southcentral Schoolcraft County about four miles northwest of Manistique. The U.P.'s fourth-largest and Michigan's 14th-biggest lake is also one of its shallowest, with about 90 percent of its volume less than 15 feet deep. The Big Indian River enters from the lake's northwest side and outlets on the northeast side before joining the Manistique River about five miles below Indian Lake. Other inlets include Dufour, Dead, Silver and Smith creeks along with Big Spring.

Although weedbeds are sparse in the south portion of the lake, dense pondweed occurs in the west and northwest basin. Rock cobble and gravel are found in two locations — near the golf course above the Indian River outflow in the southcentral region (an area known locally as the Middle Shoal) and in the southwest corner. Some northern pike spawning occurs near the mouth of the Big Indian River and in Dead and Smith creeks.

Surveys/Stocking: A spring 1988 DNR net survey revealed that 50 percent

of the relatively high numbers of walleyes and yellow perch collected were of catchable size. Also plentiful were smallmouth bass. Biologists netted smaller numbers of northern pike, pumpkinseed sunfish and trout.

Lake sturgeon exist in low numbers, although the lake has served up fish in excess of 100 pounds in recent years. USFS biologists periodically sample the lake for sturgeon. In the fall of 1982, they collected and tagged 13 fish ranging from 34 to 63 inches, and in 1991 they tagged 15 more fish to 65 inches each. Anyone catching a sturgeon with a cattle ear tag in its dorsal fin should contact the USFS Ranger District Office in Manistique at (906) 341-5666.

Managers with the DNR stocked 29,400 walleye fingerlings and 245,000 fry in 1991. In 1992 they released 58,750 fingerlings and 250,000 fry, and in 1993 they planted out an estimated 20,000 fingerlings.

Tactics to Try: Jigs and minnows are hands-down favorites of walleye anglers working the weedline. Those drifting or trolling with crawler harnesses also take occasional jumbo perch. Small Fuzz-E Grub jigs and

various tube jigs tipped with a small minnow are productive for crappies

The lake consistently throws good-size northern pike and muskies for anglers tossing spinnerbaits, crankbaits or bucktail spinners. The lake serves up muskies to 30 pounds nearly every winter to spearers.

During the day plastic worms, Ratt-L-Traps and spinner baits rate high for largemouth bass; after dark try topwater baits in dark colors. Floating Rapalas, pencil plug-type lures, and live bait score on smallmouths

The DNR installed more than 100 jackstraw fish shelters in the south basin in 1975.

Access: Sites at Indian Lake State Park (both South and West Units) and Palms Book State Park include improved boat launch ramps and attendant facilities. Also, a boat launch site exists off CR-441, immediately north of the Indian River outlet, and numerous county road endings occur around the lake. To rent a boat, contact Anchorage Resort (906-341-5838) or these businesses listed under Bait & Tackle: Gerometta's Resort, Mountain Ash Resort, Renk's Four Seasons Resort and Sequoya Resort.

ISLAND LAKE

Fishing Opportunities: Largemouth Bass, Northern Pike, Yellow Perch and Bluegills—Good; Rainbow Trout and Splake— Fair.

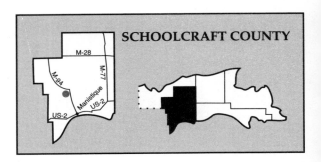

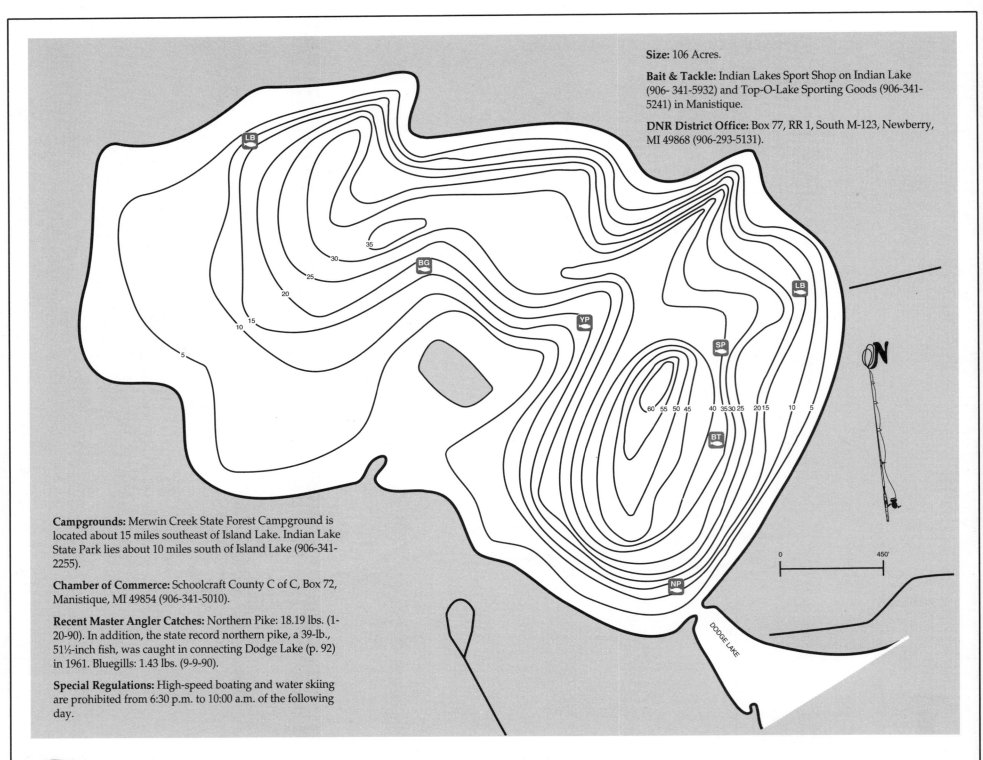

Size: 106 Acres.

Bait & Tackle: Indian Lakes Sport Shop on Indian Lake (906- 341-5932) and Top-O-Lake Sporting Goods (906-341-5241) in Manistique.

DNR District Office: Box 77, RR 1, South M-123, Newberry, MI 49868 (906-293-5131).

Campgrounds: Merwin Creek State Forest Campground is located about 15 miles southeast of Island Lake. Indian Lake State Park lies about 10 miles south of Island Lake (906-341-2255).

Chamber of Commerce: Schoolcraft County C of C, Box 72, Manistique, MI 49854 (906-341-5010).

Recent Master Angler Catches: Northern Pike: 18.19 lbs. (1-20-90). In addition, the state record northern pike, a 39-lb., 51½-inch fish, was caught in connecting Dodge Lake (p. 92) in 1961. Bluegills: 1.43 lbs. (9-9-90).

Special Regulations: High-speed boating and water skiing are prohibited from 6:30 p.m. to 10:00 a.m. of the following day.

island Lake is located in southwest Schoolcraft County about 12 miles northwest of Manistique. It is connected to Dodge Lake (p. 92) by a channel. Wooded hills of birch, maple and evergreens surround the lake, which contains sand in the shallow areas and pulpy peat in deeper reaches.

Similar in size and characteristics to Dodge, Island Lake features stairstep contour breaks, which encourage its residents — both warm- and cold-water species — to suspend and take advantage of the lake's two-story personality.

Surveys/Stocking: The lake has a long history of rainbow trout stocking dating to 1942. Steelhead and northern muskies are other species released as late as the early 1980s.

A June 1992 fyke, gill and trap net survey was disrupted by severe storms; however, the information gathered indicates that, like Dodge Lake, Island Lake receives considerable fishing pressure. Of 45 largemouth bass collected, only two were legal size. A large number of small bluegills is evidence that the lake needs thinning, although fish to 10 inches were also collected.

Three splake collected averaged 25 inches each, proof that survival exists and that lunker fish are available. In addition, researchers measured six yearling rainbows along with yellow perch, pumpkinseed sunfish, northern pike and rock bass.

In 1991 managers stocked 1,875 rainbow trout and 2,650 splake; in 1992 they released 2,675 fish of each species; and in 1993 they planted out an estimated 2,680 rainbows and 1,875 splake. All fish were fingerlings.

Tactics to Try: The same techniques for bass, pike, bluegills and trout recommended for Dodge Lake work well in Island Lake. In addition, one resource we interviewed has done well on largemouths by tossing a black-and-white jig and pig along the weedline. Plastic crawlers in dark colors (purple, blue or black) are reported to be effective, too.

Island Lake periodically produces nice catches of perch. Start at the weedlines and pockets and move into progressively deeper water until you find them. Sonar helps and minnows pinned to Russian hooks in winter or small drift rigs in summer work best.

Access: There is no public access on Island Lake. Fishermen enter through the channel connecting to Dodge Lake after launching their boats on the southwest shore of the latter. The only place to rent a boat is at Brady's Resort on Island Lake (906-341-6400), but rental units are limited and there are no motors.

PETES LAKE

Fishing Opportunities: Smallmouth Bass and Walleyes—Good to Excellent; Yellow Perch, Northern Pike and Bluegills—Fair to Good.

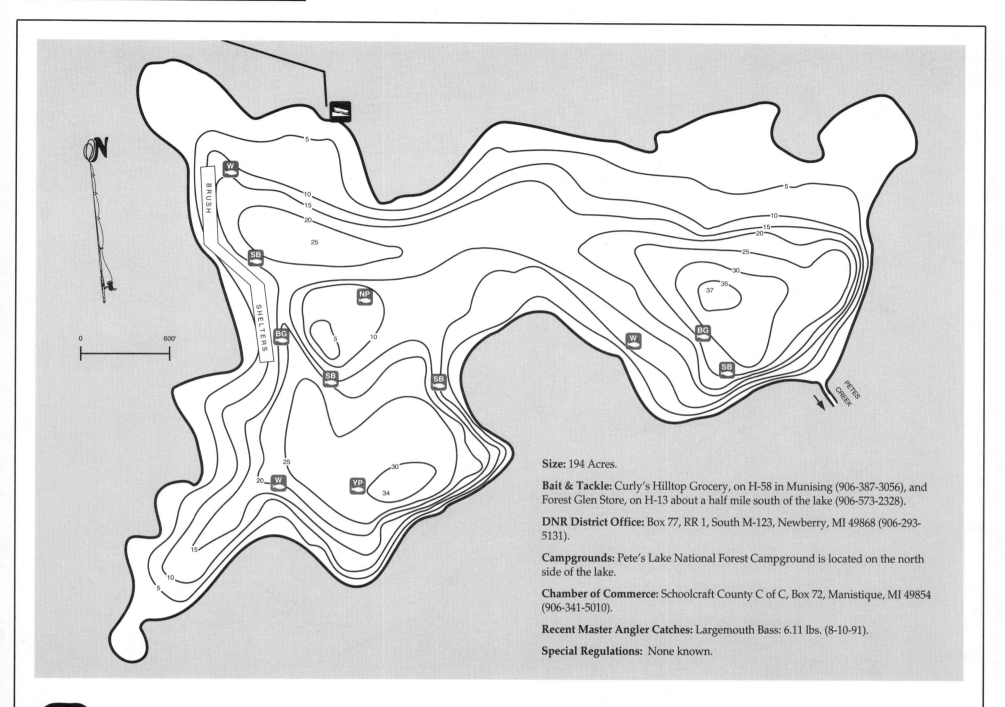

Size: 194 Acres.

Bait & Tackle: Curly's Hilltop Grocery, on H-58 in Munising (906-387-3056), and Forest Glen Store, on H-13 about a half mile south of the lake (906-573-2328).

DNR District Office: Box 77, RR 1, South M-123, Newberry, MI 49868 (906-293-5131).

Campgrounds: Pete's Lake National Forest Campground is located on the north side of the lake.

Chamber of Commerce: Schoolcraft County C of C, Box 72, Manistique, MI 49854 (906-341-5010).

Recent Master Angler Catches: Largemouth Bass: 6.11 lbs. (8-10-91).

Special Regulations: None known.

Petes Lake is located among sandy hills of mixed hardwood, pine and hemlock in westcentral Schoolcraft County near the border with Delta and Alger counties about eight miles northwest of Steuben. The lake features two distinct basins, which are separated by a large sand bar resembling a sunken island. The southwest basin is 35 to 40 feet deep, and the east basin is 40 to 45 feet deep. The shoal bottom is mostly sand with marl; organic material shows up in deeper reaches.

The lake's outflow is Petes Creek, a 4- to 10-foot-wide tributary that passes from the southeast corner into a small creek from Grassy Lake. Eventually it joins the Indian River.

Petes Lake has a long history of producing smallmouth and largemouth bass along with yellow perch and northern pike.

Surveys/Stocking: Stocking records indicate the lake received hatchery-reared bluegills and walleyes as early as 1937, but no fish were released from 1939 until recently when managers stocked 5,000 walleye fingerlings each in 1991 and 1992 and an estimated 5,500 more in 1993.

A crew of DNR researchers surveyed the lake in June 1988 with trap and fyke nets to determine how the lake had fared since a manual removal of undesirable species four years earlier. Although the average size of yellow perch had improved since 1984, growth rates were poor. On the other hand, smallmouth reproduction was good, although an active sport fishery tends to crop adults shortly after they become legal size.

In 1990 USFS biologists removed 2,500 pounds of white suckers and determined that the lake held many small yellow perch. Returning in the fall of 1992 with a boomshocker, managers discovered good numbers of smallmouth bass and walleyes. One three-year-old walleye was nearly 20 inches long, indicating excellent growth rates.

Tactics to Try: Fifty-two fish shelters installed in 1972 in the 10- to 15-foot-deep contour along the western shoreline — from the north end to the lake's center — continue to provide some habitat and should not be overlooked for all species.

Red jigs tipped with worms and fished during summer along steep drops in 15 to 20 feet of water are productive for walleyes. Crawler harnesses and Lindy Rigs, either drifted or trolled, are also rated. Orange blades and black- and-orange beads are hot harness colors.

Color seems to be less important when fishing for smallmouths, which tend to scatter widely. Minnows are the first choice, with crawlers and leeches also productive.

The lake is capable of throwing magnum bluegills for small-leech fishermen in summer and those using tiny white or chartreuse spoons and larvae in winter. Finesse fishing is a must to catch jumbo 'gills.

Most northern pike are taken incidentally by anglers after other species. Still, the lake is home to 10-pound-plus pike as evidenced by winter spearers and tip-up fishermen.

Access: The public access site is located on the lake's northcentral shore. Features include a hard-surfaced boat launch ramp and toilets, but parking is severely limited. There is no place to rent a boat.

SWAN LAKE

Fishing Opportunities: Smallmouth Bass, Northern Pike, Bluegills and Yellow Perch—Fair to Excellent.

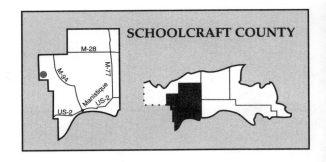
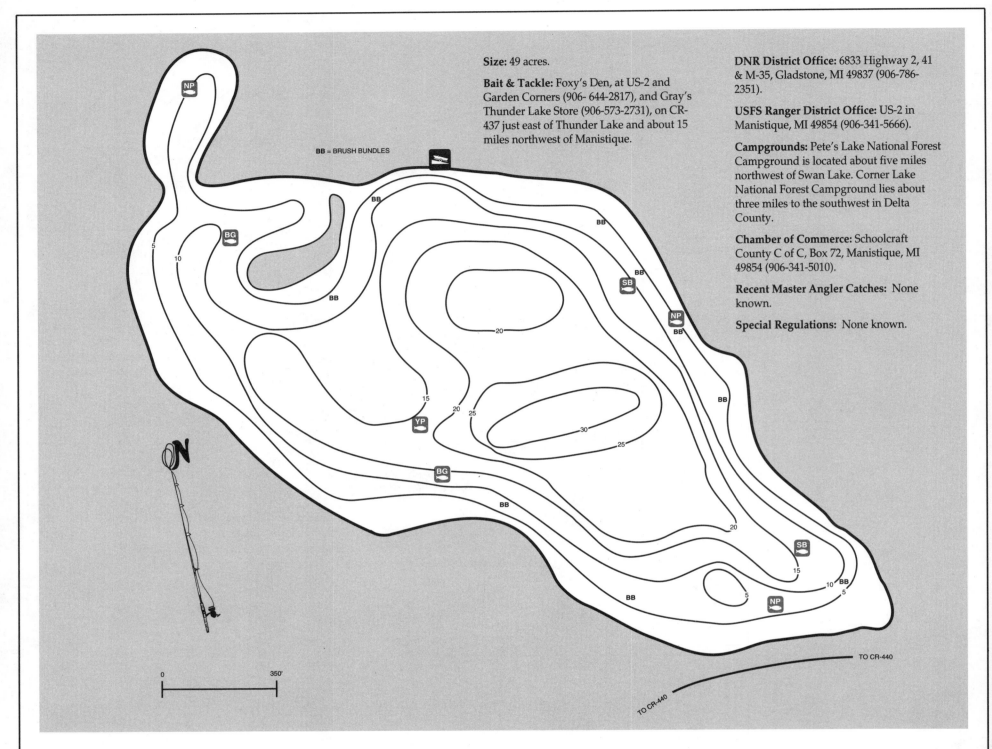

Size: 49 acres.

Bait & Tackle: Foxy's Den, at US-2 and Garden Corners (906-644-2817), and Gray's Thunder Lake Store (906-573-2731), on CR-437 just east of Thunder Lake and about 15 miles northwest of Manistique.

DNR District Office: 6833 Highway 2, 41 & M-35, Gladstone, MI 49837 (906-786-2351).

USFS Ranger District Office: US-2 in Manistique, MI 49854 (906-341-5666).

Campgrounds: Pete's Lake National Forest Campground is located about five miles northwest of Swan Lake. Corner Lake National Forest Campground lies about three miles to the southwest in Delta County.

Chamber of Commerce: Schoolcraft County C of C, Box 72, Manistique, MI 49854 (906-341-5010).

Recent Master Angler Catches: None known.

Special Regulations: None known.

BB = BRUSH BUNDLES

S wan Lake is located in westcentral Schoolcraft County within the Hiawatha National Forest and just north of the Delta County line. Technicians with the USFS mapped the undeveloped lake in 1979. Most of the shoreline is wooded with maple, aspen, tamarack and jack, red and white pine. The shoreline consists of gentle slopes with some erosion problems showing due to fluctuations in the water level, which seems odd because the lake has no inlets nor outlets.

Bottom composition along the 5- to 10-foot-deep contour is mostly sand; deeper areas feature muck. The water is clear and virtually colorless, due in part to its depth (maximum of 36½ feet) and lack of vegetation in deeper water. Weeds are limited to bulrushes, water lilies, cabbage, coontail and milfoil in the shallows.

Surveys/Stocking: A 1975 DNR Fisheries Division survey showed good numbers of northern pike, smallmouth bass and panfish. By 1982, however, bullheads dominated the catch. After chemically reclaiming the lake in 1985, biologists began to manage it for a two-story fishery, stocking both smallmouth bass and trout (rainbows and browns).

A 1988 DNR survey showed great smallmouth bass survival but poor trout survival. The nets also collected a few yellow perch, bluegills and pumpkinseed sunfish.

In the summer of 1993, USFS techicians found a large number of 4- to 8-inch bluegills and good numbers of smallmouth bass including some fish in the 15- to 18-inch category. Perch were small but abundant. Only one bullhead was captured, indicating that the manual removal project was successful. Fishing should improve as a result.

The DNR has not stocked the lake in recent years.

Tactics to Try: Best smallmouth bass action occurs in the southeast corner and along the east side. Try a copper-colored, tandem-blade spinnerbait, or toss Bass Busters. For northern pike, troll or spincast Dardevle spoons along weedlines or over drop-offs, especially during the period from 10:00 a.m. to 4:00 p.m. The best spots for bluegills and perch are along the west and north sides.

A good place to find most gamefish is around the brush shelters and spawning boxes installed by the USFS in 7 to 10 feet of water at the locations indicated on the map.

Access: The public access site is located via USFS-2258 and CR-440, and the shallow boat launch ramp is best suited for canoes and cartoppers. A second access site is located at the southeast corner of the lake. There is no place to rent a boat.

THUNDER LAKE

Fishing Opportunities: Bluegills, Pumpkinseed Sunfish and Black Crappies—Good to Excellent; Walleyes, Yellow Perch, Northern Pike and Smallmouth Bass—Good; Largemouth

Size: 340 acres.

Bait & Tackle: Gray's Thunder Lake Store (906-573-2731) is located just east of Thunder Lake on CR-437.

DNR District Office: 6833 Highway 2, 41 & M-35, Gladstone, MI 49837 (906-786-2351).

USFS Ranger District Office: US-2 in Manistique, MI 49854 (906-341-5666).

Campgrounds: Indian Lake State Park is located about 10 miles southeast of Thunder Lake (906-341-2355). Indian River National Forest Campground lies five miles northeast, and Camp Seven National Forest Campground is about five miles to the southwest of Thunder Lake.

Chamber of Commerce: Schoolcraft County C of C, Box 72, Manistique, MI 49854 (906-341-5010).

Recent Master Angler Catches: Bluegills: 1.19 lbs. (7-1-93), 1.25 lbs. (6-2-92), 1.19 lbs. (3-28-92), 1.06 lbs. (6-21-91) and 1.12 lbs. (8-22-90). Black Crappies: 2.0 lbs. (8-22-90).

Special Regulations: None known.

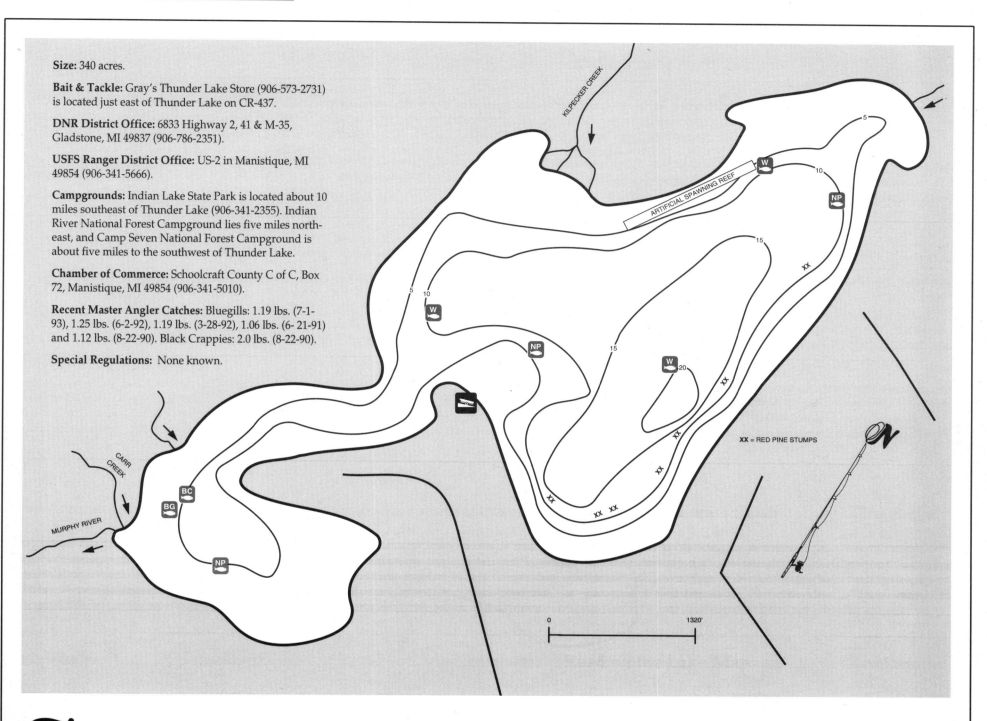

Thunder Lake is located in southwest Schoolcraft County about 15 miles northwest of Manistique. The lake is about 1½ miles long by a mile wide and is fed by four inlets, including Carr and Kilpecker creeks. The latter is rated as a trout stream. The lake's outlet is Murphy Creek, which also contains trout.

Shoreline shallows of the fairly well-developed lake consist of sand, gravel, mud and clay. Deep-water areas contain silt and pulpy peat. Abundant vegetation covers much of the lake except for the east shore. Rolling hills of birch, maple and pine surround the lake along with lowland cover types that include spruce and balsam in the northwest region.

Surveys/Stocking: Stocking records date from 1923 when smallmouth bass were introduced. Through 1940 the planting program shifted to walleyes and yellow perch. Early surveys indicated good populations of northern pike, walleyes, largemouth and smallmouth bass, perch, bluegills and sunfish.

A May 1983 DNR net survey showed an over-abundance of suckers and bullheads and too many small, slow-growing pike. Walleyes, bass and panfish were of average size but low in numbers.

The USFS surveyed the lake shallows with trap and fyke nets in the summer of 1993 and found good numbers of big bluegills averaging about 7 inches. Thunder Lake has a good population of rock bass and pumpkinseed sunfish, and bullheads appear to be under control. The nets also revealed black crappies to 13 inches and a few northern pike.

A major management prescription a few years ago called for manually removing small northern pike and building a 1,700 square-foot artificial reef along the 5-foot-deep contour of the west shore just north of the Kilpecker Creek inlet. That work has now been completed, along with installing 14 red-pine stumps along the northeast shore.

In 1992 DNR managers released 12,000 walleye fingerlings.

Tactics to Try: The lake receives fairly heavy fishing pressure, and that may be why some of the year's best catches of walleye, pike and panfish occur in winter, when fewer anglers are out. At most, only a half-dozen ice fishing shacks dot the lake.

Average size of keeper walleyes is 15 to 20 inches, and the best baits in spring, summer and fall are leeches or minnows. Some anglers score by trolling with night crawlers.

For bluegills, fish waxworms on a tiny ice fly or tear drop spoon and concentrate efforts at the south end or along the northeast shore around the fish shelters.

Access: The public access site is located on the lake's east side off CR-437, and the launch ramp can accommodate small- to medium-size boats. There are no toilet facilities and a limited amount of parking space. To rent a boat, contact Gray's Thunder Lake Store (see Bait & Tackle listing). Whispering Pines Resort (906-573-2480) and Thunder Lake Resort (906-573-2468) rent boats along with cabins.

ALPHABETICAL LIST OF LAKES

Antoine (Dickinson Co.), 21
Arrowhead (Delta Co.) — see *Norway*
Au Train (Alger Co.), 1

Bar (Alger Co.), 2
Bass (Houghton Co.), 40
Beaver (Alger Co.), 3
Belle (Luce Co.), 63
Big Badwater (Dickinson Co) — see *Twin Falls Flowage*
Big Island (Schoolcraft Co.), 91
Big Manistique (Mackinac Co.), 71
Big Trout (Chippewa Co.) — see *Carp*
Bluegill (Schoolcraft Co.), 91
Blush (Schoolcraft Co.), 91
Bob (Houghton Co.), 39
Brevoort (Mackinac Co.), 72
Brule (Iron Co.), 48
Byers (Schoolcraft Co.), 91

Camp 7 (Delta Co.), 18
Caribou (Chippewa Co.), 15
Carp (Chippewa Co.), 16
Center (Schoolcraft Co.), 91
Chalk Hills Flowage (Menominee Co.), 85
Chicagon (Iron Co.), 49
Cisco (Gogebic Co.), 23
Clark (Gogebic Co.), 24
Clear (Houghton Co.), 40
Clearwater (Gogebic Co.), 25
Coattail (Schoolcraft Co.), 91
Courtney (Ontonagon Co.), 87
Craig (Baraga Co.), 7
Crooked (Baraga Co.), 8
Crooked (Gogebic Co.), 26
Cub (Gogebic Co.), 29
Cucumber (Schoolcraft Co.), 91

Deer Island (Gogebic Co.), 27
Deer Lake Basin (Marquette Co.), 77
Dodge (Schoolcraft Co.), 92
Duck (Gogebic Co.), 28
Dutch Fred (Schoolcraft Co.), 93

East Bear (Gogebic Co.), 29
Emily (Iron Co.), 52

Fence (Baraba Co.), 9
Fish (Alger Co.), 4
Frenchman's (Chippewa Co.), 17

Gerald (Houghton Co.), 41
Gogebic (Gogebic Co.), 32
Golden (Iron Co.), 50
Goose (Marquette Co.), 78
Grand Sable (Alger Co.), 5
Gratiot (Iron Co.), 59
Greenwood Reservoir (Marquette Co.), 79
Gulliver (Schoolcraft Co.), 94

Hagerman (Iron Co.), 51

Imp (Gogebic Co.), 30
Independence (Marquette Co.), 80
Indian (Schoolcraft Co.), 95
Island (Marquette Co.), 96

Kidney (Iron Co.) — see *Ste. Kathryn*
King (Baraga Co.), 10
Klondyke (Schoolcraft Co.), 91

Lac La Belle (Keweenaw Co.), 91
Lac Vieux Desert (Gogebic Co.), 31
Little Brevoort (Mackinac Co.), 73
Long (Luce Co.), 68
Loon (Gogebic Co.), 33

Manganese (Keweenaw Co.), 62
Marion (Gogebic Co.), 34
Marsh (Gogebic Co.), 29
McInnes (Schoolcraft Co.), 91
Medora (Keweenaw Co.), 61
Michigamme (Marquette Co.), 81
Mid (Schoolcraft Co.), 91
Milakokia (Mackinac Co.), 74
Millecoquin (Mackinac Co.), 75
Mirror (Ontonagon Co.), 88
Moon (Luce Co.), 64
Muskallonge (Luce Co.), 65

Nawakwa (Alger Co.), 6
Neds (Schoolcraft Co.), 91
North Manistique (Luce Co.), 69
Norway (Delta Co.), 19

Parent (Baraga Co.), 11
Peavy Reservoir (Iron Co.), 55
Perch (Iron Co.), 56
Perch (Luce Co.), 66
Perrault (Houghton Co.), 44
Petes (Schoolcraft Co.), 97
Pike (Luce Co.), 67
Pomeroy (Gogebic Co.), 35
Portage (Houghton Co.), 45
Pretty (Luce Co.), 68
Prickett Dam Backwater (Baraga Co.), 12

Rice (Houghton Co.), 46
Roland (Baraga Co.), 13
Roland (Houghton Co.), 42
Round (Delta Co.), 20
Round (Luce Co.), 69

South Manistique (Mackinac Co.), 76
Squaw (Marquette Co.), 82
Stanley (Iron Co.), 57
Ste. Kathryn (Iron Co.), 53
Sucker (Alger Co.) — see *Nawakwa*
Sudden (Ontonagon Co.), 89
Sunset (Iron Co.), 58
Swan (Schoolcraft Co.), 98

Tamarack (Gogebic Co.), 36
Teal (Marquette Co.), 83
Thousand Island (Gogebic Co.), 37
Thunder (Schoolcraft Co.), 99
Torch (Houghton Co.), 47
Townline (Schoolcraft Co.), 91
Trout (Chippewa Co.) — see *Carp*
Twilight (Schoolcraft Co.), 91
Twin (Luce Co.), 70
Twin Falls Flowage (Dickinson Co.), 22

Vance (Schoolcraft Co.), 91
Vermilac (Baraga Co.), 14
Victoria Dam Backwater (Ontonagon Co.), 90

West Bear (Gogebic Co.), 29
Whitefish (Gogebic Co.), 38
Whitefish (Mackinac Co.)—see *South Manistique*
White Rapids Flowage (Menominee Co.), 86
Witch (Marquette Co.), 84

THE AUTHOR

Tom Huggler is a fulltime freelance writer and book author who lives in the Lansing area. The Michigan Editor and National Camping Editor for *Outdoor Life* magazine also writes monthly columns for *Michigan Out-of-Doors* ("Michigan Meanders"), *Woods-N-Water News* ("Kicking Back") and *North American Fisherman* ("Great Lakes").

Huggler fished throughout the Upper Peninsula and researched all the information for this, his tenth book. Many of his popular other works are now out of print and considered collector's items. They include:

Westwind Woods (out of print)

Midwest Meanders (out of print)

Hunt Michigan (out of print)

Fish Michigan — Great Lakes (out of print)

Cannon's Guide to Freshwater Fishing with Downriggers

Quail Hunting in America

Grouse of North America

Fish Michigan — 100 Southern Michigan Lakes

Fish Michigan — 100 Northern Lower Michigan Lakes

Walleye Tactics with Tom Huggler (video)

Information on these and other forthcoming titles by Tom Huggler is available from:

Outdoor Images
P.O. Box 250
Sunfield, MI 48890
(517) 566-8155

Photo by Boyd Pfeiffer

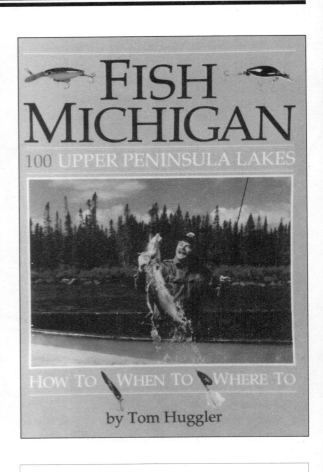